# REGULATION
# LEGAL FORM AND ECONOMIC THEORY

# REGULATION
## Legal Form and Economic Theory

ANTHONY OGUS

·HART·
PUBLISHING

OXFORD – PORTLAND OREGON
2004

Hart Publishing
Oxford and Portland, Oregon

Published in North America (US and Canada) by
Hart Publishing c/o
International Specialized Book Services
5804 NE Hassalo Street
Portland, Oregon
97213-3644
USA

Hart Publishing is a specialist legal publisher based in Oxford, England.
To order further copies of this book or to request a list of other
publications please write to:

Hart Publishing, Salter's Boatyard, Folly Bridge,
Abingdon Road, Oxford OX1 4LB
Telephone: +44 (0)1865 245533 or Fax: +44 (0)1865 794882
e-mail: mail@hartpub.co.uk
WEBSITE: http://www.hartpub.co.uk

British Library Cataloguing in Publication Data
Data Available
ISBN 1 84113–530–5 (paperback)


Printed and bound in Great Britain by
Lightning Source UK Ltd

# Preface

This book has its origin in a conviction that conventional approaches to public law and administrative law have failed to address some key issues pertaining to the regulation of industrial and commercial behaviour. Those nurtured within the British, particularly the Diceyan, tradition are obsessed with the institutional dimension of public law: how the powers to control behaviour are allocated between different public and semi-public authorities; and how the exercise of such powers may be constrained by principles of accountability. But public law is not only about preventing the abuse of power; it is also about selecting legal forms which can best achieve the instrumental goals of collective choice. If, for example, the agreed objective is to limit industrial pollution, to achieve certain standards of safety in our factories, or to control the prices of the privatized utilities, we need critically to compare the legal instruments which are available or can be devised.

Hitherto we have tended to assume that this task is not for a 'public' lawyer, but rather for a specialist in environmental law, health and safety law, or utilities law. My perception is that specialism of this kind hinders, rather than facilitates, the evaluative analysis of the legal framework which is required. A more complete understanding of the legal forms is acquired only when specific instruments are related to more general goals and thus cross the boundaries between different regulatory areas.

The aim of this book is, then, to classify and explain regulatory forms and to evaluate their capacity and record of achievement in meeting collective goals. Clearly, a theoretical framework is necessary to analyse the goals and to provide some criteria for evaluation. The framework that I have adopted has been drawn predominantly, but not exclusively, from economics. In the last two decades, economics has made a major contribution to the study of private law; its impact on public law scholarship has been much less marked, particularly this side of the Atlantic. In attempting to redress the balance, I have been much influenced by the rich (and sometimes controversial) American literature which adopts this approach. However, while the modes of analysis formulated by American authors may, without undue difficulty, be applied to British regulation, the conclusions which they reach have to be treated with considerable caution, since American regulatory institutions, processes, and styles are often very different from their British counterparts.

As colleagues have been only too ready to point out, and as I have increasingly appreciated throughout the lengthy period of writing this book, it is a very ambitious undertaking. The volume of legislation which comes within my definition of regulation is enormous and the range of activities governed by the instruments is highly diverse. Of course, my coverage is far from comprehensive, and my accounts of the law in specific areas are not—and are not intended to be—definitive. My aim has been to select from the mass of material examples which illustrate my general themes.

My debt to those who provided me with assistance, encouragement, and stimulus is considerable. Parts of the book were written during periods most happily spent at the Universities of Antwerp, and California at Berkeley, the latter with financial assistance from the John M. Olin Foundation and the Fulbright Commission. Discussions with colleagues at these institutions provided me with a much-needed comparative perspective. On home territory, lawyers and economists at the University of Manchester responded patiently, and sometimes even enthusiastically, to my pleas for help.

Sections of the book were critically scrutinized by Andrew Bell, Richard Bragg, Paul Burrows, Martin Currie, Martin Davey, Neil Duxbury, Tom Gibbons, Morten Hviid, Tim Jones, Michael Jones-Lee, Diana Kloss, Bob Millward, Mick Moran, Genevra Richardson, Peter Stubbs, John Tillotson and Martin Wasik. I acknowledge my gratitude to all of them. My greatest debt is to Martin Loughlin. Having (with difficulty) overcome his aversion to a work adopting an economic approach to public law, he bravely read the whole work in typescript: his critical, but constructive, comments were invaluable. Preparation of the final manuscript was assisted by Christina Malkowski-Zaba and Robert Ritter. Richard Hart and John Whelan, from the Oxford University Press, and Peter Cane and Jane Stapleton, as editors of the Clarendon Series, gave me encouragement and guidance. Julie Froud assisted with the checking of proofs and the remarkable secretarial skills of Mary Platt were a constant support.

It remains only to thank my wife, Catherine. When the task ahead seemed to be too hard to accomplish and when my spirits were in consequence at a low ebb, she provided the best possible remedy: *la bonne cuisine française*.

A. O.

*Dobcross*
*March 1994*

# Contents

# Table of United Kingdom Statutes

# Table of Statutory Instruments

# Table of European Legislation and Treaties

# Table of United Kingdom Cases

# Table of Cases from other Jurisdictions

# I

# Introduction

## I. NATURE OF REGULATION

The expression 'regulation' is frequently found in both legal and non-legal contexts. It is not a term of art, and unfortunately it has acquired a bewildering variety of meanings.[1] Sometimes it is used to indicate any form of behavioural control, whatever the origin. But when, in the rhetoric of the day, politicians and others refer to the stifling effect on industry of 'regulation' and the need to 'deregulate',[2] they clearly do not have such a broad concept in mind. They may be assumed instead to be referring to what one American social scientist has described as the 'central meaning' of regulation: a 'sustained and focused control exercised by a public agency over activities that are valued by a community'.[3]

The emphasis on 'valued activities' serves to exclude from the concept of regulation the traditional areas of criminal law and the concerns of the criminal justice system.[4] But, for the purposes of describing the subject-matter of this book, the concept must be narrowed still further. We need to recognize that 'regulation' is fundamentally a politico-economic concept and, as such, can best be understood by reference to different systems of economic organization and the legal forms which maintain them.[5]

In all industrialized societies there is a tension between two systems of economic organization. Under the first, which may be called the *market* system and which is fully explored in Chapter 2, individuals and groups are left free, subject only to certain basic restraints, to pursue their own welfare goals. The legal system underpins these arrangements but predominantly through instruments of private law; regulation, as we shall understand it, has no significant role. The second is the *collectivist* system: the state seeks to direct or encourage behaviour which (it is assumed)

---

[1] For a valiant attempt to provide a taxonomy of the various meanings, see B. M. Mitnick, *The Political Economy of Regulation* (1980), ch. 1.

[2] Cf. White Paper, *Lifting the Burden* (1985, Cmnd. 9571), para. 1.5: 'The amount of regulation which new and established firms face acts as a brake on enterprise and the wealth and job creating process.'

[3] P. Selznick, 'Focusing Organizational Research on Regulation' in R. Noll (ed.), *Regulatory Policy and the Social Sciences* (1985), p. 363.

[4] Cf. below, pp. 79–98.

[5] Cf. G. Majone, 'Introduction', in G. Majone (ed.), *Deregulation or Re-regulation? Regulatory Reform in Europe and the United States* (1990), pp. 1–2.

would not occur without such intervention. The aim is to correct perceived deficiencies in the market system in meeting collective or public interest goals—these will be analysed in Chapter 3. Some legal cultures have a specific concept or concepts to designate the instruments used for this purpose and the law governing them, for example, the German *Wirtschaftsverwaltungsrecht*[6] and the French *droit public économique*.[7] There is no equivalent term of art in our legal culture,[8] and we thus have to fall back on admittedly imprecise expressions, such as 'regulation' and 'regulatory law', to fill the gap.[9]

If, then, the term 'regulation' is used to denote the law which implements the collectivist system, what are its characteristics and how do these compare with the characteristics of law under the market system? First, regulation contains the idea of control by a superior; it has a *directive* function. To achieve the desired ends, individuals are compelled by a superior authority—the state—to behave in particular ways with the threat of sanctions if they do not comply. Secondly, it is *public* law in the sense that in general it is for the state (or its agents) to enforce the obligations which cannot be overreached by private agreement between the parties concerned. Thirdly, because the state plays a fundamental role in the formulation, as well as the enforcement, of the law, it is typically *centralized*.

In contrast, under the market model, the law has a primarily *facilitative* function: it offers a set of formalized arrangements with which individuals can 'clothe' their welfare-seeking activities and relationships. The arrangements carry with them mutual rights and obligations which, if necessary, a court will enforce. Although the law may be said to control conduct, the fact that it is *private* renders it distinct from regulation in two fundamental respects: it is left to individuals and not the state to enforce rights; and obligations are incurred voluntarily in the sense that they can always be displaced by agreements between the affected parties, if they are found to be inappropriate. For the same reasons, the law is largely *decentralized*.

In drawing these basic distinctions, of course, we risk oversimplifying the

---

[6] See H. D. Jarass, *Wirtschaftsverwaltungsrecht und Wirtschaftsverfassungsrecht* (2nd edn., 1984), pp. 3–32.

[7] See A. de Laubadère and P. Delvolvé, *Droit public économique* (5th edn., 1986), pp. 13–20.

[8] Cf. the problems encountered by a German in locating *Wirtschaftsrecht* within the classifications of English Law: H. W. Goldschmidt, *English Law from a Foreign Standpoint* (1937), pp. 90–2.

[9] 'Administrative law' is sometimes used in this sense (e.g. F. A. Hayek, *Law, Legislation and Liberty*, i. (1973), p. 137), but under the predominant 'normativist' tradition of British public law the term usually refers to the principles governing the allocation of power and is thus primarily concerned with the legal bounds of executive action: e.g. H. W. R. Wade, *Administrative Law* (6th edn., 1988), pp. 4–5. For discussion of this and the rival 'functionalist' tradition, see M. Loughlin, *Public Law and Political Theory* (1992).

complex and multi-faceted function of law which is a necessary consequence of any system of economic organization.[10] Clearly, it is wrong to
identify the market system exclusively with private, facilitative, and
decentralized law. No society can exist without the state providing a
minimum degree of order and security by imposing and enforcing some
obligations and, if necessary, overriding private agreements. That is the
task of the traditional, non-regulatory, criminal law.

Conversely, regulation is not always directive, public, and centralized.
In some areas it is formulated and enforced by self-regulatory agencies,
rather than by a public body.[11] Occasionally, collective goals are pursued
by means of instruments, such as franchise contracts, which resemble
private legal obligations.[12] Finally, although rarely used in Britain,
regulation can take the form of an 'economic instrument' which is not
directive: individuals or firms are legally free to undertake certain activities
which, from a public interest perspective, are regarded as undesirable, but
if they do so, they must pay a tax or charge.[13]

## 2. THEORIES OF REGULATION AND ECONOMIC REASONING

Identifying regulation with the collectivist system of economic organization
also provides us with a theory to explain and evaluate regulation. We can
attempt to specify collective goals and to identify the circumstances in
which those goals are unlikely to be met by the unregulated market.
Armed with these justifications for intervention, we can then apply them to
different areas and forms of regulation, in an attempt to determine
whether the law is consistent with them. The first of these tasks, the
elaboration of the *public interest theory of regulation*, will be undertaken in
Chapter 3, and that theory will be used as an explanatory hypothesis and
evaluative tool in Parts II, III, and IV of this book.

The public interest theory attributes to legislators and others responsible
for the design of regulation a desire to pursue collective goals. It is
obviously extremely difficult to validate this assumption. The study of
motivation is an elusive and perhaps an impossible task. Laws, particularly
in the form of legislation, are rarely the work of a single mind, and there
are often conflicting expressions of what was intended. Even when there is
no such conflict and the intention is apparently clear, how can we know
that it genuinely motivated the passing of the law? Perhaps it was used to
disguise some private motive?

---

[10] R. S. Summers, 'The Technique Element in Law' (1971) 59 Calif. L. Rev. 733; R. C.
Ellickson, 'A Critique of Economic and Sociological Theories of Social Control' (1987) 16 J.
Legal Stud. 67.
[11] See generally below, pp. 107–11.
[12] Below, pp. 330–3.
[13] Below, Ch. 11.

A sceptical attitude to the assumed 'public-interestedness' of legislators and a recognition that regulation typically benefits particular groups in society—not always those groups that it was apparently designed to benefit—has led to an alternative, *private interest theory of regulation*. Scholars, mainly American, who subscribe to this theory analyse the way in which the political and law-making processes can be used by private interest groups to secure for themselves regulatory benefits. This theory, which is the focus of Chapter 4, thus provides a hypothetical explanation for the incidence and form of regulation which is very different from that of the public interest theory. Both theories should be treated with respect and both will be used as analytical tools in our exploration of regulation.

This is perhaps a convenient point for alerting the reader to the use of economic reasoning in this book. The public interest and private interest theories are each, to some extent at least, built on economic concepts. This should not prove an obstacle to readers unfamiliar with economics, provided that they read, in addition to the exposition of the theories (Chapters 3 and 4), Chapter 2, where an explanation of some of the key economic concepts is given.

### 3. SCOPE AND FORM OF REGULATION

Regulation, in the sense in which we are using the term, covers a huge variety of industrial and non-industrial activities and involves a number of different legal forms.[14] In this book we adopt the broad distinction which is often made between *social regulation* (the subject-matter of Part III) and *economic regulation* (the subject-matter of Part IV).[15]

### (a) Social Regulation

The public interest justifications for social regulation, which deals with such matters as health and safety, environmental protection, and consumer protection, tend to centre on two types of market failure. First, individuals in an existing, or potential, contractual relationship with firms supplying goods or services often have inadequate information concerning the quality offered by suppliers; in consequence, the unregulated market may fail to meet their preferences.[16] Secondly, even if this information problem does not exist, market transactions may have spillover effects (or externalities) which adversely affect individuals who are not involved in the transactions.

---

[14] For a (dated) attempt to provide a comprehensive account of such activities and forms, see E. Freund, *Legislative Regulation: A Study of the Ways and Means of Written Law* (1932).
[15] Cf. L. Graymer and F. Thompson, 'Introduction', in L. Graymer and F. Thompson (eds)., *Reforming Social Regulation* (1982), pp. 9–10; D. Swann, 'The Regulatory Scene: An Overview', in K. Button and D. Swann (eds.), *The Age of Regulatory Reform* (1989), pp. 5–6.                                                                       [16] Below, pp. 38–41.

To deal with these problems, policy-makers can choose from a range of regulatory instruments, classifiable according to the degree of state intervention required.[17] At the end of the spectrum associated with low intervention, we can identify three regulatory forms: information regulation (Chapter 7), forcing suppliers to disclose details concerning the quality of their goods or services; 'private' regulation (Chapter 12), imposing obligations which nevertheless can be enforced only by the individuals for whose benefit they have been created; and economic instruments (Chapter 11) which, as explained above, are not coercive but rather induce desirable behaviour by financial incentives. At the other end of the spectrum, we find the highly interventionist instrument of prior approval (Chapter 10); this prohibits the undertaking of an activity without a licence or authorization issued by an agency. Between the extremes lies the most frequently employed form of regulation—sometimes referred to as 'command-and-control'—in which standards, backed by criminal sanctions, are imposed on suppliers (Chapters 8 and 9).

### (b) Economic Regulation

What is generally designated as 'economic' regulation covers a much narrower range of activities than social regulation. It applies primarily to industries with monopolistic tendencies. For reasons which are examined in Chapter 2,[18] monopolies are in general regarded as undesirable and are prohibited by competition law. But under certain special conditions there may exist a 'natural monopoly'[19] where it is economically preferable for there to be a single supplier. If, in such circumstances, a firm is granted monopoly rights, it will not be subject to the discipline normally provided by competition and in consequence may overprice its products, fail to meet consumer preferences regarding quality, and lapse into inefficiency.

The principal function of economic regulation is, then, to provide a substitute for competition in relation to natural monopolies. Broadly speaking, there are three alternative forms. First, the firm can be publicly owned (Chapter 13), the expectation being that the mechanics of political direction and accountability will be sufficient to meet public interest goals. Secondly, the firm may remain in, or be transferred to, private ownership but be subjected to external constraints in the form of price and quality regulation (Chapter 14). Thirdly, firms desiring to obtain a monopoly right may be forced to compete for it (Chapter 15). As part of their competitive bid, they are required to stipulate proposed conditions of supply, relating especially to prices and quality; and those conditions then become terms of the licence or franchise under which they exercise the monopoly right.

---

[17] Cf. below, p. 151.    [18] Below, p. 23.    [19] Below, pp. 30–3.

## 4. HISTORICAL DEVELOPMENT OF REGULATION
### IN BRITAIN

*(a) Regulation in the Tudor and Stuart Periods*

It is usual to trace the origins of modern regulatory law to the nineteenth century, but the roots lie much deeper, particularly in the highly interventionist regimes of the Tudor and Stuart periods.[20] Almost all areas of industry and trade were at that time subject to very detailed legislative controls, although some were governed by what we would now call 'self-regulation', since guilds were given monopoly rights of supply with powers to regulate the methods of production. Regulation was not grounded in any general theory of the role of the state in economic affairs.[21] But since, equally, there was no notion of an inherent 'freedom of trade', controls on trade were seen neither as exceptional nor as antithetical to a market-based economy. Notwithstanding the profound changes to the economic and political environment which have occurred since, the Tudor and Stuart regimes provide some important parallels to the dilemmas which have beset modern regulatory policy.

The need to respond swiftly to the political demands for intervention created a challenge for legislative rule-making which was not always successfully met. As a result of crude drafting, statutory controls were often either over-inclusive, incurring the hostility of those unintentionally caught by the provisions, or under-inclusive, leading to avoidance behaviour by those intended to be caught.[22] In consequence, many areas of regulation underwent an evolutionary process, statutory definitions requiring constant amendment to meet the more obvious deficiencies.[23]

Although regulation was predominantly an act of central government, enforcement was a matter for local administration and often ineffective.[24] Legislation was thus as much concerned with the symbolic function of appeasing those aggrieved or responding to political demands as it was with the pursuit of instrumental goals.[25] The nature of those demands itself provides an early illustration of one of the central themes of this book, the

---

[20] A. I. Ogus, 'Regulatory Law: Some Lessons from the Past' (1992) 12 Legal Stud. 1.

[21] The notion that it was inspired by what was to be later called 'mercantilism' (the protection of domestic industries, combined with notions of just prices and fair wages) is now largely discredited by historians: C. Clay, *Economic Expansion and Social Change: England 1500–1700*, (1984), p. 206.

[22] Ogus, above, n. 20, p. 13; cf. below, pp. 164–70.

[23] For an excellent illustration see L. Harper, *The English Navigation Laws: A Seventeenth Century Experiment in Social Engineering* (1939).

[24] In principle, the responsibility for enforcement generally lay with local constables and justices; in practice, private prosecution by common informers (who took a share in the proceeds of a successful prosecution) was of much greater importance: M. Beresford, 'The Common Informer, the Penal Statute and Economic Regulation' (1957–8) 10 Econ. Hist. Rev. (2nd ser.) 221.          [25] P. Williams, *The Tudor Regime* (1979), p. 156.

tension between public interest aims and private interest ambitions. Regulatory controls were typically justified, often explicitly in the Preamble to an Act of Parliament, by reference to the 'common profit of the Realm'.[26] It is nevertheless clear from historical sources that many were actively sought by guilds of the trades whose activities were being controlled, to protect the profits of their members from outside competition.[27]

### (b) Nineteenth-Century Regulation

By the middle of the eighteenth century, the fabric of trade regulation erected in the Tudor and Stuart periods had largely disappeared. Its re-emergence in the nineteenth century coincided with industrialization and urbanization.[28] In his famous study of the subject, Dicey saw the growth of regulation as a late nineteenth century development, reflecting a collectivist disenchantment—fuelled by the expansion of the electoral franchise—with the dominant *laissez-faire* ideology.[29] Modern historians discredit this view.[30] There never was an 'age of *laissez-faire*', and state intervention did not result from any abrupt shift to collectivist ideology but rather emerged gradually, throughout the nineteenth century, as a pragmatic response to social problems: 'England stumbled into the modern administrative State without design.'[31]

The key factor in this development, and that which distinguished it so markedly from the regulation of earlier periods, was the emergence of administrative structures capable of diagnosing the problems and formulating solutions to deal with them.[32] Although there was some growth in central government bureaucracy, that was not as significant as other institutional developments: the creation of *ad hoc* commissions to investigate social conditions, of professional draftsmen to formulate legislative solutions, and, above all, of permanent Boards or Inspectorates to administer the new law. Indeed, the existence of specialist bodies served to inject an almost unstoppable momentum into the growth of regulatory law.[33] In carrying out their responsibilities, these administrators would

---

[26] See e.g. the Preamble to 5 & 6 Edward VI, c. 6 (1552).

[27] E. Lipson, *The Economic History of England* (6th edn., 1956), vol. iii, pp. 332–3. Sharp criticism of regulation of this kind is to be found in Adam Smith's *Wealth of Nations* (ed. W. Todd, 1976), bk. iv.

[28] See generally, A. Taylor, *Laissez-faire and State Intervention in Nineteenth-century Britain* (1972).

[29] A. V. Dicey, *Law and Public Opinion in England during the Nineteenth Century* (2nd edn., ed. E. C. S. Wade, 1962).

[30] Taylor, above, n. 28, ch. 8. See also P. Atiyah, *The Rise and Fall of the Freedom of Contract* (1979), pp. 231–7. [31] Ibid. p. 236.

[32] H. Arthurs, *Without the Law: Administrative Justice and Legal Pluralism in the Nineteenth Century* (1985); P. Craig, *Administrative Law* (2nd edn., 1989), pp. 34–50.

[33] O. MacDonagh, 'The Nineteenth-Century Revolution in Government: A Reappraisal' (1958) 1 Historical J. 52.

often find defects in the legislative provisions, perhaps caused by the political necessity of reaching compromises. To correct the defects, they would demand amendments to the provisions or an extension to their own rule-making powers. The creation of more detailed rules might lead to the identification of new loopholes and the cycle would be repeated, perhaps indefinitely.

The legal status of some of the specialist bodies (or 'regulatory agencies', as we would now call them) was problematic.[34] The majority were independent of government and thus not answerable to Parliament. Moreover, when they engaged in rule-making, it was not always clear to what extent this activity came within the powers conferred by the legislation. Their relationship with traditional legal institutions was not facilitated by the fact that when, for purposes of enforcement, resort was had to local courts, they found it difficult to obtain convictions.[35] Criticisms, both from politicians and from lawyers, led eventually to the decline of the independent regulatory agencies. The powers of some were transferred to central or local government; others retained their identity but were subject to more formalized arrangements regarding both the legislative definition of their powers and their accountability to Ministers (and through them to Parliament).

This period also saw the emergence of distinctive forms of social and economic regulation. Prominent among the former was the large number of measures dealing with public health[36] and the conditions of employment.[37] In addition, there were some early forms of consumer protection,[38] although these tended to concentrate on combating fraud (e.g. through weights and measures and anti-adulteration controls) rather than on providing mandatory product or service standards. The need for economic regulation arose with the creation of the railways and the mass supply of water, gas, and electricity, when it became clear that competition in these industries was not feasible.[39] So long as the ownership of the enterprise remained in private hands or municipal corporations, there was legislative regulation of prices, the quality of service, and safety.

## (c) Twentieth-Century Growth of Regulation

There has been a steady growth of regulation throughout most of the present century, reaching a high point at the end of the 1970s. Several factors influenced this growth. First, it can be linked to the changed perception of the role of the state in relation to the economy, resulting

---

[34] Arthurs, above, n. 32, ch. 4.                      [35] Ibid. p. 105.
[36] C. Brockington, *Public Health in the Nineteenth Century* (1965).
[37] M. Thomas, *Early Factory Legislation* (1948).
[38] Atiyah, above, n. 30, pp. 545–50.
[39] J. Sleeman, *British Public Utilities* (1953), ch. 4.

from Keynesian ideas, although the latter had a greater impact on government investment in, and control of, industrial development[40] than on regulation as we use the term here.[41] Secondly, as a result of universal suffrage, governments came under pressure to adopt policies which appealed to a broader section of the population and, in particular, to be seen to respond quickly to problems when they emerged in an acute form and thus were given extensive media coverage. Regulation often provided a convenient solution, not least because, as Dicey had observed, 'the beneficial effect of State intervention, especially in the form of legislation, is direct, immediate, and, so to speak, visible, whilst its evil effects are gradual and indirect, and lie out of sight'.[42] Thirdly, rapid advances in technology constituted greater threats to health and safety and also created problems for individual consumer choice. It seemed rash to leave matters to the combination of an unregulated market and private law remedies when the necessary expertise and experience could be accumulated in centralized public agencies. Fourthly, there occurred in the 1960s and 1970s what has been described in the American context as a 'rights revolution':[43] groups representing, for example, the environment, consumers, and disadvantaged members of the community emerged as a significant political force and demanded, if only rhetorically, 'rights' to increased protection.

The scope of social regulation expanded enormously but, for our purposes, developments in the methods and forms of control were equally important. Perhaps because of an increased acceptance of the state's power to limit, in the public interest, traditional property rights and freedom of economic activity, greater use was made of the most interventionist of regulatory forms, the requirement of prior approval. The town and country planning legislation, controlling developments in land use, is the most obvious example.[44] Confidence in the knowledge and expertise of centralized agencies and in their ability to formulate appropriate regulatory solutions for a huge variety of industrial circumstances led, in some areas, to a proliferation of highly detailed and complex standards regimes, many of them requiring firms to use specific processes or specific materials.[45]

During the first part of the century, economic regulation, in the form of price and quality controls, persisted and indeed was extended to some industries (e.g. bus and coach services) which were not obviously natural

---

[40] S. Young and A. Lowe, *Intervention in the Mixed Economy* (1974).

[41] In contrast, in the USA, the New Deal, which was partly inspired by Keynesian doctrine is considered to have constituted a breakthrough in the development of regulatory systems: C. Sunstein, *After the Rights Revolution: Reconceiving the Regulatory State* (1990), pp. 18–24.

[42] Above, n. 29, p. 257.

[43] Sunstein, above, n. 41, pp. 24–31.                    [44] Below, pp. 238–44.

[45] What we call 'specification' standards: below, p. 151.

monopolies.[46] The key development occurred after the Second World War, when the major utilities were transferred to public ownership. In this sector, legal forms of constraint disappeared and were replaced by (some) government direction and political accountability.

### (d) Deregulation and Privatization

The period since the end of the 1970s has generally been perceived as one of 'deregulation'.[47] While the use of this term is not inapposite, it is also misleading. Certainly within the area of social regulation, the Deregulation Initiative, inaugurated in 1985,[48] has resulted in the abolition of a number of controls.[49] A renewed impetus was given to the Initiative from 1993–94 with the Deregulation and Contracting Out Bill[50] and the publication of a long list of deregulatory proposals.[51] But many so-called 'deregulating' measures have involved not the removal of external constraints but rather a change to less interventionist methods and forms. For example, the standards governing occupational health and safety and consumer products have become less prescriptive; detailed mandatory requirements have been replaced by general targets, employers and manufacturers being left free either to conform to recommended standards or else to devise alternative means of meeting the targets.[52]

Some areas of social regulation have continued to grow, notably those pertaining to the environment[53] and financial services.[54] But the most dramatic developments have occurred in the realm of economic regulation. The privatization of the leading public utilities has necessitated the creation of elaborate new regulatory structures which, though resembling in some respects their nineteenth-century ancestors, are considerably more sophisticated.[55] At the same time, it has been government policy to inject competition, or more competition, into the relevant industries,[56] and were this to be achieved the need for regulation would be reduced. The more

---

[46] Below, pp. 321–2.

[47] There is already a huge literature on the developments described in this section. See particularly: J. Kay, C. Mayer, and D. Thompson (eds.), *Privatisation and Regulation: The UK Experience* (1986); D. Swann, *The Retreat of the State: Deregulation and Privatisation in the UK and US* (1988); K. Button and D. Swann (eds.), *The Age of Regulatory Reform* (1989); Majone, above, n. 5.

[48] *Lifting the Burden*, above, n. 2.

[49] For details, see White Paper, *Releasing Enterprise* (1988, Cm. 512), Annexe 1, and Dept. of Trade and Industry, *Cutting Red Tape for Business* (1991).

[50] See further below, p. 338.

[51] Dept. of Trade and Industry, *Deregulation: Cutting Red Tape* (1994).

[52] Below, pp. 185–7 and 201–3.

[53] Below, pp. 204–11.

[54] Only some aspects are covered in this book (below, pp. 138–41). For a more general account see A. Page and R. Ferguson, *Investor Protection* (1992), and for critical evaluation, A. Seldon (ed.), *Financial Regulation—or Over-Regulation?* (1988).

[55] Below, pp. 305–17.                                    [56] Below, pp. 290–3.

extensive use of public franchising within broadcasting and its future application to railways[57] suggest that it is gaining in political popularity as an alternative method of dealing with natural monopolies. Nevertheless, doubts persist concerning the nature of the bidding process and its ability to generate services which meet public interest goals.[58]

It is clear that the shift in political and economic ideology associated, in Britain, with Mrs Thatcher's assumption of power has been a major inspiration for these developments.[59] The reaffirmation of faith in the efficiency of competitive markets and the commitment to controlling public expenditure and limiting the public sector have obviously had a very significant impact on regulatory policies. But other factors have also contributed to the search for new regulatory forms, particularly in relation to social regulation.

Although the strident criticisms of 'regulatory failure' which abounded in the 1970s[60] may well have been exaggerated, there was a general perception that industry had been subjected to an unnecessarily complex and inflexible body of detailed rules, some of which were difficult to reconcile with public interest goals. This perception was combined with a growing scepticism concerning the ability of centralized bureaucracies, whether a government department or a regulatory agency, to prescribe technical standards which were appropriate for varying local circumstances.[61] These institutions might, indeed, be motivated to over-regulate: while they would derive benefits—notably an enhancement of prestige—from being seen to respond vigorously to a problem attracting public concern, others—shareholders, employees, consumers, taxpayers—would have to pay the cost.[62]

Finally, account must be taken of the evolution towards a Single European Market and its impact on regulatory policy.[63] The fact that differences between national regulatory regimes constituted a barrier to the creation of an integrated market was not, by itself, sufficient to justify deregulation. It could be, and idealistically was, envisaged that the regimes could be harmonized. In those areas where there has. been effective harmonization—food standards is a good example[64]—the form of regulation is little affected, although decision-making has to some extent been transferred to a different forum. But harmonization proved to be a lengthy process, too easily frustrated by the assertion of national interests, and in

---

[57] Below, pp. 325 and 327.
[58] Below, pp. 324–7.
[59] For a more detailed discussion of the origins of privatization, see below, pp. 288–9.
[60] Below, pp. 55–6.
[61] For a theoretical justification of this scepticism, see Hayek, above, n. 9, and below, pp. 56–7.                                                                    [62] Below, p. 173.
[63] For more detailed discussion, see below, pp. 174–9.
[64] Below, p. 193.

1985 a new policy emerged. Harmonization would be limited to general principles; Member States could retain their own regulatory systems but, for the purpose of intra-Community trade, would have to recognize the validity of the regulatory requirements of other Member States. As a consequence of this principle of mutual recognition, and to preserve the competitiveness of domestic industries, governments have come under pressure to reduce the burden of national regulation.

# PART I
# THEORIES OF REGULATION

# The Context of Regulation: The Market and Private Law

In Chapter 1, reference was made to two basic systems of economic organization: the market system and the collectivist system, identifiable with, respectively, private law and regulation. According to the public interest theory, regulation is to be justified as a corrective to perceived deficiencies in the operation of the market. An understanding of the latter, and its limitations, is thus an essential prelude to our exploration of the public interest theory in Chapter 3. It also provides a useful context for introducing the reader to the economic concepts which will be used as analytical tools throughout this book.

### 1. CO-OPERATION AND TRANSACTIONS

We begin by examining certain features which will be found in any form of social organization. The first is that individuals must co-operate if they are to satisfy fundamental human needs. In anything other than the purest of 'Robinson Crusoe' societies, individuals are not capable by personal efforts alone of satisfying their wants. This is because the wants can be met only by different skills and different resources, neither of which are evenly spread among the population. It follows that individuals naturally become 'specialists' in various areas of production, depending on their attributes and access to resources. The surplus produced by an individual in his or her own specialist activity can be exchanged with the surpluses created by others. Jack has the aptitude to construct shelters and exchanges one such dwelling for food produced by Jill's agricultural efforts which generate more than she needs. To facilitate exchanges of this kind, it becomes convenient to use a common denominator—money—by means of which individuals can communicate how they value one product against another. Prices play a key role in this process, since they enable potential buyers to indicate the intensity of their demand for particular products and potential suppliers to compare what they would earn from putting their resources to that use, as opposed to other uses. In the language of economics, supply is determined by 'opportunity cost'.[1]

---

[1] A. I. Ogus and C. Veljanovski (eds.), *Readings in the Economics of Law and Regulation* (1984), pp. 24–30.

Trade is, then, essential for human welfare. What social, and therefore legal, institutions are necessary for trade in this simple form to take place? The most basic need is for the establishment of a system of government to enforce these essential arrangements. Clearly, each producer must have the power to exclude others from the resources, notably the raw materials and the human faculties (body and mind), necessary for the productive process, and also from the fruits of productive efforts. If, for example, Jill cannot herself dispose of the corn which she is able to grow, she will receive no reward for her efforts and consequently she has no incentive to produce. Protection against such interference can be provided by a system of *property rights*: institutions within a society are given authority to define the extent of an individual's power of exclusion, and to enforce that power against intruders, ultimately by threatening physical compulsion. The institutional arrangements for defining, adjudicating and enforcing the rights are the province of *constitutional law*. The rights themselves may be purely private in character: that is, initiative for their enforcement lies exclusively with the right-holder. Additionally or alternatively, public officials (e.g. the police) may be entrusted with the enforcement role, usually by means of the *criminal law*. The latter, as a public law instrument, constitutes part of the institutional framework of the market system because in any society there must be a minimum level of protection of liberty, life, limb, property, and order.

Trade is normally carried out by agreements and the *law of contract* provides the necessary institutional support. The pivotal role of agreements, and therefore of contract law, to the market system is not difficult to understand.[2] The upholding of contracts makes economic sense because, assuming rational behaviour, both parties gain by the transaction, and so, therefore, does society. Take a simple contract whereby Bill agrees to sell a car to Ben for £5,000. In normal circumstances it is appropriate to infer that Bill values the car at less than £5,000 (say £4,500) and Ben values it at more than £5,000 (say £5,500). If the contract is performed, both parties will gain £500 and therefore there is a gain to society—the car has moved to a more valuable use in the hands of Ben—of £1,000. In the language of economics, this is said to be an allocatively 'efficient' consequence, because someone is made better off and no-one is made worse off.[3] *Freedom of contract* is a natural corollary of this reasoning. On the assumption that individuals know what is best for themselves and behave rationally to maximize their utility (what gives them satisfaction), they should be left free to make what agreements they wish.

---

[2] Cf. A. Kronman and R. A. Posner (eds.), *The Economics of Contract Law* (1979), pp. 1–4; J. Adams and R. Brownsword, 'The Ideologies of Contract Law' (1987) 7 Legal Stud. 205.

[3] See further below, pp. 24–5.

## 2. REDUCING TRANSACTION COSTS

By a further extension of the reasoning, we can explain much of private law, the legal apparatus of the market system, as a series of utility-maximizing but surrogate contracts between relevant individuals. In theory, we can envisage that almost all conceivable welfare goals can be pursued by individuals trading with one another.[4] The problem is that negotiating, formulating, and (if necessary) enforcing the contracts required for this trade involves expenditure or 'transaction costs'. Such costs may be particularly high if more than two parties are involved, or if it is necessary to deal specifically with a large number of contingencies. To some extent, the legal system can assist by making available devices which serve to reduce these transaction costs. These can be thought of as 'surrogate' contracts: legislation and/or case-law may enunciate a set of rights and obligations which will apply to particular situations unless the parties expressly provide otherwise.

### (a) Implied Terms

The first example forms part of the law of contract itself. For many types of commonly encountered agreements, for example, employment, sale, carriage, insurance, credit, there are implied terms which are incorporated into individual contracts, subject to the manifestation by the parties of a contrary intention. (These must be carefully distinguished from *mandatory* implied terms, which are intended to meet collectivist goals, and as such are properly to be treated as analogous to regulation).[5] Implied terms clearly reduce the transaction costs of contracting and, since they may be superseded by contrary agreement, are consistent with the individualist, utility-maximizing assumptions of the market system. Indeed, they serve to further its aims: the welfare goals of the parties are achieved at lower cost.[6]

### (b) Fiduciary Obligations

Similar devices exist outside the law of contract, one prominent example being the creation of fiduciary obligations. In a wide variety of circumstances one party (the 'principal') delegates some decision-making power over resources to another (the 'agent'). In an ideal world, where the principal had appropriate knowledge and expertise, he could, in a highly detailed contract, lay down specifically how the agent was to exercise the

---

[4] This is the basis of the Coase Theorem which argues that if the cost of making market transactions is ignored, social welfare will be maximized however the law allocates rights: R. Coase, 'The Problem of Social Cost' (1960) 3 J. Law & Econ. 1.

[5] Cf. below, pp. 257–8.

[6] C. J. Goetz and R. E. Scott, 'The Limits of Expanded Choice: An Analysis of the Interactions between Express and Implied Contract Terms' (1985) 73 Calif. LR 261.

power. Typically, however, the information available to, and the expertise of, the agent is much greater and as a second-best, transaction-cost-saving solution, the law in such cases imposes, subject to overriding contracts, a fiduciary obligation on the agent, requiring him to act in the best interests of the principal, according to standards worked out in the case-law. Such standards reflect what would have been in a detailed contract, if such had been made.[7]

## (c) Forms of Organization

There are different ways in which individuals can co-operate for the purposes of productive activity.[8] The parties can contract across the market (Jack enters into a one-off contract with Jill to buy corn), one party can employ another with power to direct how that other is to work (Jack enters into a contract of employment with Jill for a fixed period, whereby she agrees to carry out his instructions), they can form a partnership, or they can form a company. The choice between these various forms is primarily determined by which is cheaper in terms of transaction costs.[9] Further, each form carries with it a concomitant set of mutual rights and duties, the majority of which are nevertheless subject to being overridden by explicit provision in contracts or other legal instruments, such as the company articles or memorandum. The function of the law is again clear: to achieve a saving on the transaction costs associated with detailed contracting, it provides a number of alternative forms designed to suit different types of enterprises. Adoption of any one such form communicates a signal to the parties involved, and to those dealing with them, that certain legal consequences (e.g. fiduciary duties or limited liability) will arise unless steps are taken to make alternative provision in a relevant legal instrument. As has been observed, forms of organization are 'like ready-to-wear clothes: if they fit well they can be worn without alteration, or they can be modified until they fit better. With the right legal craftsmanship or tailoring, any form can be modified to suit the needs of any group of clients'.[10]

### 3. THIRD PARTY EFFECTS

As we have seen, contracting with others will normally be economically efficient, because one or all parties gain and no-one loses. But clearly some behaviour, whether or not it involves contracts, may adversely affect

---

[7] F. Easterbrook and D. Fischel, 'Contract and Fiduciary Duty' (1993) J. Law & Econ. 425.

[8] O. Williamson, *The Economic Institutions of Capitalism* (1985), chs. 1–3.

[9] R. Coase, 'The Nature of the Firm' (1937) 4 Economica (NS) 386; H. Demsetz, *Ownership, Control and the Firm* 1. (1988).

[10] R. Hessen, 'The Modern Corporation and Private Property: A Reappraisal' (1983) 26 J. Law & Econ. 273, 283.

others and thus will not satisfy this test. For example, to facilitate the cultivation of crops Jill may use a fertilizer, some of which drains into a river and impairs the quality of water available to downstream users. If Jill does not have to cover the costs thereby imposed on others in the pricing of her corn—or, as economists describe it, 'external costs' have not been 'internalized'—there will be a misallocation of resources. The price will be lower than if it had reflected the true social cost of production; at that lower price, more will be demanded and hence a larger number of the products will be manufactured and sold. From society's point of view, it would have been better if some of the resources employed in growing and selling the corn at this lower price had been put to another, more valuable use.[11]

What are the solutions to such problems within the context of the market system? In theory, it is possible for the misallocation to be corrected through utility-maximizing contracts made with all third parties affected. Thus, neighbouring landowners may extract an undertaking from Jill not to pollute. The price that they are prepared to pay for this (say £x) will reflect how much they value the water free from the pollutant. The price that Jill is prepared to accept to stop the pollution (say £y) will, in its turn, reflect the value to her of using the fertilizer and allowing it to drain into the river. If the bargain is struck, £x will exceed £y, with the important implication that it is socially more valuable for the water to be pollutant-free. If the bargain is not struck, because £y exceeds £x, then the result is equally appropriate from society's point of view, because the bargaining process has revealed that Jill's use of the water (for draining fertilizer) is more valuable than that of the landowners. In either case, there will be no misallocation of resources.[12]

If in theory the process of contracting can solve the problem of third party effects, in practice it is rarely able to do so. The transaction costs of bargaining between two parties are often high; when larger numbers are involved they quickly become astronomical. Consider what would happen if twenty downstream users had to agree on what they would pay Jill.[13] Moreover, the problem of dispersion of third party effects may be exacerbated by time and uncertainty. For example, the harm arising from Jill's pollution, if it is toxic, may adversely affect an indeterminate number of people over an indeterminate time-period. Alternative legal solutions are obviously necessary. As we shall see, there are a number of regulatory

[11] See further, below, pp. 35–8.
[12] Coase, above n. 4.
[13] One reason why it will be difficult (and expensive) to reach an agreement is the 'free rider' problem: each of the downstream users will be motivated to make a minimum contribution to the price payable, knowing that if a deal is struck he will gain the same benefit, however much (or little) he pays.

devices for dealing with externalities; here we must examine the methods which are consistent with the market system.

## (a) Refinement of Property Rights

Hitherto we have treated property rights as conferring unlimited power on owners to use and exploit resources as they wish. But the principles governing the extent of property rights can be refined to deal with the externality problem by limiting use to accord with what would have been contained in a contract between the owner and the affected third parties if transaction costs had not prevented them from reaching such an agreement. The device of restrictive covenants provides a straightforward example. In selling part of my land, I may wish to restrict the purchaser's use of it. Obviously, I can achieve this aim by a term in my contract with him. But it would be very costly if I had to reach an equivalent agreement with all subsequent owners, or users, of his land. Subject to certain constraints, the law treats the restrictive covenant with my purchaser as a property right which automatically runs with the land and is enforceable against subsequent owners and users. The law of private nuisance can be rationalized in a similar way. The principles governing liability typically require that one landowner's user should not *unreasonably* interfere with the interests of neighbours. This may be construed as conferring power on judges to aim at imposing standards of environmental amenity which the relevant parties would have agreed to in the light of the value they attribute to such amenity.[14]

## (b) Principles of Tort Law

Much of tort law consists of principles determining when one person is entitled to compensation for injuries caused by another. As such, its content is often considered to reflect notions of corrective justice based on theories of moral entitlement: where Jill's rights are transgressed by Jack's 'wrongful' conduct and she suffers a loss in consequence, he is bound to repair the damage.[15] But without undue distortion, tort law might also be viewed as a series of 'surrogate' contracts to deal with problems of externalities.[16] Some accidents, for example those arising within the context of an employment relationship, may occur in situations already governed by a contractual relationship, and the contract in question may indicate what standard of care is to be exercised by the potential injurer, thereby reflecting the utilities of the parties concerned. In other cases, no

[14] A. I. Ogus and G. M. Richardson, 'Economics and the Environment: A Study of Private Nuisance' (1977) 36 Camb. LJ 284.

[15] See the papers collected in R. L. Rabin, *Perspectives on Tort Law* (1976).

[16] R. Cooter, 'Unity in Tort, Contract and Property: The Model of Precaution' (1985) 73 Calif. LR 1.

doubt the majority, it is impossible to determine this *ex ante* because the transaction costs of contracting are infinitely high: clearly a pedestrian wishing to cross a road cannot enter into contracts with all motorists that happen to be passing! The law of tort may then attempt to lay down standards of care which, predictably, the relevant parties would have agreed to if contracting had been possible. To this it may be objected that, since people do not typically reach agreements about the standard of care to be taken in relation to risks about which they know nothing, an attempt to 'mimic' such agreements is futile. If, however, we objectivize the issue, we would expect individuals in society rationally to agree on what may be described as the 'socially optimal level of care', that is where the marginal benefits of care taken (reduction in the costs of accidents) are approximately equal to the marginal costs of taking such care. From this perspective, therefore, the law of tort will be formulated to induce risk-creators to behave in such a way as will minimize the costs both of accidents and of accident avoidance.[17]

### (c) External Benefits

Externalities can be positive as well as negative. If a third party acquires a benefit from a producer's activity without having to pay for it, that benefit will not be reflected in the income the producer receives and will not, therefore, be taken into account in making decisions as to how much to produce. If we can assume that the third party would have been prepared to pay for the benefit, a misallocation results, because the signal of aggregate demand for the commodity to which the producer responds (the income realizable from those who have to pay) does not represent the true social demand for the commodity; in consequence, there will be under-production of the commodity. For example, if I knew that it would be possible to copy this book without me, the author, receiving any payment either directly or indirectly (via the publishers), I would have less incentive to produce the book than if the copiers were forced to pay for it.

This very example indicates the solution often available under private law. I am given a property right in what I produce, enabling me to prevent third parties from copying my work and thus forcing them to transact with, and pay, me if they wish to copy: the externality is internalized. The formulation and enforcement of property rights are, however, far from costless. In relation to some resources, it is impracticable (i.e. transaction costs are infinitely high) to create property rights. Suppose—doubtless, a heroic assumption—that this book contains a novel idea or theory that is freely used by scholars and practitioners. I can assert no property right over it (theories, unlike industrial inventions, are not patentable[18]), the

---

[17] See generally S. Shavell, *The Economics of Accident Law* (1987).
[18] Patent Act 1977, s. 1(2)(a).

main reason being that it would be almost impossible in practice to determine the extent to which others had made use of the theory. Further, it is a physical characteristic of some resources, known as 'public goods', that the benefit is shared by a group and it is impossible to exclude a member of that group from the benefit, classic examples being defence, and law and order. In such cases, private property rights are of no avail, and, as we shall see,[19] regulatory institutions have to decide questions of supply and financing.

### 4. COMPETITION

Our brief survey of the market system must be completed by an account of competition. Competition is an essential feature of the system for reasons both political and economic. The political justification is that it decentralizes and disperses power. When decision-making power is concentrated in a small number of hands, whether public or private, individuals' freedom to choose how they wish to use resources is limited. But it is the economic function of competition which has attracted most attention. Economic theory posits that when an industry is 'perfectly competitive' it will generate allocative efficiency, the resources of society being put to their most valuable use. 'Perfect competition' exists 'when the number of firms selling a homogeneous commodity is so large, and each individual firm's share of the market is so small, that no individual firm finds itself able to influence appreciably the commodity's price by varying the quantity of output it sells'.[20] In such circumstances, each firm will produce up to the point where the marginal revenue of production (the price paid by buyers for the last unit of output at that point) equals the marginal cost (the cost to the firm of producing that last unit). Each consumer will demand the commodity up to the point where her marginal valuation of the commodity is equal to the market price. Thus, in a competitive equilibrium, the marginal valuation of consumers will be equal to the marginal cost of producing the commodity and, in the absence of externalities, the marginal social benefit and the marginal social cost of producing the commodity are equal; and allocative efficiency will result.

If a firm tries to sell the product at a price above its cost, it will lose sales to other firms; in the long run, and given freedom to enter the industry, each firm will produce at the lowest point on its average cost curve. For this reason, perfect competition is said to lead also to 'productive efficiency', which maximizes output relative to input costs.

[19] Below, pp. 33–5.
[20] F. M. Scherer, *Industrial Market Structure and Economic Performance* (2nd edn., 1980), p. 10.

At the other extreme from perfect competition is pure monopoly. A monopolist firm, because it is the sole producer of a commodity, is able to determine both the quantity produced and the price at which it is sold. Unlike a competitive firm, it will be able to maximize profits by selling at a price greater than the marginal cost of producing the relevant number of units of the commodity.[21] Output will be lower than it would have been if the competitive equilibrium price had been charged (equal to marginal cost), and those who would have purchased the commodity at that price are thus deprived of the benefit that would have accrued to them. The result is allocative inefficiency: the potential purchasers will use the money they would have spent on the monopolized commodity in ways which give them less satisfaction. This is often called the 'deadweight loss' of monopoly. Also, the lack of competition is assumed to dull the incentive on the firm to minimize the costs of production, thus leading to productive inefficiency.

Between the extremes of perfect competition and pure monopoly there is, of course, a wide spectrum of situations and practices (for example, oligopolies and cartels) which to a greater or lesser extent inhibit competition. We cannot here explore the highly complex question of what degree of imperfect competition should be controlled and by what means. For present purposes it is sufficient to note that private legal instruments are available to enhance competition, for example, by rendering void contracts in restraint of trade or by conferring rights in tort law on third parties suffering losses as a result of anti-competitive practices.[22] Nevertheless, in most legal systems, such instruments are overshadowed by public, regulatory devices which have been considered necessary, given the difficulties and shortcomings of private enforcement.

## 5. ASSUMPTIONS AND LIMITATIONS OF THE MARKET SYSTEM

We have been considering the market system as a form of organization which, as reinforced by certain (normally private) legal institutions, is supposed to advance economic welfare, more specifically allocative efficiency. That contention now needs to be examined in more depth, to render explicit the assumptions on which it is based and the limitations to which it gives rise.

*Individualism.* The model assumes that social welfare can be understood only as the aggregate of all individual welfare; what is 'valuable to society' can have no other meaning.

[21] For a technical explanation, see ibid. pp. 14–20.
[22] See R. Whish, *Competition Law* (3rd edn., 1993), ch. 2.

*Utility-Maximizing Behaviour.* Individuals are assumed to behave 'rationally' by choosing courses of action which maximize their utility. With the possible exception of the very young and the mentally handicapped, no allowance is made for incompetence or the inability to process information.

*Information.* Individuals are further assumed to have the information necessary to make utility-maximizing choices. Although agreements resulting from a misrepresentation by one party to another will not, in general, be enforced, the mere absence of information is not considered to be an obstacle.

*Absence of Externalities.* Allocative efficiency will result only if decision-making in the production process takes account of external costs and benefits. As we have seen, there are private legal devices available, notably contract, property rights, and tort, which may internalize such externalities, but their use is constrained by transaction costs. These may be so high that misallocations are not corrected.

*Competitive Markets.* Finally, the market system depends crucially on the existence of competition in relation to resources. It is far from clear that the private legal means of controlling anti-competitive practices and situations are adequate.

The concept of 'allocative efficiency' is itself problematic as a normative goal for economic welfare. In the first place, there is no general agreement among economists on the test to be applied.[23] In the discussion so far we have implicitly been adopting the *Pareto* test, which holds that the allocation of resources is efficient when it is impossible to make any one individual better off without, at the same time, making someone else worse off. Put another way, a 'Pareto improvement' to welfare occurs when at least one individual gains and no-one loses. As we have seen, a simple transaction may constitute a Pareto improvement if the only parties affected by it gain as a result. But the narrowness of the test which effectively allows any one individual to veto a change which would benefit the rest of society obviously makes it of limited use for policy purposes: it is almost impossible to conceive of a reform which would not engender at least one loser. It is for this reason that many economists tend to adopt the alternative *Kaldor-Hicks* criterion. This stipulates as efficient a policy which results in sufficient benefits for those who gain such that *potentially* they can compensate fully all the losers and still remain better off. The fact that under this test the gainers are not *required* to compensate the losers means that in practice it is satisfied when the gains (to whomsoever) exceed

---

[23] Ogus and Veljanovski, above n. 1, pp. 19-22.

the losses (to whomsoever)—and thus provides a theoretical base for standard cost-benefit analysis.

While the looser character of the Kaldor-Hicks test enables it to be used in a wide variety of circumstances—and it is certainly helpful for the policy-maker to know whether the benefits of a given course of action exceed its costs—it is nevertheless subject to several powerful objections, at least as a conclusive criterion of social welfare. First, it allows for the coercive imposition of losses on individuals. Secondly, because it balances gains against losses in terms of money, it assumes that one unit of the currency has the same value whoever owns it or may receive it. Such an assumption must in many circumstances be false: £1 is clearly worth more to a poor person than to a rich person. This leads inexorably to the third and perhaps most fundamental objection which, unlike the other two, also applies to Pareto efficiency: the tests take no account of distributional justice, a value which has considerable importance in some societies.

Take a policy which, by taxing some part of higher earnings and conferring some benefits on poorer people, attempts a (mild) degree of progressive redistribution. Clearly, such a policy can never satisfy the Pareto test, as higher earners are deprived of some of their property against their will. Application of the Kaldor-Hicks test would appear to lead to the same conclusion. While society's resources should not be diminished merely by the transfer of wealth from richer to poorer people,[24] nevertheless such transfers impose a real and substantial cost in terms of administration. In economic terms, to justify such measures, it would then be necessary to show that the earners' gain in utility from seeing the poorer people benefit exceeded that cost.[25] Similar arguments may be made about less overt forms of redistribution. Suppose that the policymaker had to choose between (A) a policy that increased society's wealth by £1 million and benefited the poor more than the rich, and (B) a policy that increased its wealth by £2 million, the great bulk of which devolved on the rich? Many would argue for (A) on grounds of fairness[26] but (B) would be considered to be superior in Kaldor-Hicks terms.

## 6. CONCLUSIONS

We need now to reach some general conclusions on the nature of law within the context of the market system. Since social welfare is understood in terms only of individual utility, the law is constructed on the basis of private interests. Its fundamental role is to preserve economic liberty, the

---

[24] Though some argue that such transfers lead to work disincentives, thus leading to reduced productivity: L. D. McClements, *The Economics of Social Security* (1978), ch. 4.

[25] A. J. Culyer, *The Political Economy of Social Policy* (1980).

[26] Cf. J. Rawls, *A Theory of Justice* (1972).

freedom to produce, acquire, use, or consume whatever the individual wants. It is coercive only to the extent that force is necessary to achieve this goal. In consequence, public law has a limited scope: criminal law to maintain order and defend the person, property, and liberty against aggression; and constitutional law to secure the institutional arrangements necessary both for the exercise of that power and for the formulation, adjudication, and enforcement of private rights. The private law is predominantly facilitative in character. Its foundational concepts are property, enabling society's resources to be exploited and enjoyed by individuals, and contract, which gives security to the processes required for those resources to shift to their most valuable uses. Although private law also lays down general obligations and duties, these can be ousted by contract where they inhibit specific individualist goals. The legal system enshrines a principle of abstract equality and equivalence between individuals. This means that, on the one hand, no groups are singled out for more favourable or less favourable treatment, and, on the other, that the state, save only for its monopoly of force, is a legal subject like any other.

The law that we are here describing lends itself easily to coherence.[27] The rules which it contains are not designed instrumentally to achieve particular social goals, a characteristic which would seem inevitably to lead them to transcend different perceptions of just outcomes. Rather, they are derivable deductively from a set of principles which in its turn is referable to the underlying value of individual autonomy implicit in the market system. The *outcomes* are necessarily treated as 'just' if the *processes* by which they are reached (inheritance, trade, etc.) are 'just', that is, consistent with the moral value of individual autonomy.[28]

Admittedly, this perception of private law is not universally held. Some scholars purport to find, particularly in contemporary judicial doctrine, a tendency to adapt principles to meet distributional and paternalist concerns.[29] As will be seen in Chapter 12, private law, at least to the extent that it is not modifiable by contract, can be accommodated to collective goals of this kind. But its capacity to perform this role in a coherent and consistent manner is necessarily limited and it would be misleading to give undue prominence to it.

In English-speaking jurisdictions, the law associated with the market system has been predominantly customary, or common law, that is, has

---

[27] S. F. C. Milsom, 'The Nature of Blackstone's Achievement' (1981) 1 Ox. J. Legal Stud. 1, 3; N. E. Simmonds, *The Decline of Juridical Reason* (1984), ch. 2.
[28] Cf. R. Nozick, *Anarchy, State and Utopia* (1974).
[29] e.g. D. Kennedy, 'Distributive and Paternalist Motives in Contract and Tort Law, with Special Reference to Compulsory Terms and Unequal Bargaining Power' (1982) 41 Maryland LR 563.

been formulated and developed primarily by judicial decisions. The codification of private law in other jurisdictions shows that there is no inherent contradiction between legislation and the market system; indeed, as Bentham among others argued, the very process of codification should enhance the coherence of the system.[30] On the other hand, a powerful theory has been advanced asserting that the evolutionary character of the common law is essential for the realization of the economic goals implicit in the market system. Hayek identifies both the market and the common law with what he calls 'spontaneous order', a social organization which is not deliberately brought about and which has no specific purpose, but which enables individuals (including judges) to make decisions about courses of action within an environment of limited information and certainty.[31] Just as the competitive market rewards those who, with their decentralized and fragmented knowledge, experiment most successfully in meeting changing patterns of demand, so the common law relying on the individual judge functioning more as an 'unwitting tool . . . than a conscious initiator'[32] enables the principles guiding human conduct to evolve in an unplanned way to what will most suit society's changing needs.

Whatever the merits of this theory,[33] no industrialized society has ever relied exclusively on a system of private law general principles, emanating from judicial decisons (or a Code). It is not difficult to discern the reasons.[34] The chief problem afflicting private law is that of transaction costs. Rationally, individuals and firms will only seek to enforce rights where the expected benefits exceed the expected costs, which include not only legal expenses but also time and trouble. Given the general principle that compensation for the infringement of private rights should not exceed the losses sustained by the plaintiff, many legitimate claims are for this reason not pursued. Thus externalities which affect large numbers but which impose only a small loss on each individual right-holder will not be 'internalized' by private law instruments and serious misallocations will remain uncorrected.[35] The inhibitory impact of the costs of private

---

[30] J. Bentham, *An Introduction to the Principles of Morals and Legislation* (ed. J. H. Burns and H. L. A. Hart, 1982), pp. 302–8.

[31] F. A. Hayek, *Law, Legislation and Liberty* (3 vols., 1973–9).

[32] Ibid. i. p. 66.

[33] For critical evaluation, see A. I. Ogus, 'Law and Spontaneous Order: Hayek's Contribution to Legal Theory' (1989) 16 J. Law & Soc. 393.

[34] See generally E. Freund, *Standards of American Legislation* (2nd edn., 1965), pp. 68–71; D. L. Horowitz, *The Courts and Social Policy* (1977); A. I. Ogus, 'Social Costs in a Private Law Setting' (1983) 3 Int. Rev. Law & Econ. 27; S. Shavell, 'Liability for Harm versus Regulation of Safety' (1984) 13 J. Legal Stud. 357.

[35] The problem may be alleviated to some extent by allowing class actions or by creating additional financial incentives for successful plaintiffs, such as punitive damages. The English legal system, in contrast to its American counterpart, has, however, been slow to adopt devices of this kind: cf. J. A. Jolowicz, 'Protection of Diffuse, Fragmented and Collective Interests in Civil Litigation: English Law' (1983) 42 Camb. LJ 227.

enforcement is exacerbated in cases where it is difficult to acquire the information necessary to pursue a successful claim, particularly where high technology is involved, and where complex causation questions arise. The traditional systems of adjudicating and enforcing private rights also have inherent limitations. Normally the courts have jurisdiction to enforce rights only *ex post*, that is, only after an interference has taken place and damage has been inflicted.[36] Of course, the prospect of being sued *ex post* will often constitute an adequate deterrence *ex ante*, but if the infringer will only be subjected to making compensatory payments she may be able effectively to avoid the sanction by insolvency.[37] Finally, to the extent that the courts are responsible not only for enforcing rights but also for specifying the content of those rights, notably by formulating 'efficient' standards of conduct under the rubric of what is 'reasonable', the adversarial nature of the proceedings will impose constraints on the information available to them.

If, then, 'market failure' is accompanied by 'private law failure', of the kind described above, there is on public interest grounds a prima facie case for regulatory intervention. This forms the subject-matter of Chapter 3, where non-economic justifications, for example distributional justice and paternalism, will also be considered.

[36] On the cautious use of *quia timet* injunctions, see R. J. Sharpe, *Injunctions and Specific Performance* (1983), pp. 30–7.

[37] P. Brodeur, *Outrageous Misconduct: The Asbestos Industry on Trial* (1985); Shavell, above, n. 17, chs. 7, 10.

# 3

# Public Interest Grounds
# for Regulation

## 1. INTRODUCTION

In the previous chapter we examined the market system of economic organization in which the state plays only a residual role and in which problems are resolved primarily through private law. We also considered the limitations of that system in terms of its capacity to generate outcomes consistent with economic welfare. In this chapter, we explore the public interest arguments for the collectivist alternative.

Any attempt to formulate a comprehensive list of public interest goals which may be used to justify regulation would be futile, since what constitutes the 'public interest' will vary according to time, place, and the specific values held by a particular society.[1] In this chapter, we shall nevertheless examine those goals which in modern Western societies have typically been asserted as reasons for collectivist measures, and which are derived from the perceived shortcomings of the market system. In company with others who have explored this area,[2] we shall distinguish between economic and non-economic goals.

## 2. ECONOMIC GOALS

In the last chapter we construed economic welfare in terms of allocative efficiency, a situation in which resources are put to their most valuable uses. We also observed how, on certain key assumptions, the unrestricted interaction of market forces generates such efficiency. In the real world in many sets of circumstances these assumptions, notably adequate information, competition, and the absence of externalities, are not fulfilled—in short, there is 'market failure'. Many instances of market failure are remediable, in theory at least, by private law and thus by instruments

---

[1] See generally C. J. Friedrich (ed.), *The Public Interest* (1962), esp. ch. 17.

[2] Cf. B. Mitnick, *The Political Economy of Regulation* (1980), ch. 5; S. Breyer, *Regulation and its Reform* (1982), ch. 1; R. B. Stewart, 'Regulation and the Crisis of Legalisation in the United States', in T. Daintith (ed.), *Law as an Instrument of Economic Policy: Comparative and Critical Approaches* (1988), pp. 110–15; I. Ramsay, *Consumer Protection: Text and Materials* (1989), ch. 2; J. Kay and J. Vickers, 'Regulatory Reform: An Appraisal', in G. Majone (ed.), *Deregulation or Re-regulation* (1990), pp. 225–30; C. Sunstein, *After the Rights Revolution: Reconceiving the Regulatory State* (1990), ch. 2.

which are compatible with the market system in the sense that collective action is not required. But, as we have seen,[3] private law cannot always provide an effective solution.

Where, then, 'market failure' is accompanied by 'private law failure', of the kind described above, there is a prima facie case for regulatory intervention in the public interest. It is important to stress that it is only a prima facie, and not a conclusive, case for such intervention. The reason is that either the regulatory solution may be no more successful in correcting the inefficiencies than the market or private law, or that any efficiency gains to which it does give rise may be outweighed by increased transaction costs or misallocations created in other sectors of the economy. In other words, 'market failure' and 'private law failure' have to be compared with 'regulatory failure'.

### (a) Monopolies and Natural Monopolies

Competition is a crucial assumption of the market model. Where it is seriously impaired by monopolies and anti-competitive practices there is market failure. Competition (or antitrust) law is the principal instrument for dealing with this problem.[4] Since such law serves to reinforce rather than overreach the market system, by attempting to preserve competition, detailed consideration of it does not come within the scope of this book.

A 'natural monopoly' is a special kind of monopoly which calls for very different treatment. While the undesirable consequences (that goods are overpriced and underproduced relative to their true social value) arise equally in relation to natural monopolies, the remedy for the latter lies not in competition. Rather, the monopoly is allowed to prevail; and some form of (economic) regulation is necessary to control those consequences.

A natural monopoly occurs where it is less costly to society for production to be carried out by one firm, rather than by several or many.[5] In most industries there are economies of scale: since part of a firm's costs are fixed, it is proportionally cheaper to increase output. But this is normally true only up to a certain point, beyond which the marginal costs of a firm's production tend to rise. The classic instance of a natural monopoly is where the marginal costs—and hence also average costs—of a single firm's production continue, in the long run, to decline. The monopoly tends to develop 'naturally' as it becomes apparent that a single

---

[3] Above, pp. 27–8.

[4] There is a huge literature on the area. For standard textbook treatment, see: R. Whish, *Competition Law* (3rd edn., 1993) for the UK and EC; and, for a comparative study of EC and US law, J. Fejo, *Monopoly, Law and Market* (1990).

[5] A. E. Kahn, *The Economics of Regulation* (1971), ii. ch. 4; M. Waterson, *Regulation of the Firm and Natural Monopoly* (1988), ch. 2; W. K. Viscusi, J. Vernon, and J. Harrington, *Economics of Regulation and Antitrust* (1992), ch. 11.

firm can supply the total output of an industry more cheaply than more than one firm. Such a situation typically occurs when fixed costs, that is, those that are necessarily incurred whatever the level of output, are high relative to demand. Thus, for example, the supply of electricity requires an enormous initial investment in plant and cables and so forth before even the smallest demand can be met. On the assumption that these fixed costs constitute a high proportion of the total costs of supply, then once the initial investment has been made, the average cost of additional units declines as more are produced.[6]

Even if the marginal costs of production begin to rise at a certain point, thus giving rise to what is sometimes called a 'temporary' natural monopoly, there may be features in the market which still make it cheaper for one firm to produce the total output of an industry.[7] For example, demand may vary considerably according to time and season—there are peak consumption periods of electricity during certain winter hours—and yet the supplier must respond instantaneously to the demand. A second feature, which applies particularly to systems of communication, is interdependence of demand. If one person wishes to speak by telephone to another, and/or receive calls from him, both must subscribe to the same network; there is clearly an economy of scale in a single network.[8] Intuitively, too, it would seem that the duplication of facilities, for example the laying of railway tracks or the construction of grid systems, is itself wasteful and therefore economically to be avoided. The essence of the problem is, however, not the duplication itself—there is such duplication in all competitive markets—but rather the ability, or inability, of the suppliers to achieve economies of scale through the use of a single set of facilities.[9]

In considering what are to be treated as natural monopolies on the basis of this analysis, account must be taken of some further factors. The economies-of-scale phenomenon might affect only one part of the supply process. For example, the arguments which we have considered in relation to the supply of electricity most certainly apply to the *transmission* of power, but less obviously to its *generation*.[10] Moreover, technological developments may substantially transform a natural monopoly into an

---

[6] P. L. Joskow and R. Schmalensee, *Markets for Power: An Analysis of Electrical Utility Deregulation* (1983), ch. 6.            [7] Viscusi *et al.*, above n. 5, pp. 331-335.

[8] J. Vickers and G. Yarrow, 'Telecommunications: Liberalisation and the Privatisation of British Telecom', in J. Kay, C. Mayer, and D. Thompson (eds.), *Privatisation and Regulation: The UK Experience* (1986), pp. 223-4.

[9] Kahn, above, n. 5, pp. 121-2. As he notes, the facilities can in fact be said to be 'duplicated' only when there are no such economies of scale.

[10] Joskow and Schmalensee, above n. 6, ch. 5; G. Yarrow, 'Regulation and Competition in the Electricity Supply Industry', in J. Kay, C. Mayer and D. Thompson (eds.), above, n. 8, ch. 10; White Paper, *Privatising Electricity* (1988, Cm. 322), paras. 32-43.

industry where competition between suppliers is more efficient. This is true of parts of the telecommunications industry where satellites and microwave systems have created alternatives to traditional cable networks, and where a wide range of terminal apparatus can be connected to existing networks.[11]

The existence of what is sometimes called 'cream-skimming' may enhance the case for treating certain industries as natural monopolies.[12] Where entry is free, a competitive firm has an incentive to concentrate on those areas of the market where, for geographical or other reasons, the costs of supply are lowest. The effect of competition is to render it increasingly less profitable to supply the poorer and thinner areas of the market and services in such areas will suffer. Potentially, most markets are affected to some extent at least by this phenomenon and in economic terms the consequences are not undesirable if it reduces the amount of cross-subsidization. Clearly because of problems of transport and scale economies it costs a supplier more to deliver products of the same description and quality to a remote area of low demand than to a neighbouring area of high demand, and that should be reflected in the prices charged. Uniformity of price normally implies cross-subsidization which is allocatively inefficient, demand and supply in the remote area being higher than is economically justified. There are, however, products and services which, it is assumed, should be available at certain minimum standards of frequency and quality in all areas, and in an unregulated market, where suppliers operate on a marginal cost basis, they will not be able to supply to such standards. Utilities and certain modes of transport are typical examples. We may expect electricity to be available at the turn of the switch and an ambulance to take us to and from the nearest hospital, whatever the time of day or night and irrespective of the level of demand. Without regulation, cream-skimming will deprive certain localities of such services.

The account which we have provided of natural monopoly reflects the traditional economic analysis of the problem; and that has been used to justify the forms of economic regulation—public ownership, price and quality regulation, and public franchising—which we consider in Part IV of this book. In recent years a theory of 'contestable markets' has been espoused to challenge this orthodoxy.[13] The gist of the argument is that efficient pricing and production can be forced upon a supplier by the *threat* of competition, just as much as by actual competition. If, for example, in

---

[11] Vickers and Yarrow, above n. 8; G. Knieps, 'Deregulation in Europe: Telecommunications and Transportation', in Majone, above, n. 2, ch. 3.

[12] Kahn, above, n. 5, pp. 7–10.

[13] W. Baumol, J. Panzar and R. Willig, *Contestable Markets and the Theory of Industrial Structure* (1982); W. Brock, 'Contestable Markets and the Theory of Industrial Structure: A Review Article' (1984) 91 J. Pol. Econ. 1055. For a succinct description and evaluation of the theory, see Waterson, above, n. 5, pp. 28–30.

conditions of a temporary natural monopoly[14] a rival supplier is free to enter the market, meet the demand at a lower price, and leave again, that threat should exercise a sufficient constraint on the behaviour of the monopolist to render regulation unnecessary. As an abstract construct, the theory has gained considerable currency. Its impact on regulatory policy in relation to natural monopolies has been much less significant, simply because the assumptions of 'perfect contestability' on which it is based, notably that the entrant can costlessly leave the market when it is no longer profitable to remain, are rarely encountered in practice.[15]

### (b) Public Goods

The second instance of market failure arises in relation to public goods.[16] As its name would suggest, a public good is a commodity the benefit from which is shared by the public as a whole, or by some group within it. More specifically, it combines two characteristics: first, consumption by one person does not leave less for others to consume; and, secondly, it is impossible or too costly for the supplier to exclude those who do not pay from the benefit. Take the often-cited example of a national defence system which provides collective security. That all citizens of Manchester will benefit from such a system will not diminish the benefit that will be enjoyed by citizens of Salford and it is not possible to prevent any citizen of Salford—say, one who does not pay his taxes—from the protection which the system provides. The example should make it obvious why the market method of allocation cannot be used to determine supply of a public good. Suppose a private firm offered to provide a community with protection according to the level of demand for such protection, as expressed by the willingness to pay. Each individual in the community would know that however much she was willing to pay for the protection would not affect the amount of protection actually supplied, because each would be able to benefit to the same degree however much she paid. If she paid nothing, she would still be able to 'free-ride'. Willingness to pay, in other words, cannot be used to measure demand and will thus fail to provide incentives for suppliers to produce.

National (or local) security is an example of a pure public good. Such goods are typically provided by suppliers which are publicly owned—in our example, the armed forces and the police. In fact this is not (economically) essential; a private firm could supply the good, but a public agency is required both to raise sufficient money to secure the supply and to make decisions determining the quantity and quality of the public good. The first of these functions must be carried out by a public institution because, to

---

[14] Above, p. 31.                    [15] Waterson, above, n. 5, pp. 28–9.
[16] R. B. McKenzie and G. Tullock, *Modern Political Economy* (1978), pp. 24–6, 48–9, 341–4.

overcome the free-rider problem, it must have police power to impose taxes. The second requires the political authority to make decisions representing the will of the community, given that demand cannot be determined through individual preferences, as reflected in willingness to pay. However, that very inability to measure demand by reference to individual preferences makes it virtually impossible to devise 'rational' institutional structures for ascertaining the will of the community with any precision.[17] If a policy-maker has to decide how much collective security to 'purchase', he should in theory ascertain the aggregate social demand by a summation of what all individuals within the community would be prepared, by way of taxes, to pay for it. Even if this information could be gathered at reasonable cost, it would be unreliable, since, given the free-rider problem referred to above, each individual would know that the amount which she stipulates that she is ready to pay would not affect the level of provision.[18] Conventional democratic processes cannot fare much better. Voting in a referendum cannot reflect the intensity of preferences—each voter can say only 'yes' or 'no' to a proposed programme—and electing representatives of a legislature invariably involves expressing preferences between different packages of policies.

There are many commodities which, though not pure public goods, nevertheless contain some public good dimension—they are sometimes referred to as 'impure' public goods. Such goods may be supplied and bought in the market but, unless corrected by regulatory interventions, they are subject to a degree of market failure. Education and training constitute examples. Clearly the person who receives this commodity is the primary beneficiary and the price that she is willing to pay for it should, in theory at least, reflect that benefit, principally the increase to her earning capacity. But other members of society also gain from the provision of education and training. For example, there are assumed to be material gains to present and future generations from a better-trained workforce; education may encourage socially responsible behaviour and political

---

[17] C. Sunstein, 'Endogenous Preferences, Environmental Law' (1993) 22 J. Legal Stud. 217.

[18] For a bold attempt to overcome this problem, see T. N. Tideman and G. Tullock, 'A New and Superior Process for Making Social Choices' (1976) 84 J. Pol. Econ. 1145. The suggested process would involve: (i) asking voters to indicate a price that they would be willing to pay for various levels of provision; (ii) aggregating these prices and choosing the highest price option; (iii) identifying those voters whose bids were essential for the winning option, because without the contribution that option would not have been chosen; (iv) compelling each voter identified in (iii) to pay the minimum amount necessary, over and above the sum of prices indicated by non-(iii) voters, to make the winning option the highest priced one; (v) repeating the process for all voters who bid a positive amount for the winning option. The very complexity of the process and the high transaction costs involved make this a model of theoretical, rather than practical, interest.

stability through a more informed electorate; and—though these may be difficult to define and to locate—'cultural heritage' may be enriched.[19]

Granted the existence of these consequences, a misallocation of resources will result from the unfettered operation of the market: the price which suppliers are able to obtain will not reflect the true social value of the education and training and, in consequence, there will be underproduction. The simplest regulatory corrective is for the payment of a public subsidy which will reflect this divergence between the private value of the product and its social value. But the public good hypothesis may also provide a justification for other forms of intervention. If society derives a benefit from education and training over and above that acquired by the immediate recipient, then it also has an interest in the quality of the product, and that may justify subjecting the contract between supplier and purchaser to the imposition of public quality standards.

### (c) Other Externalities

Public goods constitute one type of externality, a form of market failure which was discussed in the previous chapter.[20] We saw there that if a producer's activity imposes costs on third parties that are not reflected (or 'internalized') in the prices which he charges for his products a misallocation of resources results: purchasers of the product do not pay for its true social cost and hence more units of the product are supplied than is socially appropriate. We saw, too, that private law instruments may fail to correct the misallocation. We must now explore some aspects of externalities and the problems that are posed for effective regulation.

Much traditional analysis tends to concentrate on relatively simple examples of externalities: an industrial polluter imposing costs on a neighbouring landowner should be made to 'internalize' that cost—the 'polluter-pay principle'—by means either of private law (for example, an action in nuisance) or of regulation (imposing environmental standards or taxing discharges). But externalities may have widespread effects, leading to considerable complexities for policy-makers concerned to devise appropriate legal corrections. Suppose that the pollution involves irreversible ecological changes, which have a presumed adverse impact only on future generations. The misallocation cannot be corrected by private legal instruments because of the time-lag in the private rights accruing. On public interest grounds, regulation may be called for. But, 'rationally', how is the appropriate level of intervention to be determined?

Take next the following example. A road bridge is poorly constructed and has to be closed for two weeks for repairs to be effected. Traffic is

[19] M. Blaug, *An Introduction to the Economics of Education* (1972), ch. 4.
[20] Above, pp. 21–2.

diverted through a peaceful village, causing disamenities to residents there; the congestion creates delays to road users leading to productivity losses and inconvenience; and businesses (e.g. a petrol station) adjacent to the bridge may lose custom during the two weeks. On the face of it, we have here a series of externalities requiring some form of correction. Typically when situations like this have generated private law claims for compensation they have been rejected, and judges and academic commentators have struggled in efforts to articulate policy and formulate principles justifying such conclusions.[21] Regulatory systems faced with similar problems have not reached different solutions.[22]

There are several reasons why it may be inappropriate to attempt to correct apparent externalities, such as those described. In the first place, the third party on whom the cost is imposed may have received *ex ante*, or will receive *ex post*, indirect compensation for the loss.[23] In these circumstances, no misallocation occurs. The facts of the bridge case may be adapted to provide an illustration of *ex post* compensation. If the petrol station suffers short-term losses while the bridge is being repaired but gains in the long term from an increased traffic flow when improvements are complete, no intervention is required: in a rough and ready way, the external cost has been cancelled out by an external benefit. As regards *ex ante* compensation, suppose that I purchase property in the knowledge that a firm nearby is engaged in a polluting activity which will to some extent reduce the amenities attaching to my land. Rationally, I will pay less for the property than would otherwise have been the case. In such circumstances, the pollution does not constitute an externality, for the capital value of my purchase has not been depreciated; through the reduced price, the market has already taken account of the cost.

This pollution example also illustrates another problem in the definition of externalities, and this leads us to the second reason why a corrective measure may be inappropriate. We tend to envisage the externalities as unilaterally imposed by one person (or firm) on another. In fact the causation issue is more subtle and the policy implications, in consequence, more complex. It can be argued that the cost, the disamenity attaching to my land, is as much the result of my presence there as it is of the firm polluting the environment. No problem would, of course, arise if the firm did not pollute; but equally no problem would arise if I (or someone else) were not there to receive the pollution. Understood in this way, the language of 'externalities' disguises the basic nature of the problem, that

---

[21] Cf. M. Furmston (ed.), *The Law of Tort: Policies and Trends in Liability for Damage to Property and Economic Loss* (1986).

[22] Cf. *Argyle Motors (Birkenhead) Ltd* v. *Birkenhead Corp.* [1974] 1 All ER 201.

[23] A. I. Ogus, 'Limits of Liability for Compensation', in Furmston, above, n. 21, pp. 219–20.

there is a friction arising from the competing and conflicting claim of two parties (the firm and me) for use of a single resource—the atmosphere.[24] How should the conflict be resolved? Applying the criterion of allocative efficiency, the economic answer is that the burden of avoiding or eliminating the friction should be imposed on whichever of the parties can achieve this at lowest cost.[25] If it costs the firm more to abate the pollution than for me not to locate my home in the vicinity, or to relocate if my purchase of the property predates the industrial activity, then economically it is inappropriate for the law, public or private, to restrain the pollution.[26] Of course, for the purpose of this calculation, care must be taken to include all the costs arising from the avoidance or elimination of the friction. In the typical atmospheric pollution situation, large numbers (including possibly future generations) compete with the polluter for use of the environment, and, given the very high aggregate of their avoidance costs, abatement of the pollution will usually be the cheaper solution.[27]

Thirdly, it is not appropriate on economic grounds to eliminate what are often referred to as 'pecuniary' externalities; these, unlike 'technological' externalities, do not give rise to a misallocation of resources.[28] What we have hitherto considered as externalities are 'technological' externalities: they are harmful or beneficial effects on one party's productive activity or utility directly resulting from another party's behaviour. 'Pecuniary' externalities, on the other hand, are

pure value (financial) changes borne by third parties which result from changes in technology or in consumer preferences. They involve indirect effects which alter the demand faced by the harmed or benefited third party. Pecuniary externalities are the result of the natural play of market forces. They involve wealth transfers which cancel out and not increases in the costs faced by society.[29]

An example may help to clarify the important distinction. Alf is in the music-recording business; he sells tapes recorded in his studio. Celia, a neighbour, who manufactures widgets, installs new machinery which increases her productivity but is very noisy. Alf, as a result, has to add soundproofing to his studio. Bert markets a new recording device which is bought by some of Alf's competitors and enables them to sell tapes at a reduced price; in consequence, the demand for Alf's tapes drops dramatically. Alf purchases Bert's device to reduce his costs. Celia's noise

[24] R. Coase, 'The Problem of Social Cost' (1960) 3 J. Law & Econ. 1.

[25] P. Burrows, *The Economic Theory of Pollution Control* (1979), ch. 2.

[26] See the American case, *Spur Industries* v. *Del E. Webb Developments* 494 P 2d 701 (1972).          [27] Burrows, above n. 25, pp. 95–6.

[26] For a useful account of the distinction, see R. N. McKean, *Efficiency in Government Through Systems Analysis* (6th ptg. 1967).

[29] D. R. Harris and C. Veljanovski, 'Liability for Economic Loss in Tort', in Furmston, above n. 21, p. 48.

is a technological externality since it increases social costs. Bert's device, on the other hand, while it may impose a loss on Alf, is a pecuniary externality: it does not add to social costs; rather, it enables resources to move to a more valuable use.

Finally, account must, of course, be taken of transaction costs. An externality may give rise to a misallocation but the administrative and other costs of correcting it may outweigh the social benefits arising from such action. It is for this reason that many trivial, or relatively trivial, externalities are ignored. However, what may lead to a trivial cost for each individual affected may in aggregate involve non-trivial and even substantial costs. The series of bomb hoaxes which at the time of writing are afflicting the operation of the main London railway termini illustrates the point well. If the time (opportunity) costs of all travellers who are delayed are added to (i) their anxiety and hassle costs, (ii) the costs to travellers not directly involved but who in the light of the hoax choose a less preferred mode of transport, and (iii) the costs of security searches, the total must be considerable and would thus justify a substantial outlay in regulating the conduct.

### (d) Information Deficits and Bounded Rationality

Consumer choice lies at the heart of the economic notion of allocative efficiency. To aim at a state in which resources move to their most highly valued uses implies that choices between sets of alternatives may be exercised; individuals prefer some commodities to others and such preferences are reflected in demand. The market system of allocation is fuelled by an infinite number of expressions of these preferences. However, the assertion that observed market behaviour in the form of expressed preferences leads to allocative efficiency depends crucially on two fundamental assumptions: that decision-makers have adequate information on the set of alternatives available, including the consequences to them of exercising choice in different ways; and that they are capable of processing that information and of 'rationally' behaving in a way that maximizes their expected utility. A significant failure of either assumption may set up a prima facie case for regulatory intervention.[30]

Although traditional economic analysis of markets often assumes 'perfect' information, clearly the phenomenon never exists in the real world; some degree of uncertainty as to present or future facts must always be present. Equally clearly, from a public interest perspective, the absence of 'perfect' information cannot by itself justify intervention. Given that

[30] See generally: H. Beales, R. Craswell, and S. Salop, 'The Efficient Regulation of Consumer Information' (1981) 24 J. Law & Econ. 491; E. Mackaay, *Economics of Information and Law* (1982), chs. 6–7; P. Asch, *Consumer Safety Regulation* (1988), pp. 35–43, 48–59.

information is costly to supply and to assimilate, the relevant policy question is rather whether the unregulated market generates 'optimal' information in relation to a particular area of decision-making, that is, where the marginal costs of supplying and processing the level and quality of information in question are approximately equal to the marginal benefits that are engendered.

An analogy can usefully be drawn with the way in which an individual makes decisions on acquiring further information by means of comparative shopping.[31] Suppose that I want to trade in the car I currently possess for a new car of a particular model. As I set out, I have no information on the likely price I will pay. The first dealer I visit offers me the new car for a certain sum $(L)$ plus my car. Should I proceed to other dealers to obtain comparable information? Rationally, I should do so only if the benefit, the chance of obtaining a better price—that is the difference between the first offer $(L)$ and the second offer $(M)$ discounted by the probability $(p)$ of the second offer being lower than the first—exceeds my marginal cost $(MC)$ in terms of time and travel etc. in visiting the second dealer, thus only if $p(L - M) > MC$. Indeed, I should go on obtaining further price quotations up to the point where the marginal cost of obtaining the last quotation equals the marginal benefit—I shall then have obtained the 'optimal' information for that transaction.[32]

The concept of 'optimal' information is a useful theoretical device for indicating how the public interest in information flows may be determined. But there are major difficulties in applying it in practice. Most of these arise from the special attributes of information as a commodity. The first is the paradox that the value of the information cannot often be known with certainty until it has been acquired.[33] In my car example, I will not know until I reach the second dealer whether $M$ will be lower than $L$—the probability of it being lower $(p)$ is a matter of pure speculation. Secondly, assessment of the benefits to be derived from increased information flows is often problematic. In the car example this would be relatively easy since the information in question related to *price*. Had it related to the *quality* of the product, it would be necessary to quantify any potential gains to the purchaser's utility. And when the context of inquiry is shifted from an individual transaction to market-wide trade in particular commodities, the problem is compounded, as an estimate has to be made of how aggregate demand would be affected by different hypothetical levels of information.[34]

---

[31] G. Stigler, 'The Economics of Information' (1961) 69 J. Pol. Econ. 213.

[32] For an empirical study applying this model, see B. F. Hall, 'Price Dispersion and the Gains from Search in Local Food Markets' (1983) 17 J. Consumer Affairs 388.

[33] K. Arrow, 'Economic Welfare and the Allocation of Resources for Invention', in Universities National Bureau for Economic Research, *The Rate and Direction of Inventive Activity* (1962), p. 615.     [34] Asch, above n. 30, p. 49.

While, for these reasons, precise estimations of 'optimal' information are unattainable, nevertheless it is possible to identify situations in which the information generated by the unregulated market is likely to be substantially sub-optimal, thus locating areas of 'information failure' for possible interventionist measures.

The costs to consumers of acquiring adequate information on which to make purchasing decisions are often substantial. By means of advertising, sellers can typically provide this information more cheaply because economies of scale are involved and, in a competitive market, they have an incentive to do this, in order to distinguish their products from those of their competitors. There are, however, several factors which may blunt this incentive, or else lead to countervailing inefficiencies. First, the fact that information typically has a public good dimension[35]—it is difficult at low cost to restrict its transmission to those who directly or indirectly pay for it and consumption by one user does not lower its value to other users— implies that there will be an underprovision of such information in the unregulated market. Secondly, a seller's effort to distinguish his products from those of his competitors may lead to artificial product differentiation. This is a process in which potential buyers are led to believe that a particular commodity has special characteristics which either do not exist or are insignificant in relation to its use or consumption. The consequence is that the seller obtains a degree of monopolistic power over the product which is economically undesirable. Thirdly, the seller's incentive may extend to supplying false or misleading information, as well as accurate information, if he believes that that will enhance his profits. Such a practice may, of course, give rise to private law remedies for misrepresentation, and the prospect of a contract being held unenforceable, or damages being ordered, will reduce the incentive to cheat. For this purpose, it is important to appreciate that not all purchasers need to sue, or threaten to sue, for the private law sanction to be effective. The existence of a sufficient number of individua!s at the margin—estimated to be about one-third of all customers—able to detect the deception and threaten effective action will ensure that competitive pressures are sufficient to discipline traders.[36] Nevertheless, there may not be a sufficient number at the margin able to detect the deception, and for those who do the transaction costs incurred in taking steps to complain and threaten legal action may be high relative to their individual losses. To meet such contingencies, regulatory controls may be prima facie justifiable. Fourthly, competition may induce sellers to provide information as to a product's positive qualities, but what about

---

[35] Above, p. 33.
[36] A. Schwartz and L. Wilde, 'Intervening in Markets on the Basis of Imperfect Information: A Legal and Economic Analysis' (1970) 84 U. Penn. LR 630.

negative qualities, that is, potential defects and risks? For obvious reasons, they are unlikely to be alluded to in advertising materials.

Another problem arises from the fact that information as to quality is more costly to supply and process than information as to price. Prices are calculated by reference to objective criteria (currency) and, in general,[37] are easily communicated. Qualities are to some degree subjective and, particularly in the case of professional services and technologically more complex commodities, may not be discoverable by pre-purchase inspection. It follows that although consumers rationally trade price off against quality—they will be prepared to pay more for superior quality—if, on the information readily available to them, they can discriminate between prices but not between qualities, traders with higher-quality products will be driven out of the market, and there will be a general lowering of standards.[38]

The assumption that individuals are capable of processing the information available to them and of making 'rational' utility-maximizing choices on the basis of it may be essential to the operation of the market model, but exploration of it lies largely outside the parameters of economic analysis. Most economists accept the notion that human behaviour is constrained by 'bounded rationality', that is, that the capacity of individuals to receive, store, and process information is limited.[39] There has been some attempt to erect a model of decision-making based not on finding a utility-maximizing solution but rather on 'satisficing', that is, searching until the most satisfactory solution is found from among the limited perceived alternatives.[40] But work of this kind has mainly been the province of psychologists, and mainstream economists have not refined their models of human behaviour to accommodate the problem. We shall return to the subject when considering non-economic justifications for regulation later in this chapter.[41]

### (e) Co-ordination Problems

In the previous chapter, we saw how the private law was used to facilitate the co-ordination of utility-maximizing activities. Contracts and legal forms of organization, notably corporations, are used overtly for this purpose. Such specific legal arrangements give rise, of course, to significant transactions costs; and other private-law concepts, particularly torts and property rights, can be treated as transaction-cost savings devices to the

---

[37] This may not be the case where prices include interest charges: below, p. 128.

[38] G. Akerlof, 'The Market for "Lemons": Qualitative Uncertainty and the Market Mechanism' (1970) 84 Q. J. Econ. 488.

[39] H. Simon, *Administrative Behaviour* (1975).

[40] See the symposium, 'Papers in Honor of Herbert A. Simon' (1978) 9 Bell J. Econ. 491–608.     [41] Below, pp. 51–3.

extent that they lay down standards of behaviour that it is assumed the parties would have agreed to in contracts if transaction costs had not inhibited them.[42]

Some co-ordination problems are so complex, having regard to the numbers involved or the detail of the solutions, that in terms of transaction costs it is cheaper for public law to provide the appropriate conduct-controlling mechanism.[43] The regulation of road traffic provides an excellent illustration.[44] To most of us it is presumably a matter of indifference whether we drive on the right or the left of a road; our sole concern is that all other road users should behave in the same way. It is obviously inconceivable that this concern should be met by mutually enforceable contracts. In theory, no doubt, we could deal with the problem through tort law: those not driving on the left in the United Kingdom would be 'negligent', and if loss or damage results the victim could recover compensation by means of a private claim. But there are clear advantages to a regulatory system of control: information regarding the content of the rules may more cheaply be communicated to drivers through public channels (e.g. the Highway Code); economies of scale are achieved by a public agency responsible for monitoring and enforcement; and criminal sanctions can solve the difficulties of maintaining incentives when drivers do not have the means of satisfying a civil judgment.

There are many other examples of 'co-ordinating' intervention, including the adoption of standard systems of weights and measures.[45] Although coercion is invariably involved, regulation justified on this basis 'is not really forcing people to do what they don't want to do, but rather enabling them to do what they want to do by forcing them to do it'.[46]

### (f) Exceptional Market Conditions and Macro-Economic Considerations

This section must conclude with some account of a set of more controversial economic arguments which have been used to justify various forms of interventions in, or management of, the market. The latter range from temporary measures thought necessary to deal with exceptional market conditions to broadly based systems of economic planning; as such they reflect different ideological stances.

Acute and sudden shortages in the supply of commodities for which demand is inelastic, that is, for which individuals will not readily be able to find satisfactory alternatives, has often led to calls for regulation, typically

[42] Above, pp. 20–1.
[43] R. Hardin, *Collective Action* (1982), esp. ch. 4.
[44] R. Sugden, *The Economics of Rights, Co-operation and Welfare* (1986), pp. 5–6.
[45] Below, pp. 130–1.
[46] T. Nagel, 'Moral Conflict and Political Legitimacy' (1987) 16 Phil. & Pub. Affairs 215, 224.

in the form of rationing. Wartime controls on the sales of food and clothing furnish the best examples.[47] The argument is not, it should be noted, one based on allocative efficiency. The 'efficient' solution is to allow the market to prevail: the rise in price will then choke off the demand. With the commodity now being available only to those who can afford the much higher price, the social consequences may nevertheless be regarded as unacceptable in distributional terms, or dangerous, in that social unrest may ensue.

Much of the economy is subject to cyclical patterns of demand. During troughs in these cycles, competition between firms will force down prices, leading them to reduce capacity by laying-off or dismissing labour and closing plants. When there is an upturn in demand it will then be necessary to re-engage employees and reopen the plants.[48] Such a process would seem to engender waste which could be avoided by interventionist measures, such as subsidies or the fixing of minimum prices, the cost of such measures being less than that involved in reducing and then increasing capacity. This, however, assumes a failure of capital markets.[49] If such markets operate as economists predict, in anticipating recoveries in demand and the profits thereby engendered, they will furnish sufficient funds during the trough to maintain the firm's capacity.

The problems arising from cyclical demand must clearly be distinguished from structural changes in the economy, or sectors of it. The latter are caused by a number of factors, including: changes in the pattern of demand (as a result, for example, of increased prosperity); technological innovation; resource availability; and international competition. Structural changes can give rise to high levels of unemployment and typically have a differential impact on individual regions, as each has its own industrial structure. If allowed to prevail, these consequences lead to an inefficient allocation of resources: there is a surplus of labour and of capital equipment in some regions and a shortage in others.[50] According to conventional theory, the market can be left to solve the problem. Firms should be attracted to move to areas of high unemployment by the prospect of low wage costs, and the unemployed will have an incentive to move to areas where demand, employment, and wages are higher. In practice, there are obstacles to the market processes. Neither labour nor capital is perfectly mobile, as a result of the lack of information of opportunities or of the assumed high costs of rehousing and severing family or social ties. There may also, through collective agreements or otherwise, be minimum wage levels which blunt mobility incentives. Clearly,

[47] D. Lee, *Control of the Economy* (1974).

[48] See generally A. R. G. Heesterman, *Macro-economic Market Regulation* (1974), pp. 125–33.          [49] Breyer, above n. 2, p. 31.

[50] J. Le Grand and R. Robinson, *The Economics of Social Problems: The Market versus the State* (2nd edn., 1984), ch. 9.

governments can seek to remove such impediments and may facilitate labour mobility through information flows and retraining programmes. Such measures serve to enhance the market mechanism and thus should not be characterized as regulation, in the sense in which we are using that term in this work.

An alternative theory suggests, however, that the market aggravates, rather than reduces, regional disparities.[51] The argument is that as richer areas attract workers from less prosperous areas, this leads to an increase in demand for goods and services in those areas, and to meet the increase, further workers are needed. A reverse-spiralling effect occurs in the depressed regions as the departure of workers reduces demand and output. Proponents of this theory thus argue for more active forms of intervention, such as regional subsidies, grants, and investment incentives.

The control of inflation has been a policy goal common to all recent governments, of whatever political composition, and yet the reasons are rarely rendered entirely explicit. If the future rate of inflation is anticipated perfectly—and this is more nearly approached when the current rate is small and stable—adjustments can be made in contracts and rates of interest. Where such adjustments are made, the costs attributable to inflation are relatively insignificant, since they relate mainly to the administrative costs of transacting business.[52] Given that inflation will be reflected in high rates of interest, holdings of currency should be kept to a minimum, thus requiring firms and individuals to engage in more frequent transactions into and out of interest-earning accounts. Also, of course, more frequent changes have to be made to the prices of goods and services, and the provision of appropriate information to purchasers involves expenditure of time and money. If the future rate of inflation is only imperfectly anticipated—this typically occurring when the current rate is high or volatile—adjustments cannot so easily be made and more serious consequences ensue. Some of these are redistributional in character and do not affect allocative efficiency. So, for example, those with benefits deriving from long-term contracts, such as pensions, lose relative to those whose income is derived from shorter-term or renegotiable contracts.[53] Other effects do give rise to significant allocative inefficiencies.[54] Un-anticipated high or variable rates of inflation increase the risks of, and therefore reduce the incentives for, investment. They also make it more difficult for individuals and firms to distinguish between price rises that

[51] G. Myrdal, *Economic Theory and Underdeveloped Regions* (1957).

[52] H. R. Vane and J. L. Thompson, *An Introduction to Macroeconomic Policy* (2nd edn., 1987), pp. 148–9.

[53] D. Piachaud, 'Inflation and Income Distribution', in F. Hirsch and J. H. Goldthorpe (eds.), *The Political Economy of Inflation* (1978), ch. 4.

[54] M. Friedman, 'Inflation and Unemployment' (1977) 85 J. Pol. Econ. 3.

reflect changes in supply or demand for particular products or services (i.e. *relative* price changes) and those that are attributable to general inflation. If this problem does arise, decision-makers in the market will not so readily allocate resources to meet the changes in supply or demand, and inefficiency will ensue.

While most policy-makers have agreed on the need to control inflation, there has been considerable disagreement on how this is to be achieved. During the 1970s, various attempts were made directly to regulate prices and incomes—a form of regulation which, as we shall see,[55] gave rise to considerable legal and economic problems. Under the influence of monetarist theory, the strategy of more recent governments has been to control public expenditure and the money supply.

The shift from prices and incomes controls to monetarist policies may be seen as part of a more general disenchantment with economic planning and the theories on which it was based. Industrial decline and recession, particularly in the mid-twentieth century, had provoked more broadly based perceptions of market failure.[56] First, there was the Keynesian argument that recession was caused by insufficient aggregate private demand, leading to the view that the government should take measures, typically fiscal or monetary, to stimulate demand in the private sector. This was complemented by a second, parallel, argument that concentrated on the supply side of the market: serious insufficiencies in the supply of certain goods and services could lead to shortages which in turn produced recession and inflation. Thirdly, some contended that the very existence of competing units in the market generated inefficiency because each unit did not co-ordinate its activities with those of others, the result being either surplus production or shortages. Fourthly, attention was directed to the productive inefficiencies of the firms themselves: it seemed that many were prepared to resist expansion in times of high demand, to tolerate over-manning and restrictive labour practices, and to use outdated technology. These, and other arguments, led to calls for more broadly based and intrusive interventions in the market. National economic planning of this kind took a variety of forms: from public ownership, involving overall state management, through selective taxes, and trade and price controls, to facilitative measures, such as public investment programmes and subsidies.[57]

There is not the place in this work to give detailed consideration to the arguments for state economic planning, but it is clear that, in several

[55] Below, pp. 300–5.
[56] T. Smith, *The Politics of the Corporate Economy* (1979).
[57] A. Skuse, *Government Intervention and Industrial Policy* (2nd edn., 1972); R. A. Bowles and D. K. Whynes, *Macroeconomic Planning* (1979), pp. 56–64; P. J. Devine *et al.*, *An Introduction to Industrial Economics* (4th edn., 1985), pp. 370–88.

respects, they typically fail to recognize and address problems inherent in managing the economy.[58] State agencies must acquire and process huge amounts of data on particular markets and, indeed, interaction between particular markets. That information must reflect the frequency of changes in market conditions, and there are inevitably time-lags between the perception of these changes and the adaptation of interventionist measures. Effective policy-making has to anticipate how industry will respond to those measures; in particular, steps have to be taken to constrain the efforts of firms to avoid or distort the policy objectives. Finally, and perhaps most significantly, the state agencies are vulnerable to pressure from interest groups who will seek to obtain private advantages from the formulation and implementation of the planning instruments.

### 3. NON-ECONOMIC GOALS

#### (a) Distributional Justice

The economic goal of allocative efficiency is, as we have seen, directed to the maximization of social welfare. It is not concerned with how that welfare is distributed between people or groups within society, except in the limited sense that if individuals with adequate resources experience disutility from observing poverty in others or the effects of gross inequalities then measures taken to eliminate such phenomena may enhance social welfare.[59] Regulation may be inspired by a desire, which is quite distinct from efficiency aims, to achieve a 'fair' or 'just' distribution of resources. But very different views are held on what is to be regarded as 'fair' or 'just'. Let us first explore some important schools of thought.

For *libertarians* such as Nozick[60] distributions are just so long as the process by which the resources were acquired was just. An acquisition is just, on this view, if it was the subject of an exchange transaction, for money, goods, or labour, or if, having previously been so subject, was inherited. Interventions by the state to redistribute resources, other than to confiscate holdings not justly acquired, are unwarranted as constituting an infringement of personal liberty; hence income tax is regarded as equivalent to theft.[61] Some libertarians do, however, recognize the appropriateness of measures for the relief of extreme poverty; not because it is 'just' to do so, but rather because it is 'in the interest of all' that destitution should be avoided.[62]

[58] F. A. Hayek, *Individualism and Economic Order* (1949), chs. 7–9; S. Young and A. V. Lowe, *Intervention in the Mixed Economy* (1974), ch. 16; Bowles and Whynes, above n. 57, pp. 71–82; J. E. Stiglitz *et al.*, *The Economic Role of the State* (1989), pp. 33–6.
[59] Above, p. 25.                    [60] R. Nozick, *Anarchy, State and Utopia* (1974).
[61] Ibid. 169–72.
[62] F. A. Hayek, *Law, Legislation and Liberty*, ii (1976), p. 87.

Exponents of *liberal* theories temper a respect for individual liberty and acceptance of distributions resulting from the market processes with a concern for unjust outcomes. Some insist that social arrangements should enable all within a society to have access to a minimum level of resources.[63] This approach necessarily involves some criterion of need, for example a 'decent' or 'civilized' standard of living. The perception of need may relate to the standards prevailing generally in the particular society—the minimum standard should thus take some account of increasing general affluence—but does not imply any concern with inequality as such. Other liberal theorists have taken the latter as their principal target. According to Rawls,[64] what is 'just' may best be determined by hypothesizing what principles governing society people would rationally agree to if placed behind a 'veil of ignorance', not knowing what place in society they would occupy or what abilities or endowments they would possess. One such principle is that resources should be distributed equally unless an unequal distribution benefits those individuals who are the least advantaged.[65] So formulated, justice allows for the unequal distributions resulting from market processes, but only if they can be shown to benefit the least well-off; it also favours a policy of redistribution by means of taxation and transfer payments.[66]

*Socialist* thought has given rise to various conceptions of distributional justice.[67] Pursuit of equality is a common theme, if by this is meant the abolition of advantages conferred by power, privilege, and wealth and the entitlement of individuals to resources such as will enable them to participate equally and fully in the community. For some, these aims are incompatible with private property and market processes—total state control of the means of production and distribution is therefore the only solution; for others, the market and private ownership can continue to play a role in the economy, though subject to the regulatory controls necessary to achieve appropriate outcomes.[68] For some, need alone can justify inequality of outcome; for others, some differential degree of 'rewards' according to contributions made to the common purpose is considered desirable.

Each of these theories, except some versions of the first, indicates that distributions resulting from market processes are not necessarily to be considered fair or just. As such, they influence regulatory policy both

---

[63] e.g. W. Beveridge, *Report on Social Insurance and Allied Services* (1942, Cmd. 6404). For general discussion, see V. George and P. Wilding, *Ideology and Social Welfare* (rev. edn., 1985), ch. 3.          [64] J. Rawls, *A Theory of Justice* (1972).

[65] Ibid. 83, 303. This principle, it should be noted, ranks in priority above efficiency but below that of liberty.          [66] Ibid. 278–80.

[67] George and Wilding, above, n. 63, ch. 4.

[68] D. Miller, *Market, State and Community: Theoretical Foundations of Market Socialism* (1984).

directly and indirectly. The indirect influence occurs where intervention is primarily justified on some other ground, for example market failure. Here the distributional theories suggest that the policy-maker should attempt to predict the distributional consequences of proposed measures and adopt a form of regulation which will lead to outcomes consistent with what is perceived to be fair or just.[69] By way of simple illustration, take the case of pollution. To deal with the externality to which this often gives rise, public funds might be used to subsidize the installing of pollution abatement equipment or polluters might be taxed for discharges into the environment, the proceeds being made available to compensate those who suffer disamenities. Distributionally, the first policy would benefit shareholders and consumers of the firm's products or services at the expense of taxpayers, while the second would benefit (presumably less affluent) householders at the expense of shareholders and consumers.

The direct influence of the theories may be perceived in relation to regulatory instruments primarily designed to pursue redistributional goals. Reducing inequality of income and wealth may be considered the most important such goal, but there are other redistributional policies which should not be overlooked. Some theories of justice, for example, are concerned with equality of opportunity rather than equality of outcome. The aim is accordingly to eliminate or reduce handicaps which affect abilities to enter and participate in market processes. Determining what kind of handicaps should be subject to interventionist measures is, however, not so easy.[70] There might be broad agreement that there should be no discrimination based on race or gender, and that access to education and training should not depend on wealth and thus should not be allocated by the market. But should differences in natural abilities be compensated for? And what steps should be taken to counter the effect of differences in such factors as parental care and health?

Redistributive policies may operate within a geographical or temporal dimension. As regards the former, perceptions of 'territorial justice' suggest some equalization of resources between regions, typically by financing or subsidizing services from central funds.[71] There are two distinct forms of temporal redistribution. The first occurs over the life-span of an individual. Peoples' needs do not correlate well with their earning capacities; most obviously they will normally earn nothing during old age. Of course, individuals should rationally recognize this and, through pension or other schemes, make appropriate savings from earnings'

---

[69] Stiglitz, above n. 58, pp. 28–30. Le Grand and Robinson, above, n. 50, examine a range of regulatory policies from this perspective.

[70] A. Okun, *Equality and Efficiency: The Big Tradeoff* (1975), pp. 75–87.

[71] D. King, *Fiscal Tiers. The Economics of Multi-Level Government* (1984), pp. 140–3. Equalization can also be rationalized on economic grounds: ibid. 122–34.

surpluses. Some may, however, not act rationally in this sense; hence the existence of compulsory pension schemes.[72] The second form of temporal redistribution, between present and future generations, raises greater theoretical difficulties.[73] The use or consumption of some resources may vitally affect what is available in the distant future. This applies particularly to non-renewable sources of energy but extends more generally to assets which are the subject of irreversible decisions (allowing animal species or cultural monuments to be destroyed).[74] The market system of allocation obviously fails to deal with this problem since the preferences of future generations for the relevant resources are not reflected in current demand. The argument for compulsory preservation may seem overwhelming, but how are we to determine the likely preferences of future generations—a function, *inter alia*, of what alternatives will then be available—and over what timescale should the redistribution occur?[75]

Another goal is to transfer resources to those who have been the victim of some misfortune, such as a physical injury, illness, or unemployment.[76] Regulation may not be necessary for this purpose. Loss insurance is available in the market for most of these risks and effectively gives rise to redistribution to those who suffer the misfortune from those who do not. The law of tort confers rights to compensation on some such victims. Although in essence the rights are designed to correct individual wrongdoing, modern developments indicate that they can be used for collective purposes: liability to compensate can be targeted on those who are in a good position to distribute the loss more widely within the community through insurance or through the prices of goods and services.[77] As redistributional devices, however, both market insurance and tort law have their limitations.[78] Some risks, such as unemployment, are not insurable. Others give rise to the problem of 'adverse selection'.[79] An insurance company unable to distinguish between high risks and low risks will charge an average premium which low-risk individuals may consider too costly for their needs. If the latter leave the insurance pool, the average premium, to cover those who remain, may then have to be raised to a level which some cannot afford—and a vicious cycle ensues.

---

[72] A. Forder, *Concepts in Social Administration* (1974), p. 67. Compulsion may also be rationalized on paternalist (below, pp. 51–3) or efficiency (above, p. 25) grounds.

[73] Rawls, above, n. 64, pp. 284–93.

[74] E. Partridge (ed.), *Responsibilities to Future Generations* (1981).

[75] R. Lecomber, *The Economics of Natural Resources* (1979).

[76] A. I. Ogus, 'Do We Have a General Theory of Compensation?' (1984) 37 Current Legal Prob. 29.

[77] P. Cane, *Atiyah's Accidents, Compensation and the Law* (4th edn., 1987), pp. 476–80.

[78] R. M. Titmuss, *Social Policy: An Introduction* (1974), chs. 6–7.

[79] H. Gravelle, 'Insurance Law and Adverse Selection' (1991) 11 Int. Rev. Law and Econ. 23.

Regulation rendering insurance compulsory can achieve an appropriate balance between high and low risks.

The most direct and most frequently encountered redistributional policy is between individuals on the basis of income and wealth, in short from the richer to the poorer. To be well-targeted, the policy requires that the resources of both transferors and transferees should be assessed. While the methods of assessment adopted for income and wealth taxes have been relatively uncontroversial, the means tests used to identify recipients have given rise to criticisms that they lead to stigma and social divisiveness.[80] To meet the problem, certain non-financial criteria such as family size, old age, unemployment, or disability can be used as proxy indicators of need and payments can then be made to, or services provided for, all those within the defined categories. Clearly some of the recipients will not be below the poverty threshold but money can be 'clawed back' from them by fiscal means.

It was suggested above that regulatory measures designed to correct economic inefficiency should be subject to constraints resulting from perceptions of distributional justice. We must now examine the converse proposition, that redistributional measures should be constrained by considerations of economic efficiency. What potential efficiency losses can arise from such measures? On the face of it, the only major such loss from shifting resources between groups or individuals is the administrative cost of determining liabilities and entitlements and effecting the transfers.[81] Nevertheless, it is generally assumed—though the empirical evidence is ambivalent[82]—that welfare transfers create disincentives for transferees to work and the marginal tax rates necessary to finance them have the same effect on transferors.[83]

How then is the balance to be struck between distributional justice and efficiency? The answer must depend on ideology. Libertarians would argue that efficiency must never be sacrificed. Others would argue that justice should be given priority and a strong version of this view is expressed in terms of 'rights': an individual's need for a minimum amount of income, education, housing, health care, and safety is regarded as so essential for human development and dignity that entitlement should be guaranteed by

---

[80] R. Titmuss, *Commitment to Welfare* (2nd edn, 1976), ch. 10; B. P. Davies, *Universality, Selectivity and Effectiveness in Social Policy* (1978), ch. 7.

[81] If the test of efficiency is couched in terms of utility, no definitive conclusions can be drawn because of the difficulty of making interpersonal comparisons: A. J. Culyer, *The Political Economy of Social Policy* (1980), p. 23. Intuitively, however, it is not unreasonable to assume that a poor person derives more utility from each unit of currency than a rich person; and, if this is true, redistributional measures give rise to additions in aggregate social utility: ibid. 84–7.

[82] For a summary, see A. Auerbach and M. Feldstein (eds.), *Handbook of Public Economics* (1985), chs. 4, 5, 13.

[83] L. McClements, *The Economics of Social Security* (1979), ch. 4.

constitutional means, alongside more traditional rights, such as political liberty.[84] The implication is that such minimum standards should be achieved, by regulatory action if necessary, whatever the economic cost: 'rights' are 'trumps'.[85] Some liberals adopt a more compromising stance. The appropriate trade-off between distributional equity and efficiency should vary according to social and economic circumstances, in particular on the degree of inequality which a particular measure attempts to correct and the absolute level of deprivation which might otherwise result. For example, Okun, writing in 1975, considered that the social cost of redistributing from families in the top 5 per cent (with an average net annual income of $45,000) to those in the bottom 20 per cent (with an average net annual income of $5,000) could be up to 60 per cent of the amount transferred and still be justifiable. On the other hand, if the transfers were from $18,000 families to $10,000 families, a tolerable loss, in his view, would be no greater than 15 per cent.[86]

## (b) Paternalism

Earlier in this chapter we observed how the goal of allocative efficiency was based on individual preferences and how this, in turn, depended on assumptions of adequate information and the ability to process that information.[87] While economists acknowledge that problems arise from information deficits and generally concede that decision-making is constrained by 'bounded rationality', they nevertheless are reluctant to abandon the criterion of individual choice. In consequence, they believe that the problems are best dealt with by improving information flows. Paternalistic interventions are much more radical: the individual's choices are overridden. He or she is prevented by law, for example, from travelling in a motor vehicle without wearing safety belts, entering into a credit contract on other than certain terms, or working under a contract of employment without contributing to a pension scheme.

Paternalism is in essence 'the interference with a person's liberty of action justified by reasons referring exclusively to the welfare, good, happiness, needs, interests or values of the person being coerced'.[88] It is important to keep the concept distinct from justifications for behavioural control which have regard to the impact of individual decisions on the

---

[84] H. Laski, *A Grammar of Politics* (1925), pp. 102–30; C. Reich, 'The New Property' (1964) 73 Yale LJ 733; F. Michelman, 'In Pursuit of Constitutional Welfare Rights: One View of Rawls' Theory of Justice' (1973) 121 U. Pa. LR 962; R. Stewart and C. Sunstein, 'Public Programs and Private Rights' (1982) 95 Harv. LR 1193; A. Gewirth, *Human Rights* (1982); Asch, above, n. 30, pp. 64–9.

[85] R. Dworkin, *Taking Rights Seriously* (1977), ch. 4.

[86] Above, n. 70, pp. 88–95.　　　　　　　　　　　　[87] Above, pp. 38–9.

[88] G. Dworkin, 'Paternalism', in R. Wasserstrom (ed.), *Morality and the Law* (1971), p. 108.

welfare of others. We have already considered such justifications under the heading of 'externalities'.[89] There are many instances of regulation which would seem to be motivated by paternalistic concerns but which might, alternatively, be justified as market failures because of externalities. The failure to wear a seat belt, and indeed any other conduct which has an adverse effect on an individual's health, may give rise to medical care costs which are borne not by the individual but by the taxpayer (through the National Health Service). The taxpayer thus has an interest in reducing those costs and behavioural controls constitute one way of achieving this. Taxpayers may also have to come to the rescue—in the form of social security—when an individual is left destitute as a result of unwise financial decisions, such as an over-commitment to creditors or a reluctance to save for years when paid employment is no longer possible.

Although paternalism is not often invoked in policy discussions, it may be safely assumed that it remains a powerful motivation for regulation even when other justifications, such as externalities, are also appropriate. Its theoretical base and content nevertheless remain controversial. We may usefully distinguish between arguments that attempt to reconcile paternalism with liberal notions of individualism and those that seek legitimacy for the concept in anti-individualist ideals.

Some liberals who advocate the primacy of individual choice argue that in certain contexts, where for a variety of reasons decision-making is particularly difficult, individuals may rationally delegate choices to others.[90] For example, they may recognise that they will be subject to temptations, such as alcohol or drug consumption, which they will find difficult to resist. To succumb may provide pleasure in the short term, but in the long term will give them cause to regret, when ill health or other costs have to be borne. Individual utility is then maximized if they consent in advance to being deprived of the temptation.[91] The reasoning has been extended to areas of problematic decision-making where individuals notoriously make 'irrational' choices: if, it is argued, they had been able to perceive what was in their own best interests, they would have consented to that outcome being imposed on them.[92] There is, indeed, empirical evidence generated by psychologists showing that people commonly underestimate personal risks ('it can't happen to me') and tend to prefer current gratification to postponed gratification, even when they know that the latter will yield a greater benefit.[93]

[89] Above, pp. 35–8.
[90] B. Barry, *Political Argument* (1965), pp. 226–7; J. Kleinig, *Paternalism* (1983), pp. 55–67.
[91] G. Loomes and R. Sugden, 'Regret Theory: An Alternative Theory of Rational Choice Under Uncertainty' (1982) 92 Econ. J. 805.     [92] Dworkin, above, n. 88, pp. 120-1.
[93] See the studies discussed in T. H. Jackson, 'The Fresh Start Policy in Bankruptcy Law' (1983) 98 Harv. LR 1393, 1408–14, and P. Asch, above, n. 30, pp. 74–9.

At root, these arguments assume that there is a distinction between an individual's 'real' and 'apparent' desires and by imposing choices a paternalist law is merely striving to give effect to the former. However, this very attempt to reconcile paternalism with liberal values also reveals the weaknesses in the assumption: 'not only does it represent as "real" what can at best be inferred, but it opens the door to reconstructions that permit the overriding of any actual desire by a fictional one with a quite different character'.[94]

The rival arguments for paternalism, from an anti-individualist perspective, dispense with the fiction that the individual's own desires have primacy. The choice is a social one but opinions differ on how the intervention may be justified. One approach is to assert that, in some situations at least, 'experts' within society know better than the individual what serves his or her own interest and should determine outcomes accordingly. This view conflicts with basic notions of liberty and slides all too easily into authoritarianism. Another approach is posited on notions of personal integrity.[95] Some individuals, particularly when young, lack the ability to structure their capacity for self-development: the liberal ideal of individuality is therefore inapposite and intervention is required so that the capacity for self-development is not jeopardized. A third version is located in the ideals of altruism and compassion.[96] Those imposing choices are assumed to empathize with individuals in problematic decision-making situations and on this basis to reach solutions which are compatible with the individuals' own feelings and perceptions.

These versions of anti-individualist paternalism are subject to considerable problems of indeterminacy; in particular, no clear guidance is provided on when intervention is appropriate. Obviously, individuals differ widely in their capacity to acquire and process information and to make utility-maximizing decisions on the basis of that information. Although in theory interventionist measures can be formulated so that choices are imposed only where it is demonstrated in the particular circumstances that an individual's decision-making abilities are inadequate, such a case-by-case approach would be impracticable because of the high transaction costs involved. Paternalist regulation, therefore, has to proceed by applying uniform controls on certain activities where it is assumed that many individuals make unwise decisions. The imprecision of targeting means that some individuals who are well equipped in the relevant areas to make decisions in their own best interests are deprived of choice.

[94] Kleinig, above, n. 90, p. 59.         [95] Ibid. pp. 67–73.
[96] D. Kennedy, 'Distributive and Paternalist Motives in Contract and Tort Law, with Special Reference to Compulsory Terms and Unequal Bargaining Power' (1982) 41 Maryland LR 563.

## (c) Community Values

The diversity of non-economic values which might be invoked to justify regulation is strikingly wide and further exploration into the realms of social theory would overreach both the aims of this work and the author's competence. Nevertheless, some reference ought to be made to a set of public interest goals which may loosely be described as 'community values'.

Social ordering may reflect not only what people want for themselves but also what they want for the community as a whole.[97] Those who do not go to the theatre may wish to see the Royal Shakespeare Company flourish; those who prefer urban community life may nevertheless vote to preserve rural amenities; and it is not 'irrational' to support measures to preserve endangered species for a period in the future when one will not be alive. The desires in question are not to be identified with the production of commodities which the individuals themselves want to consume or use, but rather with expanding the social, intellectual, and physical environment in which they and others live. As such, the emphasis is on providing the opportunities for members of the community to develop and pursue different conceptions of the 'good', and on fostering this through a mutuality of concern and respect, as well as by increased participation in the decision-making processes of collective affairs.[98]

The unregulated market has only a limited capacity to achieve these goals. In the first place, as we have seen,[99] it fails to take account of the demands likely to be made by future generations. Secondly, while altruistic motives are not necessarily incompatible with market processes, a 'free rider' problem often emerges. Many people may be prepared to give up some of their assets for altruistic purposes only if they can be assured that a large number of others will do the same. Given the problems and costs of co-ordination, the dilemma is likely to be solved only by regulatory compulsion.

[97] R. Stewart, 'Regulation in a Liberal State: The Role of Non-Commodity Values' (1983) 92 Yale LJ 1537, 1555–90; Sunstein, above, n. 2, pp. 57–61.

[98] Stewart, above, n. 97, p. 1557.          [99] Above, p. 49.

# 4

# Regulation and the Pursuit
# of Private Interest

## I. INTRODUCTION

Until relatively recently, public interest explanations of regulation have been accepted as the orthodoxy by lawyers, if only implicitly. When a question of interpreting a regulatory statute arises for determination, it is trite law that the courts, in ascertaining the intention of Parliament, may have regard to the 'mischief' which the legislation was intended to remedy, at least where the meaning of the relevant words is not clear.[1] The notion that 'the *social* purpose of the statute must be found out in the light of the previous law, the specific defect unprovided for by that law, the specific remedy decided on by Parliament, and the true reason of the reform'[2] clearly carries the necessary implication that there is such a social purpose. So also the elaborate institutional structures created for decision-making in public law, particularly judicial review and the requirements of public participation, are generally regarded as desirable if 'policies and practices which advance the good of all citizens' are to be adopted.[3]

### (a) Regulatory Failure

Challenges to the orthodoxy began to proliferate in the 1970s and from very different ideological positions. During the period 1965–75 there had been a significant growth of social and economic regulation, much of it conferring a broad discretion on agencies and officials. The courts which, on the public interest theory, could be expected to ensure by means of judicial review that such discretion was being exercised in furtherance of the public interest goals of the relevant legislation were typically reluctant to intervene.[4] Alongside discretionary regulation, there was an increasing reliance on self-regulation, particularly in the field of financial and professional services. The phenomenon threw up in an even more acute form questions as to control and accountability.[5]

---

[1] D. R. Miers and A. C. Page, *Legislation* (2nd edn., 1990), pp. 170–91.

[2] W. F. Friedmann, *Law and Social Change in Contemporary Britain* (1951), p. 240 (my italics), paraphrasing the classic statement in *Heydon's Case* (1584) 3 Co. Rep. 7a.

[3] P. McAuslan, 'Public Law and Public Choice' (1988) 51 Modern LR 681, 688.

[4] R. Baldwin and C. McCrudden, *Regulation and Public Law* (1987), pp. 56–7. The position had changed by the early 1980s: ibid. pp. 57–63.

[5] A. C. Page, 'Self-Regulation: the Constitutional Dimension' (1986) 49 Modern LR 141, and see below, pp. 107–11.

The doubts expressed by those with an interventionist ideology as to whether the formal legal structures were adequate to implement the ostensible public interest goals of the regulatory systems were matched by disappointment with the performance of those systems.[6] From the other end of the political spectrum, non-interventionists could point to the failures of regulatory systems with a somewhat different emphasis. The systems either did not succeed in achieving their ostensible aim (normally the correction of market failure) or did so inefficiently: they gave rise to misallocations in other sectors of the economy; or the administrative costs of the corrective measures exceeded the social benefits which they generated.[7]

What explanations could be offered for the defects in the design of institutional structures and for the divergence between the ostensible public interest goals and achievement (or lack of it)? One set of answers centred on what might be described as 'technical' failure: insufficient expertise and forethought was brought to bear on the methods of achieving the public interest goals.[8] Thus, poor policy analysis may have resulted from inadequate information, failure to anticipate important side-effects of regulatory instruments and avoidance behaviour. This was particularly likely to occur where the government and Parliament had to be seen to respond rapidly to widespread calls for action, following a disaster or event which had captured the public attention.[9] Alternatively, an appropriate regulatory design may have been rendered ineffectual by inadequate enforcement, whether that resulted from the relevant agency lacking insufficient resources[10] or adopting a passive, compromising approach to contraventions.[11]

## (b) Search for Theory

The emerging patterns of regulatory failure prompted a search for more general, theoretical explanations. Hayek purported to find such an

---

[6] e.g. N. Gunningham, *Pollution, Social Interest and the Law* (1974); I. Paulus, *The Search for Pure Food* (1974); C. Medawar, *The Social Audit Consumer Handbook* (1978); R. Cranston, *Regulating Business—Law and Consumer Agencies* (1979); W. Carson, *The Other Price of Britain's Oil—Safety and Control in the North Sea* (1982).

[7] e.g. C. K. Rowley and G. K. Yarrow, 'Property Rights, Regulation and Public Enterprise: The Case of the British Steel Industry 1957–1975' (1981) 1 Int. Rev. Law & Econ. 63; A. Peacock (ed.), *The Regulation Game: How British and West German Companies Bargain with Government* (1984). There is a vast American literature to similar effect. For useful summaries, see P. W. MacAvoy (ed.), *The Crisis of the Regulatory Commissions* (1970); and C. Sunstein, *After the Rights Revolution—Reconceiving the Regulatory State* (1990), ch. 3. [8] Sunstein, above, n. 7, pp. 86–96.

[9] Ibid. 86; M. Levine and J. Forrence, 'Regulatory Capture, Public Interest, and the Public Agenda: Toward a Synthesis' (1990) 6 J. Law Econ. & Org. 167, 191–4.

[10] Cranston, above, n. 6, pp. 75, 109; G. Richardson, A. Ogus, P. Burrows, *Policing Pollution* (1983), pp. 87, 105–6.

[11] Gunningham, above, n. 6, ch. 6; Cranston, above, n. 6, pp. 29–30.

explanation in the finite limits to human knowledge. The very idea of using law for specific instrumental purposes was flawed by a synoptic delusion: 'the fiction that all the relevant facts are known to some one mind, and that it is possible to construct from this knowledge of the particulars a desirable social order'.[12] The centralized pool of information on which rulers must rely for regulatory measures could never replicate the widely dispersed fragments of knowledge which individuals use in pursuance of their own ends and therefore could never be adequate to anticipate all the variety of circumstances to which specific regulations must be applied.[13]

From a very different perspective, the German sociologist Offe reached a similar conclusion. Regulation as practised in Western economies was doomed to a high probability of failure because the effort to impose public interest outcomes was inherently incompatible with the preservation and fostering of private production and profit-making.[14] Law, as the primary instrument of control, was part of the contradiction: to be consistent with the rule of law, regulatory measures had to assume a level of generality and yet that very generality rendered them incapable, without the *ad hoc* exercise of discretion, of dealing with rapidly fluctuating conditions and events.[15]

### (c) Capture Theory

A theory of regulatory failure which attracted much attention in the 1970s invoked the notion of 'capture'.[16] It stemmed from the perception that the ineffectiveness of regulatory agencies in meeting the public interest goals assigned to them could most plausibly be explained by assuming that they had been subverted by pressure, influence, and 'bribery' to protect the interests of those who were the subjects of the regulation.[17] According to one well-known version, agencies typically undergo a 'life cycle' in response to the political environment. When established, an agency attracts public attention and acts with vigour; when that attention is transferred to other subjects, public support is lacking and the agency becomes vulnerable to domination by the regulated interests.[18] There are

---

[12] F. A. Hayek, *Law, Legislation and Liberty* i. (1973), p. 14.     [13] Ibid. p. 51.
[14] C. Offe, *Contradictions of the Welfare State* (ed. J. Keane, 1984), ch. 1. See also G. Teubner, 'After Legal Instrumentalism? Strategic Models of Post-Regulatory Law' (1984) 12 Int. J. Soc. Law 375.     [15] Offe, above, n. 14, p. 280.
[16] For a critical survey of the literature, see G. Wilson, 'Social Regulation and Explanations of Regulatory Failure' (1984) 32 Pol. Stud. 203.
[17] M. A. Bernstein, *Regulating Business by Independent Commission* (1955); J. S. Turner, *The Chemical Feast* (1970); W. G. Carson, 'Symbolic and Instrumental Dimensions of Early Factory Legislation', in R. Hood (ed.), *Crime, Criminology and Public Policy* (1974), pp. 107–38; P. Sabatier, 'Social Movements and Regulatory Agencies: Toward a More Adequate—and Less Pessimistic—Theory of "Clientele" Capture' (1975) 6 Pol. Sci. 301; E. Bardach and R. A. Kagan, *Going by the Book: The Problem of Regulatory Unreasonableness* (1982).
[18] Bernstein, above, n. 17.

various hypothesized methods of influencing agency policy: the information required by the agency may be obtainable only from the regulated industries; lack of expertise in the subject-matter may mean that the agency has to recruit its officials from those industries; and the industries may threaten the agency with costly, or even trivial, time-wasting appeals should it fail to be 'co-operative'.[19]

The capture theory nevertheless threw up as many questions as it purported to answer.[20] Why should agencies succumb to capture? Why should they alone constitute the target? If an interest group is strong enough to pervert an agency, why does it not turn its attention to politicians and attempt to influence regulation at the legislative stage?[21] What was needed was nothing less than a general theory which could explain how private interests operate in the public domain.

## 2. PUBLIC CHOICE THEORY: THE MAIN IDEAS

### (a) General

Economists have devoted much attention to these questions in recent years,[22] and it is not difficult to understand why. Welfare economics has traditionally focused on the preferences of individuals, assuming that what is good for society is the aggregate of those preferences. In most contexts, individual preferences are adequately revealed in market behaviour, but, as we have seen, it is wrong to assume that what is socially desirable in terms of resource allocation, can always be left to individual market decisions. In the first place, there are areas of market failure, such as 'pure' public goods,[23] the resolution of which can be determined only by collective choice. Secondly, individual preferences, as revealed in market behaviour, are a function not only of what people want but also of their income and wealth, what is sometimes referred to as the 'starting position'.[24] Now that position is the consequence of entitlements (for example, the right to inherit) conferred by the law, and the law is determined, or at least subject to amendment, by collective choice.

These phenomena have led economists to extend their field of inquiry. They have developed a 'public choice' theory to explain, positively, how

[19] P. J. Quirk, *Industry Influence in Federal Regulatory Agencies* (1981), pp. 16–19.
[20] R. Posner, 'Theories of Economic Regulation' (1974) 5 Bell J. Econ. 335; A. Fels, 'The Political Economy of Regulation' (1982) 5 UNSW LJ 29.
[21] Cf. G. Kolko, *The Triumph of Conservatism* (1963); J. Q. Wilson, *The Politics of Regulation* (1980).
[22] See generally: I. McLean, *Public Choice—An Introduction* (1987); D. C. Mueller, *Public Choice II* (1989); P. Dunleavy, *Bureaucracy and Public Choice: Economic Explanations in Political Science* (1991); D. Farber and P. Frickey, *Law and Public Choice: A Critical Introduction* (1991).
[23] Above, pp. 83–4.                                        [24] Cf. above, p. 25.

individual preferences are reflected in the voting and other procedures adopted by the institutions used for collective choice and to evaluate, normatively, the consequences for social welfare. In so doing, they assume that behaviour in the political arena is, in its essence, no different from behaviour in the market, the individual acting in both contexts rationally to maximize his or her own utility.[25] This means, on the one hand, that citizens and interest groups use their voting power to extract from collective decision-making the maximum benefits for themselves, and, on the other, that politicians and political parties act as entrepreneurs to provide those benefits in exchange for voting them into power.[26] The exchange relationship which lies at the heart of, and fuels, the market system of production, is thus perceived to play an equally crucial role in the political system.

### (b) Conventional Markets and Political Markets

There are, nevertheless, important differences between conventional market transactions and political 'trade'. First, in conventional markets, when a supplier meets a consumer demand, the transaction does not give rise to any coercion—other than to require both parties to do what they *voluntarily* agreed. Provided that the transaction does not give rise to externalities,[27] third parties are not affected. In a political context, the end result of the 'transaction' is normally legislation which has a general *coercive* effect, applying to, and often imposing costs on, those who did not vote for it or did not want it.[28] From a normative perspective, it should be noted that unless a unanimity voting rule (allowing any potential cost-bearer to veto a proposal) is adopted, the collective choice may give rise to economic inefficiency in the Pareto sense,[29] because there will be at least some who will be made worse off.[30] Of course, that does not necessarily make it socially undesirable: the choice may satisfy the Kaldor-Hicks test of efficiency[31] or fulfil distributional goals. But, in the absence of constitutional constraints, collective decisions made on the basis of less-than-unanimity voting rules can be used to oppress minorities.

A second important difference between 'trade' in conventional and political markets respectively relates to the manner in which preferences are expressed. In conventional markets consumers are able to indicate the intensity of their preferences for products by means of prices: the more they are willing to pay, the greater their desire for the product. Simply

---

[25] J. M. Buchanan and G. Tullock, *The Calculus of Consent: Legal Foundations of Constitutional Democracy* (1962), ch. 4.
[26] A. Downs, *An Economic Theory of Democracy* (1957).
[27] Cf. above, pp. 33–8.
[28] A. Breton, *The Economic Theory of Representative Government* (1974), pp. 57–9.
[29] Above, p. 24.
[30] Buchanan and Tullock, above, n. 25, pp. 88–90.     [31] Above, p. 24.

voting 'Yes' or 'No' to particular proposals in a political market does not provide an equivalent indication of the intensity of the voters' preference. Thus, the normal system of voting, under which individuals or represent-atives have only a single vote, cannot reflect the true extent of demand, and the outcomes of collective choice adopting this system will not accord with what is socially valuable.[32] Suppose, to give a simple example, a policy option had to be decided by a committee of three individuals (Leslie, Mary, and Nicola) and the costs or benefits (in £) to the individuals consequent on the adoption of the option were as follows: Leslie 30; Mary −10; Nicola −10. Clearly, if each had a single vote, the proposal would not achieve a majority; whereas, if financial transactions were possible, Leslie would be prepared to pay (say) £12 to both Mary and Nicola, and the proposal would be adopted.

This problem helps to explain a third difference between conventional markets and political systems. Transactions in conventional markets usually relate to *specific* products. The institutional mechanisms for making collective decisions on policy and law, whether an electorate choosing a government, a political party conference formulating a policy manifesto, or a legislature determining the content of a statute, typically involve voting on a *package* of proposals. The main reason for this might seem to be obvious: it is simply not feasible to isolate all specific issues for political decisions of this kind. But, more germane to the present discussion, the packaging facilitates the obtaining of majority support, which is necessary under a democratic system, and which might not be obtained if the issues were decided on separate votes. The benefits accruing from parts of the package may outweigh the losses arising from other parts. Suppose, in relation to our previous example, the committee were considering three policy options (A, B, and C), the costs and benefits of which were as follows:

|        | A     | B     | C     |
|--------|-------|-------|-------|
| Leslie | + 30  | − 10  | − 10  |
| Mary   | − 10  | + 30  | − 10  |
| Nicola | − 10  | − 10  | + 30  |

If the policy options were voted on separately none would obtain a majority and therefore succeed, but if all three were voted on as a package they would all be accepted.

However, the very process of combining issues gives rise to a problem of collective choice, because the content of the package has itself to be determined by voting rules. It has been demonstrated that no voting mechanism, whether it involves voting for a single preference, or ranking

---

[32] Buchanan and Tullock, above, n. 25, pp. 125–6.

preferences ordinally or cardinally, can adequately reflect the totality of individual preferences.[33] Outcomes will vary according to the voting procedure adopted and the order in which the issues are presented for decision.[34]

Suppose that our committee were formulating a policy statement which included a commitment to reduce traffic congestion in a town and that there were three policy options: reducing public parking space (A); subsidizing public transport (B); and limiting access to certain licensed vehicles (C). Suppose, further, that the committee members ranked their preferences as follows.

|        | A | B | C |
|--------|---|---|---|
| Leslie | 1 | 2 | 3 |
| Mary   | 3 | 1 | 2 |
| Nicola | 2 | 3 | 1 |

If the committee proceeded by voting on a choice between two different options, each would obtain a majority of two to one, but the majority would be a different one in each case, and stopping after any particular vote would be arbitrary.

Analysis of this kind gives rise to the bleak—if also unsurprising—conclusion that voting procedures for policy packages (and therefore democratic systems in general) cannot match the assumed operation of prices in conventional markets in signalling the intensity of demand for particular products and thereby activating producers to supply the appropriate quantity of those products.

### (c) Logrolling

Public choice theorists have drawn attention to the device of 'logrolling', or trading in votes, which can mitigate the problem arising from voting procedures and which is likely to exist, to a greater or lesser extent, in any political system.[35] The basic concept is easily understood: Jack agrees to vote for a proposition which is favoured by Jill but not Jack, in return for which Jill votes for a proposition which is favoured by Jack but not by Jill. An explicit bargain to this effect may well be illegal[36], but the prohibition is a difficult one to police. Logrolling is unexceptional in the American political system where legislative voting is by no means tied to party lines.[37]

---

[33] The seminal analysis in K. J. Arrow, *Social Choice and Individual Values* (1951; 2nd edn., 1971), has led to a considerable literature. For a useful summary, see McLean, above, n. 22, ch. 8.

[34] M. Dummett, *Voting Procedures* (1984), pp. 15–28.

[35] Buchanan and Tullock, above, n. 25, ch. 10; Mueller, above, n. 22, pp. 82–94.

[36] *Allen* v. *Hearn* (1785) 1 Term Rep. 56.

[37] C. K. Rowley, 'Rent-Seeking in Constitutional Perspective', in C. K. Rowley, R. D. Tollison, and G. Tullock (eds.), *The Political Economy of Rent-Seeking* (1988), pp. 455–7.

It occurs much less frequently in the United Kingdom Parliament where party discipline is strict.[38] But, of course, it may, and presumably does, frequently occur in relation to policy decisions *within* parties, given that each party will contain a number of sectional interests but must produce a common manifesto.[39]

Clearly, the trading of votes cannot be equated with utility-maximizing transactions in conventional markets. In particular, given the difficulty of monitoring and policing agreements, voters are motivated to misrepresent preferences and renege on promises.[40] Subject to this, however, logrolling may enable preferences to generate appropriate outcomes. To see this, let us consider a variant on an earlier example.

|        | A     | B     |
|--------|-------|-------|
| Leslie | + 30  | − 10  |
| Mary   | − 10  | + 30  |
| Nicola | − 10  | − 10  |

If propositions A and B are determined by separate votes neither will succeed, even though there will be a gain to Leslie and Mary if both are adopted. The latter result will be achieved on separate votes if Leslie agrees with Mary to vote for B, in return for Mary voting for A. In normative terms, the agreement will be economically efficient according to the Kaldor-Hicks test, since the gain to Leslie and Mary will exceed Nicola's losses.[41] On the other hand, trading of this nature can lead to an inefficient outcome, as can be illustrated by altering the figures in the example.

|        | A     | B     |
|--------|-------|-------|
| Leslie | + 30  | − 10  |
| Mary   | − 10  | + 30  |
| Nicola | − 30  | − 30  |

It is still in the interests of Leslie and Mary to trade votes, and that will create the necessary majority for A and B, but the result is a net aggregate loss. Some public choice theorists have generalized from examples like this to predict that allowing legislatures to determine budgets by majority votes (and logrolling) will lead to excessive public expenditure.[42]

[38] It can occur on 'free votes' or when a government majority is very small. In 1979 a 'deal' was implicitly struck between the Callaghan government and Welsh Nationalist MPs whereby the support of the latter was acquired in return for the Pneumoconiosis (Workers Compensation) Act which conferred rights to compensation on a group of predominantly Welsh quarrymen: see A. I. Ogus, 'Legislation, the Courts and the Demand for Compensation', in R. C. O. Matthews (ed.), *Economy and Democracy* (1985), pp. 157–8.
[39] Ogus, above, n. 38, pp. 161–2.          [40] Mueller, above, n. 22, p. 85.
[41] But it will not be efficient on the Pareto test: cf. above, pp. 24–5.
[42] Notably, G. Tullock, 'Problems of Majority Voting' (1959) 67 J. Pol. Econ. 571.

### (d) Summary

It may be helpful at this stage to summarize the main thrust of the analysis. From a public choice perspective, legislation is a product which is supplied by politicians in response to the demand of private interests. Within a democratic system, that demand is expressed in voting behaviour (including logrolling). Although votes cannot be treated as an exact analogy to prices in conventional markets, primarily because they cannot indicate the intensity of preferences, nevertheless a study of voting procedures and practices can serve to predict the amount and nature of regulation which will be supplied for private interests.

In the light of these general considerations, we may now explore in greater detail how individual preferences affects different stages of the legislative process. That process is complex[43] but at its core are two fundamental voting exercises:

(1) the electorate choosing Members of Parliament (and thus also the government of the day);

(2) the Members of Parliament assenting to, or rejecting, specific legislative proposals.

Around the core are two important sets of influences which reflect individual preferences not normally identified with democratic processes but which, predictably, will participate in the political market:

(3) bureaucracies which provide information for government and legislatures and which also help to formulate legislative proposals;

(4) interest groups which, *inter alia*, lobby Parliament.

The various forms of political trade will now be examined in turn.

### 3. PUBLIC CHOICE THEORY: FORMS OF POLITICAL TRADE

### (a) Electing MPs and Government

The first type of 'transaction' in the political market envisaged by public choice theory is that between politicians supplying policy promises and the electorate which has a demand for particular policies, the 'price' being votes cast at a General Election. The assumption that individuals cast such votes as a rational act of self-interest may appear to be a reasonable starting-point for this analysis, but it seems hardly adequate, by itself, to explain why they actually vote.[44] The possibility that any single vote will

---

[43] Miers and Page, above, n. 1, chs. 2–8.
[44] Downs, above, n. 26, chs. 3, 14; McLean, above, n. 22, pp. 45–9; Mueller, above, n. 22, ch. 18.

determine the outcome of the particular election is generally tiny, and in cost-benefit terms the personal benefit accruing to the voter from the preferred candidate succeeding must be very large for the act of voting to be rational.[45] It would seem necessary, therefore, to hypothesize that most individuals aim to secure from voting a benefit which extends beyond their self-interest. For example, they may derive utility from the satisfaction of participating in a democratic process; or from the knowledge that if their party is elected other individuals (perhaps of the same social class as themselves) will benefit financially. In other words, they may be motivated by altruism, as well as self-interest. Empirical studies carried out in North America and Western Europe tend to support the hypothesis.[46]

Whether voters' intentions are governed by self-interest or something broader, they may be expected to respond to what candidates offer and vote for that candidate whose goals most closely approximate to their own. The candidates themselves may offer themselves for election for a variety of motives. Their ultimate objective may be a narrow, self-interested enjoyment of power;[47] or a more altruistic concern to improve social welfare. At this stage, however, it is necessary only to assume that their primary initial objective is election or re-election.[48]

Candidates seeking to maximize their prospects of election by attracting voters to their product are, like producers in more traditional markets, confronted with problems of information: they require information on the nature of the demand, and they need to communicate information to voters on what they are willing to supply.[49] A special feature of the electoral 'market' is the heterogeneous nature of the product: given the diversity of the voters' demands, candidates have to offer a package of policies on a large number of issues, and no single voter will be offered exactly what he wants.[50] Thus each voter is expected rationally to vote for the package which, as a whole, is likely to generate more utility for himself than the packages offered by other candidates.

The principal method used by candidates to reduce the costs of information flows is by organizing themselves into parties.[51] Considerable economies of scale are achieved by a party formulating and communicating to the electorate generally a manifesto, to which individual candidates

---

[45] e.g. if the chance of the election in the particular constituency ending in a tie is 0.00003, and that of a one-seat majority in the House of Commons is 0.005, an individual perceiving that she would benefit by £5,000 from her party winning the General Election would rationally vote only if it cost her less than 0.03p to do so: McLean, above, n. 22, p. 46.

[46] L. Lewin, *Self-Interest and Public Interest in Western Politics* (1991), ch. 2.

[47] For definitions of this concept, see Mueller, above, n. 22, pp. 247–50.

[48] Downs, above, n. 26, pp. 23–32; Breton, above, n. 28, pp. 124–6.

[49] See generally M. J. Trebilcock and D. G. Hartle, 'The Choice of Governing Instrument' (1982) 2 Int. Rev. Law & Econ. 29, 37–40.

[50] What Breton, above, n. 28, pp. 50–1, refers to as the 'full-line supply' problem.

[51] See generally ibid. pp. 125–30.

agree to adhere. Further advantages are gained by providing that manifesto with a coherent ideological core (i.e. with a set of policies which flow from a single set or from related sets of political values).[52] On the one hand, this makes it easier for voters to identify the product; on the other hand, for the purpose of communicating with the electorate, it enables a candidate to classify voters on the assumption that their demand on a number of politically related issues will be consistent with the ideology. There is generally assumed to be a single-dimensional Left-Right spectrum with substantial consensus on most major political issues among those on a particular point of the spectrum;[53] so, for example, those voting for Labour candidates are likely to have similar views on unemployment and public housing. Finally, electing candidates *qua* members of a political party provides voters with an indirect means of controlling politicians who shirk on their electoral promises.[54] Actions for breach of contract are not available for breaches of promises in political markets, unlike conventional markets. Such breaches would, of course, reduce the politician's prospects of re-election but she may not wish to be returned for a second term. When she carries a party label, however, she risks jeopardizing the future votes for that party and thus members of that party who wish to be elected for the next term will be motivated to monitor and discipline her performance.

A 'first-past-the-post' electoral system, like that currently used in Britain and the United States, has the effect of reducing the number of viable political parties and thereby simplifying voters' choices.[55] If there are only two parties contesting the election, to maximize its vote each should design its policy package to attract the median voter and, in consequence, there will be a tendency for the product offered to converge.[56] If three or more parties are involved, the situation is more complex and each will have some incentive to move away from the middle ground.[57]

In devising an electoral strategy, a party will recognise that, in broad terms, potential voters fall into two categories: either they are marginal voters who are uncommitted; or they are infra-marginal voters who remain committed to the party. To attract marginal voters, rationally it will offer

---

[52] Downs, above, n. 26, pp. 100–2.

[53] Ibid. pp. 115–7. The assumption has been challenged in e.g. D. Stokes, 'Spatial Models of Party Competition' (1963) 57 Am. Pol. Sc. Rev. 368. It is true that voters are likely to diverge from the spectrum on some issues, e.g. abortion, capital punishment; but these issues may impact less on voting behaviour at General Elections than the issues for which the assumption remains valid.

[54] R. J. Barro, 'The Control of Politicians: An Economic Model' (1973) 14 Public Choice 19; W. R. Dougan and M. C. Munger, 'The Rationality of Ideology' (1989) 32 J. Law & Econ. 119.

[55] For the effect of different proportional representation systems, see: Downs, above, n. 26, ch. 8; Mueller, above, n. 22, ch. 12.

[56] Downs, above, n. 26, ch. 8; Mueller, above, n. 22, ch. 10. For criticism that this is too simplistic, see Dunleavy, above n. 22, pp. 90–8.

[57] Dunleavy, above, n. 22, p. 143.

policies which concentrate benefits on that group, the costs being borne either by infra-marginal voters or those who would, in any event, not contemplate voting for the party.[58] Such a strategy will, however, be affected by considerations relating to the information flows between parties and the electorate. In the last chapter we saw how the problems of obtaining and assimilating information impaired consumer choice in conventional markets.[59] The problems are no less acute in political markets, having regard, in particular, to the difficulties voters encounter in ascertaining the extent to which they will gain or lose from specific policies. The distribution of such information among the electorate is likely to be highly asymmetric: in general producers, because of their business interests, are likely to be much better informed than consumers.[60] Moreover, political parties will be motivated to select policy instruments which, on the one hand, enhance the size and visibility of benefits offered to marginal voters and, on the other, diversify the costs of providing those benefits in such a way as to render them less visible.[61] Thus, for example, marginal voters may clearly perceive the benefits to them resulting from an increase to state retirement pensions but be less aware of the extent to which they will bear the cost, since that will be shared by all contributors to the National Insurance Fund.[62]

The content of a political party's manifesto itself normally results from a set of committee and/or conference decisions, each subject to voting procedures. Although it is to be envisaged that many members of these decision-making bodies will wish to maximize the electoral prospects of the party and thus seek to render the manifesto package attractive to median and marginal voters, others with a greater degree of ideological commitment are likely to remain loyal to values and policies which appeal to infra-marginal voters.[63] Given the problems (outlined above) arising from voting and logrolling procedures, the outcome of the ensuing struggle is difficult to predict.

### (b) Voting for Legislative Proposals

Public choice theorists, predominantly Americans, have attributed to individual legislators a key entrepreneurial role in supplying legislative

---

[58] Trebilcock and Hartle, above, n. 49, pp. 35–7.

[59] Above, pp. 38–41.

[60] P. Aranson, 'Theories of Economic Regulation: From Clarity to Confusion' (1990) 6 J. Law & Pol. 247, 273–4.

[61] M. Olson, *The Logic of Collective Action* (1965), pp. 141–3; Trebilcock and Hartle, above, n. 49, p. 40.

[62] J. A. Brittain, *The Payroll Tax for Social Security* (1978), pp. 6–13; and see, more generally, S. Brittan, 'The Wenceslas Myth', in *The Role and Limits of Government: Essays in Political Economy* (1983), ch. 1.

[63] R. C. O. Matthews, 'Competition in Economy and Polity', in Matthews, above, n. 38, pp. 11–12.

benefits to constituents (or particular groups of constituents), on the assumption that they are primarily motivated by a desire to maximize their chances of re-election.[64] While recognizing the importance of the re-election goal, some have nevertheless argued that the behaviour of legislators results from a wider range of self-interested motives, including personal power, a desire to make an imprint on history and, more generally, ideology.[65]

The tight party discipline operating in the British Parliament reduces the influence of individual legislators and attention must therefore be focused on the government which, given also the small number of political parties, dominates the supply of legislation. The party which gains the majority of seats in the House of Commons is then, effectively, a 'monopoly supplier'.[66] Like any other monopolist, it will presumably aim to discourage the entry of rival suppliers as well as maximize its utility or profit.[67] That suggests that its main concern will be re-election and, to that end, it will seek to implement the promises made in the manifesto at the previous election, particularly to benefit those who were perceived to be median or marginal voters. This can be done by tying-in to general 'public good' legislation benefits destined for special interests, just as in conventional markets monopolists are able to increase their profits by incorporating features which most consumers do not want into the products sold.[68] Such measures will not, of course, accord with the exact preferences of all the government's (existing and potential) supporters, but the problem can be mitigated by implicit logrolling: those supporters will be prepared to tolerate some legislation which they do not want provided they obtain some of the legislation they do want.[69] The government's control over significant sources of information will also enable it, to some extent, to influence what its supporters want, and thus to alter preferences either to accord with what is being provided or at least to render the preferences more homogeneous, so as to reduce the cost of supply.[70]

There is, nevertheless, an important difference between an entrepreneur operating in a conventional market and a government supplying legislative

---

[64] See esp. R. E. McCormick and R. E. Tollison, *Politicians, Legislation and the Economy* (1981); B. R. Weingast, 'Regulation, Reregulation, and Deregulation: The Political Foundations of Agency Clientele Relationships' (1981) 44 Law & Contemp. Prob. 147. For the impact on the analysis of different constitutional and institutional arrangements, see Dunleavy, above, n. 22, pp. 136–41.

[65] Breton, above, n. 28, pp. 124–6; E. L. Rubin, 'Beyond Public Choice: Comprehensive Rationality in the Writing and Reading of Statutes' (1991) 66 NYU LR 1; Farber and Frickey, above, n. 22, pp. 21–4.                    [66] Breton, above, n. 28, pp. 136–9.

[67] For the argument that the monopolist government will aim at maximizing revenue primarily through taxation, see G. Brennan and J. Buchanan, *The Power to Tax: Analytical Foundations of a Fiscal Constitution* (1980), pp. 17–24.

[68] Mueller, above, n. 22, p. 266.

[69] Breton, above, n. 28, pp. 155–7.                    [70] Ibid. p. 157.

benefits in a political market. In the former, there is a continual interaction between supply and demand; in the latter, 'transactions' can take place only at discrete intervals, at the time of general elections.[71] Provided that a government has a working majority for the period between elections, it can therefore adjust its policies so as to maximize the meeting of demand towards the end of a term of office. This will enable it, in particular, to indulge in measures which have a greater ideological content during the earlier part of that period.[72]

### (c)  The Influence of Bureaucracies

According to the Weberian idealized theory of public administration, bureaucracies should implement but not influence government policy.[73] Modern political theorists are sceptical of this conception,[74] as are exponents of public choice, who assume that bureaucrats, like all other individuals, must be motivated by self-interest, and that in the pursuit of that interest they will significantly influence government policy and, therefore, the form and content of legislation.[75] Their ability to do this arises from their key role in policy-making.[76] They are typically assigned the responsibility of exploring policy options to a given set of problems and in discharging this responsibility they can set the agenda on what can and cannot be done. Further, their control of relevant information enables them to be selective in what is communicated to politicians, so that, for example, budget proposals for particular options can be presented on a 'take-it-or-leave-it' basis.

Niskanen has provided the classic public choice analysis of bureaucracies.[77] He argues that the hypothesized elements of bureaucrats' self-interest, which include salary, perquisites, reputation, and power, can be achieved primarily through maximizing the *budget* of the bureau, and that therefore that must be their assumed goal. This contrasts with the goal of *profit* maximization which conventionally is attributed to managers in private, competitive firms. The difference is significant because whereas

---

[71] Breton, above, n. 28, pp. 131–5.

[72] For other variables governing legislative output, see: W. M. Crain, 'Cost and Output in the Legislative Firm' (1979) 8 J. Legal Stud. 607; J. K. Smith, 'Production of Licensing Legislation: An Economic Analysis of Interstate Differences' (1982) 11 J. Legal Stud. 117.

[73] M. Weber, *Economy and Society* (tr. G. Roth and C. Wittich, 1968), pp. 957–9.

[74] P. M. Blau and M. W. Meyer, *Bureaucracy in Modern Society* (2nd edn., 1971); R. Brown, E. Kamenka, M. Krygier, and A. E.-S. Tay, *Bureaucracy: The Career of a Concept* (1978).

[75] G. Tullock, *The Politics of Bureaucracy* (1965); W. Niskanen, *Bureaucracy and Representative Government* (1971); A. Breton and R. Wintrobe, *The Logic of Bureaucratic Conduct* (1982); P. M. Jackson, *The Political Economy of Bureaucracy* (1982). For an excellent survey of the literature, see Dunleavy, above, n. 22, ch. 6.

[76] R. Rose, *The Problem of Party Government* (1974).          [77] Above, n. 75.

private managers to achieve profits, must assess the marginal costs and benefits of their decisions, bureaucrats have no means of making an equivalent assessment. In a competitive setting, private managers will typically be rewarded according to performance; but, despite the British government's recent attempts,[78] the salaries of civil servants can rarely be determined by such criteria. The problem is exacerbated by the bilateral monopoly relationship which exists between the bureau as 'supplier' and the government as 'purchaser' of services, and which means that there is no competitive pressure on bureaux to be efficient.

On the basis of his analysis, Niskanen predicts that the total output (and budget) of a bureau is likely to exceed that of a firm in a competitive industry faced with the same demand and cost conditions by up to 100 per cent, and that its activities are likely to be marred by productive inefficiency.[79] However, both his assumptions and his conclusions have been challenged.[80] In the first place, empirical research suggests that governments have greater power to control budgets than Niskanen recognises.[81] Indeed, since political parties in power must attempt to convince the electorate that they can control public expenditure and bureaucratic inefficiency better than opposition parties, some efforts in this respect must be envisaged.[82] Secondly, it has been alleged that Niskanen underestimates the impact of competition *within* bureaucracies. Different bureaux have to compete for budget allocation; and there is competition between bureaucrats for promotion and prestigious positions.[83] Thirdly, and most fundamentally, Dunleavy has suggested that bureaucrats' self-interest in power and prestige is best secured not by budget maximization but rather by 'bureau-shaping strategies' which enable them to enjoy high status and agreeable work tasks.[84]

### (d) The Influence of Interest Groups

The thrust of the above analysis suggests that, subject to some important qualifications, including, notably, the impact of bureaucratic influences, governments will supply legislation to meet the demand of voters, particularly median and marginal voters. Many public choice theorists, however, argue that special-interest groups have such a powerful influence

---

[78] Cf. P. Jowett and G. Rothwell, *Performance Indicators in the Public Sector* (1988).

[79] On productive inefficiency, see above, p. 22.

[80] See, for surveys of the literature, Mueller, above, n. 22, pp. 255–68; Lewin, above, n. 46, pp. 78–97

[81] R. Goodin, 'Rational Politicians and Rational Bureaucrats in Washington and Whitehall' (1982) 60 Pub. Admin. 23; R. Rose, *Understanding Big Government: The Programme Approach* (1984).

[82] Breton and Wintrobe, above, n. 75, p. 152.

[83] Ibid. pp. 97–9, 111–21.      [84] Above, n. 22, chs. 7–8.

on politicians that their efforts to obtain legislative favours override more general preferences.[85]

The political influence of interest groups has a long history and has been the subject of many studies.[86] As these reveal, there is a variety of ways in which groups affect political decision-making. On the one hand, they can influence the voting behaviour of the electorate by providing (sometimes selective) information on how measures under discussion might affect individuals and on how assiduous particular politicians are in serving the interests of those individuals. On the other hand, they can influence the voting behaviour of politicians by providing (again sometimes selectively) information on the degree of support within the electorate for particular measures, as well as technical information on the details of such measures. More directly, interest groups can help pay politicians' expenses or even, in Britain at least,[87] employ them in some capacity.

Broadly speaking, there are two types of groups: those representing particular sectional interests (e.g. professional or producer associations, trade unions) and those representing 'causes' or ideologies (e.g. environmentalists, feminists).[88] A seminal study by Olson in 1965[89] sought to identify what made a group more or less effective in influencing political decisions. Each group is subject to the classic 'public good' problem:[90] members will benefit from any successful activity, whether or not they have contributed to the group's efforts—in short, they have an incentive to 'free ride' on others' efforts. Two important conclusions follow from this. First, it is easier to form an effective group from a smaller, rather than larger, number of potential members. However, in so far as the group seeks to demonstrate to politicians that its views are held by a significant number of electoral voters, there is a countervailing advantage in size. Secondly, the effectiveness of a group will depend, to some extent at least, on its ability to exercise control over its members; and this, in turn, is likely to be a function of the homogeneity of the common interests of the group and the transaction costs incurred in organization. Obviously, effectiveness will be maximized when the ability to require substantial financial contributions as a condition of membership is combined with the acquisition of monopoly rights to engage in profitable undertakings. Thus, professional associations with powers of self-regulation which include the right to determine who may engage in the professional practice have always been highly effective

---

[85] Rowley, Tollison, and Tullock, above, n. 37.

[86] For refs. (mainly American), see Farber and Frickey, above, n. 22, ch. 1. On Britain, see esp. J. Richardson and A. Jordan, *Governing Under Pressure* (1985); G. Alderman, *Pressure Groups and Government in Great Britain* (1984).

[87] British MPs must register such interests: see E. May, *Parliamentary Practice* (20th edn., 1983), pp. 435–9.

[88] For this and other taxonomies, see: Fels, above, n. 20, pp. 32–5; N. Craig Smith, *Morality and the Market* (1990), ch. 4.

[89] Above, n. 61.          [90] Cf. above, p. 33.

pressure groups.[91] In short, Olson's theory predicts that groups representing producers are likely to exert a greater influence on legislation than those representing consumers and other 'public' interests, such as the environment.[92]

Just as in conventional market settings individuals and firms rationally channel their investments to yield the highest rate of return, so in political markets interest groups will predictably invest in lobbying and similar activities if that generates benefits which exceed those from other forms of investment.[93] If, say, the creation of a legislative monopoly in teddy bear manufacturing would result in additional profits of £1 million to members of the teddy bear producers' association, then the latter should be prepared to pay up to that sum on lobbying, provided that the benefit to be derived is higher than that which could be obtained by the same expenditure on a different investment.

## 4. PRIVATE INTEREST THEORIES OF REGULATION

### (a) Positive Theory

On the basis of public choice analysis there has emerged, particularly in the American literature, an 'economic' theory of regulation according to which the existence and form of regulation may be predicted as a response by politicians to the demands of interest groups who will derive benefits from the measure.[94] Given the advantages referred to above, of homogeneity of interest and relatively low organization costs, producer groups will typically be able to exert more influence than those representing consumers or ideologies. Hence, the central thesis that 'as a rule, regulation is acquired by the industry and is designed and operated primarily for its benefit'.[95]

The theory seeks to provide an explanation not only for regulation which overtly confers benefits on producers (e.g. subsidies) but also measures which ostensibly protect more generalized interests, such as consumers or the environment, but which serve to generate profits for the industries or firms (or some of them) which are regulated. (Of course, if the generalized

---

[91] M. Trebilcock, 'Regulating Service Quality in Professional Markets', in D. Dewees (ed.), *The Regulation of Quality* (1983), ch. 4. The power of trade unions operating a 'closed shop' in particular industries is analogous: Olson, above, n. 61, p. 39, and ch. 3.

[92] For an evaluation, see McLean, above n. 22, pp. 63–80.

[93] A 'profession' of lobbyists has emerged to meet the increasing demand for such investment: M. Case, *The Power of the Lobbyist: Regulation and Vested Interest*, Hume Occasional Paper No. 32 (1991).

[94] G. Stigler, 'The Theory of Economic Regulation' (1971) 2 Bell J. Econ. 3; Posner, above, n. 20; S. Peltzman, 'Towards a More General Theory of Regulation' (1976) 19 J. Law & Econ. 211; F. McChesney 'Rent Extraction and Rent Creation in the Economic Theory of Regulation' (1987) 16 J. Legal Stud. 1; Aranson, above, n. 60.

[95] Stigler, above n. 94, p. 3.

interests—or a sufficiently influential group from within them—can be persuaded to support the measure, politicians will be even more motivated to supply it.)[96] Some such measures may enhance the profits of incumbent firms in an industry if they restrict the entry of newcomers. Most obviously, a licensing system often has this effect;[97] but other forms of regulation can also impede competition. Suppose that legislation were to prohibit a certain manufacturing process on the basis of its harmful pollutant effects but that, to minimize the cost for those already engaged in the process, the ban were to apply only to new manufacturing plants. Clearly, the legislation would constitute a barrier to entry and, as such, would generate benefits for existing manufacturers.[98] Regulation may also be anti-competitive if the costs of complying with it are proportionally higher for a smaller firm than for a larger firm, because similar costs must be incurred whatever the level of output.[99]

The 'economic' theory of regulation, as propounded by its principal exponents, does not normally encompass the private interests of bureaucrats. As we have seen, the latter play an important role in public choice analysis, and a private interest theory of regulation would be incomplete without some reference to them. The main implications of that analysis for the creation and content of regulation would seem to be as follows. First, the interests of bureaucrats, whether they are identified with budget maximization or bureau-shaping, may impinge on, and sometimes over-ride, preferences of voters expressed through democratic processes. Secondly, in so far as those interests are promoted by interventionist measures and an enlarged public sector, the influence of bureaucrats is likely to yield a greater volume of regulation than is justified on public interest grounds. Thirdly, as regards the form of regulatory intervention, the interests may generate pressure for systems which maximize bureau-cratic power and prestige, such as public ownership.

## (b) Normative Theory

As we have already seen,[100] legislation can almost never be allocatively efficient in the Pareto sense, because it will invariably impose losses on some individuals. If legislation is the result of democratic processes and reflects, in broad terms, the range and extent of economic interests in a society at a given time, there is nevertheless a good chance that it will be Kaldor-Hicks efficient,[101] the aggregate gains from the measure exceeding

---

[96] B. Yandle, 'Bootleggers and Baptists in the Market for Regulation', in J. Shogren (ed.), *The Political Economy of Government Regulation* (1989), ch. 3.

[97] Below, pp. 219–20                               [98] Below, pp. 168–9.

[99] Below, p. 172.                                   [100] Above, p. 59.

[101] Cf. above, p. 29.

the aggregate losses.[102] On the public choice hypothesis, however, private interest groups thwart the democratic process and concentrated, minority economic interests prevail over the more widespread, majority economic interests; and the Kaldor-Hicks test of efficiency is not satisfied.

The normative criticism of regulation serving producer interests has been extended in a branch of public choice theory which is generally referred to as 'rent seeking' theory.[103] 'Rent' in this context refers to the difference between revenue from producing a good and the cost of production.[104] Competition between producers eliminates rent; in the absence of such competition, the rent is retained by monopolists. To the extent that regulation protects producers from competition they acquire rents and some wealth is transferred to them from consumers.

Such wealth transfer may be condemned on *distributional* grounds, particularly if the legislation results from the activities of groups representing producers, rather than from the preferences of electoral voters generally. But, from their narrower *economic* perspective, rent seeking theorists focus on another objection: the waste engendered by devoting resources to capturing the wealth transfers, an activity which from society's point of view, is entirely unproductive.[105]

### (c) Criticisms of the Theories

The private interest theories of regulation have been criticized on a number of grounds. Let us first examine the assumption that self-interest motivates the behaviour of all those engaging in political trade. Self-interest tends to be narrowly interpreted and is invariably identified with the maximization of wealth. As such, it is plausible more for producers and groups representing producers than for individual voters and politicians.[106] The broader and vaguer desires and needs which enter into the utility function of such individuals (e.g. altruism, ideology) cannot be ignored, but they pose problems for economists since they generate hypotheses which are not capable of being measured and tested by conventional means. There is, too, the obvious danger that when the model which is

[102] H. Hovenkamp, 'Legislation, Well-Being, and Public Choice' (1990) 57 U. Chicago LR 63, 86.

[103] See generally: R. D. Tollison, 'Rent Seeking: A Survey' (1982) 35 Kyklos 575; Rowley, Tollison, and Tullock, above, n. 37; Mueller, above, n. 22, ch. 13.

[104] Strictly speaking, the 'opportunity cost', i.e., the most highly valued alternative use of the resources employed in producing the good.

[105] The point was first made in G. Tullock, 'The Welfare Costs of Tariffs, Monopolies and Theft' (1967) 5 Western Econ. J. 224.

[106] M. Kelman, 'On Democracy-Bashing: A Skeptical Look at the Theoretical and "Empirical" Practice of the Public Choice Movement' (1988) 74 Virginia LR 199, 214–23; Rubin, above n. 65, pp. 14–23; Hovenkamp, above, n. 102, pp. 81–5; Farber and Frickey, above, n. 22, pp. 26–33.

used to analyse political behaviour is enlarged to reflect a wide diversity of human motivations its predictions become tautologous: they explain everything and thus also nothing.[107] If, for example, a particular regulatory measure is seen not to accord with the wealth-maximizing aims of groups which influenced its enactment, the explanation is doubtless to be found in the non-financial utility which such groups derive from the measure. But then the model becomes useless as a predictive tool: 'the concept of rational egotism has predictive value only if one defines utility strictly in terms of definitive material interests rather than indeterminate psychological rewards'.[108]

The unduly narrow interpretation of self-interest also affects the normative conclusions of public choice analysis. If social welfare is identified solely with wealth-maximization, then regulation which leads to the transfer of wealth between different groups, rather than the increase of aggregate wealth, must be treated as economically inefficient, particularly when substantial resources are spent in securing such transfers. On the other hand, if the gains to the utility of certain members of society generated by the measure exceed its costs—a result which may occur even though it cannot be demonstrated mathematically—the charge of inefficiency is misplaced.[109]

Empirical studies, particularly those carried out by political scientists, do not always confirm the predictions made by public choice theorists on the basis of the wealth-maximizing assumption.[110] Some surveys of voting behaviour in elections suggest that there is an imperfect correlation between what would benefit individuals in financial terms and how they cast their votes.[111] Further, there is evidence to doubt the overwhelming influence attributed to groups representing industrial producers. It would seem that the impact of such groups tends to be most pronounced in relation to statutory provisions which are technical or narrow in scope, and which are not inconsistent with the ideology of the government of the day.[112] Some regulation, particularly that introduced in the 1970s, appears to have reflected the pressures exerted by general, ideologically-orientated

---

[107] Rubin, above, n. 65, p. 17.                                                [108] Ibid.

[109] Hovenkamp, above, n. 102, judging 'efficiency' by the Kaldor-Hicks test: cf. above, p. 24.

[110] '[P]ublic choice theory is strong on a priori reasoning but short on empiricism': A. Dunsire, K. Hartley, D. Parker, and B. Dimitriou, 'Organizational Status and Performance: A Conceptual Framework for Testing Public Choice Theories' (1988) 66 Pub. Admin. 363, 365. For a general survey, see Lewin, above, n. 46.

[111] For the USA: D. R. Kinder and D. R. Kiwiet, 'Economic Discontent and Political Behavior: The Role of Personal Grievances and Collective Economic Judgments in Congressional Voting' (1979) 23 Am. J. Pol. Sc. 495; for the UK: D. Butler and D. Stokes, *Political Change in Britain* (1969).

[112] A. T. Denzau and M. C. Munger, 'Legislators and Interest Groups: How Unorganized Interests Get Represented' (1986) 80 Am. Pol. Sci. Rev. 89.

groups, notwithstanding the free-rider problem which, it is argued, constrains their efforts.[113] Nor is it clear how the theories can be used to explain the large number of deregulatory measures which have been passed in recent years.

### (d) Conclusions

We may reach the conclusion, on the basis of the above criticisms, that the economic theory of regulation cannot provide a conclusive explanation for the large variety of interventionist measures which we shall be considering in this book. This is not to imply that the theory should be rejected out of hand, still less that we should necessarily fall back on the public interest theory of regulation.

As we shall see, the forms of regulation adopted in certain areas can plausibly be explained only on the basis that they served to generate profits for firms within the regulated industry. In other instances, no such benefits to the firms can be detected, but the measures still diverge significantly from what would be required by reference to public interest goals. Here, a private interest theory of regulation may have considerable explanatory power if we are prepared to give a wider ambit to the notion of 'private interest' and to the motivations of those responsible for creating regulation, and to recognize that much depends on how issues reach the political agenda.[114]

For example, politicians or bureaucrats, in devising a regulatory instrument, may gain prestige, and therefore satisfaction, from being seen to respond swiftly and positively to problems that suddenly receive prominent media attention—perhaps as a result of some crisis or disaster. This will sometimes lead to what is, from a public interest perspective, over-regulation, the costs of the measure exceeding the benefits. But in terms of the politicians' or bureaucrats' private interest, the action is rational: they receive credit for having initiated action, while the costs may be widely spread and barely perceived.

Finally and most importantly, public choice theory, and its various offshoots, rightly focus our attention on the way in which regulation affects a variety of private interests. The distributional impact of interventionist measures may be concealed behind the public interest rhetoric which usually accompanies them, but it remains crucial to normative evaluation.[115]

---

[113] For the USA, see the studies cited in Hovenkamp, above, n. 102, p. 88, n. 56; for the UK, see McLean, above, n. 22, pp. 78–80. For criticisms of empirical studies by American economists which purport to demonstrate the contrary, see Kelman, above, n. 106.

[114] See esp. Levine and Forrence, above n. 9. They refer to their own approach as an e.g. (see also Denzau and Munger, above, n. 112) of 'postrevisionist agency theory'.

[115] Fels, above, n. 20.

# PART II

# GENERAL ISSUES

# 5

# Use of the Criminal Law

## 1. INTRODUCTION

The great majority[1] of regulatory forms adopted in Britain are coercive and hence are commonly styled 'command-and-control'. Failure to comply may lead to the imposition of penal sanctions, if only as a last resort. The sanction may be inherent in the form (a person who contravenes a regulatory standard commits a punishable offence) or ancillary to it (for certain activities a licence must be obtained—engaging in the activity without a licence is a punishable offence). Most regulation is, therefore, underpinned by the criminal law.

The identification of regulation with the criminal law has, nevertheless, proved to be problematic.[2] Regulatory offences are not easily reconciled with the popular notion of crime, nor indeed that commonly espoused by criminologists, in so far as it correlates with moral delinquency.[3] There is perceived to be a distinction between *mala in se*, conduct which is 'wrongful in itself' and which is thus treated as 'criminal' in societies with very different social and economic values, and *mala prohibita*, which cannot be so characterized, and which is the subject of specific proscription.[4]

The moral basis of mainstream criminal law is reflected in the requirement that the prosecution prove not only the wrongful act (*actus reus*) but also some degree of mental responsibility (*mens rea*). As we shall see, for both theoretical and practical reasons, regulatory law generally dispenses with *mens rea*. The need to rationalize this has led some judges to refer to regulatory offences as 'not criminal in any real sense'[5]

---

[1] The exceptions are economic instruments, private regulation and public ownership (below, chs. 11, 12, and 13, respectively).

[2] G. Williams, 'The Definition of Crime' [1955] Current Legal Prob. 107; S. Kadish, 'Some Observations on the Use of Criminal Sanctions in Enforcing Economic Regulation' (1963) 30 U Chicago LR 432; H. V. Ball and L. M. Friedman, 'The Use of Criminal Sanctions in the Enforcement of Economic Legislation: A Sociological View' (1965) 17 Stan. LR 197; G. Richardson, A. Ogus, P. Burrows, *Policing Pollution: A Study of Regulation and Enforcement* (1983), pp. 14–18.

[3] S. Cohen, 'Footprints on the Sand: A Further Report on Criminology and the Sociology of Deviance in Britain', in A. Fitzgerald *et al.* (eds.), *Crime and Society* (1981), ch. 13.

[4] See C. Wells, *Corporations and Criminal Responsibility* (1993), pp. 7–8.

[5] *Sherras* v. *De Rutzen* [1895] 1 QB 918, 922, per Wright J.; see also *Provincial Motor Cab Company* v. *Dunning* [1909] 2 KB 594, 602, per Lord Alverstone CJ.

or as 'quasi-criminal'.[6] One leading Canadian judge has said that

[a]lthough enforced as penal laws through the utilization of the machinery of the criminal law, the offences are in substance of a civil nature and might well be regarded as a branch of administrative law to which traditional principles of criminal law have but limited application.[7]

Some commentators argue that the use of the language and the processes of traditional criminal law for regulatory purposes devalues their significance in relation to mainstream crime.[8] Others hold that regulation is not morally neutral and that it is symbolically and instrumentally valuable to stigmatize areas of it as genuinely 'criminal'.[9]

In other legal systems, terminology and procedures have been used to differentiate regulation from traditional criminal law. For example, in Germany liability for regulatory offences (*Ordnungswidrigkeit*) is procedurally distinct from criminal liability (*Straflichkeit*).[10] The American Federal Administrative Agencies have power, in many areas, to issue civil penalties as an alternative to instituting criminal prosecutions.[11] In Britain, although powerful arguments have been made for the use of civil penalties,[12] they appear to have been unequivocally adopted only in relation to evasions of tax liability.[13] The adherence to criminal law language and processes may be explained, at least in part, by the historical roots of modern regulation.

A prohibition combined with a criminal sanction was the standard form used for the extensive economic regulation of the Tudor and Stuart periods.[14] In general, the legislature (or Crown, in the case of proclamations) was content to stipulate the sanction which the justices of the peace could impose, and leave it to constables, other local officials, and above all

---

[6] *Pearks, Guston and Tee* v. *Ward* [1902] 2 KB 1, 11, per Channell J. See also *Re the Board of Commerce Act 1919* [1922] 1 AC 191, 198–9 ('not within the province of criminal jurisprudence'), per Viscount Haldane.

[7] Dickson J. in *R* v. *City of Sault Ste. Marie* (1978) 40 CCC (2d) 353, 357. See, to similar effect, Lord Scarman in *Wings Ltd.* v. *Ellis* [1985] AC 272, 293.

[8] Williams, above, n. 2, pp. 114–16; Kadish, above, n. 2, pp. 443–6.

[9] Wells, above, n. 4, pp. 29–30.

[10] J. Baumann and U. Weber, *Strafrecht* (9th edn., 1985), pp. 38–41. For theoretical discussion, see H. Mattes, *Untersuchungen zur Lehre von den Ordnungswidrigkeiten* (1982).

[11] See generally C. S. Diver, 'The Assessment and Mitigation of Civil Money Penalties by Federal Administrative Agencies' (1979) 79 Columbia LR 1435.

[12] See esp. D. Tench, *Towards a Middle System of Law* (1981). He argues that enforcement would be facilitated since less stigma would attach to liability and agencies would be less reluctant to take proceedings.

[13] Taxes Management Act 1970, Part X (Inland Revenue); Finance Act 1985, s. 13 (Customs and Excise in relation to VAT). The system of penalty points which are imposed for certain lesser road traffic offences (under Road Traffic Offenders Act 1988) and which may lead to licence disqualification can also be so treated.

[14] W. Holdsworth, *A History of English Law*, iv (1929), pp. 134–9; A. I. Ogus, 'Regulatory Law: Some Lessons from the Past' (1992) 12 Leg. Stud. 1, 13–17.

private individuals,[15] to bring prosecutions. The system lasted well into the eighteenth century[16], but was clearly inappropriate for the new forms of social legislation which emerged in the nineteenth century.

Inspectorates were then created to enforce the Factories Acts and other health and safety measures, but unlike equivalent agencies in other jurisdictions[17] they were not themselves given power to impose penalties or other sanctions.[18] The resistance to the notion that non-judicial institutions should perform such a function had a strong constitutional basis in the separation of powers doctrine. Other influences were doubtless at work: local justices were notoriously reluctant to convict reputable fellow members of the upper middle class and the industrialist lobby therefore had an interest in preserving their monopoly over adjudication.[19] Nevertheless, especially after it had been enshrined in Dicey's classic statement,[20] the constitutional orthodoxy prevailed, and the residual jurisdiction of the ordinary courts was seen as the cornerstone of English administrative law.[21] The consequence was that criminal law remained the framework for the bulk of regulatory law, although—as we shall see— regulatory agencies, denied the opportunity of imposing formal sanctions themselves, developed an enforcement strategy in which ultimate resort to the courts played only a small role.

## 2. LEGAL FRAMEWORK FOR REGULATORY OFFENCES

### (a) The Nature of Criminal Liability: General Principles

The *actus reus* of regulatory offences varies according to the type of control used; this will be considered in the ensuing chapters. Here we are concerned mainly with the issue of *mens rea* and, since regulation applies predominantly to firms, the problems of locating criminal responsibility within corporate structures.

The need to adapt traditional principles of criminal liability, with its

---

[15] So-called 'common informers' who played a significant role in early forms of regulation: M. W. Beresford, 'The Common Informer, the Penal Statute and Economic Regulation' (1957–8) 10 Econ. Hist. Rev. (2nd ser.) 22.

[16] Holdsworth, above, n. 14, vol. x (1938), pp. 159–65.

[17] E. Freund, *Administrative Powers over Persons and Property: A Comparative Survey* (1928), ch. 10.

[18] For a brief and experimental period the Factory Inspectorate had limited such powers: Factories Act 1833, s. 34.

[19] H. Arthurs, *Without the Law: Administrative Justice and Legal Pluralism in Nineteenth-Century England* (1985), p. 140.

[20] *Law of the Constitution* (1885), pp. 215–6. Dicey's views should be contrasted with the American doctrine—regulatory agencies with broad powers, though subject to judicial review—which received its classic statement in J. M. Landis, *The Administrative Process* (1938), chs. 3–4.

[21] P. Craig, *Administrative Law* (2nd edn., 1989), pp. 4–11.

strong emphasis on moral responsibility, to the very different context of command-and-control regulation as it affects mainly firms may be self-evident, but it has not proved to be an easy task.[22] The first question that arises is whether a corporate body can be convicted of an offence which requires *mens rea*. After some initial hesitation the courts decided that it could be so liable,[23] the guilty intent being found in a person (e.g. a managing director) who is seen to act 'as the company'.[24]

A more fundamental issue is whether *mens rea* should be required for regulatory contraventions. Whatever the strength of the moral arguments against strict liability,[25] economic considerations would seem to favour it, at least in the corporate sphere. Although the existence of an intention, recklessness, or negligence in relation to the prohibited act might indicate an increased likelihood of that act occurring and thus enable enforcement strategies to be better targeted,[26] proof of these mental states can impose prohibitively high administrative costs.

Recent regulatory legislation tends to indicate what degree of *mens rea* (if any) is required, usually by specifying circumstances in which lack of fault on the part of the defendant may constitute a defence.[27] Where a statute is ambiguous on the point, it is for judges to determine the nature of liability. In 1978 the Law Commission drew from case-law the following principles.[28] There is a presumption that *mens rea* is a requirement of a statutory offence, but that is rebutted where (1) an explicit indication in the statute, or (2) the social object of the provision, or (3) the nature of the penalty imposed, points to strict liability.[29]

The application of (1) has given rise to some problems of interpretation[30] but is otherwise unexceptional. The presumed moral neutrality of

---

[22] See generally Wells, above, n. 4.

[23] *R* v. *ICR Haulage Co* [1944] KB 551.

[24] Lord Reid in *Tesco Supermarkets* v *Nattrass* [1972] AC 153, 170, applying what has been referred to as 'managerial *mens rea*': B. Fisse, 'Reconstructing Corporate Criminal Law: Deterrence, Retribution, Fault, and Sanctions' (1982) 54 S. Calif. LR 1141. Fisse distinguishes two other theories of corporate *mens rea*: composite *mens rea* (aggregating the knowledge of various individuals within the corporation); and strategic *mens rea* (the explicit and implicit corporate policy).

[25] Cp. G. Williams, *Textbook of Criminal Law* (2nd edn., 1983), pp. 927–33, with R. Wasserstrom, 'Strict Liability in the Criminal Law' (1960) 12 Stan. LR 730.

[26] R. Posner, *Economic Analysis of Law* (3rd edn., 1986), pp. 218–19.

[27] Below, pp. 94–6.

[28] Law Commission, *Criminal Law: Report on the Mental Element in Crime*, No. 89, (1978 HC 499), para. 30.

[29] A distinct, but related, question is whether a provision may give rise to vicarious liability, i.e. the employer being held criminally liable for the acts of an employee. In determining this, courts have adopted similar interpretative principles to those used in relation to strict liability: L. Leigh, *Strict and Vicarious Liability: A Study in Administrative Criminal Law* (1982), pp. 44–50.

[30] e.g. on whether the use of the phrase 'permitting' in relation to the prohibited activity implies some degree of *mens rea*: ibid. 36–7.

regulation motivates (3): judges clearly think that proof of *mens rea* is desirable where the penalty is severe (e.g. imprisonment) or where moral stigma is likely to attach to conviction.[31] Strict liability may then be tolerated where the penalty is financial and perhaps only modest.[32] What then of (2), the 'social object'? To indicate the type of offence for which strict liability is appropriate, judges tend to use language like 'the regulation for the public welfare of a particular activity'.[33] They clearly have in mind the notion of 'regulation' which is the subject-matter of this book,[34] but that is hardly precise enough for a legal definition. To assist further in delimiting the appropriate area, recourse is then typically had to instrumental reasons why the legislature may have intended strict liability. Sometimes reference is made to the seriousness of the harm which the legislation was concerned to prevent.[35] The futility of this indicator is clear from the fact that actions causing the most serious harms, such as death, tend to give rise to traditional crimes which attract very severe penalties and are associated with moral stigma.

Two other indicators are potentially more helpful and correlate with the economic considerations mentioned above. The first is where a defendant, although not directly carrying out the prohibited activity, is well placed to control or prevent its occurrence.[36] This most obviously applies where the offence is committed within an enterprise, and is thus a major justification for corporate strict liability.[37] The second is where proof of a mental state would be very difficult (and costly).[38] This has a general ambit, but again applies particularly to enterprises.

In Australia and Canada, the conjunction of judicial opposition to strict liability and recognition of the administrative burden of proving *mens rea* has led to a compromise solution. A statute may be construed as giving rise to prima facie strict liability, in that the prosecution need prove nothing more than the *actus reus*, but allowing the defendant to avoid liability by proving that he took all reasonable care in the circumstances, or that he had an honest and reasonable belief in a state of facts which, if they

---

[31] *Warner* v. *Metropolitan Police Commissioner* [1969] 2 AC 256, 278, per Lord Reid.

[32] Cf. *Laird* v. *Dobell* [1906] 1 KB 131.

[33] *Lim Chin Aik* v. *R* [1963] AC 160, 174, per Lord Evershed. See also: Lord Reid in the *Warner* case, above n. 31, p. 271; Lord Diplock in the *Tesco* case, above n. 24, p. 194; and Dickson J. in *R* v. *City of Sault Ste. Marie*, above, n. 7, pp. 362–3.

[34] Cf. above, pp. 1–3.

[35] e.g. *R* v. *St. Margaret's Trust* [1958] 2 All ER 289, 293, per Donovan J.; *Seaboard Offshore Ltd* v. *Secretary of State for Transport* [1993] 3 All ER 25, 30, per Staughton LJ.

[36] Cf. Lord Diplock in the *Tesco* case, above. n. 24, p. 194; Lord Evershed in *Lim Chin Aik* v. *R* [1963] AC 160, 174.

[37] Fisse, above n. 24.

[38] Cf. Dickson J. in *R* v. *City of Sault Ste. Marie*, above, n. 7, p. 363; Lord Reid in the *Tesco* case, above, n. 24, p. 159.

existed, would make his conduct lawful.[39] Some English judges have been attracted by these ideas, but any temptation to adopt them has been resisted, primarily because it is thought that legislation would be required to effect the necessary reform.[40] In fact, the case for importing such a general principle into the law is relatively weak, for, as we shall now see, modern legislation frequently provides for *specific* defences which are presumptively designed to target liability where it is considered to be most cost-effective. Moreover, empirical studies have shown that enforcement agencies rarely initiate proceedings for strict liability offences when contraventions occur without any negligence.[41]

## (b) The Nature of Criminal Liability: Statutory Defences

Until the late 1970s, regulatory legislation typically imposed, or was interpreted as imposing, strict liability.[42] In the period since then, there has been a reaction to this traditional approach, perhaps motivated by a concern that imposing responsibility on those that had no knowledge of the act or could not have avoided it is inconsistent with the moral basis of the criminal law.[43] Recent regulatory legislation therefore attempts to find some compromise between that principle and the undesirability of placing too great a burden on enforcement agencies.

A variety of defences have been made available to exculpate blameless defendants. Some which would appear to come within this category, for example that the defendant has used the 'best practicable means' or the 'best available techniques not entailing excessive cost' are concerned more with standards of behaviour (i.e. *actus reus*) than with culpability (*mens rea*) and, as such, are reserved for discussion later in this book.[44]

The most frequently encountered defence relating to *mens rea* requires the defendant to prove, on a balance of probabilities, that

he took all reasonable precautions and exercised all due diligence to avoid the commission of the offence by himself or by a person under his control.[45]

---

[39] The leading cases are: *Proudman* v. *Dayman* (1943) 67 CLR 536 (Australia); and *R* v. *City of Sault Ste. Marie*, above, n. 7 (Canada). See generally C. Howard, *Strict Responsibility* (1963).

[40] See esp. *Sweet* v. *Parsley* [1970] AC 132, at 150 (Lord Reid) and 158 (Lord Pearce).

[41] W. G. Carson, 'Some Sociological Aspects of Strict Liability and the Enforcement of Factory Legislation' (1970) 33 Modern LR 396; Richardson *et al.*, above, n. 2, pp. 170–81; K. Hawkins, *Environment and Enforcement* (1987), pp. 168–9.

[42] It has been estimated that, in 1975, there were upwards of 7,000 separate criminal offences (including non-regulatory offences) and about a half of these did not require proof of *mens rea*: Justice Report, *Breaking the Rules* (1980).

[43] M. Clarke, *Business Crime: Its Nature and Control* (1990), p. 205.

[44] Below, pp. 206–7.

[45] Food Safety Act 1990, s.21(1). To similar effect see e.g. : Fire Precautions Act 1971, s.25; Weights and Measures Act 1985, s.34; Financial Services Act 1986, s.4(2). There is, of course, a considerable case-law on the meaning of the expressions 'reasonable precautions' and 'due diligence'. Most of this is concerned with what must be proved in relation to specific

In relation to some statutory offences this is all that need be proved, but for a defence to others there is an additional condition

that the commission of the offence was due to a mistake or to reliance on information supplied to him or to the act or default of another person, an accident or some other cause beyond his control.[46]

Normally, if 'reasonable precautions' and 'due diligence' are proved, it will not be difficult to satisfy this broadly phrased second condition. Nevertheless, an important question arises as to the meaning here of 'another person': does it include an employee? In *Tesco Supermarkets* v. *Nattrass*,[47] the House of Lords held that it did, provided that the employee in question was not someone who had overall supervisory responsibility and who thus could be regarded as acting in the capacity of the corporation charged with the offence.[48] Since the defendant corporation had established that it had a proper system of control which satisfied the 'reasonable precautions . . . due diligence' test, it was therefore acquitted.[49]

There is often explicit provision to deal with the converse case, where an employee does the prohibited act under orders from his superior. In such a case, it will be a defence

that he acted under instructions from his employer and neither knew nor had reason to suppose that the acts done by him constituted a contravention.[50]

Several regulatory regimes impose liability on retailers in relation to the quality or quantity of the goods sold or to the information supplied with them. The retailers may do nothing with the goods except resell them, and, particularly where there is reliance on a warranty as to quality, quantity, or the accuracy of information provided by a manufacturer or wholesaler, such liability may seem unduly harsh. The traditional policy has been to allow the retailer to invoke by way of defence that he purchased the goods with a warranty, and that he had no reason to believe that the goods did not correspond with the warranted description.[51] The current trend is to

offences. See e.g. : *Naish* v. *Gore* [1971] 3 All ER 737; *Tesco* case, above, n. 24; *R* v. *Southwood* [1987] 3 All ER 556; *R* v. *Mabbott* [1987] Crim LR 826; *Watson* v. *Molloy* [1988] 3 All ER 459. One important general point does, however, emerge: the more likely the offence, the higher the standard of care required. See also below, pp. 153–4.

[46] e.g. Trade Descriptions Act 1968, s.24(1); Registered Homes Act 1984, s.18(1).

[47] Above, n. 24.

[48] Some statutes explicitly allow the acts of a servant/agent to be a defence provided that the employer/principal proves due diligence, e.g. Building Act 1984, s. 63.

[49] For criticism, see Wells, above, n. 4, pp. 107–10. The result would, of course, have been different if the statutory provision had given rise to vicarious liability.

[50] Environmental Protection Act 1990, s. 33(7)(b).

[51] e.g. Medicines Act 1968, s. 122. For the purposes of a similar, but now repealed, provision in the Food and Drugs Act 1955, s. 115, 'warranty' has been given a broad interpretation, to include a brand name in an invoice: *Rochdale Metropolitan BC* v. *F. M. C.(Meat) Ltd* [1980] 2 All ER 303.

extend the retailer's responsibility,[52] and some statutes require the latter also to satisfy the 'reasonable precautions . . . due diligence' test which, in this context, means taking positive steps to verify that the goods correspond to the warranty.[53]

Where a warranty or the act of another person is relied on as a defence, a device is commonly used to facilitate enforcement. The defendant is required to give the prosecutor advance notice of an intention to rely on such a defence and to supply information on the identity of the third person or a copy of the warranty. Some statutes allow the defendant to be acquitted only if the third party is convicted;[54] but, more typically, supplying the warranty or identification or assistance with identification is all that is required.[55]

Finally, mention should be made of specific defences which exculpate defendants acting in emergency situations. So, for example, a person other than a midwife or medical practitioner may attend a woman in childbirth, where 'the attention is given in a case of sudden or urgent necessity'.[56] And where waste is unlawfully deposited, it is a defence to prove that

the acts were done . . . in an emergency in order to avoid danger to the public and that, as soon as practicable after they were done, particulars of them were furnished to the . . . [relevant] authority.[57]

### (c) Rights of Prosecution

The historical tradition in English criminal law has been that prosecutions are brought by private individuals.[58] When enforcement agencies have been created, duties of prosecution are invariably imposed on them, but in general the right to bring a private prosecution has not been abrogated, because it is seen to be a constitutional right, providing the citizen with a safeguard against inertia and corruption on the part of public officials.[59] The data available suggest that the number of private prosecutions brought for regulatory offences is small, about two per cent of the total.[60] On the other hand, they play a not insignificant role in the strategy of some

---

[52] See esp. the White Paper, *Food Safety—Protecting the Consumer* (1989, Cm. 732), para. 6.10.　　　　[53] See e.g. *F.Woolworth & Co.* v. *Gray* [1970] 1 All ER 953.
[54] e.g. Shops Act 1950, s. 71(6).
[55] e.g. Trade Descriptions Act 1968, s. 24(2); Weights and Measures Act 1985, s. 33; Registered Homes Act 1985, s. 18(2); Food Safety Act 1990, s. 21(5).
[56] Nurses, Midwives, and Health Visitors Act 1979, s. 17(3)(a). See also Road Traffic Act 1988, s. 34(3) (defence to the offence of driving a motor vehicle otherwise than on a road 'for the purpose of saving life or extinguishing fire or any other like emergency').
[57] Environmental Protection Act 1990, s. 33(7)(c).
[58] J. F. Stephen, *History of the Criminal Law in England* (1883), pp. 493–503.
[59] *Gouriet* v. *Union of Post Office Workers* [1978] AC 435, per Lord Wilberforce, p. 477, per Lord Diplock, p. 498.
[60] K. W. Lidstone, R. Hogg and F. Sutcliffe, *Prosecutions by Private Individuals and Non-Police Agencies*, Royal Commission on Civil Procedure Research Study No. 10 (1980).

pressure groups and are valued as such.[61] The general right of private prosecution is now enshrined in legislation,[62] but important exceptions exist. Under some statutes, prosecutions may be brought only by the relevant enforcement agency (or police)[63], or by a private individual only if she obtains the consent of the Director of Public Prosecutions, the Attorney General, or the Minister of the relevant government department.[64]

The most important arguments for limiting private prosecutions, and which are thus to be balanced against the constitutional goal described above, are that they lead to inconsistency in the application of criminal sanctions and undermine the discretion which is exercised by public agencies.[65] The exercise of such discretion can involve abuse but, as we shall see later in this chapter,[66] it can also be essential to a rational enforcement strategy.

### (d) The Consequences of Criminal Liability

The conventional sanction prescribed for conviction of a regulatory offence is a fine of a stipulated maximum amount, the level of which is assumed to reflect the gravity of the offence.[67] Imprisonment is often available as an alternative, but its use for regulatory offences, especially those involving strict liability, is almost unknown,[68] and the sanction cannot be used when a corporation is the defendant.

What distinguishes regulatory offences from those relating to mainstream criminal law is the widespread use of other formal enforcement instruments. These fall into two categories. The first comprises administrative measures which are taken prior to, and often in substitution for, the

---

[61] C. Harlow and R. Rawlings, *Pressure Through Law* (1992), ch. 5.

[62] Prosecution of Offences Act 1985, s. 6(1), following the Government's rejection of a recommendation of the Royal Commission on Criminal Procedure (1981, Cmnd. 8092), paras. 7.46–51, that private prosecutions should be abolished: White Paper, *An Independent Prosecution Service for England and Wales* (1983, Cmnd. 9074), paras. 11–12. See generally A. Samuels, 'Non-Crown Prosecutions by Non-Police Agencies and by Private Individuals' [1986] Crim. LR 33.

[63] e.g. Weights and Measures Act 1985, s. 83(1). Where two agencies have enforcement responsibilities, it is sometimes necessary for one to give notice to the other before a prosecution may proceed, e.g.: Fair Trading Act 1973, s. 130; Consumer Credit Act 1974, s. 161(2); Estate Agents Act 1979, s. 26(2).

[64] e.g. Health and Safety at Work etc. Act 1974, s. 38; Prevention of Oil Pollution Act 1971, s. 19(1); Registered Homes Act 1984, s. 53.

[65] Royal Commission on Criminal Procedure, above, n. 62, para. 7.46.

[66] Below, pp. 96–7.

[67] See the standard scale for summary offences introduced by Criminal Justice Act 1982, s. 37. Under Criminal Justice Act 1991, s. 18(1), as amended, the court is to assess an amount which 'reflects the seriousness of the offence'.

[68] A one-year suspended prison sentence was imposed in 1989 for what was thought to be the first conviction for manslaughter resulting from a breach of health and safety regulation: Wells, above, n. 4, p. 41.

criminal process. They have played an increasingly important role in regulatory law as the criminal law and its sanctions are perceived to provide too crude a solution to the problems of enforcement, and as the regulatory agencies have sought powers which they can themselves administer without infringing the constitutional monopoly which courts have on the imposition of criminal sanctions.

'Enforcement', 'abatement', or 'improvement notices' are issued by regulatory agencies stating the details of an alleged contravention and, where appropriate, of what steps should be taken to remedy the situation.[69] In some cases, there can be no conviction unless such a notice has been issued and the addressee has been given an opportunity to comply with it.[70] 'Prohibition notices' are issued where remedial action is more urgent because of some immediate risk to health or safety.[71]

Perhaps the most remarkable example of this technique is to be found in Part III of the Fair Trading Act 1973.[72] Where an individual or firm has persisted in conduct detrimental to consumers and unlawful, either in criminal or civil law, the Director General of Fair Trading is there placed under a statutory duty to seek a written assurance from that individual or firm to refrain from the conduct.[73] A failure to give such an assurance or a breach of it may then lead to formal proceedings in the Restrictive Practices Court or the county court.

At the other end of the severity scale are 'fixed penalties'. These are used for minor offences which are regularly committed, and the formal prosecution of which would unduly absorb law enforcement resources.[74] Where the relevant authority has reason to believe that an individual has committed the offence in question, the alleged offender is given a notice offering him the opportunity to discharge any liability by the payment of the fixed sum within a certain period.[75]

The second category comprises additional instruments available to the

---

[69] e.g. Health and Safety at Work etc. Act 1974, s. 21; Environmental Protection Act 1990, ss. 13, 89, 92; Food Safety Act 1990, s. 10.

[70] e.g. Town and Country Planning Act 1990, s. 172.

[71] e.g. Health and Safety at Work etc. Act 1974, s. 22; Food Safety Act 1990, s. 12; Environmental Protection Act 1990, s. 14. These should be distinguished from 'stop notices' issued by local planning authorities to complement enforcement notices where the latter have not yet come into effect: Town and Country Planning Act 1990, s. 183.

[72] This was modelled on the 'cease-and-desist' jurisdiction of the US Federal Trade Commission, on which see: T. E. Kauper, 'Cease and Desist: The History, Effect, and Scope of Clayton Act Orders of the Federal Trade Commission' (1968) 66 Mich. LR 1095.

[73] S. 34, on which see *R* v. *Director General of Fair Trading, ex parte F.H.Taylor & Co* [1981] ICR 292, and R. Cranston, *Consumers and the Law* (2nd edn., 1984), pp. 351–5. For commentary and evaluation, see A. I. Ogus and C. K. Rowley, 'The Costs and Benefits of Part III of the Fair Trading Act 1973 and Licensing under the Consumer Credit Act 1974', unpublished research paper for the Office of Fair Trading (1981).

[74] For discussion, see *Report of the Interdepartmental Working Party on Road Traffic Law* (1981).

[75] Road Traffic Offenders Act 1988, s. 51; Environmental Protection Act 1990, s. 88.

court. The first of these is designed to secure compliance where a fine has proved to be an inadequate deterrent relative to the profit accruing from the offence.[76] The High Court has an inherent residual jurisdiction to issue an injunction to restrain the persistent commission of offences,[77] and this complements specific statutory powers to similar effect.[78] Disobeying an injunction constitutes contempt of court, which can be punished by imprisonment.

Orders issued by inferior courts can be equally drastic if they effectively prevent an individual or firm from engaging in a profitable activity.[79] For certain offences, the court may suspend or revoke a licence which is required for the lawful pursuit of such an activity.[80] The forfeiture or confiscation of certain goods used or supplied in breach of regulations was a typical sanction in early law, since it acted as an incentive for private prosecution, the successful prosecutor being entitled to a share in the proceeds.[81] Forfeiture orders[82] are today part of the punishment and thus serve mainly a deterrent purpose; confiscation orders[83] may be imposed as an additional measure where the offender has made a substantial profit. The issuing of compensation orders[84] may have a deterrent effect, but they are primarily intended to provide relief for the victim of a regulatory offence.[85]

### 3. ENFORCEMENT AND COMPLIANCE

### (a) General

The use of the criminal law as the principal legal form of regulation cannot be appraised without a careful investigation of the policy and practice of

---

[76] In *Attorney-General* v. *Harris* [1961] 1 QB 74, the defendants had been convicted of 237 offences under the same statutory provision. An alternative method of dealing with persistent offences arising under consumer protection legislation is provided by Part III of the Fair Trading Act 1983: above, p. 88.

[77] *Attorney-General* v. *Harris* [1961] 1 QB 74; *Stoke-on-Trent CC* v. *B & Q (Retail) Ltd* [1984] AC 754.

[78] e. g. Local Government Act 1972, s. 222; Financial Services Act 1986, s. 6.

[79] J. Rowan-Robinson, P. Watchman, C. Barker, *Crime and Regulation: A Study of the Enforcement of Regulatory Codes* (1990), pp. 251–2.

[80] e. g. Pet Animals Act 1951, s. 5(3); Licensing Act 1964, s. 20A; Gaming Act 1968, Sched. 2, para. 48. Where professional occupations are subject to licensing regimes, the power to suspend and revoke is typically conferred on the professional self-regulatory agency: see e.g. Solicitors Act 1974, s. 47, and Opticians Act 1989, s. 14.

[81] Ogus, above, n. 14, pp. 15–17.

[82] e.g. Powers of Criminal Courts Act 1973, s. 43 (as amended).

[83] Criminal Justice Act 1988, s. 71.

[84] General powers are conferred by the Powers of Criminal Courts Act 1973, ss. 35–38, as amended. See also Financial Services Act 1986, s.6(4), which makes provision for a 'restitution order'.

[85] See S. Weatherill, 'The Powers of Criminal Courts to Make Compensation Orders' (1986) 135 NLJ 459. Orders can be made even if civil liability would not arise on the facts.

enforcement. Policy-makers long ago abandoned the notion, prevalent in the early history of regulation, that their task was simply to enact law in the appropriate form, on the assumption that the question of enforcement could be left to such institutions and agencies as were available to deal with it.[86] There is recognized to be a symbiotic relationship between the formulation of regulatory rules and their application in specific environments.[87] Indeed, as we shall see,[88] in certain areas of regulation the law cannot be defined in terms other than those which are applied at a 'grassroots' level by an agency to a particular firm or individual.

The enforcement of modern regulatory law became a matter of concern for scholars, particularly in the early 1970s. The general perception emerged that regulation had 'failed', mainly because of the pusillanimity of agencies in dealing with offenders, as reflected, in particular, in their reluctance to initiate formal prosecutions.[89] The more recent, and by now very voluminous literature, both theoretical[90] and empirical,[91] suggests that this perception was simplistic. The literature has much enriched our understanding of enforcement policy and practice, as the following discussion should reveal. The public interest and private interest theories of regulation generate very different models of enforcement policy, and, with the aid of the empirical work, these can be compared with the practice of enforcement.

## (b) The Public Interest Model of Optimal Deterrence

On the basis of the public interest theory of regulation, we must assume that the instrumental goal of an enforcement agency is to minimize the harm resulting from contraventions of regulation at lowest administrative cost. Perfect compliance is neither practicable nor desirable, given that the costs of achieving it will invariably outweigh the benefits. The appropriate target is, therefore, optimal deterrence.

[86] Cf. Holdsworth, above, n. 14, x (1938), p. 163.

[87] See generally R. Baldwin, 'Why Rules Don't Work' (1990) 53 Modern LR 321.

[88] Below, pp. 170-1.

[89] e.g. N. Gunningham, *Pollution, Social Interest and the Law* (1974); I. Paulus, *The Search for Pure Food* (1974). See generally below, pp. 93-4.

[90] See esp. R. Posner, 'The Behaviour of Administrative Agencies' (1972) 1 J. Legal Stud. 314; C. S. Diver, 'A Theory of Regulatory Enforcement' (1980) 28 Pub. Policy 257; A. J. Reiss, 'Selecting Strategies of Social Control Over Organizational Life', in K. Hawkins and J. Thomas (eds.), *Enforcing Regulation* (1984), pp. 23-35; P. Fenn and C. Veljanovski, 'A Positive Theory of Regulatory Enforcement' (1988) 98 Econ. J. 1055; I. Ayres and J. Braithwaite, *Responsive Regulation: Transcending the Deregulation Debate* (1992).

[91] The principal studies of British regulatory enforcement are to be found in: W. G. Carson, 'White-Collar Crime and the Enforcement of Factory Legislation' (1970) 6 Brit. J. Criminol. 383; R. Cranston, *Regulating Business* (1979); Richardson *et al.*, above n. 2; Hawkins, above, n. 41; B. Hutter, *The Reasonable Arm of the Law* (1988); Rowan-Robinson *et al.* above, n. 79. There are useful summaries of the findings in Rowan-Robinson *et al.*, and G. M. Richardson, 'Strict Liability for Regulatory Crime: the Empirical Research' [1987] Crim. LR 295.

The posited models of optimal deterrence presuppose rational behaviour on the part both of enforcement agencies and of those whose conduct is regulated[92]—hereafter, for the sake of simplicity, firms. Firms will comply with the law only if the expected cost to them of violation exceeds the benefit they derive from violation; more specifically when $pD > U$, where p is the perceived probability of apprehension and conviction, $D$ the costs incurred as a result of apprehension and conviction, and $U$ the benefits accruing from violation.[93] $D$ includes, most importantly, $F$, the fine payable (or financial equivalent of an alternative sanction), $L$, any business losses caused by adverse publicity, and $M$, the costs associated with defending a criminal prosecution.

For its part, the agency should spend enforcement resources up to the point where the marginal cost ($MC$) of those resources is approximately equal to the marginal benefit ($MB$) arising from such expenditure and defined in terms of reduced violations.[94] $MC$ here includes the costs not only to the public purse of monitoring behaviour, conducting prosecutions, and administering sanctions, but also to firms in being subjected to these processes and, indeed, in modifying their behaviour to comply with the law. Now, as we have seen from the model of firm behaviour, the functional relationship between $MB$ and $MC$—the deterrent impact of enforcement expenditure—is determined by two variables $p$ (the perceived probability of apprehension and conviction) and $D$ (the costs to the firms arising from apprehension and conviction). What is represented by $D$ lies largely outside the control of the enforcement agency, since $F$ is determined by a combination of the legislature (specifying the maximum level) and the judge. On the other hand, $p$ is a consequence of how the agency within its budgetary constraints deploys its resources.

The model of optimal deterrence thus suggests how an agency should formulate its policy in relation to the problems of enforcement strategy, choosing, for example, between occasional monitoring of all regulated firms and intensive monitoring of firms suspected of contraventions, and between systematically prosecuting all known offenders and merely cautioning all but the most recalcitrant. The theoretical attractiveness of the model should not, however, be allowed to conceal the enormous

[92] Scepticism has often been expressed as to the reality of this assumption as regards individual criminals (esp. in relation to 'mainstream' crime): e.g. White Paper, *Crime, Justice and Protecting the Public* (1989, Cm. 965), para. 2.8; and, more generally, T. Gibbons, 'The Utility of Economic Analysis of Crime' (1982) 2 Int. Rev. Law & Econ. 173. In relation to corporate crime, it has been shown to have much greater predictive power: J. Braithwaite and G. Geis, 'On Theory and Action for Corporate Crime Control' (1982) 28 Crime & Delinquency 292.

[93] Cf. G. Becker, 'Crime and Punishment: An Economic Approach' (1968) 76 J. Pol. Econ. 169; I. Ehrlich, 'The Economic Approach to Crime—a Preliminary Assessment', in S. Messinger and E. Bittner, *Criminology Yearbook*, i (1979), pp. 25–60.

[94] Cf. Posner, above, n. 90.

practical difficulties arising from its application to real world situations.[95] Predicting the deterrent impact of various policies is hazardous, not the least because it cannot be assumed that all regulated firms will respond in the same way, and predicting $U$ (the benefit to the firms from contravention) may be a matter of guesswork. Even more problematic is the assessment of the social harm which will be avoided by different instances of compliance: how, for example, should an enforcement officer weigh the relative costs of one human death or mildly harming fifty individuals; of destroying wildlife habitat or rendering water undrinkable?[96]

There are a number of ways in which agencies may respond to these difficulties without totally forsaking the model.[97] It will suffice to mention three examples of how its requirements may be simplified. First, instead of formulating the enforcement policy on the basis of marginal analysis (comparing the relative deterrent effectiveness of different enforcement techniques at different levels of enforcement activity) an agency may rest content with average analysis (assuming that the costs and benefits of each technique will not vary according to the level of activity). Secondly, as a substitute for the minimization of aggregate social harm, it may take as its goal the minimization of political or social criticism, on the questionable assumption that the latter will be a good proxy for the former. Thirdly, rather than engage in the cost-benefit analysis inherent in the model, it may adopt a cost-effectiveness strategy, that is, specify a goal (e.g. reducing accidents by ten per cent) and then select policies which will predictably achieve that goal at lowest cost.[98] All three examples may be seen to accord with a well-known theory, that administrators making decisions in an environment of inadequate information adopt a 'satisficing' strategy: instead of searching for an optimal solution, they establish a standard of what is acceptable and then review alternatives until one is found which satisfies that standard.[99]

### (c) Failure of the Public Interest Model of Optimal Deterrence

Even with the adaptations considered in the last paragraph, the public interest model of optimal deterrence has proved to be a poor predictor of enforcement agency behaviour. We must now examine the problems of reconciling it with agency practice and explore how it may be modified.

We have seen that the level of deterrence is a function of two main variables, $p$, the perceived probability of apprehension and conviction, and $D$, the costs to the firms arising from apprehension and conviction which

---

[95] Diver, above, n. 90, pp. 264–71.
[96] Cf. below, pp. 156–8 and 204.                    [97] Diver, above, n. 90, pp. 271–9.
[98] L. B. Lave, *The Strategy of Social Regulation: Decision Frameworks for Policy* (1981), pp. 19–21. On the distinction between cost-benefit analysis and cost-effectiveness analysis, see below, pp. 153–62.          [99] H. Simon, *Administrative Behavior* (3rd edn., 1976).

comprise $F$ (the formal sanction), $L$ (the losses from adverse publicity), and $M$ (the cost of defending the case). The interaction of $p$ and $D$ means that if $D$ is relatively low, to achieve the same amount of deterrence, $p$ must be relatively high—and vice versa. Thus if the sum needed to deter *ex ante* a given activity was £10,000 because the anticipated profit to the firm of the activity was £9,999 and $D$ was £20,000, then $p$ would have to be 0.5. In other words, the firm would have to perceive that there was a one-in-two probability that it would be apprehended and convicted for the unlawful activity.

Although it is difficult to assess the values of $L$[100] and $M$, we know that for most regulatory offences $F$ is relatively small.[101] If an offence is indictable, there is no limit to what a court can impose by way of fine. For some serious summary offences, a maximum of £20,000 is prescribed in the legislation.[102] But for many regulatory offences, the maximum is still relatively small,[103] and when it is larger, courts in exercising their discretion, often impose only a small fraction of it, perhaps a few hundred pounds.[104] Although widely condemned, small fines are not necessarily 'irrational' or the result of undue influence. The assessment of fines for corporate crime gives rise to a dilemma which has sometimes been referred to as the 'deterrence trap'.[105] The penalty must be high enough to deter when discounted by $p$, but low enough that relevant firms will be able to pay without becoming insolvent.

According to the model, if $F$ is small, and a larger value to $L$ does not compensate for this, we must expect a high value for $p$. But the evidence shows exactly the opposite: with a few marginal exceptions (significantly for offences predominantly committed by individuals rather than firms),[106]

[100] This presumably varies significantly according to the nature of the offence. The loss to a food store arising from a conviction for lack of adequate hygiene will be substantial (Hutter, above, n. 91, pp. 184–6) but that accruing to a firm overreaching the legal limit on trade effluent into sewers may be non-existent or trivial (Richardson *et al.*, above, n. 2, pp. 143–4). On reputation costs see generally Braithwaite, above, n. 92.

[101] Rowan-Robinson *et al.*, above n. 79, pp. 264–73, and the refs. there cited. $F$ is, of course, much higher when the sanction involves the suspension or revocation of a licence.

[102] e.g. Environmental Protection Act 1990, ss. 23, 33.

[103] The maxima for offences of level 1 and 2 are £200 and £500, respectively: Criminal Justice Act 1991, s. 17.

[104] *Report of the [Robens] Committee on Safety and Health at Work* (1972, Cmnd. 5034), para. 258; Third Report of the House of Commons Environment Committee, *Pollution of Rivers and Estuaries*, (1986–87 HC 183). One researcher found that enforcement officers often had to engage in 'bluff' regarding the amount of the sanction likely to be imposed: K. Hawkins, 'Bargain and Bluff: Compliance Strategy and Deterrence in the Enforcement of Regulation' (1983) 5 Law & Pol. Q. 35; also Hawkins, above, n. 41, pp. 149–53.

[105] J. C. Coffee, ' "No Soul to Damn: No Body to Kick": An Unscandalized Inquiry into the Problem of Corporate Punishment' (1981) 79 Mich. LR 386, 390. See also Fisse, above, n. 24.

[106] e.g. for social security fraud and car and television licence evasion: Rowan-Robinson *et al.*, above, n. 79, pp. 185, 209–10.

the policy of British[107] enforcement agencies is to prosecute only a very small proportion of known offenders;[108] impressionistically, $p$ is unlikely to exceed 0.05.[109] The strategy is one of persuasion and co-operation, rather than of confrontation: formal prosecution is seen very much as a last resort, when all other methods of achieving compliance have failed.[110]

## (d) Capture Theory

One possible response to the failure of the public interest model of optimal deterrence to account for the enforcement policy of regulatory agencies is to reject the assumption that the latter pursue public interest goals. Perhaps agency officials secure private benefits from their less aggressive stance. This was the hypothesis of 'capture theory', one of the precursors of public choice analysis, which proved at one time to be a popular explanation of the reluctance to prosecute.[111] It suggested that the agencies would be subverted by pressure, influence, or 'bribery' away from their statutory goal of enforcement to protect regulated firms.

The theory should not be totally discounted. Where considerable technological expertise is required of agency personnel, there is generally some interchange of employees between the agency and the regulated industries; and an enforcement officer might not wish to prejudice his prospects of employment by the latter.[112] Some agencies are accountable to, and to some extent controlled by, local government. In such circumstances, it would be surprising if the interests of regulated firms had never been allowed to influence agency behaviour.[113] Nevertheless, recent studies have found very little evidence to support the capture theory.[114] Empirical researchers report that agency officials do pursue a public interest goal, but the goal in question is to be characterized as one of 'compliance' rather than 'deterrence'.[115] 'Compliance' implies conforming

---

[107] The approach of American agencies tends to be more formal and fines are levied for violations relatively frequently: D. Vogel, *National Styles of Regulation: Environmental Policy in Great Britain and the United States* (1986), p. 220.

[108] A finding common to all the studies cited above, n. 41.

[109] The impression is drawn from the statistics reported in a number of sources, esp. Carson, above, n. 91; Richardson *et al.*, above, n. 2, p. 62; Hawkins, above, n. 41, p. 177; Lidstone *et al.*, above, n. 60; Rowan-Robinson *et al.*, above, n. 79, pp. 47, 95.

[110] The strategy, which dates back to the nineteenth century (see Report of Royal Commission on Noxious Vapours (1878, C 2159), para. 28), is often reiterated in the formal statements of agency policy: for examples, see the refs. cited in Rowan-Robinson *et al.*, above, n. 79, pp. 210–13. It has also been approved by official bodies reviewing regulatory systems, e. g. : Robens Report, above, n. 104, paras. 208, 214, 255; Fifth Report of the Royal Commission on Environmental Pollution (1976, Cmnd. 6371), para. 227.

[111] M. A. Bernstein, *Regulating Business by Independent Commission* (1955), and see above, pp. 57–8.

[112] Cf. C. C. Hood, 'Privatising UK Tax Law Enforcement' (1986) 64 Pub. Admin. 319.

[113] Cranston, above, n. 91, p. 14.

[114] Cf. Richardson, above, n. 91, p. 300.

[115] The distinction is drawn by Reiss, above, n. 90, pp. 23–4.

to the law as a result of persuasion and negotiation before the event; 'deterrence', on the other hand, depends on penalizing offenders for offences already committed and thus deterring further violations.

### (e) Public Interest Model of Optimal Compliance

To reformulate the public interest model in accordance with the compliance goal requires us to explore the reasons for the failure of the deterrence model. Agencies cannot realistically raise the value of p, on grounds both financial and behavioural. They operate within budgetary constraints which are often severe,[116] and they face a delicate problem of allocating the resources available to them in a way which will maximize effectiveness.[117] As technology has developed, so the process of monitoring has become increasingly complex. There is typically a significant variation in the size and working methods of regulated firms. In consequence, it is very difficult to predict where and when violations will occur.

In the light of these problems, a policy of rigorous enforcement involving frequent resort to prosecution would generally be irrational. In the first place, the prosecution process is itself very costly. On the basis of data derived from a study of the Health and Safety Inspectorate, Veljanovski calculated that prosecution was 'from eight to ten times more time-consuming . . . than the average factory visit'.[118] Given that the relatively low fines imposed on those convicted is unlikely to add much deterrence to that which might accrue from locating contraventions but only threatening prosecution, the marginal benefit of prosecution is typically much smaller than its marginal cost.[119] Secondly, because the cost to the enforcement officer of acquiring appropriate information on contravention is so large, some degree of co-operation from firms is essential. A policy of confrontation would inhibit such co-operation and would thus be counter-productive.[120] There are, thirdly, some additional private interest reasons why an enforcement officer should adopt a co-operative stance. It may enhance the utility he personally derives from 'educating' the offender and advising on technical problems.[121] Further, it enables him to maintain

[116] Agencies often complain of underfunding, especially when legislative changes make increased demands of them: Rowan-Robinson *et al.*, above, n. 79, pp. 215–16. In the light of the public choice hypothesis that bureaucracies seek to maximize their budgets (above, pp. 68–9), such claims should nevertheless be treated with caution.

[117] K. Hawkins and J. Thomas, 'The Enforcement Process in Regulatory Bureaucracies', in Hawkins and Thomas, above, n. 90, ch. 1; Diver, above, n. 90, pp. 280–91.

[118] C. Veljanovski, 'Regulatory Enforcement: An Economic Study of the British Factory Inspectorate' (1983) 5 Law & Pol. Q. 75, 86.

[119] Hutter, above, n. 91, pp. 79–80; Rowan-Robinson *et al.*, above, n. 79, p. 95. The benefit becomes even smaller, perhaps even negative, if an offender had been led to believe by an officer threatening prosecution that the fine would be significantly larger: Hawkins, above, n. 41, pp. 151–2.          [120] Veljanovski, above, n. 118, p. 84.

[121] Richardson *et al.*, above, n. 2, pp. 128–30.

control over the case which, if prosecution were initiated, would be transferred to a superior who might perceive such a development as an instance of failure on his part.[122]

A co-operative stance adopted by the agency is useless without the regulated firms reciprocating. Why should they respond positively to requests for compliance which are buttressed by, at the most, only veiled threats? One commentator locates the answer in a historical and cultural phenomenon: the willingness of British industry to co-operate with governmental authority.[123] But this is vague and seems hardly adequate as a total explanation. More precise reasons are available if we consider the context in which the co-operation is sought.[124]

As will be revealed in Chapter 8,[125] in general the formal standards imposed by the law (*de jure* standards) tend to be over-inclusive, that is, they render unlawful a wider range of conduct than is necessary to fulfil the public interest goal of the legislation. Strict observance of *de jure* standards would not be socially optimal. One example is the 30 m.p.h. speed limit which is imposed uniformly in urban areas. To achieve the public interest goal of optimal safety (where the marginal costs of risk avoidance—driving slowly—are approximately equal to the marginal benefits—reducing accidents), it cannot be right to insist that *all* vehicles are driven at less than 30 m.p.h. in *all* circumstances. But the uniform *de jure* standard can be tailored to different circumstances, and thus orientated toward the goal of optimal safety, if it is made the subject of selective enforcement.[126] The enforcement officer then applies a *de facto* standard which varies according to the circumstances.[127] So, for example, at times and in locations of reduced risk, the motorist might not be apprehended unless she were exceeding 40 m.p.h. As we shall also see, the same end can be achieved by a more general standard (e.g. vehicles shall not be driven faster than is 'reasonable' in urban areas), leaving it to the enforcement and adjudication authorities to determine what is 'reasonable' in the circumstances.

In situations in which an enforcement officer has at his disposal an over-inclusive offence, he can use it as a bargaining tool. Provided that he has evidence that the firm has contravened the *de jure* standard, he can offer to abstain from enforcing that standard so long as the firm complies with the

---

[122] Richardson *et al.*, above, n. 2, 185.

[123] Vogel, above, n. 107, pp. 247–59, contrasting the British with the American experience.

[124] Veljanovski, above, n. 118, pp. 82–4.          [125] Below, pp. 164–71.

[126] Richardson *et al.*, above, n. 2, pp. 41–3.

[127] The strategy may be thwarted if a private prosecution is brought to enforce the *de jure* standard: cf. above, pp. 86–7. The history of the Control of Pollution Act 1974 illustrates the problem. This *inter alia* abolished the monopoly of public agencies over prosecutions for offences arising from the discharge of effluent into rivers. Over ten years passed before the relevant section was brought into effect, in order that the authorities might revise the *de jure* standards to accord with the *de facto* standards implicit in enforcement practice: see Hawkins, above, n. 41, pp. 33–4.

*de facto* standard. The firm should rationally accept that offer if its assessment of D (the costs incurred following conviction) exceeds the profit it will make from the activity which contravenes the *de jure* standard. There is now a much smaller discount in D, since p (the perceived probability of conviction) is now significantly increased, apprehension having already taken place. We have thus arrived at a model of 'negotiated compliance' which provides a plausible explanation of the enforcement behaviour of regulatory agencies, as observed by empirical researchers.[128]

### 4. EXTENDING THE SCOPE OF CRIMINAL LIABILITY

The perceived failure of the conventional process of criminal liability and enforcement to achieve public interest goals has led commentators on both sides of the Atlantic to explore possibilities of extending its scope or sharpening its impact.

One such possibility would constitute not so much an extension of the criminal law but rather a reversion to more traditional conceptions. It has been suggested that, far from adopting a stance of moral neutrality, policy-makers should inject retributive goals into the policies and processes of regulatory systems.[129] This could have the consequence, for example, that managers whose corporate strategy gives rise to large amounts of harm would receive a prison sentence.[130]

Other proposals stem from a perception that corporate criminal liability pays too little heed to the internal structure of firms, the deficiencies of which are often responsible for contraventions and yet which remain, in relation to the legal process, a 'black box'.[131] The traditional approach assumes that the imposition (or the threat of an imposition) on the firm will force its managers, because of the risk of lost profits, to take such internal disciplinary action as is necessary to ensure compliance. But, it is argued, the managers in many firms may fail to take such action, either because they do not respond in an economically 'rational' manner, or because the structure of the firm is not conducive to the necessary discipline.[132]

The suggested remedies extend beyond the obvious one, of imposing liability on the individual wrongdoer as well as the firm. One radical proposal is for a kind of 'corporate probation': officials appointed by the court would monitor the firm and provide advice on appropriate channels

---

[128] It is formalized in Fenn and Veljanovski, above, n. 90. For the use of game theory to establish a similar model, see Ayres and Braithwaite, above, n. 90, pp. 20–44.

[129] Fisse, above, n. 24.

[130] J. C. Coffee, 'Corporate Crime and Punishment: A Non-Chicago View of the Economics of Criminal Sanctions' (1980) 17 Am. Crim. LR 419, 433–6.

[131] C. Stone, *Where the Law Ends: The Social Control of Corporate Behavior* (1975); id., 'The Place of Enterprise Liability in the Control of Corporate Conduct' (1980) 90 Yale LJ 1.

[132] Stone (1980), above, n. 131, pp. 15–16; Coffee, above, n. 105, pp. 393–400.

of information and chains of responsibility.[133] Another is to impose severe 'equity fines' on the guilty firm: it would be required to authorize and issue to a state fund such a number of shares as would have an expected market value equal to the cash fine that would be necessary to deter the illegal activity.[134] The idea is that, since ordinary shareholders would suffer, they will be motivated to ensure that managers activate a policy of compliance.[135]

[133] B. Fisse, 'Responsibility, Prevention and Corporate Crime' (1973) 5 New Zealand ULR 250, 266–73; Coffee, above, n. 105, pp. 448–57; Stone (1980), above, n. 131, pp. 40–1.

[134] Coffee, above, n. 105, pp. 413–24.

[135] Pressure on the managers would also arise indirectly from the lowering of the value of the shares. This would make the firm vulnerable to takeover, with the risk that the new owners would oust the existing management: cf. below, p. 272.

# 6

# Institutions and Accountability

All regulatory systems require a number of tasks to be performed: as an exercise of policy-making, the goals of a regime must be established; those goals must then be translated into the principles and rules which control behaviour; and there must be procedures for explicating and enforcing the principles and rules and for the adjudication of disputes arising from them. Important structural issues arise in determining how these tasks are to be allocated to different institutions. The determination of an appropriate allocation of power contains dimensions both horizontal (the extent to which authority should be conferred on institutions other than the legislature or executive) and vertical (the degree of control exercised over such institutions).

The allocation of power and the means of constraining it form the subject-matter of administrative law, as that term is normally used in Anglo-Saxon legal systems.[1] The dominant tradition in British administrative law is founded on a set of normative values, primarily concerned with preserving the rule of law—implying freedom from arbitrary government, procedural fairness, and political legitimacy.[2] In this chapter, we adopt a somewhat different focus: we shall be concerned to examine the extent to which the institutional arrangements can assist the implementation of the public interest goals of regulation and the extent to which they offer protection against the subversion of the law to meet the demands of private interests.

There is a hierarchy of institutions on which the relevant powers of policy-formation, law-making, adjudication, and enforcement can be conferred: (a) the European Community; (b) the national legislature; (c) government departments; (d) special agencies, more or less independent of government; and (e) the courts. We begin by exploring in Section 1 the relationship between (a) and (b). There follows in Section 2 a discussion of the relative merits of delegating rule-making powers to (c) or (d). In Section 3 we address the question of using self-regulatory agencies to perform the functions of (d). The chapter concludes with consideration of the accountability of the various institutions and, particularly, of the role of (e) in this respect.

[1] H. W. R. Wade, *Administrative Law* (6th edn., 1988), pp. 4–5.
[2] See M. Loughlin, *Public Law and Political Theory* (1992), esp. ch. 4. He contrasts this tradition ('normativism') with a rival mode of thought ('functionalism') which stresses the instrumentalist character of law, facilitating public policy goals.

### I. JURISDICTIONAL LEVEL OF REGULATORY LAW

In 1973 the United Kingdom acceded to the European Community and thereby to a system under which EC law was to have supremacy. The existence of the system raises the important issue of whether the appropriate source of regulatory rule-making should be at Brussels or Westminster. In fact, the question does not always have this dichotomous character. While under the Treaty of Rome European law is to prevail over domestic law where there is a conflict, nevertheless the relevant European norms may be very general in character, leaving it to national institutions to formulate detailed rules. It becomes then a matter of determining the relative rule intensity of regulatory law at the Community level, and the extent to which it imposes detailed uniform requirements and precludes Member States from adopting alternative strategies or standards.

### (a) Rudimentary Arguments for Centralized and Decentralized Regulation

In addressing this issue, it is helpful for heuristic purposes to contrast the arguments for centralized and decentralized regulatory powers in their most extreme form. Take first the case for European regulation. *If* the aim were to create a wholly integrated European market and *if* citizen preferences were homogeneous across that market and *if* there were no political obstacles, detailed uniform rules would be made at Community level. The reasons are clear. On the assumption of homogeneity there would be a common incidence of market failure and a common commitment to redistribution and other non-economic justifications for regulation. In implementing the common objective, there would be economies of scale in having a single set of regulatory rules; more importantly, the absence of different national regulatory requirements would facilitate intra-Community trade and remove anti-competitive obstacles.[3]

Of course, the hypothesized conditions do not, and will never, exist.[4] The starting point is not federal unity but that of a number of states making concessions to their national sovereignty: the political obstacles to complete economic integration are, in consequence, formidable. Nor can it be assumed that citizen preferences are homogeneous. Social, cultural, and economic differences may lead to a very wide variation in the price that citizens are prepared to pay for, say, a cleaner environment or safer products; and a common view on what is a 'fair' distribution of resources is even less likely.

The problem of tying regulatory solutions to citizen preferences has led

---

[3] Cf. below, pp. 174–6.

[4] For general discussion, see J. Pelkmans, 'The Assignment of Public Functions in Economic Integration' (1982) 21 J. Common Market Stud. 97.

some economists to argue for the diametrically opposite solution: regulatory regimes should be highly decentralized.[5] Social welfare is maximized, it is claimed, the closer the boundaries of regulatory jurisdictions are set to areas of homogeneous populations with similar preferences. And the ability of disaffected citizens to move to jurisdictions where the regulatory package accords more with their preferences minimizes waste. But these arguments also rely on unreal assumptions:[6] migration is not an easy option and citizens have imperfect information on the content of regulatory regimes. Account must also be taken of the possibility that the regimes in one jurisdiction may adversely affect citizens in another jurisdiction, for example by allowing trans-boundary pollution or inhibiting the free movement of goods.

### (b) Compromise Solutions: 'Integration' or 'Co-ordination'?

Some compromise between these two extreme positions is clearly necessary. One way of reaching an appropriate compromise is through bargaining between national governments.[7] Such bargaining plays a fundamental role in the formulation of European law.[8] Community regulation is not imposed on Member States by an autonomous institution, but rather results from agreements between national governments who are themselves accountable to their own electorates. While that accountability should imply a general responsiveness to citizen preferences, a government can also take advantage of the fuller information it possesses concerning the content and consequences of regulation. Armed with such information, it may perceive that the sacrifice of some particular characteristics of national regulation for a European regime will confer on its electorate an *aggregate* benefit by, for example, increasing trans-boundary trade. If other governments share this perception, agreement on integrated regulation at Community level may result.

The integration solution will not, however, be reached easily if—as was the case until recently[9]—the unanimous consent of all national governments is required before the Community instrument can be issued. Each government will be tempted to hold out for a form of regulation which will minimize any loss to its electorate, perhaps by creating escape clauses and loopholes under which some discretion on the implementation of the

---

[5] e.g. C. Tiebout, 'A Pure Theory of Local Expenditure' (1956) 64 J. Pol. Econ. 416.

[6] For general discussion, see: T Heller and J. Pelkmans, 'The Federal Economy: Law and Economic Integration and the Positive State—The USA and Europe Compared in an Economic Perspective', in M. Cappelletti, M. Seccomble, and J. Weiler (eds.), *Integration Through Law* (1986), i; and J. R. Prichard and T. Benedickson, 'Securing the Canadian Economic Union: Federalism and Internal Barriers to Trade', in M. Trebilcock *et al.* (eds.), *Federalism and the Canadian Economic Union* (1983), pp. 15–27.

[7] Prichard and Benedickson, above, n. 6, pp. 27–33.

[8] F. Scharpf, 'The Joint Decision Trap: Lessons from German Federalism and European Integration' (1988) 66 Pub. Admin. 239.   [9] Cf. below, p. 176.

regulation is retained.[10] An alternative, and less ambitious, bargaining compromise is possible. If governments wish to preserve the political advantages of domestic regulation and yet also pursue the gains to be made from intra-Community trade, they may be able to agree on what we shall refer to as 'co-ordination'. This solution takes the form of framework regulation at Community level which does nothing more than state broad policy goals. A Member State may retain its own regulatory packages to implement those goals, but, for the purposes of intra-Community trade, it must recognise that compliance with the regulatory requirements of another Member State will also suffice.

As will be seen in Chapter 8,[11] progress with the integration approach proved to be very slow, and since the mid-1980s it has been largely superseded by efforts at co-ordination. This development has been reinforced by a formal commitment to the principle of 'subsidiarity': 'the Community shall take action . . . only if and in so far as the objectives of the proposed action cannot be sufficiently achieved by the Member States.'[12] The principle is explicitly linked to the desirability of decisions being 'taken as closely as possible to the citizen',[13] this rhetoric perhaps serving as an *ex post* public interest rationalization of the limited success of the integration approach.

From a public interest perspective, the consequences of the co-ordination approach are nevertheless ambiguous.[14] It cannot deal effectively with externalities unilaterally imposed by one Member State on another (e.g. trans-boundary pollution). Also, there are diseconomies of scale in the existence of multiple regulatory regimes. Against these costs must be weighed the benefits of the regimes' assumed closer approximation to citizens' preferences. However, in the longer term these benefits may diminish.[15] The principle of mutual recognition of national regimes will mean that traders complying with the regulations imposed by one Member State may have to compete with foreigners subject to less stringent requirements or less effective enforcement. To eliminate the competitive disadvantage, the traders may exert pressure on their national government to deregulate.[16] The process may result in the reduction of unnecessary constraints and thus to more efficient national regulation;[17]

---

[10] Pelkmans, above, n. 4, p. 89.   [11] Below, pp. 176–9.

[12] Treaty of Rome, Art. 3b, inserted by the [Maastricht] Treaty on European Union.

[13] Preamble to the [Maastricht] Treaty on European Union.

[14] G. Majone, 'Market Integration and Regulation: Europe after 1992' (1992) 43 Metroeconomica 131.

[15] G. Majone, 'Regulating Europe: Problems and Prospects' (1989) 3 Jahrbuch zur Staats- und Verwaltungswissenschaft 159.   [16] See further below, p. 178.

[17] J. Kay and J. Vickers, 'Regulatory Reform: An Appraisal', in G. Majone (ed.), *Deregulation or Re-regulation? Regulatory Reform in Europe and the United States* (1990), p. 244.

but it may also lead to a government overriding the preferences of its citizens, particularly if they are less effective lobbyists.

### (c) Private Interest Considerations

This last observation suggests that private interests may have an important impact on decisions about whether to regulate at Community or national level. It is reasonable to assume that a group interested in a certain area of regulation will have a preference for the rules being formulated at the level at which its strength is greatest relative to that of other groups with a divergent interest in the same area.[18] So, for example, the German environmentally sensitive industries, competing with a powerful Green lobby within their own country, strive for regulation at the Community level, where they can find allies from industries in other states, and where the strength of environmentalists is much diluted.[19] Moreover, as this example suggests, the further removed the lobbying arena is from local activists, the greater the relative power of sectional interests (e.g. trade and professional associations) over ideological interests (e.g. environmentalists and consumerists). This is because the costs of organization for the latter increase much more dramatically as regional and national diversity of interests have to be accommodated.

On the basis of this analysis, we would expect a higher density of rules by centralized institutions to govern regulatory regimes which have an impact on powerful and well-organized sectional interests. While this prediction receives empirical support from some American studies,[20] it does not seem to accord well with the general European trend away from regulation at Community level.[21] There are at least two possible explanations for this. First, however receptive to interest groups the authorities at Brussels may appear to be,[22] they do not have the same motivation to respond to the demands as governments at a national level or, indeed, the US Federal Government. This is because the European Commission and Council of Ministers are not voted into power and therefore do not need to 'purchase' electoral support through the promise of legislative favours.[23] Secondly, on the reasonable hypothesis that the transfer of rule-making power to European institutions will deprive national bureaucracies of power, prestige, and budgetary allocations, they will have a strong interest in resisting such a transfer. National governments negotiating at Brussels are

---

[18] E. Noam, 'The Choice of Governmental Level in Regulation' (1982) 35 Kyklos 278.
[19] W. Grant, *Pressure Groups, Politics and Democracy in Britain* (1989), pp. 91–2.
[20] e.g. Noam, above, n. 18, pp. 286–9.
[21] There are, however, some significant exceptions to the trend, notably in relation to food (below, p. 193) and road vehicle safety (below, p. 199). In both instances, the trading lobby was particularly powerful.
[22] Cf. Grant, above, n. 19, pp. 98–108.     [23] Cf. above, pp. 63–6.

much dependent, particularly for information, on their bureaucracies, and are thus likely to be vulnerable to their influence.[24]

## 2. DELEGATION OF REGULATORY RULE-MAKING

### (a) UK Patterns of Delegation

Subject to the dictates of European instruments, the primary source of regulatory law in Britain is parliamentary legislation. The issue to be addressed in this section is how and why regulatory rule-making powers are delegated to other institutions. If we had to provide a succinct and over-simplified statement of the typical British pattern, it would be as follows: regulatory *policy* is formulated by the government; legislative *principles* incorporating the policy are passed by Parliament; to flesh out the principles, powers are conferred on a Minister to promulgate *rules*, generally by means of a statutory instrument; those rules are subject to *enforcement* by a specialized agency; the courts are responsible for the *adjudication* of disputes and the imposition of sanctions.

In reality, the arrangements are considerably more complex.[25] There are, of course, vast differences between the various regimes, and institutional structures change over time as the nature of regulation itself evolves. But even at its level of generality, the statement above is misleading. Some, particularly recent, regulatory legislation is sparse on principles, contenting itself with setting out a procedural framework within which other institutions make the appropriate decisions. Moreover, government policy, which may not have been explicit at the legislative stage, can exert a considerable influence on these decisions.

Above all, the role of agencies tends to be much more important than that ascribed to them in the statement. There is, it must be conceded, a significant contrast to be drawn between the typical American regulatory agency and its British counterpart.[26] The former is largely independent of the Executive, derives full rule-making power directly from the legislature, and has an adjudicative as well as an enforcement function. Some shift towards the American approach can be observed in the British regimes governing the privatized utilities, the regulators having a large degree of autonomy in the setting of price caps and performance standards. But, as with the more traditional agencies who deal with social regulation, they have no formal adjudicative powers[27] and their decisions are subject to the residual control of the Minister.

[24] Cf. above, p. 68.

[25] For general accounts, see: R. Baldwin and C. McCrudden, *Regulation and Public Law* (1987), chs. 2–3; P. Craig, *Administrative Law* (2nd edn., 1989), chs. 3–6.

[26] See the (now dated) comparison in B. Schwartz and H. W. Wade, *Legal Control in Government: Administrative Law in Britain and the United States* (1972), ch. 2.

[27] The Civil Aviation Authority is a prominent exception: see below, p. 324, and R. Baldwin, *Regulating the Airlines* (1985).

The rules contained in statutory instruments issued by Ministers (although in practice formulated by government bureaucracies) continue to play a major, if diminishing, role in British regulatory law. Nevertheless, if 'rule-making' is taken to include the elaboration of norms, formal or informal, which directly constrain the behaviour of firms and individuals, then the function of agencies in this respect is of paramount importance.[28] Agency rule-making, broadly construed, can arise in a variety of contexts.[29] Most obviously, power may be conferred by Parliament on an agency to issue a set of formally binding rules, such as a Code of Conduct, although sometimes this is subject to ministerial approval. Alternatively, the formal rules may be individualized, as when an agency with power to issue licences for a certain activity may stipulate ongoing conditions which the licensee must fulfil. Increasingly in recent years, agencies have been authorized to publish Codes of Practice.[30] These are not formally binding; they serve rather as guides to the interpretation of formal provisions, although sometimes they may be used as evidence in legal proceedings. Finally, as we saw in the last chapter,[31] the practice of an agency in exercising its discretion relating to the enforcement of formal provisions may itself give rise to a set of *de facto* rules.

### (b) Public Interest Justifications

Uncontroversially, it may be assumed that the legislature has neither the time nor the expertise to engage in detailed regulatory rule-making. Further, when—as is frequently the case—technical amendments are necessary, parliamentary scrutiny would impose heavy costs and serious delays. It is thus appropriate that primary legislation should concentrate on the general principles of regulatory law. The crucial issue is, then, the extent to which detailed rule-making should be delegated to the Executive, or rather to an agency which is, to a greater or lesser degree, independent of government.

While rule-making by agencies creates problems of accountability (which we shall address later in this chapter), there are strong arguments for delegating this function to them.[32] First, expertise can be concentrated and accumulated in a way which is not always possible with government bureaucracies; and if the agency is also responsible for enforcement, that experience can beneficially feed back into the rule-making process. Secondly, distance from government may reduce the dangers of political

---

[28] G. Ganz, *Quasi-Legislation* (1987).

[29] See generally G. Ganz, 'Allocation of Decision-Making Functions' [1972] Public Law 215, 299.    [30] Cf. below, p. 186.

[31] Above, pp. 96–7. See also below, p. 171.

[32] Economic Council of Canada, *Responsible Regulation* (1979), pp. 53–5; J. Mashaw, 'Prodelegation: Why Administrators Should Make Political Decisions' (1985) 1 J. Law, Econ. & Org. 81; Baldwin and McCrudden, above, n. 25, pp. 4–7.

interference, encourage a longer-term perspective, and (perhaps) facilitate consultation and more open decision-making.

Whether, and to what extent, the government should have a residual power to review agency rule-making is less clear.[33] On the one hand, it may be argued that such power is necessary to ensure that the agency's decisions in a specific regulatory context are compatible with the government's more general objectives (e.g. regional or employment policy), and can be co-ordinated with the decisions of other agencies with responsibilities in related areas.[34] On the other hand, unless used sparingly, the power may create uncertainty and instability, enable the government to intervene for short-term political purposes, and thus frustrate the benefits traditionally associated with agency rule-making.[35]

### (c) Private Interest Explanations

Public choice theory[36] has spawned some important explanations of how private interests may be served by the delegation of rule-making powers to agencies. Take politicians first.[37] They may face the dilemma of having to placate powerful pressure groups with conflicting demands. They may recognize that a particular regulatory policy will benefit one group and impose costs on the other. A statute containing a vague principle may gain them the support of the first group, without incurring substantial opposition from the second group. The costs to the second group will become more apparent when the detailed rules are formulated; but, if this task is delegated to an agency, that institution, rather than the politicians, will bear the brunt of the criticism.[38]

Of course, groups who may potentially sustain substantial costs from the regulatory goals may themselves favour, and exert pressure for, delegation if they are confident that they can 'capture' the agency for their own ends. As we saw in Chapter 4,[39] agency capture was, for a time, a popular explanation for 'regulatory failure' in the USA and, as such, was used to discredit the public interest assertion that delegation to an independent body can insulate regulatory rule-making from political pressure. Capture theory has had some adherents among British critics of regulatory

[33] Economic Council of Canada, above, n. 32, pp. 61–8; Baldwin and McCrudden, above, n. 25, pp. 40–5.

[34] C. Sunstein, 'Constitutionalism After the New Deal' (1987) 101 Harv. LR 421, 452–3.

[35] For a valuable illustration, see the account of the 'Skytrain' decision in Baldwin, above, n. 27, ch. 9. See also below, p. 328.          [36] Above, pp. 58–75.

[37] M. Fiorina, 'Legislative Choice of Regulatory Forms: Legal Process or Administrative Process' (1982) 39 Public Choice 33; P. Aranson, E. Gellhorn and G. Robinson, 'A Theory of Legislative Delegation' (1983) 68 Cornell LR 1.

[38] The argument, derived from American writers, may not have the same explanatory power for the UK where the agencies are less independent: W. Bishop, 'A Theory of Administrative Law' (1990) 19 J. Legal Stud. 489, 500.

[39] Above, pp. 57–8.

agencies,[40] but most writers consider that it provides too crude an account of the complex relationships between agencies and those that they regulate.[41]

### 3. SELF-REGULATORY AGENCIES

Views may differ on the degree to which regulatory agencies should be independent of government, but it would appear to be obvious that they should be independent of the interests that are being regulated. There is, nevertheless, a long tradition that the rights of practice, and the rules of conduct, for professional occupations are determined by bodies drawn exclusively or predominantly from members of the profession;[42] and in recent times self-regulation has extended into other areas.[43] Can the phenomenon be reconciled with the public interest arguments for delegation? Or is it a clear example of the subversion of regulation to private interests?

### (a) Traditional Public Interest Justifications

There are a number of arguments which suggest that, at least when applied to professional regulation, a self-regulatory agency (hereafter SRA) may be a cheaper and more effective rule-maker than a public, independent agency.[44] First, since SRAs can normally command a greater degree of expertise and technical knowledge of practices and innovatory possibilities within the relevant area than independent agencies, information costs for the formulation and interpretation of standards are lower. Secondly, for the same reasons, monitoring and enforcement costs are also reduced, as are the costs to practitioners of dealing with regulators, given that such interaction is likely to be fostered by mutual trust. Thirdly, to the extent that the processes of, and rules issued by, SRAs are less formalized than those of public regulatory regimes, there are savings in the costs (including those attributable to delay) of amending standards. Fourthly, the administrative costs of the regime are normally internalized in the trade or activity which is subject to regulation; in the case of independent, public agencies, they are typically borne by taxpayers.

---

[40] e.g. N. Gunningham, *Pollution, Social Interest and the Law* (1974).

[41] e.g. C. Rowley and G. Yarrow, 'Property Rights, Regulation and Private Enterprise: The Case of the British Steel Industry 1957–75' (1981) 1 Int. Rev. Law & Econ. 63, 66–7; R. Ferguson and A. Page, 'The Development of Investor Protection in Britain' (1984) 12 Int. J. Soc. Law 287, 288–9. [42] Below, pp. 220–2.

[43] Most notably in relation to financial regulation: A. Page and R. Ferguson, *Investor Protection* (1992), pp. 82–4. More generally, see R. Baggott, 'Regulatory Reform in Britain: The Changing Face of Self-Regulation' (1989) 67 Pub. Admin. 435.

[44] Cf. P. Cane, 'Self Regulation and Judicial Review' (1987) 6 Civil Justice Q. 324, 328–33.

## (b) Traditional Criticisms

Lawyers and economists have been equally scathing in their criticisms of self-regulation. From a legal perspective, it is seen as an example of modern 'corporatism', the acquisition of power by groups which are not accountable to the body politic through the conventional constitutional channels.[45] The capacity of an SRA to make rules governing the activities of an association or profession may itself constitute an abuse if it lacks democratic legitimacy in relation to members of the association or profession.[46] The potential for abuse becomes intolerable if, and to the extent that, the rules affect third parties.[47] Further, if—as often occurs— the SRA's functions cover policy formulation, interpretation of the rules, adjudication, and enforcement (including the imposition of sanctions) as well as rule-making, there is a fundamental breach of the separation of powers doctrine.[48]

Economists have concentrated on the ability of SRAs to exploit their regulatory powers to establish anti-competitive conditions and thus generate rents (exorbitant profits) for existing practitioners.[49] Barriers to entry can be created by imposing stringent qualifications for a licence to practise and, under the guise of 'professional ethics' and 'quality control', restrictive ongoing conditions can be prescribed which distort competition and inflict unnecessary costs on consumers. These consequences can, of course, arise under a conventional regulatory regime if an independent agency responsible for rule-making is persuaded by practitioners that stringent controls are required. If an SRA possesses the relevant powers and is largely free of external constraints, rent-seeking becomes much easier: 'with self-regulation, regulatory capture is there from the outset'.[50]

## (c) Nature of Self-Regulation

One problem with the traditional criticisms of self-regulation is that they are based on a narrow, stereotyped conception of the phenomenon. In fact, self-regulation is a broad concept, covering a wide range of institutional arrangements.[51] Regimes differ according to several

[45] P. C. Schmitter, 'Neo-Corporatism and the State', in W. Grant (ed.), *The Political Economy of Corporatism* (1985), pp. 32–62; N. Lewis, 'Corporatism and Accountability: The Democratic Dilemma', in C. Crouch and R. Dore (eds.), *Corporatism and Accountability: Organized Interests in British Public Life* (1990), ch. 3.

[46] A. C. Page, 'Self-Regulation: The Constitutional Dimension' (1986) 49 Modern LR 141, 163.

[47] Cane, above, n. 44, pp. 325–6; and see *R* v. *Panel on Take-overs and Mergers, ex parte Datafin plc* [1987] QB 815, 838, per Sir John Donaldson MR.

[48] I. Harden and N. Lewis, *The Noble Lie: The British Constitution and the Rule of Law* (1986), ch. 6      [49] Below, pp. 219–20.

[50] J. Kay, 'The Forms of Regulation' in A. Seldon, *Financial Regulation—or Over-Regulation* (1988), p. 34.

[51] Page, above, n. 46, pp. 144–8; Cane, above, n. 44, pp. 324–8.

variables,[52] notably: the degree of monopolistic power (whether or not they regulate all suppliers in a given market); the degree of formality (whether or not they derive legitimacy from a legislative framework); their legal status (whether or not the rules have binding force); and the degree to which outsiders participate in rule formulation and enforcement, or in other ways supervise the system. Thus, for example, at one extreme 'self-regulation' may simply refer to standards which are established within an individual (competitive) firm or within an industry but which are not legally binding (although they may have been formulated to meet external 'public' regulatory requirements).[53] And, at the other extreme, there are regimes under which the rules formulated by a SRA must be approved by a government minister or some independent authority.

### (d) Optimalizing Self-Regulation

The traditional criticisms are undoubtedly justified for certain forms of self-regulation, notably where it involves a high degree of monopolistic control and a low degree of public accountability. But institutional arrangements can be envisaged which serve to meet those criticisms while, at the same time, retaining the advantages claimed for self-regulation. Two possibilities will be considered here.

The first involves the notion of bargaining between the SRA and the beneficiaries of the regulation.[54] It applies, in an admittedly restricted set of circumstances, where the preferences of the groups which the regime is designed to protect are relatively homogeneous, those preferences can be communicated through a representative at relatively low cost, and there are no significant externalities (i.e. the regulated behaviour does not have a major impact on parties outside the protected groups). A prime example is occupational health and safety.[55] Here, as will be seen in Chapter 9, a kind of negotiated self-regulatory regime is envisaged in which the detailed rules are created by an agreement between the employer and trade union safety representatives. Provided that adequate information on the relevant risks are available to both parties, the rules formulated on this basis may be better, and more cheaply, tailored to the circumstances of the individual firm than if they are imposed by an external agency.

The second possibility has its source in a simple observation: if the principal objection to SRAs is that they are able to exploit their monopolistic control of supply so as to enable practitioners to earn rents,

---

[52] Cf. Baggott, above, n. 43, pp. 436–8.

[53] e.g. E. Bardach and R. A. Kagan, *Going by the Book: The Problem of Regulatory Unreasonableness* (1982), ch. 8. See also R. E. Cheit, *Setting Standards: Regulation in the Public and Private Sectors* (1990).

[54] Bardach and Kagan, above, n. 53, and J. Braithwaite, 'Enforced Self-Regulation: A New Strategy for Corporate Crime Control' (1982) 80 Mich. LR 1466.

[55] Below, pp. 185–9.

then why not force SRAs to compete with one another, so that the rents will be eliminated?[56] Indeed, such competition is more prevalent than is often supposed. In the ordinary markets for products and services, suppliers compete to attract consumers by the quality (as well as the price) of their products and services. Quality is, to some extent at least, a consequence of 'self regulation' imposed internally by the management of a firm. If the competition is effective, efficient regulation should emerge, since it will have to match the preferences of consumers at a cost which they are prepared to pay.

In most cases, however, there is a fundamental obstacle to effective competition: information regarding quality (the consequences of self-regulation) must be communicated to consumers in a way that they can easily comprehend and use as the basis for comparison.[57] To overcome this problem, it may be necessary to create a public agency which has sufficient information to make appropriate judgments and can therefore act as proxy for average consumers. It can then be given authority formally to approve a firm's regulatory rules. The existence of such an agency naturally adds to the costs of the system; on the other hand, since rule-making remains within the firm, the traditional benefits of self-regulation are preserved.

Hitherto, we have been considering situations in which self-regulating firms are operating in competitive markets. What, then, of the more critical cases where an SRA has a monopolistic control over supply? The solution here is to create competition for the right to supply, each competing SRA being required, as part of its bid, to submit its proposed regulatory rules. A second-tier, public agency, acting as proxy for consumers in the manner described above, then determines the right to supply, which is contingent on the suppliers meeting the approved regulatory rules.

Such a system is already used for the allocation of public franchises, for example for broadcasting services or airline routes.[58] Recently, an attempt has been made to apply it to an area of traditional, monopolistic self-regulation, the provision of legal services.[59] Professional associations representing practitioners other than those—barristers and solicitors—who previously enjoyed a monopolistic right to supply certain services (primarily rights of audience in the higher courts and conveyancing respectively) may now apply for access to those rights, and the proposed regulatory rules are intended to play a key role in the application process.[60] Unfortunately, the institutional structures are unlikely to generate fully competitive self-regulation. As a result of pressure brought to bear on

---

[56] Kay and Vickers, above, n. 17, pp. 239–41.
[57] See generally on this problem, above, pp. 38–41 and below, pp. 121–3.
[58] Below, pp. 318–31.                                      [59] Below, p. 221.
[60] Courts and Legal Services Act 1990, s. 29.

politicians by practitioner groups during the legislative process,[61] the membership of the second-tier agencies is insufficiently independent and is clearly vulnerable to capture by the incumbent monopolists.[62]

## 4. ACCOUNTABILITY OF REGULATORS

### (a) Forms of Accountability

We have seen that legislatures typically delegate regulatory rule-making, in varying degrees, to Ministers (in practice, government bureaucracies) and to agencies (sometimes public, sometimes self-regulatory). Although, as we have also seen, there are strong public interest arguments for such delegation, it gives rise to the problem of accountability: regulators should be answerable for the manner in which they exercise their powers.[63]

We may usefully distinguish between three different forms of accountability.[64] First, there is *financial accountability*: regulators should satisfy certain standards of financial management. They should minimize administrative costs and not waste resources—what we have referred to elsewhere as productive efficiency.[65] Secondly, their procedures must be fair and impartial (*procedural accountability*), such that there is an appropriate framework for making rules and decisions which serve the public interest and for resisting the undue influence of private interests. The third form, *substantive accountability*, is the most ambitious. It seeks to ensure that the rules and decisions are themselves justifiable in terms of the public interest goals of the regulatory system in question, whether these be economic (e.g. allocative efficiency) or non-economic (e.g. redistributive).[66]

### (b) The Principal-Agent Problem

The problems of accountability are, in essence, no different from those frequently encountered by principals who employ expert agents to carry out certain profit-making tasks.[67] Given the greater knowledge and expertise possessed by agents, principals have to confer on them discretion as to how to perform the tasks and, unless constrained, agents may exploit the discretion to advance their own interests, rather than those of their

---

[61] Cf. S. Bailey and M. Gunn, *Smith and Bailey on the Modern English Legal System* (4th edn., 1991), p. 133.

[62] e.g. rights of audience are to be determined by the Lord Chancellor and designated judges, all of whom were formerly barristers and retain strong connections with the Bar.

[63] Cf. Bishop, above, n. 38, and Baldwin and McCrudden, above, n.25, pp. 50–4.

[64] See M. Loughlin, *Administrative Accountability in Local Government* (1992), pp. 2–3.

[65] Above, p. 22.

[66] On which see J. Mashaw, *Bureaucratic Justice* (1983), pp. 104–106.

[67] Bishop, above, n. 38, p. 489; P. Spiller, 'Politicians, Interest Groups and Regulators: A Multiple-Principals Agency Theory of Regulation or "Let Them Be Bribed" ' (1990) 33 J. Law & Econ. 65.

principals.[68] Where the problem arises in a private context, for example, as between shareholders and company directors, it is alleviated by both legal constraints (e.g. contractual terms and fiduciary duties) and market constraints, notably the competition for corporate control: poor business performance will reduce the value of the company shares, rendering it vulnerable to take-over by others who can dismiss slack managers.[69]

In a public, institutional setting, agent accountability poses greater challenges. In the first place, there is not a single, homogeneous group of principals concerned to monitor the performance of regulators, but rather a diverse set of interests, including politicians and citizens. Secondly, performance is, in any event, more difficult to monitor, there being no conventional profit-and-loss accounts. Thirdly, except for the limited experiments with competitive self-regulation described earlier in this chapter, there is no market for the control of regulators; and the principals (politicians and citizens) cannot easily dismiss ineffectual officials.

These difficulties are exacerbated by the dispersion of regulatory rule-making powers between the executive and agencies which characterizes British regimes and distinguishes them from their American counterparts. The concentration of rule-making powers in the (largely) independent American regulatory agencies facilitates the creation and targeting of control systems. The more fluid British approach invites government interference which may, nevertheless, be hard to identify. This can create instability for agencies, but also shifting targets for complainants seeking to pin down responsibility.[70]

### (c) Structural Controls

A number of structural controls are used to meet the challenge of accountability.[71] Since the principles of regulatory regimes are normally promulgated by Parliament, the membership of which is determined by the electorate, it might seem appropriate that that institution itself should exercise some form of control. Ministers are, of course, directly answerable to parliament for rules and decisions made by government bureaucracies and most agencies (though not self-regulatory agencies) are similarly accountable indirectly through a Minister and/or by a report presented annually. Regulatory rules themselves may be subject to formal Parliamentary scrutiny. Further, some regulatory activity may come within

---

[68] S. Ross, 'The Economic Theory of Agency' (1973) 63 Am. Econ. Rev. 134. See also below, pp. 216–17.

[69] For elaboration, see below, pp. 272–3.

[70] C. Veljanovski, *The Future of Industry Regulation in the UK* (1993), pp. 73–7; T. Prosser, 'Regulation of Privatized Enterprises: Institutions and Procedures', in L. Hancher and M. Moran, *Capitalism, Culture and Economic Regulation* (1989), pp. 145–8.

[71] For a detailed account, see Baldwin and McCrudden, above, n. 25, ch. 3.

the remit of a select committee, although no such specialist committee has been established for this purpose.[72]

Accountability to Parliament may force disclosure of information which would not otherwise be available, and may facilitate public debate, but it is not clear that it provides a good medium for ensuring that regulators satisfy the three criteria which we have identified. Politicians rarely have the time and expertise to absorb the data and make detailed judgments on the financial management of regulatory bodies. They may provide a valuable, generalized overview of procedural fairness, but investigation of particular grievances normally requires a specialist institution. Nor are they well placed to monitor adherence to public interest goals, since they are vulnerable to the influence of private interest lobbying. More generally, increased parliamentary scrutiny may encourage greater governmental interference, which itself may attempt to capture short-term political gains.[73]

The controls exercised by the Parliamentary Commissioner for Administration and the National Audit Office may be placed in another category. These institutions are staffed by professionals who may be assumed to be less vulnerable to influence by private interest groups. At the same time, the scope of their inquiries is, in principle, limited to particular forms of accountability. Procedural accountability is the province of the Parliamentary Commissioner, since he is concerned to investigate 'maladministration',[74] which implies incompetence, ineptitude, or some procedural irregularity.[75] The National Audit Office (which includes the Comptroller and Auditor General) examines the 'economy, efficiency and effectiveness' of public agencies[76] and is thus primarily concerned with financial accountability. It is true that, on occasions, these watchdogs seem to stray beyond the narrow confines of their jurisdiction into questions of substantive accountability;[77] but such exceptional forays cannot serve as substitutes for the general monitoring of consistency with allocative efficiency or other public interest goals.[78]

Arguably, the most significant device for inducing allocative efficiency in regulatory rule-making is the administrative requirement that government departments, when making proposals for regulatory rules, or amendments

---

[72] For discussion, see Baldwin, above, n. 27, pp. 271–3.

[73] N. Johnson, 'Editorial: Quangos and the Structure of Government' (1979) 57 Pub. Admin. 379.    [74] Parliamentary Commissioner Act 1967, ss. 5(1)(a) and 12(3).

[75] Cf. *R* v. *Local Commissioner for Administration, ex parte Bradford City Council* [1979] QB 287.

[76] National Audit Act 1983, s. 6(1), and see further below, p. 278.

[77] See e.g. Parliamentary Commissioner, *First Report, 1989-90, The Barlow Clowes Affair* 1989–90, HC, 76; and the extensive commentary in R. Gregory and G. Drewry, 'Barlow Clowes and the Ombudsman' [1991] Public Law 192, 408.

[78] Baldwin and McCrudden, above, n. 25, pp. 50–4.

to them, must undertake an assessment of the costs to industry of complying with the rules. The requirement is fully discussed in Chapter 8,[79] alongside its much more ambitious American equivalent, which compels regulatory agencies to provide a cost-*benefit* analysis of their rules. Suffice it here to note that the information generated by compliance cost assessments falls well short of that which would be required to ensure allocative efficiency, in particular, because (unlike the American model) no attempt is made to quantify the benefits of the rules, or the indirect costs of compliance. Further, the requirement is imposed only on government departments and thus not on other rule-making agencies.

## (d) Due Process

Procedural accountability can be secured by the principles of administrative law which are commonly grouped under the heading of 'due process'.[80] Where regulators make decisions affecting individuals or firms, such as the issuing of licences, they are subject to the natural justice requirement of a fair hearing.[81] In Britain, this requirement does not extend to regulatory rule-making. Although, in relation to the latter, there is an increasing tendency for *specific* legislation to impose duties to consult outside interests and to publish rules, there are no *general* obligations to this effect; and the giving of reasons is almost never required.[82] The position in the USA is very different; there the regulatory agencies are subject to stringent standards regarding hearings and the publication of formal and reasoned records.[83]

Some critics of the British approach have argued for an increased formalization of the rule-making process, in the style of the American requirements, including participation rights for interested groups.[84] Such a reform would, it is claimed, encourage administrative rationality and thus lead to better rules, in the sense of facilitating adherence to public interest goals. But is this so?[85] 'Open' rule-making procedures might inhibit attempts at cost-benefit analysis and reduce the importance of independent, expert judgments. There is an inherent difficulty in adapting an adjudicatory framework to the complexities of rule-making[86] and in deciding who should have participation rights. Nor should it be forgotten that American-style procedures generate substantial administrative costs and delays.

---

[79] Below, pp. 164–5.
[80] Cf. J. Mashaw, *Due Process in the Administrative State* (1985).
[81] Craig, above, n. 25, ch. 7.
[82] Baldwin and McCrudden, above, n. 25, pp. 45–8.
[83] Schwartz and Wade, above, n. 26, pp. 108–13.
[84] e.g. P. Birkinshaw, *Grievances, Remedies and the State* (1988), ch. 4.
[85] Cf. Baldwin and McCrudden, above, n. 25, pp. 45–6.
[86] The 'polycentric' problem: below, p. 117.

The extent to which 'open' procedures can be used to enhance or, conversely, to control, the influence of private interest groups is uncertain. On the one hand, formalization might lead to less covert influence, and participation rights might serve to reduce inequalities in the power of pressure groups. On the other hand, the closer the rule-making procedures are to an adjudication model, the more likely it is that the decision-makers will strive for outcomes which constitute a compromise between competing special interests that are represented in the proceedings; and this may force them to lose sight of a broader conception of the public interest.[87]

### (e) Judicial Control

At the heart of the British conception of administrative law lies the power of the ordinary courts to review the activities of public authorities. Judges are well-equipped to assume the tasks imposed by procedural accountability and undoubtedly have performed a valuable function in this regard. On the face of it, judges might also seem to be appropriate instruments for monitoring substantive accountability. Their independence and autonomy, as well as the rules of the judicial process, suggest that they are insulated from political pressures to a greater degree than regulatory agencies;[88] and there is a long tradition of addressing public interest issues in relation to judicial decisions.[89]

Historically, judicial review has nevertheless had a relatively small impact on regulation, a consequence no doubt of the Diceyan tradition of administrative law[90] which concentrates on the protection of individual rights against illegitimate government interference and thereby largely shuns a functionalist concern with public purposes.[91] There is a broad perception that judicial review has grown in importance in the last decade as a device for challenging public decisions generally.[92] Certainly, there has been a very significant increase in the number of applications made for

[87] For theorists who discredit the notion of 'public interest', this result is unexceptional: participation rights create a decision-making environment that mirrors the political circumstances of the legislature. See M. McCubbins, R. Noll and B. Weingast, 'Administrative Procedures as Instruments of Political Control' (1987) 3 J. Law Econ. & Org. 243, 255.

[88] Bishop, above, n. 38, pp. 491–2. Public choice theorists who have been so ready to explain the behaviour of politicians and bureaucrats in terms of their private interests have been reticent on the motivation of judges. For a not wholly convincing exception, see W. Landes and R. Posner, 'The Independent Judiciary in an Interest-Group Perspective' (1975) 18 J. Law & Econ. 875.

[89] J. Bell, *Policy Arguments in Judicial Decisions* (1983).

[90] Craig, above, n. 25, pp. 4–15; Loughlin, above, n. 2, pp. 140–59.

[91] In contrast to e.g. French administrative law, for which the advancement of the 'public interest' is the key unifying principle: J. Brèthe de la Gressaye, *Droit Administratif et Droit Privé* (1950), p. 304.

[92] JUSTICE-All Souls Committee on Administrative Law, *Administrative Justice* (1988), pp. 146–7.

such a review;[93] and it would appear this has been accompanied by a greater willingness on the part of the judiciary to overcome traditional inhibitions against entering the 'political' arena.

The impact of these developments on regulatory law is, however, far from clear. There have been important decisions in which the judges have stressed the importance of bringing within their purview the activities of a wide range of regulatory agencies,[94] and of insisting that regulators, whether government departments or independent bodies, exercise their discretion in a way that is consistent with their statutory goals.[95] But such pronouncements do not necessarily imply a regime of substantive accountability, and this is for two reasons.

In the first place, any judicial scrutiny of regulators is constrained by the legislative provisions under which they operate. The difficulty here is that the discretion conferred on regulators is typically broad, and the public interest goals may not be sufficiently explicit. Of course, on the cynical public choice theory of legislation[96] this is not surprising, since the measure is designed to benefit private interests. According to this view, we must not expect judges to search for an elusive public interest but rather to interpret the legislation so as to implement the 'deal' struck between politicians and private interests.[97] Critics of public choice theory have dismissed this as being far too crude and have re-affirmed purposive interpretation as the proper judicial function.[98]

Secondly, even if the conventional view is taken and it is possible to locate the public interest goals of legislation with sufficient precision, there still remain—at least in Britain—institutional obstacles to effective judicial control. The courts here are reluctant to substitute their judgment of appropriate outcomes on regulators. Substantive review is limited to ensuring that discretion is not exercised in bad faith or for improper purposes, that only relevant considerations are taken into account, and that a decision is not 'so unreasonable that no reasonable authority could ever have come to it'.[99]

---

[93] An empirical study reveals a fourfold increase between 1981 and 1991: M. Sunkin, L. Bridges, and G. Meszaros, *Judicial Review in Perspective* (1993).

[94] See esp. the *Datafin* case, above, n. 47.

[95] See esp. *Bromley LBC* v. *GLC* [1983] 1 AC 768 (below, p. 274); *R* v. *Secretary of State for Health, ex parte US Tobacco International Inc.* [1992] QB 353.

[96] Above, pp. 71–3.

[97] Landes and Posner, above, n. 88; F. Easterbrook, 'Foreword: The Court and the Economic System' (1984) 98 Harv. LR 4, 42–58.

[98] J. Macey, 'Promoting Public-Regarding Legislation Through Statutory Construction' (1986) 86 Columbia LR 223; C. Sunstein, 'Interpreting Statutes in the Regulatory State' (1989) 103 Harv. LR 459.

[99] Lord Greene MR in *Associated Picture Houses Ltd* v. *Wednesbury Corporation* [1948] 1 KB 223, 233–4. See generally Craig, above, n. 25, pp. 281–8; J. Jowell and A. Lester, 'Beyond *Wednesbury*: Substantive Principles of Administrative Law' [1987] Public Law 368. For criticism, see Veljanovski, above, n. 70, pp. 69–70.

This cautious approach to substantive review might not be inappropriate. If the gates are opened too widely, the administrative costs of regulation may escalate and private interests will have an incentive to exploit the process for tactical purposes, thereby frustrating the implementation of public interest goals.[100] Moreover, courts do not possess the expertise normally associated with regulators. Regulatory rule-making often gives rise to what has been described as the 'polycentric problem':[101] issues cannot be resolved independently and sequentially; they are, rather, interdependent, and a choice from one set of alternatives has implications for preferences within other sets of alternatives. The decision-maker must take into account the whole network before she can reach a single decision. The adversarial setting of the judicial process does not lend itself to grappling with this problem,[102] not the least because judicial intervention is generally sought after the rules have been promulgated.[103]

## (f) Conclusions

What emerges from this survey is that there exist potentially powerful instruments for financial accountability (the National Audit Office) and procedural accountability (the Ombudsman and the courts), even though the latter may not be as extensive as some commentators may wish. Procedural accountability, in so far as it encourages bureaucratic rationality, may facilitate the pursuit of public interest goals, but it cannot guarantee outcomes which are consistent with those goals. The limitations of judicial review mean that the substantive accountability of regulators remains imperfect. But it is difficult to conceive of a strategy which would generate net improvements. At the heart of the substantive accountability issue there lies a dilemma. Particular institutions may be designated as regulators because their expertise and independence from political influence maximize the prospects of their fulfilling public interest goals. Those prospects are reduced if their judgments may be overriden by other bodies which do not combine the same degree of expertise and political independence.

[100] The judges are aware of this problem and seek to meet it, in appropriate cases, by making declaratory orders which guide regulators' future decisions but which do not quash those already made: the *Datafin* case, per Sir John Donaldson MR, above, n. 47, pp. 840–2.

[101] L. Fuller, 'The Forms and Limits of Adjudication' (1978) 92 Harv. LR 353, 393–405.

[102] D. Horowitz, *The Courts and Social Policy* (1977); A. I. Ogus, 'Social Costs in a Private Law Setting' (1983) 3 Int. Rev. Law & Econ. 27.

[103] Baldwin and McCrudden, above, n. 25, p. 55. This problem may be somewhat mitigated by the declaratory ruling device, above, n. 100.

# PART III

# FORMS OF SOCIAL REGULATION

# 7

# Information Regulation

The first type of social regulation that we shall examine applies not to primary market activity, the supply of goods or services, but rather to the flow of information which supports that activity. It is less interventionist in character than many other forms of regulation, for example quality standards, and as such is favoured by those who argue that the state's role should be reduced to a minimum.[1]

Information regulation falls into two broad categories: mandatory disclosure, which obliges suppliers to provide information relating to price, identity, composition, quantity, or quality; and the control of false or misleading information. The discussion is divided accordingly. First, however, we must consider the theoretical justifications for information regulation.

### I. JUSTIFICATIONS AND EXPLANATIONS

#### (a) Information Deficits

In an earlier chapter, we saw that in certain circumstances information deficits give rise to market failure.[2] Improving information flows in such circumstances may then increase allocative efficiency and be justified on this economic basis.[3]

Mandatory disclosure regulation can generate direct welfare gains for consumers whose purchase of goods or services is affected by inadequate information. If the unregulated market does not lead to what we have referred to as the 'optimal' amount of information, that is where the marginal benefit arising from that amount of information is approximately equal to the marginal cost of producing and communicating it,[4] consumers sustain a welfare loss: the difference between the utility derived from the transaction without the optimal amount of information and the utility they would have derived if that amount of information had been supplied. Forcing the seller to supply that amount of information may eliminate the loss.

---

[1] e.g. F. Hayek, *Law, Legislation and Liberty*, iii (1979), p. 62.

[2] Above, pp. 38–41.

[3] See generally: A. Schwartz and L. Wilde, 'Intervening in Markets on the Basis of Imperfect Information: A Legal and Economic Analysis' (1979) 127 U. Penn LR. 630; H. Beales, R. Craswell, and S. Salop, 'The Efficient Regulation of Consumer Information' (1981) 24 J. Law & Econ. 491.                                        [4] Above, p. 39.

This can be illustrated by a simple example of the frequently encountered information problem of hidden costs. Some products create risks for consumers, but, particularly where the risks are small, they may not be disclosed by the manufacturer. Suppose that I have to choose between two brands of suntan lotion. Brand A costs me £1.00 but its use carries a small risk ($1/1,000$) of a skin disorder. Brand B is identical except that there is no such risk and it costs me £1.20. Assuming that I evaluate the average adverse consequences of a skin disorder at £300 and am risk-neutral, which brand will I choose? If I remain uninformed of the risk I will certainly prefer to buy Brand A since £1.00 is less than £1.20. However, once the hidden cost (the risk of skin disorder = $0.001 \times £300 = £0.30$) is added, the real cost of Brand A to me is £1.30. If legislation forces the manufacturer of Brand A to disclose the risk and I make a rational decision on the basis of that information, I will gain £0.10 by buying Brand B.

This example may also serve to highlight an important difference between mandatory disclosure and other forms of regulation. On the stated facts, the legislature might have decided to prohibit the sale of Brand A on the ground that it created an 'unreasonable' health hazard, or, more specifically, because the average benefit to consumers from its distribution was exceeded by its average cost—$(£1.20 - £1.00) < (0.001 \times £300)$. Such a decision would, of course, prevent those consumers who if fully informed would still have preferred to buy Brand A from exercising that option. Such preference might be rational, for example, if the individual's evaluation of the health hazard was less than the average, or if he preferred to take the risk in return for the lower price.

If we accept as valid the assumption that consumers can, and in practice do, take advantage of information disclosure to make rational decisions, and if we eschew paternalism, then there are advantages to this form of regulation: choice is preserved, and the cost-benefit analysis is carried out by the individual, who may be better placed to make the calculation than a public institution.[5] The advantages are enhanced if quality regulations are, for technical or political reasons, difficult to formulate with precision. On the other hand, the balance may tip away from disclosure regulation where the relevant information cannot be communicated in an easily assimilable form, or where the risks give rise to very high costs, particularly if third parties are also affected.[6]

Improved information flows can also generate indirect welfare gains for consumers by rendering markets more competitive. If high information

---

[5] S. Breyer, *Regulation and Its Reform* (1982), p. 163; and see C. Colantoni, O. Davis and M. Swaminuthan, 'Imperfect Consumers and Welfare Comparisons of Policies Concerning Information and Regulation' (1976) 7 Bell J. Econ. 602.

[6] E. Bardach and R. A. Kagan, *Going by the Book: The Problem of Regulatory Unreasonableness* (1982), pp. 246–8.

costs prevent consumers from comparing the prices or quality offered by different suppliers in the market, the latter will be under no pressure to lower prices or improve quality—in effect, they will have monopoly power. For a market to be competitive, it is not, of course, necessary that all consumers compare prices and quality. Suppliers will respond if at the margin a significant proportion of all purchasers engage in comparison shopping. A figure of one-third has been quoted as appropriate for the general run of cases,[7] but what counts as a significant proportion for this purpose will vary according to the circumstances. It has been suggested that three considerations are relevant: the extent to which (a) sellers direct their promotional campaigns towards discriminating consumers, (b) word-of-mouth communication is frequent between the latter and less expert consumers, and (c) consumers in general react strongly to either good or bad publicity regarding products. The more these conditions exist in a particular market, the more likely it is that a sufficient number of discriminating consumers exist at the margin.[8] Even so, if suppliers are able to identify those consumers, they may be able to offer them special prices or quality, and the competition problem will not be solved.

## (b) Externalities

When regulation is used to deal with a problem of external costs, another instance of market failure,[9] it is usually in the form of a direct control or prohibition of the activity which creates the problem. In some situations, however, information disclosure may provide a more efficient solution. This is particularly the case where it is cheaper for the third party to be informed about the externality and to take appropriate steps to avoid it than for the activity to be abated or changed in a costly manner. Consider the following example. A local authority is responsible for a public lavatory, the floor of which is washed daily. For half an hour thereafter it remains slippery, creating the risk of a fall. In terms of social welfare, it is probably cheaper for a notice to be posted warning of the condition of the floor than for the lavatory to be closed for half an hour.

From external costs, we must turn to external benefits. As we have seen in an earlier chapter, the provision of information is itself subject to market failure because of its public good characteristics: consumption by the party who pays for it does not reduce the quantity available to other consumers and it is difficult to prevent such other parties 'free-riding' on its availability.[10] Where the problem is a serious one, there are therefore

---

[7] Schwartz and Wilde, above, n. 3, p. 637.

[8] P. N. Bloom, 'Identifying and Resolving Consumer Information Problems: A New Approach', in P. E. Murphy and W. Wilkie (eds.), *Marketing and Advertising Regulation: The Federal Trade Commission in the 1990s* (1990), p. 29.

[9] Cf. above, pp. 18–19 and 35–8.      [10] Above, pp. 33–4.

economic arguments for intervention. There is presumably a considerable consumer demand for intermediaries to provide independent, reliable comparisons on the prices and quality offered by different traders[11] and yet, because of the 'free-rider' problem, there is likely to be, in the unregulated market, an under-supply of such intermediaries.[12] Government may then fund a public agency, or subsidize a private agency, to provide such information.[13] Alternatively, it can establish a system of public registration or certification of traders who satisfy certain minimum standards of quality. Such a system is to be distinguished from a licensing regime which prohibits those without a licence from practising the trade or profession.[14] Registration or certification does not control conduct; it simply provides information. Like disclosure regulation, it preserves consumer choice.

### (c) Non-Economic Justifications

In modern constitutional theory, the citizen's 'right' to information has assumed a considerable importance.[15] Some writers have attempted to endow the concept with a very broad application, in order that individuals be given access to a wide range of private, as well as public, information affecting their lives and welfare.[16] Such a view might justify forcing suppliers to disclose details relating to their products,[17] quite independently of the economic arguments considered above. More orthodox theory and legal practice suggest a narrower interpretation, limiting the 'right' to two categories: first, where the information is personal to the right-holder (e.g. medical records) and thus part of the moral right to personal integrity; and, secondly, where it is germane to political decision-making and thus a corollary to the democratic rights of participation and voting.[18] Both categories, particularly the second, are mainly invoked in relation to information held by public institutions, and may be seen to justify an array

---

[11] e.g. the Consumer Association and its journal, *Which?*, on which see B. Harvey and D. Parry, *The Law of Consumer Protection and Fair Trading* (3rd edn., 1992), pp. 52–4.

[12] H. E. Leland, 'Quacks, Lemons, and Licensing: A Theory of Minimum Quality Standards' (1979) 87 J. Pol. Econ. 1328, 1343; A. Duggan, *The Economics of Consumer Protection: A Critique of the Chicago School Case Against Intervention* (1982), pp. 33–6.

[13] There is not space in this book for consideration of systems of public information provision. For general discussion, see: Schwartz and Wilde, above, n. 3, pp. 673–7; and Beales *et al.*, above, n. 3, pp. 523–31.        [14] Below, pp. 216–33.

[15] P. Trudel, J. Boucher, R. Piotte, J.-M. Brisson, *Le droit à l'information* (1981); P. Birkinshaw, *Freedom of Information: The Law, the Practice and the Ideal* (1988).

[16] T. Emerson, 'Legal Foundations of the Right to Know' [1976] Wash. ULQ 1; Trudel *et al.*, above, n. 15, pp. 268–70.

[17] Cf. S. Hadden, *A Citizen's Right to Know: Risk Communications and Public Policy* (1990); R. Vaughan, 'Common Access to Product Safety Information and the Future of the Freedom of Information Act' (1991) 5 Adm. LJ 673.

[18] Birkinshaw, above, n. 15, pp. 10–21.

of disclosure requirements imposed on government and other public agencies which, however, will not be examined in this work.[19]

Distributional goals may also be relevant to information regulation. If it is the case that the poorer sections of the community are also the less well-informed, then mandatory disclosure may increase their welfare relative to that of groups who do not need the information but who, because suppliers will pass on to them the cost of providing the information, have to pay for it.[20] The justification has particular force where a transaction involves financial or technological complexities which have to be communicated in simpler language, or where the disclosure relates to legal rights which can assist in post-purchase complaints.[21]

Finally, information regulation may be a relatively low-cost and liberal method of pursuing paternalist goals. Warnings of health hazards on cigarette packets and of the financial risks of over-indebtedness in advertisements for credit constitute obvious examples. More generally, there may be arguments for encouraging consumers to take account of certain information even though its mandatory disclosure cannot be justified on narrower economic grounds.[22]

### (d) Private Interest Explanations

In Chapter 4, we explored the hypothesis that regulation is introduced to benefit not the public interest but rather the firms and industries subjected to the regulatory regime. In what ways can such firms and industries benefit from information regulation? Three examples should suffice to indicate the importance of the rival explanatory theory.

In the first place, information regulation, like most other forms of regulation, gives rise to compliance costs, the impact of which may vary with the size of the firm. If for example, the cost of formulating accurate labels describing the content of a product is largely fixed, independent of the size of the firm's output, the compliance cost per unit will be greater for a firm with a small output than for one with a large output. In other words, the disclosure regulation will benefit large firms at the expense of small firms and, at the margin, may well drive some of the latter out of the market.[23]

---

[19] For a detailed survey, see P. Birkinshaw, *Government and Information: The Law relating to Access, Disclosure and Regulation* (1990).

[20] Cf. Schwartz and Wilde, above, n. 3, p. 669.

[21] K. McNeil, J. Nevin, D. Trubek, R. Miller, 'Market Discrimination Against the Poor and the Impact of Consumer Disclosure Laws: the Used Car Industry' (1979) 13 Law & Soc. Rev. 695. The empirical study there reported revealed, however, that poorer consumers did not benefit from disclosure.

[22] W. Whitford, 'The Functions of Disclosure Regulation in Consumer Transactions' [1973] Wisc. LR 400, 435-9.

[23] R. Higgins and F. McChesney, 'Truth and Consequences: The Federal Trade Commission's Ad Substantiation Program' (1986) 6 Int. Rev. Law & Econ. 149, 155.

Some forms of information regulation may also discourage innovation and consequently protect firms which adopt traditional manufacturing processes.[24] As we shall see,[25] to assist consumers in identifying products which they wish to purchase, regulations may insist that a particular designation (e.g. 'Scotch Whisky') be used only in relation to products with specified ingredients, or which have undergone specified processes. Manufacturers who develop cheaper substitutes for the ingredients or processes are thereby prevented from marketing the product with the same designation, even though the consumer might be equally satisfied with the 'new' product which would cost less.[26] Of course, the regulatory authority might amend the specifications, but there might be a lengthy delay before this occurred, and manufacturers using traditional specifications would have the opportunity to resist change.

On the face of it, mandatory price disclosure would seem to benefit consumers rather than suppliers, but this form of regulation, too, may give rise to anti-competitive effects.[27] Excessive emphasis on price information and insufficient emphasis on quality information may entice large numbers of consumers away from higher quality, higher price suppliers to lower quality, lower price suppliers. This may drive high quality, specialist suppliers out of the market.

## 2. MANDATORY PRICE DISCLOSURE

### (a) General

Information on prices (or 'price transparency', as it is sometimes called) is, of course, crucial for consumer choice and for efficient, competitive markets. If there is a substantial dispersion of prices set by suppliers for a single, homogeneous product, the market is performing poorly: the demand for the product at the lower prices should force down the higher prices. Such price dispersion may result from heavy search costs. Price disclosure regulation may reduce those costs and thus be justified economically.[28]

In English law, until recently, mandatory price disclosure was limited to a few special areas, such as foodstuffs, petrol, hotels, bars, and

---

[24] R. Merrill and E. Collier, ' "Like Mother Used To Make": An Analysis of FDA Food Standards of Identity' (1974) 74 Columbia LR 561, 600–8; Bardach and Kagan, above, n. 6, pp. 260–2.                                                                     [25] Below, pp. 135–7.

[26] Cf. R. Urban and R. Mancke, 'Federal Regulation of Whiskey Labelling: From the Repeal of Prohibition to the Present' (1972) 15 J. Law & Econ. 411.

[27] K. Grunert, 'Price Transparency, Competition and the Consumer Interest: Economic Reasoning and Behavioral Evidence', in M. Goyens (ed.), *Price Information and Public Price Controls, Consumers and Market Performance* (1985), pp. 29–31.

[28] A. Schwartz, 'Unconscionability and Imperfect Information: A Research Agenda' (1991) 19 Can. Bus. LJ 437, 441–2.

restaurants.[29] In other European systems a much wider range of products was covered[30] and, following two EC Directives of 1988,[31] the Price Marking Order 1991 now requires, with only a few minor exceptions, that retailers of all types of goods display or mark the selling price so that it is 'unambiguous and easily identifiable . . . and clearly legible'.[32] In the case of goods sold from bulk or goods pre-packed in variable quantities, the unit price (in prescribed standards of measurement) must be indicated. The supply of services and the sale of goods to traders are excluded.

The current law throws up an intriguing basic question: given the fact that most suppliers are under competitive pressure *voluntarily* to disclose prices, why is it necessary to *force* them to do so? From a public interest perspective, the answer probably lies in the mode of disclosure rather than its existence. Prices may voluntarily be disclosed, but unless they are in a form which facilitates comparisons with those set by other traders, they impede the competitive goal. In other words, the most significant welfare gains are likely to result from the requirement that prices be indicated with reference to standardized units, and the absence of such units in relation to services explains why the latter are excluded from the 1991 Order.

The broad ambit of the EC Directives and the 1991 Order in relation to goods might be explained by reference to the private interest hypothesis. In an oligopolistic market (i.e. a market dominated by only a few suppliers), a high degree of price transparency will facilitate collusive behaviour and cartels.[33] Further, as suggested above,[34] suppliers with a high output and those concentrating on lower quality, lower price products (e.g. supermarket chains) may benefit from regulation of this kind, at the expense of small firms and high quality specialists. Groups representing the advantaged suppliers could have exerted influence on governments in those EC countries to introduce mandatory price disclosure throughout the retail sector. The strategy thereafter would be to persuade the EC Commission to extend the system to retailers across the European Community, in order that all of them should incur an equivalent level of compliance costs.

There is some empirical evidence which shows that, in food markets at least, higher price transparency leads to lower product prices.[35] The

---

[29] e.g. Tourism (Sleeping Accommodation Price Display) Order, SI 1977/1877; Price Marking (Food and Drinks on Premises) Order, SI 1979/361; Price Marking (Petrol) Order, SI 1980/1121.

[30] Cf. L. Krämer, 'Legislative Means of Consumer Information on Prices', in Goyens, above, n. 27, pp. 13–17.     [31] 88/314 and 88/315.

[32] SI 1991/1382, on which see *Allen* v. *Redbridge London BC* [1994] 1 All ER 728. Special provisions apply to motor fuels: SI 1991/1382, arts. 13–16 and Sched. 2.

[33] Grunert, above, n. 27, p. 30.     [34] Above, p. 125.

[35] See the studies cited in Grunert, above, n. 27, pp. 31–2.

findings must, however, be treated with caution. In the first place, only the short-term effects were studied; the disclosure measures may have less impact in the longer term.[36] Secondly, a reduction in product prices will only unambiguously give rise to consumer welfare gains if it is not accompanied by a reduction in product quality.[37] Such gains are, therefore, most likely where quality is relatively easily ascertainable (as with food?) or unlikely to vary (as with motor fuel). Thirdly, the cost of formulating and enforcing disclosure regulation must be set off against the welfare gains.

Some self-regulatory professional bodies, far from subjecting practitioners to mandatory price disclosure, have actually prohibited price advertising.[38] The most frequently expressed argument to defend the prohibition has been that competition would threaten the integrity and ethical responsibilities of the profession.[39] Whatever the merits of that argument, the ban on advertising leads to higher consumer search costs and higher prices of services, conferring monopoly rents on the suppliers. Since 1985, when the prohibition on solicitors advertising was lifted, there has been a substantial fall in the prices charged for conveyancing.[40]

### (b) Credit Transactions

Mandatory disclosure in relation to credit transactions has assumed particular importance in recent years, and thus merits special consideration. For most consumer debtors, the search cost of obtaining accurate and comprehensible information on the 'real' total price (including interest and other payments) of credit is high. The principal concern of earlier legislation was the performance of the agreement, the perception being that this would be facilitated if the debtor was made fully aware of the degree of his commitment at the outset. The emphasis then shifted to the classic economic issues of pre-contract consumer choice and competitive markets. There was evidence of significant price dispersion in the rates of

---

[36] Grunert, above, n. 27, p. 32.

[37] Cf. S. Kimball and M. Rapaport, 'What Price "Price Disclosure"? The Trend to Consumer Protection in Life Insurance' [1972] Wisc. LR 1025, 1031–2.

[38] See the Monopolies Commission's *Report on the General Effect on the Public Interest of Certain Restrictive Practices . . . In Relation to the Supply of Professional Services* (1970, Cmnd. 4463), ch. 6 and its specific reports on restrictions on advertising by barristers (1975–6 HC 559), solicitors (1975–6 HC 653), stockbrokers (1976, Cmnd. 6571), veterinary surgeons (1976, Cmnd. 6572) and accountants (1976, Cmnd. 6573).

[39] See the 1970 Report of the Monopolies Commission, above, n. 38, para. 252. For other arguments, see M. Trebilcock, 'Competitive Advertising', in R. Evans and M. Trebilcock (eds.), *Lawyers and the Consumer Interest* (1982), ch. 5.

[40] S. Domberger and A. Sherr, 'The Impact of Competition on Pricing and Quality of Legal Services' (1989) 9 Int. Rev. Law & Econ. 41. See also J. Schroeter, S. Smith and S. Cox, 'Advertising and Competition in Routine Legal Services' (1987) 36 J. Industrial Econ. 49. For an analogous study and findings, see L. Benham, 'The Effect of Advertising on the Price of Eyeglasses' (1972) 15 J. Law & Econ. 337.

consumer credit.[41] Information in a standardized form would enable creditors not only to decide whether to purchase with cash or on credit (or not at all), but also to compare the terms offered by different creditors.[42]

Instruments made under the Consumer Credit Act 1974 lay down highly detailed requirements for information in advertisements and quotations, as well as in the contractual document itself.[43] The most important of these is a statement of the annual percentage rate of charge (APR), a standardized measure of the relative annual cost of the agreement, calculated on a prescribed formula which takes account of such variables as repayment frequency as well as interest.[44] In advertisements the APR is to be 'afforded . . . greater prominence than a statement relating to any other charge'.[45]

The APR disclosure requirement serves the same purpose as the unit price provision under the Price Marking Order, and yet its specification and calculation is both complex and costly. Moreover, as a standard measure, it is imperfect: for example, in relation to 'running account agreements' (i.e. where the amount of credit is not fixed), the APR takes no account of variations in the level of credit limit, nor the existence of any interest-free period of credit.[46]

Evaluative studies have been attempted both of the British regulatory system and of the American 'Truth-in-Lending' Act[47] which inspired it. Perhaps unsurprisingly, these reveal that only a small minority of debtors had a clear understanding of the meaning of the APR figures, although in the USA that minority had increased in size over time.[48] Further, lower-income groups took little account of the information in entering credit transactions. To the extent, therefore, that the rate disclosure requirements were motivated by distributional considerations or the paternalist goal that individuals should not overcommit themselves to credit, these

[41] Report of the [Crowther] Committee on Consumer Credit (1971, Cmnd. 4596), para. 3.3.3.                                                                          [42] Ibid. 3.8.3.
[43] Consumer Credit (Agreement) Regulations, SI 1983/1553; Consumer Credit (Advertisements) Regulations, SI 1989/1125; Consumer Credit (Quotations) Regulations, SI 1989/1126.
[44] See Consumer Credit (Total Charge for Credit) Regulations, SI 1980/51.
[45] SI 1989/1125, Reg. 8(1).
[46] Cf. A. Duggan, 'Consumer Credit Rate Disclosure in the United Kingdom and Australia: A Functional and Comparative Appraisal' (1986) 35 Int. Comp. Law Q. 87, 93–5.
[47] On which, see: A. Stone, *Economic Regulation and the Public Interest: The Federal Trade Commission in Theory and Practice* (1977), pp. 240–6; J. Landers and R. Rohner, 'Functional Analysis of Truth in Lending' (1979) 26 UCLA LR 711; R. Rohner, 'Truth in Lending "Simplified" Simplified?' (1981) 56 NYU LR 997.
[48] USA: F. Angell, 'Some Effects of Truth in Lending Legislation' (1971) 44 J. Business 78; Federal Reserve Board, *1977 Consumer Credit Survey* (1978). UK: National Consumer Council, *Consumers and Credit* (1980), pp. 45–74 and App. I; Office of Fair Trading, *Overindebtedness* (1989); see also the 1990 study commissioned by the Consumers Association and cited in J. Eaglesham, 'The Regulation of Credit Marketing and Credit Cost Transparency in the UK' (1992) 2 Cons. Pol. Rev. 111, 113.

studies suggest that the regulations have failed. Conclusions as to allocative efficiency are less easily reached. Hitherto, the studies have concentrated on consumer awareness, and little is known as to the impact of the disclosure requirements on the dispersion of market credit rates. As we have seen,[49] the crucial determinant of supplier behaviour is the demand of marginal consumers, rather than that of consumers in general. If those able to understand APR have 'shopped around' to find the most favourable rate, some suppliers will have been forced to lower their charges, and the welfare gain might well have been sufficient to justify the cost of the disclosure system.

### 3. QUANTITY DISCLOSURE

For many types of product, price is meaningless without reference to quantity. If I am to compare the prices of two packets of soap powder I need to know how much powder each packet contains. Quantity disclosure thus serves the same economic purposes and has the same consequences as price disclosure: it reduces search costs and enhances the competitiveness of the market.[50] Regulation relating to quantity disclosure falls into two categories: that which defines the units of measurement which *may* be used; and that which determines what *must* be disclosed.

### (a) Weights and Measures

For the purposes of disclosure, buyers and sellers of products need a common language of quantity; and there is an obvious economic justification for the public regulation of the units of weights and measures, as this avoids the huge costs of co-ordination which would arise if traders and trade associations were to devise such units voluntarily.[51]

The current British system is contained in the Weights and Measures Act 1985. This Act, and instruments made under it,[52] specify and define the only units which may be used in lawful trade. Notwithstanding the British entry into the EC, the traditional imperial units remain alongside metric units as lawful measures. It is only recently that the government has announced an intention to phase out use of the imperial system.[53] Undoubtedly, having a single measurement system and the one used by other EC Member States must be more efficient than a dual system; but

---

[49] Above, p. 123.

[50] Report of the Committee on Weights and Measures Legislation (1951, Cmd. 8219), para. 245.         [51] Cf. above, pp. 41–2.

[52] Notably: Weights and Measures Regulations, SI 1963/1710 (as amended); Weights and Measures (Packaged Goods) Regulations, SI 1986/2049.

[53] Under draft regulations circulated for comment in 1993, the mandatory use of metric units (and a prohibition of imperial units) would come into force for some products in 1995, and for others in 2000.

the public interest justification for regulation forcing conversion in all cases is less clear. The market demand may be such that most producers will voluntarily convert; and the marginal costs to some firms of being obliged to convert at a particular time will almost certainly exceed the marginal benefits, particularly when account is taken of the capital investment in existing stock.[54]

From a private interest perspective, one would expect mandatory conversion legislation to be favoured by tool manufacturers, publishers, and educators, all of whom would make substantial short-term gains from the demand generated by the requirements of metrication.[55] There is, indeed, some evidence that representatives of these categories were involved in (unsuccessful) lobbying activities.[56]

### (b) Mandatory Disclosure

Traders have an obvious market incentive to disclose quantity. At the same time, they may also be tempted to gain competitive advantages by providing misleading information; for example, the weight disclosed on the soap powder packet may include that of the carton. Efforts to constrain such behaviour have a long history,[57] and unsurprisingly under modern law have given rise to a huge body of complex regulation, covering not only pre-packaged goods and a wide variety of foodstuffs but also such other articles as solid and liquid fuel, ribbons and tapes, ready mixed concrete, and cigars.[58]

While the existence of mandatory quantity regulation is, in general, uncontroversial, it may be less easy to justify its present form on public interest grounds: the cost of administering, and complying with, its bulk and complexity might not be matched by an equivalent increase in welfare. A private interest explanation may be sought in the fact that there are specialist officers appointed to enforce the weights-and-measures legislation and other quantity standards.[59] They benefit when resources (and powers) have to be allocated to them to cope with the voluminous demands of the regulations.[60]

EC law, which has sought to harmonize disclosure requirements for pre-packaged products, has nevertheless forced on Britain a change which may serve to lower administrative and compliance costs. Traditional British

---

[54] R. L. Faith, R. E. McCormick and R. D. Tollison, 'Economics and Metrology: Give 'Em an Inch and They'll Take a Kilometer' (1981) 1 Int. Rev. Law & Econ. 207.

[55] Ibid. 215–16.

[56] N. Stone, 'Metrication and the Consumer', in D. Morris (ed.), *Economics of Consumer Protection* (1980), pp. 96–7.

[57] J. O'Keefe, *The Law of Weights and Measures* (2nd edn., 1977), pp. 1–23.

[58] For a useful overview, see Harvey and Parry, above, n. 11, pp. 398–413.

[59] Trading Standards Officers, on which see G. Rhodes, *Inspectorates in British Government* (1981), pp. 42–50.            [60] Cf. above, pp. 68–9.

quantity regulation was couched in terms of minimum weight (or other units)—'no less than . . .'[61] As a consequence of EC Directives,[62] the system has now been altered to one in which the manufacturer's product need satisfy the requirement only 'on average', a specific degree of tolerated error being allowed under the regulations.[63] The change enables the enforcement agency to test in bulk at the factory rather than at random in retail outlets. The reform attracted the support of British manufacturers because it allows them to fill packages with lesser quantities than would have satisfied the minimum system.[64]

## 4. IDENTITY AND QUALITY DISCLOSURE

### (a) General

Information relating to quality is as important as information relating to price and quantity. In a famous paper, Akerlof demonstrates how asymmetry in the search costs of the two types of information can lead to seriously detrimental consequences.[65] Suppose that the market selling price of a 'high quality' used car of a particular model is £5,000, and that of a 'low quality' equivalent is £2,000. If potential purchasers have information as to the prices set by different dealers but cannot distinguish between 'high quality' and 'low quality' cars, they will assume an 'average' quality for all cars on offer, for which they may be prepared to pay only £3,500. This will force down the market price for *all* used cars to that amount, and dealers will no longer be able to make a profit on 'high quality' cars. Unless, therefore, appropriate information can be communicated to buyers, 'high quality' cars will disappear from the market.[66]

Technological development and the broadening of consumer choice have increased the importance of quality information; but its communication is problematic. In the first place, although some dimensions of quality, such as reliability and durability, can be objectively determined, others involve a high degree of subjectivity. Secondly, while the quality of some products ('search goods') can be ascertained on inspection prior to purchase, others ('experience goods'), including almost all types of services, can be evaluated only in the process of receipt, use, or

---

[61] See e.g. the Butter Regulations, SI 1966/1074, Reg. 4.

[62] 76/106 and 76/211.

[63] Weights and Measures (Packaged Goods) Regulations, SI 1986/2049.

[64] Harvey and Parry, above, n. 11, p. 411.

[65] G. A. Akerlof, 'The Market for "Lemons": Quality Uncertainty and the Market Mechanism' (1970) 89 Q. J. Econ 488.

[66] Another explanation of the same problem is that higher-quality sellers who market high quality goods, which cannot be identified as such, have to share with other sellers the increase in prices which sellers generally are now able to charge—an external benefit: Leland, above, n. 12, p. 1339.

consumption.[67] In some cases ('credence goods'), the effects of use or consumption are known only years later.[68] Thirdly, some indicators of quality cannot be stated succinctly, and given the difficulty of assimilating technical data, large amounts of information may be counter-productive.[69]

A variety of quality information channels is available to suppliers.[70] Advertisements constitute the most obvious method of communicating quality information, but, equally obviously, they can be used to make false or misleading claims. Contractual terms, such as product warranties, may be a more reliable signal of quality, but there is a limit to the types of attributes which can be made the subject of legal obligations. Where direct communication of quality is too difficult or costly, suppliers and purchasers tend to rely on proxies. The most important of these is the supplier's reputation: consumers may, over time, accumulate trust in the quality of a particular firm's output or a particular brand name and, to preserve goodwill, it will be in the interest of the supplier or brand manufacturer to maintain quality. The latter motivation will not apply in relation to one-off transactions; but even here, reputation may have a value when recommendations are made by friends or relatives.

From a public interest perspective, when should regulation require the disclosure of quality information? Given the administrative and compliance costs attaching to such regulation, and the fact that some of it will not significantly enhance consumer choice, the question provokes a cost-benefit analysis of some complexity.[71] Such analysis is likely to take account of the following considerations.

In the first place, the products in question must give rise to problems of consumer choice of a sufficient magnitude. This may occur either because

---

[67] The distinction was drawn in P. Nelson, 'Information and Consumer Behavior' (1970) 78 J. Pol. Econ. 311.

[68] The term was coined in M. R. Darby and E. Karni, 'Free Competition and the Optimal Amount of Fraud' (1973) 16 J. Law & Econ. 67, 68.

[69] Bardach and Kagan, above, n. 6, pp. 249–56. The authors cite (p. 254) the example of a bank which, to meet disclosure requirements, issued to all its customers a 4,500-word booklet describing its electronic funds transfer services. A sentence was inserted in the middle of the booklet offering $10 to any customer who would write 'Regulation E' on a postcard and send it to the bank. Not one person answered. For empirical support of the general proposition, see W. A. Magat and W. K. Viscusi, *Informational Approaches to Regulation* (1992), pp. 102. For a sceptical view, see D. Grether, A. Schwartz and L. Wilde, 'The Irrelevence of Information Overload: An Analysis of Search and Disclosure' (1986) 59 So. Calif. LR 277.

[70] E. Mackaay, *Economics of Information and Law* (1982), pp. 155–60.

[71] Cf. R. Reich, 'Toward a New Consumer Protection' (1979) 128 U. Penn LR 1, 26–39; R. Gage, 'The Discriminating Use of Information Disclosure Rules and the Federal Trade Commission' (1979) 26 UCLA LR 1037, 1065–83; Beales *et al.*, above, n. 3, pp. 521–31; Schwartz and Wilde, above, n. 3, pp. 651–66; Bloom, above, n. 8, pp. 293–7. See also Final Report of the [Molony] Committee on Consumer Protection (1962, Cmnd. 1781), p. 290, and J. Ferguson et al., 'Consumer Ignorance as a Source of Monopoly Power: FTC Staff Report on Self-Regulation, Standardization and Product Differentiation' (1971–2) 5 Antitrust Law & Econ. Rev., No. 2, 79, No. 3, 55.

they generate risks to health or safety, or because they involve major expenditure, or because they are purchased by a large proportion of the community. Secondly, the case for mandatory disclosure is weak where, as a consequence of market competition, producers—other than 'fly-by-nighters'—have an incentive to disclose relevant information voluntarily. Such market discipline will normally be adequate in relation to 'search goods', particularly if there is a significant number of discriminating consumers purchasing at the margin. The market discipline will be weaker in relation to 'experience goods', but even here, producers will often have large investments in a brand name and they will not want to lose the goodwill attaching to it. This suggests that there is an important distinction between attributes which apply to a whole class of products and those which are associated only with particular brands.[72] The incentive to the producer to provide information is much greater in the latter than in the former case, because the information distinguishes his product from that of his rivals. Voluntary disclosure is least likely in relation to 'credence goods', because for reasons of competition, sellers will not be motivated to refer to *negative* qualities, such as a very small risk of ill-health, particularly when that risk is so remote that consumers will be unable to establish a tort claim for product liability.[73]

Thirdly, the information which producers will be bound to disclose must relate to attributes which are considered by typical consumers to be important, and which therefore conclusively determine their choice to a significant degree. Further a substantial number of consumers must make use of the information. A problem here is the expectation, confirmed by some empirical studies,[74] that information printed on product labels or notices is predominantly used by middle-class consumers. Of course, the effectiveness of communication can be maximized by sagacious decisions on the timing and placing of the information and the comprehensibility of its content.[75]

Fourthly, account must be taken of the costs of mandatory disclosure. These include not only the administrative costs of formulating and enforcing the regulations, and the direct cost to firms from complying with them, but also any indirect costs which may arise if the disclosed information leads to an over-reaction by consumers. If, for example, a

---

[72] Beales *et al.*, above, n. 3, p. 527.

[73] Cf. P. Asch, *Consumer Safety Regulation* (1988), pp. 51–2. The Consumer Protection Act 1987 has significantly expanded tort liability for injuries resulting from defective products but the existence of remote risks may not render a product 'defective' in accordance with the criterion prescribed in s. 3.

[74] Cf. Gage, above, n. 71, p. 1052; W. A. Magat and W. K. Viscusi, *Informational Approaches to Regulation* (1992), pp. 121–3, 157.

[75] See generally W. K. Viscusi, 'Predicting the Effects of Food Cancer Risk Warnings on Consumers' (1988) 43 Food Drug Cosmetic LJ 283.

warning notice has to be given considerable prominence and yet it relates to an extremely tiny risk, consumers may be misled and choice distorted.[76]

## (b) Composition and Designation

The mandatory disclosure of the composition or ingredients of a product may substantially reduce the information costs incurred in relation to 'experience' and 'credence' goods. If, for example, I am committed to a low-fat diet, I will have no means of ascertaining whether a particular processed food product will be suitable unless it is labelled accordingly. Regulations requiring the disclosure of ingredients or composition were originally designed to prevent adulteration and fraud in relation to staple products.[77] Today, given the much greater diversity of taste and the broader range of articles available, particularly synthetics, the emphasis is more on consumer choice.

Ingredients as indicators of quality have the advantage of being objective in character. This reduces the cost of formulating and administering the system, and helps to explain the popularity of the technique in relation to food, pharmaceutical, and textile products.[78] Although the regulations specifically require that the lists on the label should be 'easy to understand',[79] this can hardly be realistic in many cases.[80] Indeed, one problem of required composition listing is that it may tilt consumer preferences in favour of products with ingredients with which they are familiar, however well or ill those ingredients serve their needs. To that extent, this form of regulation may discourage innovation and thus have some anti-competitive consequences.[81] The point should not, however, be exaggerated and, provided that the measures do not invade the domain of trade secrets,[82] their relatively low cost ensures that they remain uncontroversial.

The measures so far considered in this section permit a product to be marketed under whatever name is considered appropriate, requiring only that the ingredients be specified. An alternative technique to deal with the

---

[76] Viscusi, above, n. 75.

[77] W. E. Forte, 'Definitions and Standards of Identity for Foods' (1967) 14 UCLA LR 796, 798–801; R. Cranston, *Consumers and the Law* (2nd edn., 1984), pp. 290–1.

[78] Food Labelling Regulations, SI 1984/1305; Medicines (Labelling) Regulations, SI 1976/1726; Textile Products (Indication of Fibre Content) Regulations, SI 1986/26—all as amended. For EC instruments, see Directives 79/112, 65/65, and 71/307 respectively.

[79] SI 1984/1305, Reg. 34(1).

[80] Regulations designed to assist the consumer in ascertaining the nutritional content of foods, implementing EC Directive 90/146, require that numerical values be given to e.g. the fat and sugar content. A study revealed that one half of the consumers questioned were unable to understand these: *The Independent*, 28 October 1993.

[81] Cf. Stone, above, n. 47, pp. 224–31.

[82] Cf. J. O'Reilly, 'Knowledge is Power: Legislative Control of Drug Industry Trade Secrets' (1985) 54 U. Cinc. LR 1.

information problem is to prohibit the marketing of a product using a generic product name unless it conforms to a specific description, contains a specified set of ingredients, and/or has undergone specified processes. The technique is widely used in relation to food and drink products.[83] For example, anything marketed as 'whipped cream' must contain not less than 35 per cent milk fat and have been whipped—it may also contain nitrous oxide and no more than 13 per cent sugar;[84] and there is a detailed specification of the processes of manufacturing what is to be sold as 'Scotch Whisky'.[85]

The public interest rationalization is clear.[86] The designations of such products themselves serve as signals of quality, or at least give rise to expectations that they possess certain attributes. Now, of course, a disclosed list of ingredients should provide a better indicator of such quality or attributes, but many purchasers may not read or comprehend the list. Designation regulation then provides a model which, by and large, will correspond to the average consumer's expectations, or more precisely, to that consumer's *minimum* expectations.

Designation regulation arguably proceeds from a more realistic assumption of consumer behaviour than composition regulation, and yet potentially its cost is much greater. The model of consumers' expectations is derived historically—that is the way that traditionally Scotch Whisky has been manufactured—and there is clearly a risk that the regulations will be very slow to adapt to new (and cheaper) possibilities of manufacturing the same quality product. Designation regulation, designed to facilitate consumer choice, slides all too easily into mandatory product regulation,[87] restricting that choice. Further, the stifling of innovation may serve to erect barriers to entry around existing producers, thus enabling them to earn supra-competitive rents. As private interest theory would predict, there is evidence that producers with vested interests in traditional manufacturing processes have sought to protect those interests by lobbying for appropriate regulation.[88]

The anti-competitive effects of designation regulation have been a major concern of EC Law.[89] The average German consumer's expectations when the word 'beer' is used may be somewhat different from those of a consumer in Britain or Belgium, but if everything marketed as 'beer' in

---

[83] Cranston, above, n. 77, pp. 323–9. For European law, see L. Krämer, *EEC Consumer Law* (1986), paras. 155–9.

[84] Food Labelling Regulations, above, n. 78, Reg. 15(3), and the Cream Regulations, SI 1970/752, Reg. 4(1)(d).

[85] See Scotch Whisky Order SI 1990/998 and Scotch Whisky Act 1988, ss. 2 and 3(1).

[86] Merrill and Collier, above, n. 24.          [87] Below, pp. 192–204.

[88] Urban and Mancke, above, n. 26; Stone, above, n. 47, ch. 9.

[89] S. Weatherill and P. Beaumont, *EC Law* (1993), pp. 446–50; Krämer, above, n. 83, pp. 114–20.

Germany has to conform to the traditional German 'purity' specifications, clearly German brewers will be protected against those from other member states. The European Court has held such legislation to be incompatible with Article 30 of the Treaty of Rome (free movement of goods).[90] Some efforts have, in consequence, been made in Community directives to harmonize national designation regulation,[91] though with occasional reservations where a state's consumption pattern is significantly different from the rest.[92]

### (c) Other Quality Indicators

Producers of higher-quality goods have an incentive voluntarily to provide information in labels and advertisements which will convince consumers of that quality. The problem is that most claims to quality can only be expressed in subjective or at least non-verifiable language, and the consumer response may be one of scepticism. One way of addressing the problem is to adopt scoring systems, analogous to weights and measures systems, which use objective criteria and which relate to attributes of quality.[93] Such systems are unlikely to emerge without government intervention because the cost of competing firms agreeing will be very high, as different producers will wish to focus on different product attributes.

The grading of foodstuffs under EC regulations[94] is typical of a system which comes closest to classical weights and measures, focusing on such attributes as size and condition. More recently, there have been attempts to harmonize national provisions for specific nutritional characteristics and the energy consumption of certain household appliances.[95] As regards the more elusive attributes of durability, reliability, and safety, the British Standards Institution, a private body independent of government and financed by industry, has for many years operated a system of standards; its symbol—the 'Kitemark'—is an indicator to consumers that the product complies with the relevant standard and that the manufacturing process and sample items are periodically tested.[96] To similar effect, products which satisfy standards formulated by equivalent European institutions

[90] *Commission* v. *Germany (Re Beer Purity Laws)* [1988] 1 CMLR 780. The case follows the principle established in the *Cassis de Dijon* case [1979] 3 CMLR 494. See further below, pp. 177–9.

[91] e.g. Directives 74/409 (honey), 75/726 (fruit juices), 79/693 (jellies and marmalade). Directly applicable Council Regulations tend now to be adopted: see e.g. Regulation 2333/92 on the designation of 'sparkling wine'.

[92] e.g. Directive 73/241 on chocolate allows the UK and Ireland to include as 'milk chocolate' products containing only 20% cocoa, whereas for other states the requirement is 25%.          [93] Reales *et al.*, above, n. 3, pp. 523–7.

[94] e.g. Regulation 2772/75 (eggs). For general discussion, see Krämer, above, n. 83, pp. 301–5.          [95] Directives 77/94 and 79/530 respectively.

[96] Harvey and Parry, above, n. 11, p. 55.

(e.g. the European Committee on Standardization—CEN) may bear an appropriate marking.[97] Such standards are, however, necessarily minimum standards.

The benefit to both producers and consumers of information systems of this kind may be self-evident, but some attention should also be given to their potential costs. Over and above the usual administrative and compliance costs, these may include some welfare losses which occur as a result of the scoring system singling out only certain attributes. This may induce consumers to overrate the importance of these attributes, and neglect others which they would otherwise value highly, but for which no objective measurements exist.[98]

### (d) Securities and Financial Disclosure

Mandatory disclosure of information under financial and securities regulation merits special consideration both because of its special characteristics, and because of the controversy to which it has given rise, as reflected in the critical literature.[99] While this literature is predominantly American, it has important implications for the British regulatory system.[100]

That system underwent major changes as a result of the Financial Services Act 1986. This was inspired by the Gower Report which had, *inter alia*, criticized the previous law for its structural defects and its failure to provide investors with adequate protection.[101] Much of the emphasis in the current legislation is on *ex ante* control by the screening of individuals and institutions in the investment industry.[102] Nevertheless, the requirements of disclosure have been extended and play a significant role within the system.[103] The following provisions exemplify the technique.[104]

---

[97] Below, p. 178.                                    [98] Beales *et al.*, above, n. 3, pp. 524–5.

[99] See esp. : G. J. Benston, *Corporate Financial Disclosure in the UK and the USA* (1976); W. Beaver, 'The Nature of Mandated Disclosure', Report of Advisory Committee on Corporate Disclosure to the Securities and Exchange Commission (1977), reproduced in R. Posner and K. Scott (eds.), *Economics of Corporation Law and Securities Regulation* (1980), pp. 317–31; H. Kripke, *The SEC and Corporate Disclosure: Regulation in Search of a Purpose* (1979); F. Easterbrook and D. Fischel, 'Mandatory Disclosure and the Protection of Investors' (1984) 70 Virginia LR 669; J. C. Coffee, 'Market Failure and the Economic Case for a Mandatory Disclosure System', ibid. 717; J. Gordon and L. Kornhauser, 'Efficient Markets, Costly Information and Securities Research' (1985) 60 NYU LR 761. The literature reveals a 'cycle' of theory for and against mandatory disclosure: Coffee, loc. cit., pp. 717–20.

[100] Cf. A. Page and R. Ferguson, *Investor Protection* (1992), pp. 45–9.

[101] *Review of Investor Protection* (1984, Cmnd. 9125); see also the White Paper, *Financial Services in the United Kingdom—A New Framework for Investor Protection* (1985, Cmnd. 9432).                                    [102] See below, pp. 220–2.

[103] See generally R. Pennington, *Law of the Investment Markets* (1990). For the history of disclosure regulation within this area, see ibid, ch. 2.

[104] These are, of course, additional to the duties of a company to lay before its shareholders annually a statement of accounts, a director's report and an auditor's report: Companies Act 1985, Part VII.

Where securities are offered to the public, there is a general duty to disclose

all such information as investors and their professional advisers would reasonably require, and reasonably expect to find there, for the purpose of making an informed assessment of—(a) the assets and liabilities, financial position, profits and losses, and prospects of the issuer of the securities; and (b) the rights attaching to those securities.[105]

Such duty complements more specific duties imposed by the Rules of the Stock Exchange (now a regulatory agency under the 1986 Act) if the security is listed there, and by government-determined regulations in the case of unlisted securities. The Stock Exchange requirements are very detailed. At admission, they include, for example: audited annual financial statements of the issuer for the past five years; information on the trend of business since the period of the last published financial statement; and a forecast of prospects for at least the current financial year, including a statement of the principal assumptions underlying such a forecast.[106]

As regards continuing obligations, a listed company must issue an annual report which, in addition to a financial statement, must contain information on a large range of items, including a statement of any differences between operating results and previous forecasts, a geographical analysis of operations, and biographical information on the company's outside directors.[107] Another important set of requirements is imposed in relation to merger and takeover bids. The Takeover Code issued by another regulatory agency, the Panel on Takeovers and Mergers, is a very detailed document specifying the voluminous amount of information which must be made available to the shareholders of all companies involved.[108] Rule 28 on profit forecasts and its note alone take up seven pages of the Code.

The most usually stated public interest goal of mandatory financial disclosure is investor protection.[109] But this expression can mean several different things which ought carefully to be distinguished. One possibility is that the disclosure might enable less sophisticated investors to avoid substantial losses, should the information alert them to the possibility of bankruptcy. A variant of this is that such investors should be protected against paying a price for a security which does not reflect the company's record and prospects. Forcing an adequate disclosure of the latter would then provide investors with an opportunity to compare price and 'quality'.

---

[105] Financial Services Act 1986, s. 146(1), for securities listed on the Stock Exchange; the same duty applies to unlisted securities: ibid. s. 163(1).

[106] Stock Exchange, *Admission of Securities to Listing* (Yellow Book), paras. 3.31–3.36; and 3.41.                    [107] Ibid. 5.16–5.27.

[108] See L. Rabinowitz, *Weinberg and Blank on Take-Overs and Mergers* (5th edn., 1989), Part VIIA.

[109] e.g. the Gower *Review of Investor Protection*, above, n. 101, pp. 5–8.

The problem with both these claims is that normally the market price of securities reflects all available information on a company—the so-called 'efficient capital markets hypothesis'.[110] What is disclosed under regulatory requirements will invariably already be known to 'informed' traders whose action governed by that information will have influenced the market price. To the extent that the hypothesis is correct, mandatory disclosure cannot therefore benefit investors in this way.[111]

The argument then might shift to an assertion that, having regard to notions of distributional justice, it is 'unfair' for 'informed' traders to have an advantage over ordinary members of the public by reaping the benefits of easier and earlier access to information. Equal access to information is not possible in practice. Statements in regulated disclosures are not the principal source of information regarding firms, and a system in which capital markets were to be fed on that information alone can hardly be envisaged. Traders may receive higher returns for investing (or selling) ahead of the market. Whether or not the particular rewards which they earn for engaging in that activity may be regarded as distributionally 'just', it is economically appropriate that they make a profit, since the securing of information and its communication to the rest of the market (through their trade affecting the prices of securities) facilitates the operation of capital markets.[112]

There are, nevertheless, some more promising sources of public interest benefit. First, the system of regulated disclosure may help to reduce fraud and misrepresentation. As with 'experience goods', managers have an incentive to suppress unfavourable information about their firm's 'quality'. Although there is no unequivocal empirical evidence to this effect,[113] it is not unreasonable to assume that a public system of scrutiny and enforcement is more cost-effective than one in which reliance is placed entirely on private auditing and legal actions.[114]

Secondly, as with many other types of information,[115] data regarding a firm's activity has public good characteristics: it is difficult to exclude third parties from benefiting, and what is consumed by one party does not reduce what is available to others. There will, therefore, be a sub-optimal

[110] On which see Gordon and Kornhauser, above, n. 99.

[111] Kripke, above, n. 99, pp. 97–105; Easterbrook and Fischel, above, n. 99, p. 694. For the limits to the 'efficient market hypothesis', see: Beaver, above, n. 99, pp. 329–9; Gordon and Kornhauser, above, n. 99.

[112] Easterbrook and Fischel, above, n. 99, p. 694. A distinction has nevertheless to be drawn between (1) efforts to secure profits which simply deprive others of equivalent gains, and (2) those which perfect capital markets by facilitating an entrepreneur's ability to raise capital for wealth-creating activities. (2) is economically valuable, (1) is not: J. Hirschleifer, 'The Private and Social Value of Information and the Reward to Inventive Activity' (1971) 61 Am. Econ. Rev. 561.        [113] Cf. Benston, above, n. 99, pp. 104–15.

[114] Beaver, above, n. 99, p. 319; Easterbrook and Fischel, above, n. 99, p. 677.

[115] Cf. above, p. 40.

amount of voluntary disclosure in an unregulated market. This proposition is valid but requires some greater precision.[116] When the information in question is used solely for the purposes of trading in securities, there is no public good dimension: 'consumption' by one party does indeed reduce its value to others. The private value in the information is secured by the ability of the disclosee to trade before the price of the security reflects the impact of the information. On the other hand, where the information is used by others for the purpose of other resource activity, its value may not be reduced by the first 'use'. The under-supply of such information is a genuine externality which might properly be addressed through mandatory disclosure.

Against the benefits of mandatory disclosure, so described, must be set its costs. The sheer bulk of the current requirements under the Financial Services Act suggests that the direct costs (to the firms) of compliance and (to the regulatory agencies) of rule formulation, monitoring, and enforcement must be considerable. To these may be added potential indirect costs which might be more speculative but should not be ignored.[117] Forcing disclosure of certain information might induce some firms to modify or abandon profitable projects. Also, some may find it beneficial to overload the required statements with obfuscating information, itself an item of wasted expenditure, imposing costs on those attempting to read and understand it.

The public interest justification for the current regime would depend on the outcome of this cost-benefit analysis. Private interest explanations should also be considered.[118] The familiar observation that compliance costs are proportionally much higher for small, compared with large, firms has particular force in this context. What is required may cost large firms little more than what they would in any event have spent, but for small firms it may be very onerous relative to turnover. Other groups likely to profit from the regime are the professionals, such as chartered accountants, whose services are required to fulfil the requirements; those such as stockbrokers, who derive benefit from what is disclosed without having to pay for it; and those employed by the regulatory agency to administer the requirements.

### (e) Warnings and Instructions for Use

The pressures of ordinary market competition should create incentives for producers voluntarily to provide information on how to use their products, and it is relatively easy for consumers to verify at the time of purchase that such information is given. In the light of this, regulation requiring the

---

[116] Benston, above, n. 99, pp. 141–2.
[117] Easterbrook and Fischel, above, n. 99, pp. 708–9.
[118] Cf. Benston, above, n. 99, pp. 157–8, and ch. 5.

communication of instructions is rare, and it is difficult to understand the reason for the provision in an EC Directive that instructions for use should be printed on the label of foodstuffs 'when it would be impossible to make appropriate use of the foodstuff in the absence of such instructions'.[119]

The matter is very different where use of the product gives rise to risks of illness, injury, or perhaps, as with consumer credit, severe financial hardship. The losses in question may be very large and the risks are paradigms of hidden costs which attach to experience and credence goods.[120] Information, in the form of warnings, is therefore highly valued by consumers.

Since 1980, there has been in the USA a major growth in regulation compelling warnings to be issued, mostly on labels but also on shelf displays and check-out counters.[121] This has arisen, in part, as a reaction to the perceived failure of more traditional forms of regulation such as product standards, and in part as a consequence of the emergence of the 'right to know' movement.[122] In Britain and Europe, warning requirements also proliferate, although enthusiasm for their use has not been so dramatic.[123]

When risks attach to a product or service supplied, a mandatory warning is only one of several policy options, the others being: no regulation, leaving the matter to be dealt with by the market and private law (notably tort remedies); banning the product or service; and imposing standards. From a public interest perspective, the choice of mandatory warning depends on some important cost-benefit considerations which may vary according to the nature of the risk.

Risk analysis centres on three variables: the probability of harm resulting from the activity or product $(p)$[124]; the amount of harm which occurs if the risk materializes $(D)$; and the cost of taking measures sufficient to avert the risk $(C)$. The normal economic goal is to encourage what we have already referred to as the 'socially optimal level of care'[125], where $C = pD$.[126] In addressing the question of when warnings should be used as devices to deal with risks, we should distinguish between four situations.

---

[119] Directive 79/112, Art. 3. Where different producers may use different symbols or units as part of the instructions, regulations harmonizing such symbols or units may be justified on grounds of reducing co-ordinating costs. See e.g. the problems arising from different symbols for the care of textiles cited in Krämer, above, n. 83, p. 124.

[120] Cf. above, pp. 132–3.

[121] See, generally, S. Hadden, *Read the Label: Reducing Risk by Providing Information* (1985).          [122] Magat and Viscusi, above, n. 74, pp. 1–2.

[123] Krämer, above, n. 83, pp. 124–6.

[124] This should be adjusted to take account of the degree of risk-aversion of potential victims.          [125] Above, p. 21.

[126] If the care taken reduces, but does not eliminate, the risk, the optimal level of care is where $C$ equals the reduction in $pD$.

(I) Where the *producer* alone can take the precautions necessary to avert the risk and $C < pD$. The preferable regulatory[127] solution in this case is likely to be behavioral standards requiring the producer to take the precautions. There is, however, an argument for mandatory warning as an alternative solution. The benefit of risk reduction will vary between consumers because their personal circumstances differ and—more importantly—they have different attitudes to risk: some are more risk-averse; some are more risk-preferring. A warning system, in contrast to precautionary standards, preserves freedom of choice for the latter. Nevertheless, the argument is not a strong one.[128] It is highly unlikely that the warning can provide a sufficiently clear indication of the risk for the consumer to make such a rational choice, and the costs of informational failure may be very high.

(II) Where $C < pD$, but the most significant precautions reflected in $C$ must be taken by the *consumer*. This is obviously a much stronger case for mandatory warnings, since the only practical regulatory alternative is to ban the product, behavioural controls on consumers being prohibitively expensive to enforce. Most of the British[129] and European[130] mandatory warning provisions fall into this category.

(III) If the precautionary cost will, in general, exceed the benefit from the reduced risk $(C > pD)$ no warning is economically justified, and for this purpose $C$ should include not only the cost of taking the precautions, but also that of administering and complying with the information regulation. There is, moreover, a limit to the capacity of consumers to assimilate information, so that adverting to low-value risks (i.e. where $pD$ is small) is counter-productive.[131] Empirical evidence nevertheless suggests that well-designed warnings are reasonably effective in stimulating consumer precautions, particularly where these are negative—'don't do X'—rather than positive—'do X'.[132]

(IV) In a fourth situation, there is nothing which either the producer or the consumer can do to avert the risk, other than not to sell, buy, or use the product. Where the risk is a very grave one (i.e. $pD$ is very large), regulation might impose that solution. In other cases, mandatory warnings are an attractive option because, on the assumption that they are understood, they allow individuals to make the choice of whether to take the risk or not. British and European law contain only a few examples, the

---

[127] This is, of course, to disregard the private law (tort) solution to the problem: above, p. 21.

[128] Cf. Duggan, above, n. 12, pp. 44–5; W. K. Viscusi, *Regulating Consumer Product Safety* (1984), pp. 22–3.

[129] e.g. Oil Heaters (Safety) Regulations, SI 1977/162, Reg. 5(1); Poison Rules, SI 1982/218, Sched. 7; Low Voltage Electrical Equipment (Safety) Regulations, SI 1989/728, Reg. 8(c); Toys (Safety) Regulations, SI 1989/1275, Reg. 12.

[130] e.g. Directives 75/324 (aerosol dispensers) and 88/378 (toys).

[131] Magat and Viscusi, above, n. 74, pp. 90–2.     [132] Ibid. pp. 103–4.

most notable being in relation to tobacco.[133] In Britain, health warnings on cigarette packets, and in posters and advertisements, were originally the subject of an informal agreement between government and the tobacco industries.[134] Now they are the subject of an EC Directive, the regulations requiring the issuing of both a general warning—'Tobacco seriously damages your health'—and one of six specific warnings (e.g. 'smoking causes cancer', 'smoking when pregnant harms your baby').[135]

As has been mentioned, American jurisdictions have made more extensive use of this regulatory form. The principal difficulty has been to determine when a risk is sufficiently large to justify the cost of the warning. A controversial Californian measure requires manufacturers of food products which give rise to a 'significant' risk of cancer to make such effects known to consumers by means of warning labels.[136] 'Significant' is currently construed in terms of a lifetime cancer risk of 1 in 100,000—i.e. $p = 0.00001$.[137] Apparently, consumerists argued that the threshold should have been 0.000001.[138]

It is not easy to make a rational decision on what is appropriate in this context. On the one hand, there is the 'right to know' ideology which places a high value on information, however remote the risk. On the other hand, there is the possibility that warnings of tiny risks will provoke consumers to overreact, thus depriving themselves of what they want and distorting market competition.[139] And, of course, the smaller the risk threshold, the larger the number of risks that will have to be brought to the attention of consumers. This not only adds to the cost of regulation but also reduces the impact of warnings relating to more serious risks. The question of how and where to place the warning gives rise to similar considerations, because it is important that its prominence should be commensurate with the severity of the risk.[140]

## 5. CONTROLS ON MISLEADING INFORMATION

So far in this chapter we have considered situations in which regulation has compelled the disclosure of information where the market fails to create

---

[133] Another is consumer credit. Advertisements and quotations for secured loans must carry the warning, 'YOUR HOME IS AT RISK IF YOU DO NOT KEEP UP REPAYMENTS ON A MORTGAGE OR OTHER LOAN SECURED ON IT': Consumer Credit (Advertisements) Regulations SI 1989/1125, Sched. 1; Consumer Credit (Quotations) Regulations SI 1989/1126, Sched. 1. Warnings regarding risks must also be included in investment advertisements. See Securities and Investment Board, Financial Services (Conduct of Business) Rules 1987, rule 7.20.

[134] Cranston, above, n. 77, p. 283.

[135] EC Directive 89/622; Tobacco Products Labelling (Safety) Regulations, SI 1991/1531, Regs. 3, 4, and Sched. 1.

[136] Cal. Health and Safety Code 25249. 11(c), on which see Viscusi, above, n. 75.

[137] Cal. Admin. Code, Title 22, 23703(b).          [138] Viscusi, above, n. 75, p. 289.

[139] Ibid.                                      [140] Ibid. 298–301.

incentives adequately to do this. But, whether voluntary or mandatory, information which is false is worse that no information. We must, therefore, conclude with reference to what may be called 'negative' information regulation, the prohibition or control of misleading information. In Britain, such regulation combines a highly legalized regime under the Trade Descriptions Act 1968 with a 'softer' code of conduct governing advertisements administered by a self-regulatory agency.

## (a) Trade Descriptions Legislation

The Trade Descriptions Act 1968[141] has been described by one commentator as 'a landmark in United Kingdom consumer protection. It marked a major transition from regulation according to private rights to the public regulation of the market-place'.[142] Perhaps epitomizing the confidence displayed in regulation at that time, it aimed at a specific, yet also comprehensive, legal definition of what was a 'false trade description' and therefore to be prohibited. This is exemplified by the requirement that a 'trade description' must relate to one or more of eight different attributes, including for example 'method of manufacture, production, processing or reconditioning' and 'fitness for purpose, strength, performance, behaviour or accuracy'.[143] The technique contrasts with that used in other jurisdictions where broader definitions are preferred.[144]

The problems that may arise from too great an emphasis on legal precision are well illustrated by the contorted history of those provisions in the 1968 Act which dealt with false and misleading price claims.[145] The goal was to prohibit false comparisons between a current price and one allegedly previously charged by the trader for the same product. It proved difficult to draft a provision which would hit this target but which was not too vague. What was enacted, as interpreted by the courts,[146] had the opposite defect of being too narrow: it effectively required the enforcement agency to prove that the trader had not offered the product at the higher price for a continuous period of 28 days during the previous six months.[147] Apart from creating possibilities of avoidance, this placed an impossibly high level of monitoring costs on the agency. The failure led to a radical response: the Price Marking (Bargain Offers) Order 1979 attempted

---

[141] For a detailed account of the Act, as amended by the Consumer Protection Act 1987, see R. Bragg, *Trade Descriptions* (1991).

[142] I. Ramsay, *Consumer Protection: Cases and Materials* (1989), p. 204.

[143] Trade Descriptions Act 1968, s. 2(1)(b) and (d).

[144] For European jurisdictions, see N. Reich and H.-W. Micklitz, *Consumer Legislation in the EC Countries: A Comparative Analysis* (1980), pp. 41–5; for the USA, R. Pitojsky, 'Beyond Nader: Consumer Protection and the Regulation of Advertising' (1977) 90 Harv. LR 661, 675–80.

[145] Cf. Ramsay, above, n. 142, pp. 251–7.

[146] *House of Holland Ltd* v. *Brent* [1971] 2 QB 304.

[147] Trade Descriptions Act 1968, s. 11(3)(a)(ii), since repealed.

to provide a comprehensive specification of all types of bargain offer which traders might make, prohibiting offers in any other form.[148]

The cure proved to be as detrimental as the disease. Incentives were created for finding loopholes or making claims which satisfied the Order but were actually meaningless; and the complexity arising from the exhaustiveness of the provisions rendered them difficult to understand and costly to enforce. Finally, in 1987, a new start was made. Legislation introduced an offence of giving misleading price indication, formulated in general language, of the kind typically used in other jurisdictions. The indication is

misleading . . . if . . . consumers might reasonably be expected to infer from the indication [*inter alia*] that the facts or circumstances by reference to which the consumers might reasonably be expected to judge the validity of any relevant comparison made or implied by the indication are *not what in fact they are*.[149]

To provide practical guidance and to assist in the interpretation of the legislation, there is a Code of Practice which is not binding on the courts but which may be taken into account.[150]

## (b) Advertising Standards Authority

The 'broad brush' approach of the new trade descriptions law brings the regulation of fraudulent or misleading price marking closer to the system which has dominated the control of advertising generally.[151] A Code of Advertising Practice, administered by the Advertising Standards Authority, a self-regulatory agency, includes the following provision on deception.

Advertisements should not contain any statement or visual presentation which, directly or by implication, omission, ambiguity, or exaggerated claim, is likely to mislead the consumer about the product advertised, the advertiser or about any other product or advertiser.

There appears to be a general consensus that this system of regulating advertising is satisfactory,[152] a fact which no doubt assisted the British government in persuading the European Commission that it should be retained notwithstanding pressure to conform to the European model of control, which extends beyond misleading advertising, to 'unfair' advertising and which enables complainants to bring actions in the courts. The relevant European Directive is thus confined to misleading advertising and allows a self-regulatory agency to perform the principal enforcement function.[153]

---

[148] SI 1979/364.          [149] Consumer Protection Act 1987, s. 21(1). My italics.
[150] For a comprehensive discussion, see Bragg, above, n. 141, pp. 113–39.
[151] Cranston, above, n. 77, pp. 42–59.
[152] Ramsay, above, n. 142, p. 395.
[153] Directive 84/450. See Krämer, above, n. 83, pp. 152–61. As a concession to the European model, the Control of Misleading Advertisement Regulations SI 1988/915, which

## (c) Public Interest Analysis

The difficulty of determining what should be controlled is acute for systems of negative information regulation. There is no easy distinction between what is truthful and what is false; between what is a factual claim (and therefore susceptible of objective substantiation) and what is an opinion; between what is explicit and what is merely implicit. Nor should the circumstances and behaviour of the consumer-representee be ignored. In many cases, the latter will in any event give little credence to claims, and controls will generate no benefit; in some others, one or more of the numerous private law remedies[154] will suffice.

In the light of these problems, public interest attempts to fashion regulatory instruments on the 'optimal' level of control are obviously prone to substantial error. Nevertheless some guidelines have emerged in the literature.[155] First, the benefits of controlling falsehoods must be assessed. These will be the difference ($D$) between what consumers would have gained if the claims had been true and what (if anything) they gained from them as sold, as discounted by the probability ($p$) that consumers attach credence to the claims. The further the claim is from an assertion of fact, the higher the discount for $p$, because consumers do not generally take much heed of 'puffery'. $D$ is likely to be relatively small in the case of 'search goods' or where the traders have an established market reputation to preserve, because in both cases the market is likely to constrain the incentive to deceive.

However the benefits so derived are assessed, there is obviously a substantial risk that they will be outweighed by the costs of the regulatory system. This is primarily because the direct costs to a regulatory agency of verifying the accuracy of claims in trade statements or advertisements are very high. Different regulatory systems have adopted different methods of reducing these.

Although the Advertising Standards Authority has in recent years engaged in a certain amount of prior vetting at the request of advertisers, it assumes a predominantly reactive enforcement role by relying primarily on complaints: the result must be a dulling of the deterrent effect. When a complaint is made, the burden of substantiating a claim is normally

---

implement the Directive, empower the Director-General of Fair Trading to seek a court order in relation to a misleading advertisement, but in exercising his discretion, the latter should take into account the desirability of control by self-regulatory bodies.

[154] M. P. Furmston, *Cheshire, Fifoot and Furmston's Law of Contract* (12th edn, 1991), ch. 9.

[155] Especially Beales *et al.*, above, n. 3, pp. 516–21, on which the following is based. See also E. H. Jordan and P. H. Rubin, 'Economic Analysis of the Law of False Advertising' (1979) 8 J. Legal Stud. 527, which argues from narrower assumptions and reaches different conclusions: for criticism, see Duggan, above, n. 12, pp. 23–8.

imposed on the firm making it. The effect may be to increase the costs to a firm of making (true as well as false) claims in advertisements which are capable of verification. The firm then has an incentive to substitute 'puffery' for such claims, or at least more subjective claims which are less valuable to consumers.[156]

Subject to this problem, the approach adopted in the British trades description legislation in relation to descriptions of *goods* may be the most cost-effective. The specificity of the legal technique allows for routine administration, thus reducing the cost. Moreover, while the bias to under-inclusiveness means that it fails to catch some deceptive practices, it nevertheless avoids deterring practices which are socially valuable and which might be deterred by a more general approach.[157] That bias against intervention is underpinned by the practice of narrow, literal interpretation which courts have established in this area.[158] Nevertheless, on occasions judges have taken a more robust approach, and it is striking that this has tended to occur in situations where, in terms of the above analysis, $D$ is likely to be large. So, for example, second-hand car dealers (who probably have little investment in reputation and with whom most customers have a 'one-off' relationship) have tended to be penalized for statements which might have been treated as lawful if made by (say) manufacturers of a food product.[159]

The history of British attempts at controlling misleading statements on *prices* has, contrastingly, been one of failure. In part, this was because it was not appreciated that beyond a certain point legal specificity increases, rather than reduces, administrative cost.[160] But it resulted also from a failure to recognize that many consumers may heavily discount claims made in bargain offers (i.e. $p$ is small)[161] and that therefore the potential benefits of controls are unlikely to be substantial.

### (d) Private Interest Considerations

Exponents of private interest theory who doubt the cost-effectiveness of the American control system have looked for reasons why particular groups of firms or industries might benefit from that regulation.[162] In the first place, there is the standard hypothesis that the cost of compliance

---

[156] See: Pitojsky, above, n. 144; R. Higgins and F. McChesney, 'Truth and Consequences: The Federal Trade Commission's Ad Substantiation Program' (1986) 6 Int. Rev. Law & Econ. 149.

[157] Cf. I. Ehrlich and R. Posner, 'An Economic Analysis of Legal Rulemaking' (1974) 3 J. Legal Stud. 257.          [158] Cf. Ramsay, above, n. 142, pp. 209–15.

[159] Cp. *Robertson* v. *Di Cicco* [1972] RTR 431 with *Cadbury Ltd* v. *Halliday* [1975] 1 WLR 649.

[160] Cf. A. Ogus, 'Information, Error Costs and Regulation' (1992) 12 Int. Rev. Law & Econ. 411, 417.

[161] For views and empirical evidence to this effect, see the refs. cited by Ramsay, above, n. 142, pp. 252–3.          [162] Higgins and McChesney, above, n. 156.

(which here means substantiating a claim) will be largely a fixed cost, independent of output, and therefore will benefit large firms at the expense of small firms. Secondly, firms with already established reputations can divert more of their advertising resources away from factual claims which are vulnerable to the control, to simply reminding consumers of their name. Both of these postulates suggest that negative information regulation can protect larger firms from competition by smaller, marginal firms.

# 8

# Standards: General

Quality standards which subject suppliers of goods and services to behavioural controls and which penalize those who fail to conform are, and have always been,[1] the dominant form of 'social' regulation. They have been applied, with differing goals and using diverse techniques, to a huge variety of commercial, industrial, and social activities. Our treatment of standards must necessarily be very selective, but it proceeds from a conviction that generalizations on justifications, principles, and methods are both possible and valuable.

In this chapter we explore public interest models for setting standards and how those models may be implemented by legal instruments (Sections 1–5). We also consider (Sections 6–7) the impact of private interests and of EC law. In Chapter 9, in the light of this analysis, we examine three important areas governed by standards: occupational health and safety regulation, consumer product regulation, and environmental regulation.

## I. NATURE OF STANDARDS

Regulatory techniques differ in the extent to which the public controls impede freedom of activity. To appreciate the nature of standards and their relationship to other traditional forms, we may envisage (Figure 8.1) a spectrum representing different degrees of state intervention. Standards (the subject of this chapter and Chapter 9) occupy a middle position between information measures (Chapter 7), representing low intervention, and prior approval (Chapter 10), representing high intervention.

*Information* measures require suppliers to disclose certain facts, but do not otherwise impose behavioural controls. At the other end of the spectrum, individuals or firms may be prevented from lawfully supplying a product or service without obtaining *prior approval* from an authorizing agency; and for such approval they will have to satisfy the agency that certain conditions of quality are, or are capable of being, met. The *standards* technique allows the activity to take place without any *ex ante* control, but the supplier who fails to meet certain standards of quality commits an offence. Standards can be subdivided into three categories

---

[1] Cf. A. I. Ogus, 'Regulatory Law: Some Lessons from the Past' (1992) 12 Legal Stud. 1, 13–15.

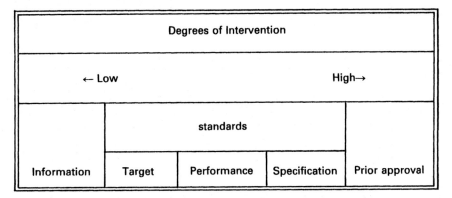

FIG. 8.1

which themselves represent different degrees of intervention.[2] A *target* standard prescribes no specific standard for the supplier's processes or output, but imposes criminal liability for certain harmful consequences arising from the output.[3] A *performance* (or output) standard requires certain conditions of quality to be met at the point of supply, but leaves the supplier free to choose how to meet those conditions. A *specification* (or input) standard can exist in either a positive or negative form: it compels the supplier to employ certain production methods or materials, or prohibits the use of certain production methods or materials. As such, it is the most interventionist of the standards techniques.

These various forms can be illustrated by reference to the regulation of products which generate risks for consumers. The information technique is used for tobacco: a health warning must be printed on all cigarette packets.[4] Prior approval is mandatory for pharmaceutical products: a manufacturer must obtain a licence before marketing a drug.[5] The requirement that toys be so designed that 'they do not present health hazards or risks of physical injury by ingestion, inhalation or contact with the skin . . .'[6] constitutes an example of a target standard. Health risks arising from pencils are governed by performance standards which, *inter alia*, prescribe that any coating of paint shall not contain soluble antimony

[2] Cf. G. Richardson, A. Ogus, P. Burrows, *Policing Pollution: A Study of Regulation and Enforcement* (1982), pp. 35–40.

[3] As will be seen (below p. 178), a target standard may also be prescribed by an EC directive (or other international instrument). This imposes an obligation on the national legal system to take appropriate steps to ensure that the target is met.

[4] Tobacco Products Labelling (Safety) Regulations, SI 1991/1531: above, p. 144.

[5] Medicines Act 1968: below, p. 236.

[6] Toys (Safety) Regulations, SI 1989/1275, Sched. 2, incorporating EC Directive 88/378, Annex II, point 3(1).

or lead exceeding 250 ppm of that coating.[7] Finally, the regulations governing the construction of motor vehicles incorporate several specification standards, one of which is the requirement that all tyres used on cars shall be pneumatic tyres.[8]

## 2. AN IDEALIZED PUBLIC INTEREST MODEL FOR STANDARD-SETTING

### (a) Public Interest Justifications

The basic economic justification for standards is that they can correct market failures, particularly information deficits[9] and externalities,[10] more effectively or more cheaply than less interventionist measures. The limits to the efficacy of private law remedies have already been mentioned;[11] what then of information regulation? As regards externalities, mandatory disclosure of risks and other hidden costs can at best only assist those third parties who have some direct contact with the source of the externality; and many of these will not be in a good position to avoid the harm. The risks of a slippery floor in a public lavatory may be cheaply averted by a suitably placed notice,[12] but we can hardly use this device to deal with motorists driving a vehicle with defective brakes.

As we saw in the last chapter, mandatory disclosure can be a most effective solution for information asymmetries between suppliers and purchasers. But it has its limits. It may be impossible to summarize the necessary information in a form which the great majority of purchasers will read and understand. The 'bounded rationality' of individuals may constitute a further obstacle:[13] there is evidence that individuals tend to overestimate risks associated with low-probability events and underestimate those arising from higher-probability events.[14] Given the often significant costs to purchasers of assimilating information and making decisions, it may be cheaper to force suppliers to adjust the product or service to what purchasers would presumptively have chosen if those intellectual processes had been completed.[15] This solution may be particularly apposite where the costs arising from consumer error are high, such as where death or serious personal injury may result. Paternalist arguments to override individual choice[16] are frequently invoked in such circumstances.

---

[7] Pencils and Graphic Instruments (Safety) Regulations, SI 1974/226, Reg. 2(1)(b).
[8] Road Vehicles (Construction and Use) Regulations, SI 1986/1078, Reg. 24.
[9] Above, pp. 38–41.
[10] Above, pp. 18–20 and 35–8.                                    [11] Above, p. 28.
[12] Cf. above, p. 123.                                           [13] Above, p. 41.
[14] B. Fischhoff et al., Acceptable Risk (1981); and see P. Asch, Consumer Safety Regulation: Putting a Price on Life and Limb (1988), pp. 70–9.
[15] Above, p. 143.                                    [16] Above, pp. 51–3.

Distributional considerations may also point to more interventionist solutions. Lack of resources may be a barrier to the use of private law remedies; and information regulation tends to discriminate against those with poor educational attainment.

## (b) Goal of Optimal Loss Abatement

To facilitate exposition of the theory of standard-setting, it is helpful to distinguish between the general *aims* of intervention and the specific *goal* which policy-makers ought rationally to pursue in designing regulatory standards.[17] The aims of intervention can be inferred from the public interest justifications discussed above. If the concern is with an information deficit afflicting buyers, the interventionist aim is to require suppliers to produce the quality that would have been demanded if there had been no such deficit. If an activity gives rise to an externality, it is to force a modification to that activity so as to internalize the externality. In short, in both cases, the aim is to eliminate an unwanted loss. That loss may be either certain (e.g. the loss of utility from a product of inferior quality or a financial loss consequent on damage to person or property) or uncertain (e.g. the risk of personal injury from a dangerous product or activity).

The specific goal of a system of regulatory standards differs from the general aims of intervention simply because the total elimination of unwanted losses is neither possible nor desirable. The avoidance of damage and harmful risks is itself a costly exercise in terms of the resources necessary both to comply with the standards and to administer the regulatory system. Some form of cost–benefit analysis therefore constitutes an indispensable part of rational regulatory policy-making.[18] At its crudest minimum, this may mean only that the benefits to society of a given standard—reduction in unwanted losses—should exceed its costs. The idealized goal, which we can refer to as 'optimal loss abatement', can be stated more precisely. Regulatory standards should be set at a level at which the total benefits exceed the total costs by the greatest amount, and at which the marginal benefits are equal to the marginal costs.

The goal of optimal loss abatement can be illustrated by an arithmetical example, using hypothetical data. Suppose a standard-setter, responsible for determining levels of safety for a certain product, had the information set out in Table 8.1. The first column represents different standards, the number of units of care to be taken by manufacturers. *MC* is the marginal

---

[17] Cf. B. Mitnick, *The Political Economy of Regulation* (1980), pp. 281–91.

[18] Economic Council of Canada, *Responsible Regulation* (1979), pp. 34–42; C. R. Sunstein, 'Cost–Benefit Analysis and the Separation of Powers' (1981) 23 Arizona LR 1267; S. Breyer, *Regulation and its Reform* (1982), p. 98; A. Peacock, *The Regulation Game: How British and West German Companies Bargain with Government* (1984), ch. 1; C. M. Heimann, 'Project: The Impact of Cost–Benefit Analysis on Federal Administrative Law' (1990) 42 Admin. LR 545.

TABLE 8.1

| Units | MC (£ m.) | TC (£ m.) | p | pD (£ m.) | MB (£ m.) | TB (£ m.) | NTB (£ m.) |
|---|---|---|---|---|---|---|---|
| 0 | 0 | 0 | 0.5 | 500 | 0 | 0 | 0 |
| 1 | 10 | 10 | 0.2 | 200 | 300 | 300 | 290 |
| 2 | 15 | 25 | 0.15 | 150 | 50 | 350 | 325 |
| 3 | 20 | 45 | 0.12 | 120 | 30 | 380 | 335 |
| 4 | 28 | 73 | 0.095 | 95 | 25 | 405 | 332 |
| 5 | 40 | 113 | 0.08 | 80 | 15 | 420 | 307 |
| 6 | 60 | 173 | 0.07 | 70 | 10 | 430 | 257 |

cost of each additional unit of care and $TC$ the total costs. $p$ is the probability of accidents resulting from use of the product (1.0 is certainty) and $D$ the average amount of harm (£1,000 million) that would result if accidents occur. Thus $pD$ is the expected damage costs of the product at each level of care.[19] $MB$ is the marginal benefit of each additional unit care, calculated as the reduction in the $pD$ at each level of care, and $TB$ is the total of such benefits. Finally, $NTB$ represents the net total benefits, i.e. $TB$-$TC$, at each level of care.

The standard-setter would require product manufacturers to take three units of care[20] because at that level the total net benefit of care is maximized (at £335 million); also, the marginal costs of care (£20 million) remain less than the marginal benefits (£30 million)—conversely, at four units, $MC$ exceeds $MB$.

The idealized cost–benefit model is easy to state and to comprehend; its implementation is quite another matter because of the enormous difficulties of specifying the magnitude of each variable.[21] These problems must now be addressed.

[19] e.g. at 1 unit of care, there is a 0.2 chance of £1,000 million damage costs and 0.8 chance of no damage costs. The expected damages costs are therefore (0.2 × £1,000 million) + (0.8 × £0) = £200 million.

[20] This is on the assumption that the provision of care is not continuous, i.e. the standard-setter has to choose between the specified units of care. If it were continuous, the optimal level would be somewhere between 3 and 4 units, where $MC = MB$.

[21] For general discussions, see: R. Sugden and A. Williams, *Principles of Practical Cost–Benefit Analysis* (1978); Economic Council of Canada, above, n. 18, pp. 34–40; D. W. Pearce and C. A. Nash, *The Social Appraisal of Projects* (1981); L. B. Lave, *The Strategy of Social Regulation* (1981), ch. 3. For valuable critical reviews of American cost–benefit analyses in different areas of social regulation, see: J. C. Miller and B. Yandle, *Benefit–Cost Analyses of Social Regulation: Case Studies from the Council on Wage and Price Stability* (1979); and Heimann, above, n. 18.

## (c) Assessing the Costs of Standards

The costs associated with regulatory standards can be subdivided into administrative costs, compliance costs, and indirect costs. *Administrative costs* are largely borne by the public agency which has the task of formulating standards, monitoring behaviour, and enforcing compliance. As will be seen, these vary significantly according to the type and style of standard adopted. Some of the administrative costs are borne by the firms who are subjected to the standards, notably acquiring relevant information, keeping records relating to compliance, and receiving and perhaps negotiating with the enforcement agency. In principle, these costs should be calculated on an 'opportunity cost' basis, that is, the loss accruing from resources not being allocated to their most highly valued alternative use. In practice, quantification does not give rise to major difficulties.

The *compliance costs* comprise, most importantly: the capital expenditure on equipment and adaptation to plant necessary to meet the standard; any additional, recurrent maintenance costs; and any productivity losses, calculated on an 'opportunity cost' basis. Again, quantification does not pose insuperable problems. One complicating factor is, however, the possible heterogeneity of the regulated firms. The marginal cost of meeting a standard may be significantly higher for one firm than for another, given that, for example, the capacity of the environment to assimilate pollution varies from one location to another, and that older equipment may be more expensive to adapt to technical requirements than new equipment. The differences may justify either individualized standards (as in some areas of environmental regulation[22]) or a less severe standard for firms which have used the same plant or production technique for a number of years.[23] On the other hand, too great a departure from uniform standards may generate significant inefficiencies: firms will be motivated to overstate their compliance costs, and will lack the incentive to reduce them. Moreover, the imposition of more stringent standards on 'newer' firms may create barriers to entry and thus protect 'older' firms from competition.

Such inefficiencies are but examples of *indirect costs*, the generally unintended,[24] and sometimes perverse, consequences of regulation. Broadly speaking, they fall into three categories: productive inefficiency,[25] a lower ratio of output to input; the inhibition of technical change; and allocative inefficiency,[26] where resources are not being put to their socially most valuable uses. The assessment of indirect costs is problematic because the relevant effects are widespread and data is difficult to obtain.

---

[22] Below, p. 210.      [23] Below, p. 169.
[24] They may, of course, be intended by those who benefit from them! Cf. below, pp. 171–173.      [25] Cf. above, p. 22.      [26] Cf. above, p. 24.

### (d) Assessing the Benefits of Standards

Some of the benefits generated by regulatory standards may be assessed with a reasonable amount of precision. If the policy-maker's aim is to eliminate a specific unwanted loss to a specific set of beneficiaries and it can be assumed that a given standard will achieve this, the gain to the beneficiaries, or at least part of it, may have an objective value. Thus, an environmental standard may increase the market value of property and a health standard may reduce the incidence of sickness, with consequent savings on medical costs and lost earnings. The risk dimension ($p$ in Table 8.1) may be objectively determined from available data—for example, the annual risk of death to a child from inflammable nightware has been assessed at 2.4 in 1,000,000 (i.e. $p = 0.0000024$)[27]; but many risks are the subject of considerable uncertainty.[28]

Nevertheless, in general, the benefits of standards are much more difficult to quantify than the costs. There are four principal reasons for this. First, it is impossible to lay out a neat taxonomy for benefits, of the kind that presented itself for costs. Many of the alleged benefits are diffuse in character and significantly removed in time and space from the regulated activity—for example, very large numbers of people may derive utility from a cleaner environment. Secondly, the causal connection between the benefits and the regulation may be disputable or complicated by the existence of other factors. Thirdly, many of the benefits are non-marketed assets which therefore cannot easily be converted into units of currency for the purpose of comparison with costs. Fourthly, the benefits may accrue over an extended timescale and some discounting method has to be used to give them a current value. The last two of these require some elaboration.

### (e) The Value of Non-Marketed Assets

For the last two decades or so, finding a solution to the problem of valuing life and other non-marketed assets has been a major concern of economists.[29] Although other methods have been postulated,[30] there has

[27] J. F. Morrall, 'A Review of the Record' (1986) 10 Regulation 30, which tabulates a number of risks of fatalities as estimated by American regulatory agencies.

[28] The range of uncertainty relative to each risk, or its confidence level, (e.g. 5% or 10%) is often quoted in the data. For UK government policy on risk assessment generally, see Dept. of Trade and Industry, *Regulation in the Balance: A Guide to Risk Assessment* (1993).

[29] See esp. : M. Jones-Lee, *The Value of Life: An Economic Analysis* (1976); id., *The Economics of Safety and Physical Risk* (1989); and W. K. Viscusi, *Fatal Tradeoffs* (1992).

[30] e.g. for the value of life, some measure of human capital represented notably by lifetime earnings (E. J. Mishan, 'Evaluation of Life and Limb: A Theoretical Approach' (1971) 79 J. Pol. Econ. 706) or that sum reduced by what is spent by the deceased for his own consumption—a method used by courts in assessing damages in fatal accident cases: A. I. Ogus, *Law of Damages* (1973), p. 268. The obvious objection to these approaches is that they cannot apply to individuals who are not active in the labour market: K. A. Clarke and A. I. Ogus, 'What is a Wife Worth?' (1978) 5 Br. J. Law & Soc. 1.

emerged a general preference for a market-orientated 'willingness-to-pay' test: the sum of money which individuals would be willing to pay to avoid the risk of damage to, or destruction of, the asset, if fully informed of the magnitude of the risk.

Suppose that a given activity generates an annual risk of death of 0.0001 for each of a group of 10,000 people; each year it will therefore be expected to cause one death within the group. Suppose further that individuals in the group would, on average, each be prepared to pay £100 to avoid the risk. On aggregate the group would be willing to pay £1 million to prevent one death; and, in this sense, the value of life for this group is taken to be £1 million. We can then use the formula:

$$V = \frac{S}{p}$$

where $V$ is the value of the asset, $S$ the sum the individual is willing to pay to avoid the risk, and $p$ the risk of damage or destruction.

The relevant information may be acquired either explicitly, by questionnaire survey, or implicitly, for example by reference to the difference between wages which are earned in jobs which give rise to a known specific risk and those earned in similar jobs without such risk by individuals with similar characteristics (e.g. training, status, and union membership).[31] It is to be expected that the survey method will generate higher values than the labour market method, because those responding to questionnaires do not have to pay the price they stipulate, and thus may overstate their true demand for protection. This is not, however, conclusively borne out by the evidence.[32] The fact that there is a vast difference between the valuations which emerge from various studies using either method—the range on the value of an individual life is roughly between £200,000 and £5 million (in 1987 terms)[33]—should not necessarily be treated as a matter for concern because the risks and populations studied are not homogeneous. If air travellers value life more than those in motor vehicles, then to achieve allocative efficiency more should be spent to protect them. On the other hand, if that higher value were predominantly a function of the greater wealth and income of air travellers, then distributional considerations might suggest a different policy.[34]

[31] Viscusi, above, n. 29, chs. 3–4.

[32] See the tables in Jones-Lee (1989), above, n. 29, pp. 91–3, which list and compare the values emerging from a number of studies of both types. Although the median value of life from 8 questionnaire surveys was (in 1987 terms) £1,060,000 and thus higher than the median value of £600,000 derived from 21 market studies, the former figure reflected two surveys of air passengers which produced very high values, both over £8 million.

[33] Jones-Lee (1989), above, n. 29, pp. 91–3. For policy purposes, the UK Dept. of Transport adopts (in 1993) a value of about £700,000: M. Jones-Lee, 'Transport Safety: Getting Value for Money' (1993) 4 Cons. Pol. Rev. 196, 200.

[34] Viscusi, above, n. 29, pp. 28–9.

Evaluating human life has understandably dominated studies under-taken in this area, since protection of life is a central goal of much safety legislation. Although in theory the same methods of evaluation can be used for a wide variety of benefits, in practice the data available is limited. In recent years, some work has been done on illness and non-fatal injuries; for example, skin poisoning from insecticide was valued at $761.[35] But in comparison with death, which has an unambiguous meaning for survey respondents, it is difficult to specify morbidity conditions with much precision, and the results are less reliable. For the purposes of environ-mental regulation, studies have also been undertaken on how freedom from pollution is valued by residents, using both the explicit survey method and the implicit market method, the latter involving analysis of residential property prices.[36] The temporal and spatial dimensions of such inquiries are, of course, limited; and quantifying the broader impact of environ-mental disamenity, like many other benefits of regulatory standards, must remain a matter for guesswork.

## (f) Discounting for the Future

Even supposing that the standard-setter were able to give accurate values to the variables in the cost–benefit equation, the major problem of discounting for future effects would still remain. In areas of social regulation concerned with environmental harm and certain diseases, this is particularly important, as the intended benefits extend over a long time period.

The method of discounting is subject to considerable debate, some of which reflects ideological differences.[37] Given that the object is to assess the opportunity cost of the resources spent to achieve the desired benefits, the simplest approach is to use a market-based measure of the cost of capital such as is reflected in the real rates (i.e. after adjustment for inflation) of return on government bonds. This is how economists assume that individuals rationally make decisions between present consumption and saving for the future. While some are prepared to apply it to public cost–benefit analysis, others consider that it fails to capture the 'social' or external benefits of investment, that is, the additional benefits which

[35] W. Evans and W. K. Viscusi, 'Estimation of State-Dependent Utility Functions Using Survey Data' (1991) 73 Rev. Econ. & Stat. 94. This result and others are summarized in Viscusi, above, n. 29, pp. 71–2. For details of a study in which respondents were invited to indicate the value to them of avoiding the risk of 'serious injury' (left undefined), see Jones-Lee (1989), above, n. 29, ch. 4.

[36] For a survey, see R. Cummings, D. Brookshore, and W. Schulze, *Valuing Environ-mental Goods: An Assessment of Contingent Valuation Method* (1986).

[37] See generally Sugden and Williams, above, n. 21, ch. 15; Pearce and Nash, above, n. 21, ch. 9.

accrue to people other than the investor, such as future generations.[38] The criticism acquires particular force in relation to regulatory policies intended to yield benefits at some distant time in the future. If discounted by traditional market-based criteria, the present value of such benefits will be only trivial. For example, at a discount rate of 6 per cent (the rate generally used in recent government policy analysis[39]), the present value of a benefit of £100 million accruing fifty years hence is only £5.43.

For certain regulatory policies, then, a 'social' discount rate is commonly adopted. But there is little consensus on how such a rate should be calculated. We cannot predict the future state of the economy, what alternative technologies will be capable of achieving, and, least of all, what utility future generations will derive from particular assets. In practice, therefore, some degree of arbitrariness inevitably enters into the analysis, especially where the impact of a regulatory programme extends over a lengthy timescale.

### (g) Distributional Considerations

Distributional considerations may affect the cost–benefit model in several ways. In the first place, even if the goal of optimal loss abatement is defined exclusively as an economic goal, the maximization of social welfare, it can be argued that the measure of welfare should explicitly take account of the relative wealth of those who, respectively, incur the costs and receive the benefits of a regulatory measure. This is because, on the traditional assumption of the diminishing marginal utility of wealth, a pound is worth more to a poor person than to a rich person.[40] On this view, it becomes necessary to locate, if only in broad terms, the sections of the community on whom the costs and benefits fall, and adjust the values by some method of weighting.[41]

Secondly, distributional considerations may implicitly intrude into the cost–benefit analysis. As we have seen, the evaluation of non-marketed assets is at best unreliable, at worst wholly arbitrary. Given the latitude of interpretation available to the standard-setter, the values adopted may reflect distributional values. For example, if an activity or product generates a risk of death to low earners, the value attributed to each life saved may be given a heavier weighting.

[38] S. A. Marglin, 'The Social Rate of Discount and the Optimal Rate of Investment' (1963) 77 Q. J. Econ 95.

[39] Dept. of the Environment, *Policy Appraisal and the Environment* (1991), Annex, para. 4.1.2.   [40] Above, p. 25.

[41] Sugden and Williams, above, n. 21, pp. 201–7. An alternative method of incorporating distributional goals into the analysis is to assume the existence of 'demoralization costs' in the population at large incurred as a result of awareness of the infliction of further disadvantages on poorer people: cf. A. I. Ogus, 'Do We Have A General Theory of Compensation?' [1984] Current Legal Prob. 29.

Thirdly, although distributional effects may be ignored in the cost-benefit analysis on the ground that the selection of an appropriate weighting factor is too problematic,[42] nevertheless policy-makers may still require information as to the distributional impact of proposed measures. This is because they wish to adopt only such measures as are consistent with their own conceptions of distributional justice, or only such measures which, given the distributional impact, will prove to be politically acceptable.[43]

### (h) Cost–Benefit Analysis: Conclusions

What emerges from the above discussion is that, in general, costs (with the exception of indirect costs) are easier to quantify than benefits. If the task of the standard-setter is simply to make a crude ordinal judgement, that the benefits of a given standard are greater or less than costs, the consequences are not so serious, since estimates of precise values are not required.[44] If, on the other hand, the idealized goal of optimal loss abatement is to be attempted and a standard set which maximizes the difference between benefits and costs (or equates costs and benefits at the margin), some degree of precision in assessment is important. That leads to a fundamental problem, sometimes referred to as Gresham's law of decision-making: quantifiable effects will tend to dominate cost–benefit analysis even when the analysts recognize that qualitative effects may be more important.[45] Where this occurs there will be a bias against regulation and in favour of market outcomes, because the quantifiable costs will tend to outweigh the quantifiable benefits.[46]

Further, forcing an essentially qualitative effect into a quantitative framework invariably involves some degree of subjective, perhaps ideological, judgement.[47] As we have seen, this enables non-economic public interest goals, such as redistribution, to be incorporated into the analysis. But, at the same time, it can also allow the public interest goals to be subverted by some private interest goals, such as wealth transfers to particular groups able to lobby effectively for a measure which has this consequence.[48] Since the legal framework for decision-making has to accommodate considerable discretion on such questions, accountability for this type of 'regulatory failure' is generally weak.

---

[42] Cf. Sugden and Williams, above, n. 21, pp. 206–7.

[43] For acknowledgement that this forms part of UK government policy analysis, see *Policy Appraisal and the Environment*, above, n. 39, para. 4.11.

[44] Cf. Lave, above, n. 21, p. 28.                    [45] Ibid. p. 32.

[46] D. Kennedy, 'Cost–Benefit Analysis of Entitlement Problems: A Critique' (1981) 33 Stan. LR 387.

[47] S. Kelman, 'Cost–Benefit Analysis: An Ethical Critique' (1981) 5 Regulation 33.

[48] See further below, p. 172.

### 3. COST-EFFECTIVENESS MODELS FOR STANDARD-SETTING

One public interest response to the information problems posed by the idealized goal is for the standard-setter to do the best she can: use what data she is able to obtain (at reasonable cost) and make reasonable guesses for what remains unknown. Another—and one currently favoured by UK regulatory policy-makers[49]—is to quantify only what is genuinely quantifiable by reliable data and simply 'describe' other effects. The ultimate decision is then based not on a precise arithmetical comparison of costs and benefit, but rather on an impressionistic balancing of the information on impact, both quantified and unquantified.

A third possibility is to substitute for the cost–benefit model one which makes fewer informational demands. The term 'cost-effectiveness' is often used to describe these 'second-best' approaches. Cost-effectiveness analysis covers a variety of techniques, most of them concerned to determine the means of accomplishing a given objective at lowest cost, or maximizing the benefits for a given amount.[50] Two main approaches can be distinguished. Under the first, a goal is specified by, for example, an EC Directive or the UK policy-maker—say, to reduce the level of fatal accidents arising from a given activity by 10 per cent—and the task of the standard-setter is then to formulate the standards so as to minimize the costs of achieving that goal.[51] For this purpose, 'costs' can be given different interpretations. As specified in the idealized cost–benefit model, they can extend beyond the direct costs of administration (both to the regulatory agency and to the regulated firms) and of compliance (calculated on an opportunity-cost basis) to indirect social welfare losses. Less ambitiously, the assessment can be confined to direct administrative and compliance costs, calculated on an accounting basis, rather than an opportunity cost basis, i.e. simply aggregating expenditure and capital depreciation.[52]

Under the second approach, the policy-maker specifies the cost—a budgetary limit—and requires the standard-setter to formulate standards so as to maximize the benefits accruing from the use of those resources. As with 'costs' in the first approach, 'benefits' here can be given a broader or narrower meaning. In theory, they could be equated with those assessed in cost–benefit analysis, but, as we have seen, much of the latter involves non-marketed assets which elude easy quantification. Cost-effectiveness analysis, therefore, tends to limit benefits to those which can be assessed on objective criteria, such as reduction in health costs and lost earnings.

---

[49] *Policy Appraisal and the Environment*, above, n. 39, para 4.7.

[50] Lave, above, n. 21, pp. 19–21; Sugden and Williams, above, n. 21, pp. 190–3.

[51] Cf. *Policy Appraisal and the Environment*, above, n. 39, para 4.2.

[52] See generally on the distinction between accounting costs and opportunity costs, Sugden and Williams, above, n. 21, ch. 3.

A practical method of accomplishing the second approach is to allocate the specified budget by appraising sequentially the marginal benefits of different standards.[53] Suppose that the regulatory goal was the abatement of death and personal injury. The first increment of the allocated budget would be 'spent' on a standard which would save most lives; the second on that which would generate the next best gain. The process would be continued until the budgetary limit was reached. At that point, the last increment should give rise to approximately the same amount of benefit across the different standards selected.

These approaches impose fewer informational demands on standard-setters than cost–benefit analysis, but their use does not mean that the problems of quantifying unquantifiables and comparing incommensurables are solved. Rather, the problems remain with the policy-maker, who establishes the parameters of standard-setting, and who is formally responsible for authorizing the standard as a legal requirement. The specified goal or budgetary limit to which the standard-setter must address her analysis may carry assumptions about, say, the value of human life. If it does not, the task of making that evaluation is merely postponed. Thus, when the standard-setter duly provides the information, that a particular set of standards can reduce fatal accidents by 10 per cent or will maximize the benefits arising from expenditure of £10 million, the judgment that those standards should be legally binding contains implicit valuations of matters which in cost–benefit analysis are rendered explicit.

### 4. MANDATORY COST–BENEFIT OR COST-EFFECTIVENESS ANALYSIS

Rational pursuit of public interests goal might imply an application of the models of cost–benefit and cost-effectiveness analysis outlined above, but is there any reason to expect that they will be used in practice? As we shall see later in this chapter, standard-setters may be diverted by considerations of private interest. One reason for the marked shift in government policy in the 1980s away from traditional interventionist measures was the perception that business had been 'over-regulated', a phenomenon which would have been avoided if standard-setters had taken more account of the economic impact of regulation.[54] To remedy the situation, attempts have been made to force government departments to assess systematically the costs of regulatory measures.

---

[53] Lave, above, n. 21, p. 20.

[54] Dept. of Trade and Industry, *Burden on Businesses: Report of a Scrutiny of Administrative and Legislative Requirements* (1985); White Papers: *Lifting the Burden* (1985, Cmnd. 9571); *Building Businesses . . . Not Barriers* (1986, Cmnd. 9794); *Releasing Enterprise* (1988, Cm. 512).

## (a) President Reagan's Executive Order 12,291

A major inspiration for this development in the UK was the obligation imposed by the American Federal Government on regulatory agencies to justify regulatory proposals by cost–benefit analysis.[55] Some experiments to this end had been made by the Nixon, Ford, and Carter Administrations,[56] but the high-water mark was reached with President Reagan's Executive Order No. 12,291 of 1981.[57] This required agencies, before promulgating new regulations, reviewing existing regulations, or developing legislative proposals relating to regulations, to submit a Regulatory Impact Analysis (RIA) for review to the Office of Management and Budget. The requirement was so far-reaching that it merits quotation. Each RIA was to contain

(1) a description of the potential benefits of the rule, including any beneficial effects that cannot be quantified in monetary terms, and the identification of those industries or individuals likely to receive the benefits;

(2) a description of the potential costs of the rule, including any adverse effects that cannot be quantified in monetary terms, and the identification of those likely to bear the costs;

(3) determination of the potential net benefits of the rule, including an evaluation of effects that cannot be quantified in monetary terms;

(4) a description of alternative approaches that could substantially achieve the same regulatory goal at lower cost, together with an analysis of the potential benefits and costs of the alternatives and a brief explanation of the legal reasons why such alternatives, if proposed, could not be adopted; and

(5) unless covered by the description required under paragraph (4) above, an explanation of any legal reasons why the rule cannot be based on the [cost-benefit] requirements.

The reader will be struck by the ambitious character of the RIA requirements; in many respects, they seem to correspond to our idealized model of cost–benefit analysis. Moreover, obliging the agency to demonstrate that the benefits of a measure exceed the costs might be interpreted as indicating that economic goals should prevail over non-economic, particularly distributional, goals.[58] Yet the absence of clear instructions on how 'costs' and 'benefits' should be calculated[59] suggests that the Order

[55] There is explicit acknowledgement of the inspiration in *Lifting the Burden*, above, n. 54, para. 8.2.　　　　[56] For details, see Heimann, above, n. 18, pp. 555–9.

[57] Reprinted in 5 USC § 601, and discussed in Sunstein, above, n. 18, and Heimann, above, n. 18, pp. 559–63.

[58] Sunstein, above, n. 18, pp. 1272–5. However, as he points out (p. 1281), such an interpretation should be rejected on constitutional grounds where the ostensible legislative goal of the regulation was redistributional.

[59] Some general and vague guidelines were issued by the Office of Management and Budget, but it was left to the agencies themselves to develop detailed interpretive criteria: Heimann, above, n. 18, pp. 560–3.

should not be taken entirely at face value. If, for example, 'benefits' are widely construed to include psychic benefits to the community at large from dealing with certain hazards, they can with relative ease be shown to exceed costs, and the cost–benefit analysis becomes little more than a tautologous, *ex post* rationalization.[60]

Order 12,291 is best understood in its political and ideological context. It clearly had rhetorical value in that it reflected the Reagan Administration's sceptical attitude to social regulation and fostered a climate in which cost–benefit analysis was to be both more prominent and more explicit. It has also generated a considerable amount of information which has proved to be beneficial to the process of regulatory reform.[61] Although the legal significance of the Order should not be exaggerated, its formal character has enabled RIAs to be used as evidence in judicial review proceedings instituted to challenge the legality of certain regulatory standards.[62]

### (b) Mrs Thatcher's Compliance Cost Assessments

In 1985, Mrs Thatcher established an Enterprise and Deregulation Unit (EDU) charged with the task, *inter alia*, of reviewing what were perceived to be the undue burdens imposed by social regulation on industry.[63] As part of this exercise, each Government Department was asked to provide: a systematic *ad hoc* account of the impact on business of existing regulations; six-monthly 'forward looks' of all new regulatory proposals to identify possible burdens; and, most significantly, a Compliance Cost Assessment (CCA) in relation to all such proposals.[64]

CCAs are expected to provide the following information:[65]

(1) an outline of the purpose and wider benefits of the measure;
(2) a list of the business sectors affected;
(3) a summary of the total estimated compliance costs of the measure for all affected sectors;
(4) a summary of the total estimated compliance costs of the measure for a 'typical' business in the sectors principally affected;
(5) a description of how any additional costs arising from the measure might affect the competitive position of UK based businesses;
(6) if a different approach would have achieved the objectives of the proposed measure at lower cost, an explanation of why this was rejected.

---

[60] Sunstein, above, n. 18, p. 1276.
[61] Heimann, above, n. 18, pp. 622–54.
[62] e.g. *Donovan* v. *Castle & Cooke Foods Inc.* 692 F 641 (1982), on which see Heimann, above, n. 18, pp. 576–8.
[63] 'The EDU acts in some sense as a proxy for the voice of business within Whitehall': *Building Businesses*, above, n. 54, para. 3.3.
[64] Ibid. ch. 3. Since Nov. 1993, CCAs have also been added to parliamentary bills.
[65] Dept. for Trade and Industry, *Checking the Cost to Business: A Guide to Compliance Cost Assessment* (1992).

CCAs differ from American RIAs in two important respects. First, they are the subject of internal administrative directives and are designed primarily to assist government policy-making. They do not impose any formal constraints on what standard-setters may lawfully do, and there is, therefore, no question of their being used in a judicial process to challenge the 'reasonableness' of regulatory standards. Secondly, Government Departments are not required themselves to engage in cost–benefit analysis.[66] Although some indication of benefits must be given,[67] the focus is on costs, and particularly compliance costs; it would seem that indirect social welfare losses, such as those resulting from reduced competition, are not included.[68] In other words, CCAs are essentially cost-effectiveness exercises. The aim is to

provide scope for improving the balance between costs and benefits. [The] procedure is intended to ensure that all proposals for new regulations to meet the Government's other policy objectives have been properly considered for the requirements they will place on business and that, taking all policy considerations into account, the new regulation is justified.[69]

It is too early to judge the impact of CCAs on UK regulatory policy in general and on standard-setting in particular. Since 1987, a large number of amendments have been made to a variety of regulatory regimes,[70] but it is unclear how far these have been tailored to meet specific cost assessments. Nevertheless, as with the American experience, CCAs have generated a considerable amount of information on particular regulatory regimes.[71] Also, they have been much used by the UK government in the process of negotiating EC Directives at Brussels.

## 5. PRINCIPLES OF STANDARD-SETTING

In pursuit of the public interest goal, the standard-setter must address a number of general issues concerning the nature and characteristics of the regulatory instrument: the type of standard; whether to apply the same

---

[66] Exceptionally, the Health and Safety Executive meets the CCA requirement by providing some cost–benefit analysis, since such analysis is regularly undertaken independently of the CCA initiative: below, p. 186.

[67] The *Guide*, above, n. 65, invites Departments to quantify benefits when appropriate information is available.

[68] Under the original plans, it was envisaged that a 'full scale analysis of the costs and benefits to business, government and the economy as a whole' would be undertaken in special cases: *Building Businesses*, above, n. 54, para. 3.12.

[69] Ibid. para. 3.11.

[70] For summaries, see *Releasing Enterprise*, above, n. 54, Annex 1, and Dept. of Trade and Industry, *Cutting Red Tape for Business: Some Recent and Forthcoming Deregulation Activities* (1991). For further proposals see id. *Deregulation: Cutting Red Tape* (1994).

[71] See e.g. the list of published CCAs in Business Briefing, 5 Apr. 1991, p. 4.

standard to all firms or to differentiate according to individual circumstances; whether to define unlawful conduct by a precise formula or to use broad language allowing for discretion in interpretation; and, if the latter, where and how the discretion is to be exercised. The discussion is structured accordingly.

### (a) Types of Standard

As indicated in Figure 8.1, there is a choice between three types of standard, each representing different degrees of state intervention. The most important variables in exercising that choice are the costs of being informed on the technological means of achieving the regulatory goals and the administrative costs of formulating appropriate standards and monitoring compliance. In principle, firms should be given choice as to how to meet the goals, since this encourages innovation in loss abatement techniques. There is thus a presumption in favour of less interventionist measures. However, the benefits of such measures might be outweighed by the costs of administering them, and/or the costs to firms of acquiring information on loss abatement technology.

At first sight, target standards, which render unlawful the causing of certain harms, might appear to be an attractive option, at least from a cost-effectiveness perspective. The stipulated goal of the regulation (for example, reduction to a certain concentration of pollutant in the environment) can be translated directly into the prohibited consequence, and it is then left to firms to determine the cheapest means of avoiding that consequence. On the other hand, in some areas of regulation (for example pollution or occupational diseases) where the harm is not closely connected in time or space to the activity, the agency costs of determining the causal connection are often very high, as the harm may also result from other activities or conditions. Moreover, the information costs to the firm on determining what quality of performance will ensure compliance with the target standard may also be high, either because account has to be taken of third party activities, or because centralized agencies have better knowledge on the aetiology of the specific harm. Even where these problems do not arise, the firm will generally be liable in tort to the damaged party and the duplication of legal proceedings will be wasteful. In some cases, however, the harm will be thinly spread over a number of victims and the costs of bringing a private action for any one victim may exceed the compensation payable. In such circumstances there is a strong argument for complementing the private right with a public target standard.

Performance (or output) standards are more costly to formulate than target standards, because the standard-setter has to relate different levels in the quality of performance to the regulatory goal. That task may nevertheless be undertaken more cheaply by the standard-setter than by individual firms, as required by target standards, and if firms (or their products) are largely homogeneous there will be significant economies of scale. Further, performance standards can normally be monitored at the firm's place of business and causation problems rarely arise; enforcement costs are therefore lower. The standard imposed on each firm will be less uncertain and therefore legal and other information costs will be reduced.[72]

The principal advantages of specification standards over performance standards[73] relate to administrative costs. It is easier for the standard-setter to predict compliance costs, since these vary little from one firm to another. As regards monitoring, the enforcement agency has simply to verify that the prescribed input has been used by firms, or, in the case of a negative standard, that a prohibited substance or process has not been used. The firms themselves do not face uncertainty as regards either the law or the action necessary to achieve particular outcomes.

Given the technological complexities of inputs, it is often necessary to lay down a series of specification standards to achieve an outcome for which, in comparison, a single performance standard would suffice. But, paradoxically, this may facilitate deterrence. Fixing an appropriate sanction for breach of a performance standard is generally difficult because of the 'deterrence trap': the problem that the fine should reflect the gravity of harm resulting from contravention and be large enough to deter breach, but not so large as to encourage firms to declare themselves insolvent.[74] Since each specification standard constitutes only one component in the aggregate of protective devices, a smaller sanction is appropriate. The aggregation of a multitude of smaller sanctions for a multitude of lesser offences provides a means of avoiding the deterrence trap.[75]

There are, on the other hand, significant disadvantages to specification standards. The fact that the standard is imposed at an earlier stage in the production process implies that the standard-setter has, perhaps inappropriately, a high level of confidence that the mandatory inputs will accomplish the regulatory goal in a cost-effective manner. The prohibition of other inputs induces technological rigidity, since it inhibits firms from innovating in general, and from developing other, cheaper means of meeting regulatory targets in particular. Specification standards become

---

[72] A. I. Ogus, 'Information, Error Costs and Regulation' (1992) 12 Int. Rev. Law & Econ. 411.

[73] For general discussion of the relative merits of specification and performance standards, see: C. Stone, 'The Place of Enterprise Liability in the Control of Corporate Conduct' (1980) 90 Yale LJ 1, 36–43; R. B. Stewart, 'Regulation, Innovation and Administrative Law: A Conceptual Framework' (1981) 69 Calif. LR 1256, 1268–73; J. Braithwaite, 'The Limits of Economism in Controlling Harmful Corporate Conduct' (1982) 16 Law & Soc. Rev. 481, 490–2; Richardson *et al.*, above, n. 2, pp. 37–40.

[74] Above, p. 93.　　　　　　　　　　　　　[75] Braithwaite, above, n. 73, p. 491.

obsolete very rapidly and there is typically a delay before technological changes are reflected in the regulations.[76] These consequences may give rise to major social welfare losses.

It follows that the case for specification standards is weak unless the standard-setter has better access than firms to information concerning the technology of production and unwanted effects, or firms (or their products) are sufficiently homogeneous that innovative activity is unlikely to occur or to generate significant social benefits.

## (b) Differentiated Standards and Optimal Specificity

Standards may be either uniform or differentiated according to region, industry, or firm. Uniform standards are very much cheaper to formulate and enforce, and they are less susceptible to being manipulated to protect private interests. But if the public interest goal is to minimize the sum of the costs arising from a given activity and of the costs of modifying that activity to reduce the harm, both sets of cost may vary according to the circumstances of the firm, its location, or the population affected by the activity. Formulating standards on the basis of 'average' costs will then inevitably lead to some mismatches and welfare losses, and standards should then be differentiated where the benefits of reducing these losses exceed the additional administrative costs of formulation and enforcement.[77] Situations in which this is likely to occur may usefully be classified as particular areas of regulation, general problems transcending areas of regulation, and specific circumstances.

As an example of a particular area of regulation, environmental protection calls for special treatment because the damage costs arising from pollution vary significantly according to the characteristics of a particular region and even within a region. This is because there are large regional differences in the assimilative capacity of watersheds and airsheds, in the desired environmental quality, and in the number of pollution sources.[78]

A general problem which transcends different areas of regulation is that compliance costs can vary considerably according to the period of time over which an activity has taken place.[79] Take, for example, a specification standard requiring certain safety equipment to be installed in a factory. The compliance cost for a firm using alternative equipment will be higher than that for a firm which is in the process of constructing a new plant.

---

[76] Report of the [Robens] Committee on Safety and Health at Work (1972, Cmnd. 5034), para. 29.

[77] See generally: Breyer, above, n. 18, p. 153; Richardson *et al.*, above, n. 2, pp. 49–55; H. Latin, 'Ideal versus Real Regulatory Efficiency: Implementation of Uniform Standards and "Fine-Tuning" Regulatory Reforms' (1985) 37 Stan. LR 1267.

[78] For further discussion of this question, see below pp. 210–11.

[79] P. Huber, 'The Old-New Division in Risk Regulation' (1983) 69 Virginia LR 1025.

Differentiation by means of a 'grandfather clause', which exempts from the standard firms engaged in the regulated activity before a certain date, is not costly to administer and is commonly encountered. It may, however, give rise to indirect social costs:[80] the application of a standard only to 'new' firms may create barriers to their entering a particular market, and thus insulate 'old' firms from competition. It may also discourage innovation (which would deprive the firm of the protection of the grandfather clause) and thus perpetuate the use of outmoded technology.

Many regulated activities may be attended by special circumstances which call for a stricter, or more relaxed, standard than is the norm. For example, the safety measures appropriate for a factory when the manufacturing process is fully operative may be inappropriate for periods of inactivity, when only maintenance work is being carried out. The problem is to find a method of differentiating standards which is neither too cumbersome, because of the huge amount of detail involved, nor too vague.

In addressing this problem, the standard-setter should recognize that there is a spectrum representing different degrees of generality of rule formulation. At one end of the spectrum, she may create a highly precise, perhaps quantitative, rule (e.g. vehicles must be driven at a speed not exceeding 30 m.p.h. in a given area); at the other end, a general rule (e.g. vehicles must be driven at a 'reasonable' speed in urban areas), requiring interpretation by both the actor and the enforcement agency. Because a precise rule eliminates discretion and uncertainty, it reduces the agency's administrative costs and the regulated firm's information costs. On the other hand, its specificity means that it is inflexible and cannot be accommodated to the variety of circumstances to which it must be applied. It is likely to be over-inclusive (deterring more than is optimal in the circumstances) or under-inclusive (deterring less than is optimal in the circumstances). Thus the 30 m.p.h. limit will unduly deter faster driving during times when few pedestrians will be present and when the optimal speed might be 40 m.p.h.; and will insufficiently deter slower driving in icy conditions, when the optimal speed might be 15 m.p.h. A more general rule, which can be interpreted to fit the special circumstances, will avoid these costs arising from mismatch, but is more expensive to administer. In theory, therefore, there is an optimal specificity for any given standard where the administrative costs are approximately equal to the costs of any potential mismatch.[81]

---

[80] Breyer, above, n. 18, pp. 115–16.

[81] I. Ehrlich and R. Posner, 'An Economic Analysis of Legal Rulemaking' (1974) 3 J. Legal Stud. 257; A. I. Ogus, 'Quantitative Rules and Judicial Decision Making', in P. Burrows and C. Veljanovski (eds.), *The Economic Approach to Law* (1981), pp. 210–25.

A related characteristic of legal rules is their complexity and access-
ibility.[82] A precise rule will often be detailed, complex, and less
transparent, thus requiring technical or legal expertise to comprehend and
apply it. A general rule may obviate the need for such expertise, although
predicting how an enforcement agency or a court will interpret its
application to a given situation may require knowledge or experience of
practice and precedent.[83]

### (e) Legal Formulation of Differentiated Standards

It follows from the above discussion that there are various legal methods of
formulating differentiated standards.[84] They raise issues of appropriate
institutional structures and accountability procedures which have already
been the subject of detailed discussion in Chapter 6. Here it will suffice to
summarize the options and the principal arguments.

The first option is to incorporate the different standards into the formal
regulatory code (normally parliamentary legislation or statutory instrument) which governs the activity. This renders the differentiation process
more certain and more open to scrutiny, but it also makes change more
difficult and liable to delay. The second option is for the regulatory code to
contain a general principle, for example that an activity must be conducted
so as not to give rise to an 'unreasonable' risk of injury, or to use the 'best
available techniques not entailing excessive cost' to prevent certain
occurrences. The general principle may be accompanied by guidelines as to
how it is to be interpreted in particular contexts, but it nevertheless
effectively confers on the enforcement agency a broad discretion to
differentiate according to the circumstances. Flexibility is achieved, but the
exercise of discretion is unlikely to be open to public scrutiny, and firms
may be uncertain as to how the differentiation will apply to them.

The third option is to confer power on an agency to create formal
differentiated standards for individual firms or groups of firms. The
technique normally used is a system of permits: the legislation prohibits the
activity unless the firm obtains from the agency a permit which contains
conditions incorporating the appropriate differentiated standard. This
option combines the advantages of both precise rules and discretion: the
rules are well defined and thus facilitate enforcement and compliance; and,
at the same time, they may be tailored to the circumstances of each case.
On the other hand, the system is, of course, very costly to operate
(standards being individually negotiated); and, unless details of the permits

---

[82] D. J. Gifford, 'Communication of Legal Standards, Policy Development and Effective
Conduct Regulation' (1971) 56 Cornell LR 409; C. S. Diver, 'The Optimal Precision of
Administrative Rules' (1983) 93 Yale LJ 65.                    [83] Ogus, above, n. 72.

[84] Cf. Richardson et al., above, n. 2, pp. 40–8; J. Rowan-Robinson, P. Watchman, and C.
Barker, Crime and Regulation: A Study of the Enforcement of Regulatory Codes (1990), pp.
188–92.

are available for public scrutiny, it is vulnerable to manipulation and abuse.

Finally, differentiation can be left to the enforcement stage.[85] The regulatory code contains uniform *de jure* standards, but the agency which has discretion to enforce that code requires compliance only with differentiated *de facto* standards. Here the flexibility is achieved at the cost (to firms) of considerable uncertainty. Courts are reluctant to interfere with the discretion relating to enforcement conferred on agencies,[86] thus raising problems of accountability. This option is also dependent on the agency having the exclusive right to prosecute. If, as is often the case, private prosecutions may be brought, they can be used to enforce the uniform *de jure* standard, and thus subvert the differentiation process.[87]

## 6. PRIVATE INTEREST CONSIDERATIONS

Our analysis of standard-setting has so far assumed an adherence to public interest goals, abstracted from the political environment. But, of course, it does not take place in a vacuum. Whether standards are set centrally or locally, by a legislature or by a regulatory agency, the process is subject to pressure from groups who seek to have their own set of private interests reflected in the law. Furthermore, we cannot ignore the private interests of the standard-setters themselves, since these too can diverge significantly from the public interest goals.

We must therefore consider how the demand from private interests may be met by regulatory standards. Such interests may usefully be classified into those which are external to the standard-setting process—groups which, respectively, incur the costs of, and derive the benefits from, the regulation—and those which are internal, notably those of politicians and bureaucrats.

### (a) External Private Interests

A simple starting point is the prediction that firms and industries will oppose the introduction of standards which will be imposed on them, or at least will invoke arguments for relaxing the stringency of the requirements or their enforcement. Typically, however, the situation is more complex because it is in the interest of some regulated firms to support standards when cast in an appropriate form.[88]

---

[85] Cf. above, pp. 96–7.

[86] While the discretion whether or not to prosecute is not absolute, the court will not in general interfere with policy decisions on how the agency deploys its enforcement resources: *R* v. *Commissioner of the Police of the Metropolis, ex parte Blackburn* [1968] 2 Q.B. 118, 136.

[87] Cf. above, p. 87.

[88] Breyer, above, n. 18, p. 115; R. Hirshhorn, 'Regulating Quality in Product Markets', in D. Dewees (ed.), *The Regulation of Quality* (1983), pp. 76–7.

First, and most obviously, a proposed regulatory standard will benefit firms which, on a voluntary basis, already adhere to it: they will gain protection from competition by firms who are able to price their lower-quality products or services more cheaply. Where the form adopted is that of a specification standard, the anti-competitive effect is enhanced because the proscribed alternative materials or processes used by rival firms may have achieved similar quality at lower cost. Secondly, as we have seen,[89] by the use of 'grandfather clauses' more stringent standards may be applied prospectively to firms not yet undertaking the particular activity. Existing suppliers, subject to more lenient standards, will benefit from this barrier to entry. Thirdly—and this applies particularly to specification standards— adaptation to the technology required by the standard may, because of economies of scale, be cheaper for larger firms than for smaller firms. Standards may thus provide larger firms with a competitive advantage.[90]

Even the assumption that firms will oppose standards which impose costs on them requires some qualification, because, in some instances, those costs can be transferred to others. Compliance with standards may lead to a rise in the price of the goods or service, a reduction in the wages paid to employees, a diminution in the firm's profits, or some combination of these. The variables which determine the outcome in relation to the particular market are the mobility of labour and capital, and the responsiveness of consumers to changes in prices and quality. The issue is too complex to be investigated here,[91] but clearly it can affect the behaviour of private interest groups in relation to standard-setting. If, for example, the main burden falls on wages, we may expect trade unions rather than firms to provide the main opposition.

Groups representing interests which a proposed standard is intended to protect—the ostensible beneficiaries—will predictably campaign for its adoption. In general, however, such action is likely to be less effective than the opposition from groups representing private interests adversely affected. This is because the benefits accruing from standards are typically conferred on more widely spread, and less homogeneous, groups (for example, consumers and environmentalists) than those which bear the costs. In consequence, co-ordinating opposition through lobbying and other such activities tends to be more problematic and costly.[92]

There are, nevertheless, groups other than the ostensible beneficiaries which will profit from the standard and which are not afflicted by the co-ordination problem. As we have just seen, these may include some of the

---

[89] Above, p. 169.

[90] This may be only temporary where the larger firms can adapt more quickly to the new requirements: Hirshhorn, above, n. 88, p. 77.

[91] For discussion, see S. Rea, 'Regulating Occupational Health and Safety', in Dewees, above, n. 88, pp. 127–8.          [92] Above, pp. 70–1.

regulated firms, particularly where the standard generates anti-competitive effects, and to these may be added firms or industries for whose products or services there is an increased demand as a result of the standard. Manufacturers of pollution abatement or safety equipment have an obvious interest in stricter standards in the relevant areas of regulation, and are likely to constitute coherent pressure groups.

### (b) Internal Private Interests

Standards are usually set by bureaucrats within a general framework of principle and policy determined by politicians and/or legislators. Politicians may be assumed to want to maximize their prospects of re-election.[93] At one level, they must be seen to respond directly to the concerns of the median voter in the general electorate. Thus, if a 'crisis' occurs, such as a serious accident, or set of serious accidents, they may be prompted to press for measures which may not be justified on cost–benefit grounds, but which accord with general public sentiment.[94] This may lead to the enactment of relatively strict standards, especially where opposition is muted because the costs will be thinly spread, or concentrated on groups without significant lobbying power.

At another level, and in less dramatic contexts, politicians will seek to placate pressure groups who, by means of informational channels which they command, are able to influence electoral voting behaviour. Given that such groups are likely to represent different private interests, some compromise, reflecting their relative weight, should normally occur.[95] Nevertheless, some unlikely coalitions of divergent interests may emerge. For example, representatives of environmentalists may attribute particular importance to long-term measures, and this will accord with the preferences of existing polluters who seek to have stricter standards applied only prospectively, to new entrants to the industry.[96]

To some extent, the bureaucrats who set standards will have to satisfy the dictates of their political masters. Subject to this, they may be expected to favour regulatory forms which necessitate larger budgetary allocations to their departments and/or add to their personal prestige and standing.[97] One implication of this is a preference for discretionary performance standards requiring expert judgement on technical feasibility and compliance costs.

---

[93] Cf. above, pp. 64–6.                    [94] Above, p. 75.

[95] A. Stone, *Economic Regulation and the Public Interest* (1977), pp. 189–93; C. J. Tuohy, 'Regulation and Scientific Complexity: Decision Rules and Processes in the Occupational Health Arena' (1982) 20 Osgoode Hall LJ 562; W. Magat, A. J. Krupnick, and W. Harrington, *Rules in the Making* (1986), ch. 4.

[96] R. W. Hahn, 'The Political Economy of Environmental Regulation: Towards a Unifying Framework' (1990) 65 Public Choice 25, 27–8.

[97] Cf. above, pp. 68–9.

## 7. THE IMPACT OF EC LAW

### (a) General

The principles and techniques of standard-setting have been profoundly affected by British membership of the European Community and by its legal provisions which have attempted to secure an integrated internal market.[98] Fundamental to the Community and its notion of an integrated market is the freedom of trade between Member States, and from the earliest it was recognized that the profusion of national regulatory regimes might constitute barriers to such trade. For example, manufacturers in State A wishing to sell their products in State B are significantly disadvantaged if they have to satisfy a set of specification standards in State B which result from negotiation between regulators and manufacturers in that jurisdiction, particularly if they also have to satisfy another set of standards in State A. The result is an increase in costs: to the manufacturers, from having to adapt production to different requirements and from additional inventory and distribution expenditure; to enforcement agencies, from duplicating monitoring procedures; and to consumers, from paying higher prices consequential on both the increase to manufacturers' costs and the reduction in competition.[99]

The key provision in the Treaty of Rome is Article 30, which prohibits 'quantitative restrictions on imports and all measures having equivalent effect', although this must be read subject to Article 36 which, under certain conditions,[100] allows Member States to justify such measures on grounds, *inter alia*, of 'public morality, public policy or public security; the protection of health and life of humans, animals or plants'.

The interpretation of these provisions by the European Court of Justice has been robust.[101] Article 30 has been construed to prohibit 'all trading rules enacted by Member States which are capable of hindering directly or indirectly, actually or potentially, intra-Community trade'.[102] 'Public policy' in Article 36 does not encompass the protection of consumers' economic interests,[103] and the Court is alert to discountenance national

---

[98] For general discussions, see: J. Pelkmans, 'Regulation and the Single Market: An Economic Perspective', in H. Siebert (ed.), *The Completion of the Internal Market* (1990), pp. 91–117; G. Majone, 'Market Integration and Regulation: Europe after 1992' (1992) 43 Metroeconomica 131.

[99] P. Cecchini, *The European Challenge: 1992, the Benefits of a Single Market* (1988); M. Emerson *et al.*, *The Economics of 1992: The EC Commission's Assessment of the Economic Effects of Completing the Internal Market* (1988).

[100] In particular that the restriction is proportionate to the risk envisaged from the import.

[101] N. Reich, *Internal Market and Diffuse Interests* (1990), ch. 2; S. Weatherill and P. Beaumont, *EC Law* (1993), chs. 15–16.

[102] *Procureur du Roi* v. *Dassonville* [1974] 2 CMLR 436, 453–4.

[103] *Kohl* v. *Ringelhan* [1985] 3 CMLR 340.

measures grounded on the 'protection of health' but designed to insulate domestic producers from competition.[104]

Article 30 must be considered an instrument for *negative* integration of the market. It prohibits national regulatory measures which constitute barriers to trade and allows such offending measures to be challenged in the courts. But it does nothing positive to promote the approximation or harmonization of national standards. Subject to the haphazard and uncertain impact of challenges in the courts, the government of a Member State which is politically sensitive to pressure from national industrial interests cannot realistically be expected voluntarily to dismantle or adjust regulatory regimes unless it is assured that other governments will do the same. Thus some form of centrally dictated *positive* integration is called for. The same need arises in relation to measures which are governed by Article 36: to the extent that, for example, national regulatory systems protecting health can be integrated, freedom of trade can be increased.

In broad terms, two options are available.[105] The first, which was favoured in the period up to 1985, involves an ambitious attempt by the centralized European authorities to formulate fully harmonized standards which would replace national systems. The second, which represents the current preferred policy, relies much less on harmonization and instead focuses on the mutual recognition of national standards. The discussion is divided accordingly.

### (b) Harmonization of Standards

A number of harmonization programmes have been undertaken in accordance with the first approach and where successfully completed they have, of course, been binding on the UK government which has had to adapt its regulatory systems in consequence. The approach has important implications for the type of standards which are adopted. The process of harmonization is thwarted if Member States lack confidence that the standards emerging would be equally applicable across the Community. The Commission, which has primary responsibility for securing compliance with European instruments, can in practice operate only on the basis of reports received from national enforcement agencies.[106] The problem of unequal compliance can be mitigated if the accountability of these agencies relates to standards that are objective in character. This would suggest a reluctance to adopt harmonized target standards (for example, that a

---

[104] *Commission* v. *United Kingdom* [1982] 3 CMLR 497.

[105] J. Pelkmans, 'The New Approach to Technical Harmonization and Standardization' (1987) 25 J. Common Market Stud. 249. For the institutional implications, see above, pp. 100–4.

[106] For general discussion of this problem, see S. Weatherill, 'Reinvigorating the Development of Community Product Safety Policy' (1991) 14 J. Cons. Pol. 171.

product should not create an 'undue' risk of personal injury), except where such standards are easily quantifiable (as with some environmental ambient standards); and a preference for specification and performance standards which confer much less discretion on enforcement agencies.

Harmonization programmes can generate considerable welfare gains: in particular, there are scale economies in having a single set of standards, and competition is enhanced. But, as became increasingly apparent when progress on the programmes faltered, there are theoretical and practical difficulties inherent in the approach. As regards theory, harmonization presupposes a homogeneity of preferences across the Community.[107] The formulation of standards involves, as we have seen, a trade-off between their costs and their benefits, the latter reflecting the values that citizens in general attach to, say, a cleaner environment or the reduced risk of personal injury. But there may be a significant divergence between the values of these benefits in the different Member States. A set of harmonized specification standards may also lead to neutral 'Euro-products' replacing the rich diversity of national cultures and traditions.[108] In the light of the welfare losses arising from over-reaching differences in national preferences, full[109] harmonization may be undesirable, at least in some areas of regulation.

Even where full harmonization is desirable, its attainment is hindered by practical difficulties.[110] Until the Treaty of Rome was amended by the Single European Act, unanimity in the Council of Ministers was required for the issuing of Directives, the primary instrument for harmonization measures.[111] The private interests which profited from the anti-competitive character of some national regulation could exert influence on their governments to exploit the opportunity this created for strategic voting behaviour, and thus thwart progress. Delay is, in any event, inevitable, given the immensity of the Commission's task in formulating detailed standards governing technologically complex processes and products. The specification standards for tractors alone required twenty years' negotiation and twenty-five separate Directives, before the work was complete.[112]

---

[107] Above, pp. 100–1.

[108] Weatherill and Beaumont, above, n. 101, pp. 456–7; and see, more generally, G. Majone, 'Preservation of Cultural Diversity in a Federal System: The Role of the Regions', in M. Tushnet (ed.), *Comparative Constitutional Federalism* (1990), ch. 3.

[109] Lesser forms of harmonization are possible, e.g. : 'partial harmonization' (Community law governs interstate transactions but Member States may impose different controls on domestic products) or 'optional harmonization' (interstate suppliers may choose to comply with either Community standards or the national standards imposed in the importing State). See E. Rehbinder and R. Stewart, *Environmental Protection Policy* (1985), pp. 7–9.

[110] A. Dashwood, 'Hastening Slowly: The Community's Path Towards Harmonization', in H. Wallace, W. Wallace, and C. Webb (eds.), *Policy Making in the EC* (1983), pp. 288–92.

[111] Treaty of Rome, Art. 100.        [112] Pelkmans, above, n. 98, p. 99.

There remains, finally, the problem of enforcement: national agencies must be educated in, and adapt their monitoring techniques to, a new set of standards, which may differ significantly as regards style and content from those to which they are accustomed and for which they have developed expertise and experience.

### (c) Limited Harmonization, Mutual Recognition, and Competitive Regulation

Dissatisfaction with the slow progress of the harmonization programme combined with a general scepticism of its appropriateness resulted in a fundamental change to Community policy. The reorientation was aided by a highly significant legal development.[113] In the *Cassis de Dijon* case,[114] the European Court of Justice had indicated that, pending the introduction of common Community rules, it was for the Member States to regulate the quality of products. Differences in regulatory regimes were not contrary to Community Law so long as they were

necessary in order to satisfy mandatory requirements relating in particular to the effectiveness of fiscal supervision, the protection of public health, the fairness of commercial transactions and the defence of the consumer.[115]

Nevertheless, if a product had been manufactured and marketed in one Member State in accordance with its national standards, unless there were 'exceptional circumstances' its importation into another Member State could not be prohibited on the ground that it failed to satisfy the national standards of the latter. In other words, recognising by implication the relative failure of the harmonization programme, the Court had admitted a policy of national regulation; but to harness that policy to market integration, it had also adumbrated a principle of mutual recognition.

The new approach to integration, as it was articulated in 1985,[116] involved four distinct, but related, strategies.[117] First, harmonization by means of Community Directives was now to be limited to 'essential safety requirements (or other requirements in the general interest)'. Secondly, to meet these requirements, Member States could continue to use and develop their own sets of national standards and it was to be presumed that such standards satisfied the requirements and thus should be the subject of mutual recognition. Thirdly, to facilitate mutual recognition, information

---

[113] Weatherill and Beaumont, above, n. 101, ch. 17.
[114] *Rewe-Zentrale AG* v. *Bundesmonopolverwaltung für Branntwein* [1979] 3 CMLR 494.
[115] Ibid. p. 509.
[116] Commission White Paper, *Completing the Internal Market*, COM (85) 310; Council Resolution of 7 May 1985 on a New Approach to Technical Harmonization and Standards (1985) OJ C1361/1.
[117] Cf. Pelkmans, above, n. 105, pp. 253–7. See also N. Burrows, 'Harmonization of Technical Standards: Reculer Pour Mieux Sauter' (1990) 53 Modern LR 597.

on national draft regulations should be circulated among Member States—this was already mandatory under a Directive of 1983.[118] Fourthly, sets of European standards were to be promoted through the activities of expert committees, notably CEN (European Standardization Committee) and CENELEC (European Standardization Committee for Electrical Products). Such standards were, however, to remain voluntary in the sense that, to meet the European 'essential requirements', trans-frontier traders would be free to comply either with the European standards or with relevant national standards.

The new approach has had a profound impact on the nature of standards, at both European and national levels. In terms of the spectrum portrayed at the beginning of this chapter,[119] it has pushed both systems towards forms involving lower degrees of intervention and has thus contributed to the general deregulation movement.[120] The Directives which impose harmonized solutions to the 'essential requirements' are cast in the form of framework legislation and thus constitute target standards.[121] The principle of mutual recognition, according to which trans-frontier traders may choose between European and national standards, goes some way towards replacing traditional quality-control regulation by information regulation.[122] The products lawfully marketed on the basis that they comply with either European (e.g. CEN) or national specifications will normally bear a certification or marking to that effect. Such certification or marking constitutes a signal to consumers as to the quality of the product, and thus enables them effectively to choose between different quality regimes. In short, the approach promotes competition between different national (and European) standards systems.[123]

Such competition itself creates a momentum for deregulation within national systems. As firms appreciate that they will not succeed in maintaining protection from external competitors by means of national standards, they will exert pressure on their national governments to reduce the costs arising from those standards and thus render their prices more attractive to consumers.

Compared with its predecessor, the new approach has obvious advantages. It substantially reduces the administrative burden on the Commission of formulating fully harmonized standards, and the problems, notably that

---

[118] Directive 83/189. *Inter alia* this enables the Commission to request a moratorium of 1 year on the implementation of the draft regulations.          [119] Above, p. 151.

[120] A. McGee and S. Weatherill, 'The Evolution of the Single Market—Harmonisation or Liberalisation' (1990) 53 Modern LR 578, 584–5.

[121] For examples, see below, pp. 203 and 209.

[122] On the latter, see above, pp. 132–8.

[123] Majone, above, n. 98 pp. 140–6. See also J. Kay and J. Vickers, 'Regulatory Reform: An Appraisal', in G. Majone (ed.), *Deregulation or Re-regulation? Regulatory Reform in Europe and the United States* (1990), pp. 239-44.

of delay, resulting from the need to reach unanimity for the promulgation of Directives (the Single European Act in any event substituted a qualified majority for this requirement in relation to most areas of regulation).[124] The task of enforcement is facilitated: national agencies are predominantly concerned with monitoring their own national standards or ensuring that products have been certified as conforming to other national (or European) standards. The approach also accommodates heterogeneity in citizen preferences, since diversity between such preferences can be reflected in different national regimes. Indeed, the envisaged competition between regulatory systems should induce standard-setters to meet the preferences more efficiently.[125]

There are, nevertheless, some disadvantages and costs which flow from abandoning the pursuit of full harmonization.[126] There are diseconomies of scale in the existence of multiple regulatory systems. Also the new approach cannot deal effectively with trans-frontier externalities, that is, where the consequences of a national regulatory regime reflecting citizen preferences in one Member State have a negative impact on citizens in another Member State. Nor is it necessarily to be assumed that competition between regulators will enhance welfare. For such competition to be effective, consumers in choosing between products complying with different regimes must be able to evaluate the relevant cost-quality trade-offs. A failure to do so may result in a 'race to the bottom': to attract consumers by lower prices, producers will choose to comply with the most lenient (and therefore the least costly) of the regulatory regimes available to them.[127]

[124] See now Treaty of Rome, Art. 100A.
[125] Kay and Vickers, above, n. 123, p. 244.
[126] Majone, above, n. 98, pp. 142–6.
[127] McGee and Weatherill, above, n. 120, loc. cit.; O. Brouwer, 'Free Movement of Foodstuffs and Quality Requirements; Has the Commission Got It Wrong?' (1988) 25 Common Market LR 237. For theoretical analysis, see G. Akerlof, 'The Market for "Lemons"; Qualitative Uncertainty and the Market Mechanism' (1970) 84 Q. J. Econ. 488, and above, p. 132.

# 9

# Standards: Specific Regulatory Regimes

Regulatory regimes involving the imposition of standards cover a very wide range of industrial and commercial activity and seek to protect an equally wide range of interests. The particular regimes which form the subject-matter of this chapter—occupational health and safety (Section 1), consumer products (Sections 2–4), and environmental pollution (Section 5)—have been selected on the basis of two principal considerations. On the one hand, they share the common characteristic of political and economic importance; they are among the most widely discussed of regulatory regimes. On the other hand, they differ significantly in so far as the phenomena which they control give rise to markedly divergent problems of market failure. In the case of occupational health and safety, there is a strong existing market relationship between the creator of the risk, the employer, and the potential victims, the employees, who form a largely homogeneous group and whose bargaining strength may be enhanced by membership of trade unions. At the other extreme is environmental protection, where there is normally no market relationship between the polluters and their victims, who are typically numerous and heterogeneous and therefore unlikely to constitute a coherent pressure group. The problem of product quality and safety lies somewhere between these two extremes: consumers often have a market relationship with producers but are less well-placed than employees to negotiate standards, both because of the diversity of their preferences and the difficulty and cost of effective organisation.

### 1. OCCUPATIONAL HEALTH AND SAFETY

### (a) General

The control of risks arising at the workplace occupies a special position among regulatory regimes. It has a long and well-documented history[1] and has served as a model for other systems of social regulation. Most obviously, this was the case in the nineteenth century, as the pioneering

[1] M. W. Thomas, *The Early Factory Legislation: A Study in Legislative and Administrative Evolution* (1948); H. P. Marvel, 'Factory Regulation: A Reinterpretation of Early English Experience' (1977) 20 J. Law & Econ. 379; W. G. Carson, 'The Conventionalisation of Early Factory Crime' (1979) 7 Int. J. Soc. Law 37; P. Bartrip and P. Fenn, 'The Administration of Safety: The Enforcement Policy of the Early Factory Inspectorate 1844–64' (1980) 58 Pub. Admin. 87.

attempts at controlling working conditions in factories and mines exerted a deep influence on the development of British regulatory law and institutions. Its impact on more recent developments has been no less remarkable. A comprehensive appraisal of occupational health and safety law in the early 1970s by the Robens Committee[2] not only led to major reforms in the system of regulating workplace risks, but also inspired a new approach to standard-setting generally.

In the last chapter, we identified optimal 'loss abatement' as the public interest economic goal of regulatory standards. In the context of occupational risks to health and safety, this becomes the optimal level of care, where the marginal benefits of the precautions are equal to the marginal costs. The optimal level of care in a given situation may theoretically be determined by reference to an idealized labour market model.[3]

According to this model, employers will agree to provide their employees with, *inter alia*, a combination of a certain level of care and a certain level of wages in return for their work. Assuming perfect competition in the labour market and perfect information regarding risks and their consequences, that combination will be equal to the marginal value to the employer of the employees' work. The relative levels of care and wages will thus reflect how the employees themselves value the benefits of care; some will prefer higher wages and lower care while others will opt for higher care and lower wages. On the given assumptions, as well as the absence of significant externalities, the level of care supplied under such an agreement will be optimal.

The assumptions of the model are, of course, rarely, if ever, fully met.[4] Individual employees often have scant knowledge of the risks involved in particular jobs[5] and even if sufficiently informed cannot be assumed to make 'rational' decisions.[6] There are major cultural and institutional obstacles to the competitiveness of labour markets.[7] In addition, industrial accidents and diseases give rise to some significant externalities including,

[2] Report of the Committee on Safety and Health at Work (1972, Cmnd. 5034).
[3] Cf. W. Y. Oi, 'On the Economics of Industrial Safety' (1974) 38 Law & Contemp. Prob. 669; W. T. Dickens, 'Occupational Safety and Health Regulation and Economic Theory', in W. Darity (ed.), *Labour Economics: Modern Views* (1982), ch. 5.
[4] Cf. S. Rea, 'Regulating Occupational Health and Safety', in D. Dewees (ed.), *The Regulation of Quality* (1983), ch. 5.
[5] A distinction may nevertheless be drawn between workers starting a job who do not have requisite knowledge and those who gain knowledge through work experience. The more experienced worker may then demand a higher level of safety, and the employer will have an incentive to provide this because the training investment in such a worker is lost if he is injured or quits the job: W. K. Viscusi, J. M. Vernon, and J. E. Harrington, *Economics of Regulation and Antitrust* (1992), ch. 22.                    [6] Cf. above, p. 52.
[7] In particular, some assert that there is segmentation into a 'primary' and 'secondary' labour market, those 'trapped' in the latter being employed in jobs which are both less well-paid and riskier: J. King, *Labour Economics* (2nd edn., 1990), pp. 147–53.

notably, the costs borne by the National Health Service and the social security system. Nor does the model take account of distributional goals.[8] These may, for example, imply some minimum standard of safety and some minimum level of income, irrespective of market outcomes. Pursuit of distributional goals may nevertheless be problematic. An employer may be able to raise safety standards only by reducing wages, and if he is not permitted to do the latter he may have to discharge some employees.

### (b) Regulatory Strategies

If the unregulated market is unlikely to generate optimal standards of occupational health and safety, how should standard-setters tackle this goal? We may identify, in broad terms, two different strategies. Under the first, which we may call the *agency approach*, an independent, public agency is entrusted with the task of determining conclusively the standards which, in its expert view, will correspond to the optimal level of care in the particular workplace circumstances. In theory, it does this by acquiring sufficient information to 'mimic' the idealized labour-market model outlined above, with or without adjustment for distributional considerations. Thus, it attempts to predict what level of care would have been agreed between an employer and 'average', fully informed, employees, operating in perfectly competitive markets. To eliminate externalities, employees would be assumed to bear the full costs of sickness or injury.

Under the alternative, which we will refer to as the *quasi-market approach*, the primary responsibility for formulating standards necessary for the optimal level of safety is cast on the employer, but in discharging that responsibility she must provide full information to, and negotiate with, representatives of the employees subject to the risks. The independent agency plays only a residual role, that of scrutinizing the standards emerging from these processes to verify that they are consistent with the goal of optimal safety, and of enforcing them, should that prove to be necessary. In other words, this approach seeks to foster market-type solutions, so far as they are feasible, and external, interventionist standards are substituted only when such solutions are presumed to fail.

### (c) The Agency Approach

The predominant tradition of occupational risk regulation both in Britain and elsewhere[9] can be identified with the agency approach. When the Robens Committee reported in 1972, there were seven agencies responsible

---

[8] For fuller discussion, see Rea, above, n. 4, pp. 127–8.

[9] See, for the USA, J. Mendeloff, *Regulating Safety: An Economic and Political Analysis of Occupational Safety and Health Policy* (1979); for Canada, G. B. Reschenthaler, *Occupational Health and Safety in Canada* (1979); and for a comparative survey, W. Szubert, 'Safety and Health at Work', International Encyclopedia of Comparative Law, xv, ch. 7 (1983).

for nine separate regulatory regimes, each containing a complex network of detailed standards.[10] The great majority of these standards were formulated in statutory instruments following consultation with, and advice from, the relevant agencies, special committees, employers' representatives, and trade unions. The content combined a huge number of performance standards, attempting to cover 'contingency after contingency' and resulting in 'a degree of elaboration, detail and complexity that deters even the most determined reader',[11] with considerable reliance on specification standards, leaving employers with little or no choice as to the method of compliance.

A few provisions may be selected to illustrate the approach. Take first the standards governing the lighting of workplaces. It might have been thought relatively unproblematic to require that employers provide illumination adequate for the work to be undertaken, but without subjecting workers to glare. The Factories (Standard of Lighting) Regulations, instead, provided that

The general illumination over those parts of the factory where persons are regularly employed shall be not less than 6 foot candles measured in the horizontal position at a level of 3 feet above the floor

and

where any source of artificial light in the factory is less than 16 feet above the floor level, no part of the source of the lighting fitting having a brightness greater than 10 candles per square inch shall be visible to persons normally employed within 100 feet of the source, except where the angle of elevation from the eye to the source or part of the fitting as the case may be exceeds 20°.[12]

Some specification standards were remarkable not only for their pedantry but also for their foreclosure of other possibilities of fulfilling the regulatory goal by means more suitable to the employer's working system (and thus less costly) or by alternative technologies. For example, the Pottery (Health and Welfare) Special Regulations insisted that

on each day between 12 noon and 2 p.m., at such time as the number of persons in the workroom is expected to be least, all clay scraps shall be removed from those parts of the floors of potters shops on which persons are liable to tread;[13]

and agricultural workers were not allowed to use ladders with wooden rungs if, inter alia, 'the grain thereof does not run lengthwise', or if

the rungs are not fixed into the stiles by rabbet, notch or mortise, and (unless tie-rods are fitted not more than 610 millimetres from each end of the ladder and not

---

[10] Robens Report, above, n. 2, App. 6.
[11] Robens Report, above, n. 2, para. 29.
[12] S R & O 1941/94, Regs. 2(a) and 3(a).   [13] SI 1950/65, Reg. 18(3)(f).

more than 2.44 metres apart throughout its length) are not through-tenoned and wedged in the stiles.[14]

The defects of this approach are apparent. Standards such as those cited above may have been justified by reference to limited cost-effectiveness criteria, in that the benefits of eliminating or reducing the particular risks envisaged would doubtless normally exceed the expenditure on compliance, but for several reasons they may have failed to satisfy the dictates of a broader cost–benefit appraisal.[15]

In the first place, given the specificity and complexity of the standards, the information costs for employers and the costs to the agency in administering and monitoring the rules were high. Secondly, in relation to specification standards, employers were prevented from fulfilling the regulatory goals by cheaper methods. Admittedly, the regulations routinely provided for certificates of exemption from the standards where the agency was satisfied that they were 'not necessary for the protection of the persons employed' or 'their application [was] impracticable in the circumstances';[16] but the process of obtaining such exemption would itself, of course, be costly. Thirdly, the individual standards might rapidly become obsolete as a result of technological developments either in the industrial processes or in the means of combating the risks; and amendment to the statutory instruments to accommodate these developments or to provide for newly perceived risks was an expensive and lengthy process. Finally, the external, centralized character of the system meant that there was little incentive for the principal actors, the employers and employees themselves, to assess the risks resulting from the working conditions and the most appropriate ways of dealing with them.

## (d) Private Interest Explanations

If, and to the extent that, the agency approach gave rise to regulatory failure, some explanation may be sought by reference to private interest considerations. A system in which highly detailed standards were formulated and enforced by a centralized agency necessarily required substantial resources to be allocated to that institution, a phenomenon which accords with the hypothesis that the personal interest of bureaucrats is best served by policies which maximize the budget available to them.[17]

Regard may also be had to the private interests of the firms subjected to the standards and their employees. As a broad generalization, it may be predicted that the typical package of detailed standards imposed under the agency approach benefited large firms (and their employees) at the

[14] Agriculture (Ladders) Regulations SI 1957/1385, Reg. 3(2), as amended.
[15] Cf. Robens Report, above, n. 2, paras. 28–9 and 138.
[16] See e.g. the Pottery Regulations, above, n. 13, Reg. 5.
[17] Above, p. 68.

expense of smaller firms (and their employees). The differential impact occurs because the ratio of compliance costs to output is higher for the smaller firms.[18] The widespread use of specification standards would enhance this effect to the extent that the prescribed mode of compliance is modelled on the typical practices of larger firms. Moreover, the cost of obtaining an exemption certificate, which permits the application of some alternative standards, is lower for larger firms, since the same cost is incurred however large the number of employees and thus irrespective of the size of output.

The prediction that the agency approach may engender anti-competitive consequences by protecting larger firms derives some empirical support from studies of the American system of occupational health and safety regulation.[19]

### (e) The Quasi-Market Approach

The new system recommended by the Robens Committee and largely implemented by the Health and Safety at Work Act 1974[20] may be seen to correspond, in many respects, with the quasi-market approach.[21] Although the system continues to be administered by a central agency, the Health and Safety Commission (HSC), it is less 'independent' than its predecessors in that its members are nominated by the CBI and the TUC, as well as the government and local authorities. The policy of encouraging consensual solutions to safety problems is furthered by the provisions in the Act for the creation, in individual firms, of safety representatives (appointed by recognized trade unions) and safety committees. The employer is under a statutory duty to consult any such representatives

with a view to the making and maintenance of arrangements which will enable him and his employees to cooperate effectively in promoting and developing measures to ensure the health and safety at work of the employees, and in checking the effectiveness of such measures;

and the safety committee has the function, *inter alia*, of reviewing those measures.[22] To counter the problem of information deficits which

---

[18] Above, p. 72.

[19] See esp. A. P. Bartel and L. G. Thomas, 'Direct and Indirect Effects of Regulation: A New Look at OSHA's Impact' (1985) 28 J. Law & Econ. 1, and 'Predation through Regulation: The Wage and Profit Effects of the Occupational Safety and Health Administration and the Environmental Protection Agency' (1987) 30 J. Law & Econ. 239.

[20] The new regime is replacing the older legislation only gradually.

[21] For general evaluative overviews, see: G. K. Wilson, *The Politics of Safety and Health: Occupational Safety and Health in the United States and Great Britain* (1985), chs. 5–6; R. Baldwin, 'Health and Safety at Work: Consensus and Self-Regulation', in R. Baldwin and C. McCrudden (eds.), *Regulation and Public Law* (1987), ch. 7.

[22] Health and Safety at Work etc. Act (hereafter HSWA) 1974, s. 2(6) and 2(7). See further The Safety Representatives and Safety Committee Regulations, SI 1977/500.

constitute a major obstacle to the pure market model, the employer is bound to make available to safety representatives information within his knowledge which is necessary to enable them to fulfil their functions;[23] and this is complemented by the employer's general[24] and specific[25] duties to provide employees with adequate information concerning the risks and the precautions which should be taken to control them.

The procedures, style, and substance of standard-setting have changed dramatically. The principal parliamentary legislation now contains only broad target standards, for example, 'the provision and maintenance of plant and systems of work that are, so far as is reasonably practicable, safe and without risks to health'.[26] As interpreted by the courts,[27] this implies a level of care which is consistent with optimal loss abatement. What is necessary to comply with the skeletal statutory duty is then typically fleshed out in other measures: statutory instruments (SIs), Authorized Codes of Practice (ACOPs), and guidance notes.

SIs are formally made by the Secretary of State and are laid before Parliament, but they generally result from an HSC initiative; and their content, together with that of a relevant ACOP, is the result of analysis of costs and benefits undertaken by the Health and Safety Executive (HSE), the body responsible for enforcing the 1974 Act, and discussion and negotiation between the HSE and representatives of both sides of industry.[28] Increasingly, too, they must conform to, and are thus influenced by, EC Directives.[29]

ACOPs provide in non-legal language a commentary on the SIs and practical guidance on how the regulations apply to different circumstances and what alternative methods may be adopted to comply with them. They are issued by the HSC, although the consent of the Secretary of State must first be obtained. An ACOP provision may be cast in the form either of a specification or of a performance standard. But in both cases it is only voluntary. This is because the failure to observe the provision does not itself give rise to liability. Rather, if the provision is relevant to a formal requirement or prohibition (normally contained in an SI), the failure is regarded as proof of the contravention of the requirement or prohibition unless it can be shown that compliance was achieved by other means.[30]

Guidance notes are sometimes issued by the HSC (or HSE) to provide

---

[23] The Safety Representatives and Safety Committee Reg. 7(2), which lists some exceptions.                                         [24] HSWA 1974, s. 2(2)(c).

[25] e.g. Control of Substances Hazardous to Health Regulations, SI 1988/1657, Reg. 12.

[26] HSWA 1974, s. 2(2)(a).

[27] See e.g. Austin Rover Group v. Her Majesty's Inspector of Factories [1990] 1 AC 619, 625–7, per Lord Goff.                                [28] Baldwin, above, n. 21, p. 138.

[29] Particularly Framework Directive 89/392. See generally on the EC dimension E. Szyszczak, '1992 and the Working Environment' [1992] J. Soc. Welfare Law 3.

[30] HSWA 1974, s. 17, and see West Cumberland By Products Ltd. v. DPP [1988] RTR 391.

information to employers. Like voluntary codes of practice, developed in particular branches of industry or even at individual plants, they have no formal legal significance.

### (f) Standard-setting under the Quasi-Market Approach

To see how the new institutional structure has affected standard-setting, we need to examine some examples. For this purpose, it is helpful to distinguish between what may loosely be described as 'regular risks' and 'special risks'.

*Regular risks* are those which are frequently encountered and which pose no special information problems for the standard-setter. In relation to such risks, employers, safety representatives, and safety committees can normally acquire relevant information at relatively low cost, and can be expected to formulate standards which are appropriate for the local circumstances—including the workforce demand for safety—more cheaply than a centralized agency. Regulatory forms which allow for considerable flexibility in their application are therefore likely to be preferable.

The new approach is intended to facilitate decentralized flexibility. To illustrate this, we may take the current provisions governing two risks the regulation of which we used as examples of the agency approach. As regards illumination of workplaces, the relevant SI requires only that 'every workplace shall have suitable and sufficient lighting';[31] and the precise quantitative standards prescribed in the old Standard of Lighting Regulations are avoided in the provisions of the relevant ACOP:[32] 'lighting should be sufficient to enable people to work, use facilities and move from place to place safely and without experiencing eye-strain . . .' and 'dazzling lights and annoying glare should be avoided.'

Similarly, to alleviate the risks arising from clay scraps left on the floors of potters' shops, and as an amplification of the general SI requirement that 'every employer shall ensure that the exposure of employees to substances hazardous to health is either prevented or, where this is not reasonably practicable, adequately controlled',[33] the specific ACOP governing the Control of Substances Hazardous to Health in the Production of Pottery does not insist on a rigid timetable but simply indicates that 'scraps and spillages should be cleaned *regularly*'.[34]

The treatment of *special risks*, that is, those which potentially may give rise to particularly drastic consequences or those for which information is less readily available or controversial, is not so easily accommodated within the quasi-market approach. There are at least three arguments here

[31] Workplace (Health, Safety and Welfare) Regulations, SI 1992/3004, Reg. 8(1).
[32] ACOP on Workplace Health, Safety and Welfare (1992), paras. 58–9.
[33] Control of Substances Hazardous to Health Regulations, SI 1988/1657, Reg. 7(1).
[34] (1990), para. 70 (my italics).

for a greater degree of intervention by centralized agencies: first, economies of scale can be achieved by those agencies accumulating and processing the information; secondly, agreements between employers and employees may be harder to reach, especially where there is some uncertainty regarding the nature of the risk; and, thirdly, the risks may affect third parties—in other words, there are significant externalities. A regulatory framework which qualifies consensualism by some reliance on the more traditional use of detailed specification and performance standards is therefore to be expected.

The provisions governing the control of hazardous substances may serve as an example. The Control of Substances Hazardous to Health Regulations include some negative specification standards: the use of some substances is prohibited absolutely or for certain purposes; and maximum exposure limits are prescribed for others.[35] One of the problems of specifications standards is that they create no incentives for employers to reduce further a given risk or to devise cheaper means of meeting a risk.[36] The problem is met in these Regulations by subjecting the employer to an overriding performance standard. The employer must, in any event, provide 'adequate' control of hazardous substances; and where maximum exposure limits are prescribed, 'adequate' means not merely complying with those limits, but also reducing the level of exposure 'so far as is reasonably practicable'.[37]

This control system may thus be interpreted as a combination of uniform minimum (specification) standards, set by the centralized agency on the basis both of its accumulated expertise and knowledge and of the tripartite consultation processes, with variable performance standards, determined by reference to localized circumstances. How then are employers and employees induced to achieve localized optimal levels of safety? An answer lies in the SI requirement of risk assessment:

an employer shall not carry on any work which is liable to expose any employees to any substance hazardous to health unless he has made a suitable and sufficient assessment of the risks created by that work to the health of those employees and of the steps that need to be taken to meet the requirements of these Regulations.[38]

The analysis so far suggests that the Health and Safety at Work Act 1974 provides a sound framework for the pursuit of public interest goals but

---

[35] SI 1988/1657, Reg. 4(1) and Sched. 2, and Reg. 7(4) and Sched. 1, respectively.
[36] Cf. above, p. 167.                                    [37] SI 1988/1657, Reg. 7(4).
[38] Ibid. Reg. 6(1). See also Management of Health and Safety at Work Regulations, SI 1992/2051, Reg. 3 (and the ACOP on these (1992), paras. 3–26). For detailed guidelines on how the assessments should be carried out and their content, see ACOP on the Control of Substances Hazardous to Health (1988), paras. 11–24; and for carcinogenic substances, see ACOP on the Control of Carcinogenic Substances (1988), paras. 6–7.

some caution needs to be exercised before any such laudatory conclusion is reached.[39]

One specific and controversial issue relates to the choice between safer working conditions and requiring employees to wear or use suitable protective personal equipment or clothing.[40] The latter option may be a substantially less costly method of meeting the risk. Nevertheless, under provisions currently in force, to provide adequate protection against risks to health the employer is bound to use means *other than* personal protective equipment, unless the requisite degree of protection by such other means is not technically feasible.[41] It may, of course, be the case that the administrative costs of verifying that the appropriate personal equipment is used outweigh the benefits of this form of protection, but the clear intention of the provision is to exclude economic considerations.

A more general problem arises from what one writer has referred to as the 'consensual paradox': consensual regulation 'is aimed at the well-informed, well-intentioned and well-organized employer who would present few problems if left wholly to self-regulate. But many hazards relate to ill-informed, ill-intentioned and ill-organized employer . . .'[42] Empirical studies of the new regime confirm that it does not adequately deal with the latter.[43] The traditional approach may have placed small firms at a competitive disadvantage but its successor, in its attempt to adapt standards to localized circumstances, may have erred in the opposite direction, particularly where those employed in the small firms are not unionized.[44]

Finally, it may be questioned whether the system deals adequately with externalities. We have seen that there tends to be a greater degree of centralized intervention where occupational risks are likely to threaten third parties, but external effects arise also in cases where the physical impact does not extend beyond the workforce. Significant costs are incurred by the National Health Service and social security systems, and yet taxpayers and National Insurance contributors are not represented in the consensual standard-setting process.[45]

---

[39] Cf. P. James, 'Reforming British Health and Safety Law: A Framework for Discussion' (1992) 21 Ind. LJ 83.

[40] Mendeloff, above, n. 9, pp. 162–4.

[41] SI 1988/1657, Reg. 7(2) and ACOP Control of Substances Hazardous to Health (1988), paras. 32–3. See also the Personal Protective Equipment at Work Regulations, SI 1992/2966.

[42] Baldwin, above, n. 21, p. 153.

[43] H. Genn, *Great Expectations: the Robens Legacy and Employer Self-Regulation* (1987, unpubl.); R. Baldwin, 'Why Rules Don't Work' (1990) 53 Modern LR 321.

[44] It should be noted that Art. 118A of the Treaty of Rome, inserted by the Single European Act, stipulates that Council Directives concerning the health and safety of workers 'shall avoid imposing administrative, financial and legal constraints in a way which would hold back the creation and development of small and medium-sized undertakings'.

[45] Cf. Baldwin, above, n. 21, p. 140.

## 2. CONSUMER PRODUCT QUALITY AND SAFETY: GENERAL

### (a) Public Interest Justifications

Purchasers of consumer products have varying preferences regarding quality and safety. If they had perfect information on the characteristics of products offered in the market and behaved rationally in accordance with their preferences, and if their purchasing decisions did not generate externalities, regulatory intervention would not be required. Clearly, in relation to many products and many consumers, these conditions are not met.[46] First, a great variety of products are 'experience' or 'credence' goods, that is, their quality can be ascertained only through consumption or use and, in some cases, the adverse impact of poor quality may take a considerable time to emerge.[47] Secondly, even where full information is made available, making decisions on the basis of it may be difficult. The information may be complex and not easy to correlate with preferences; there is empirical evidence that consumers significantly underestimate low-probability risks.[48] Thirdly, externalities are often present: persons other than the purchaser may consume or use the product; and some of the consequences of poor quality, such as health care costs, may be borne by other third parties.

Tortious liability for defective products has been strengthened in recent years,[49] but private law provides a far from complete answer to the problem.[50] Liability arises only where a 'defect' in the product causes damage to the plaintiff's person or property—poor quality as such is not covered—and the costs to the plaintiff in furnishing adequate evidence on the existence of a defect and the causal relationship with the damage may be high relative to her loss.

To meet the problem by regulatory intervention, three basic options are available. As will be seen in Chapter 10,[51] the most drastic of these, requiring the approval of an agency before the product is marketed, has been reserved for products such as drugs which are inherently dangerous in the sense that very large social losses can result if their use is not adequately controlled. For the majority of products, the choice lies between the other two options, namely information regulation (discussed

---

[46] See for general discussion: R. Hirshhorn, 'Regulating Quality in Product Markets', in Dewees, above, n. 4, ch. 3; W. K. Viscusi, *Regulating Consumer Product Safety* (1984), ch. 1; P. Asch, *Consumer Safety Regulation* (1988), chs. 3–5.

[47] Above, pp. 132–3.　　　　　　　　　　　　　　　[48] Asch, above, n. 46, ch. 5.

[49] A regime of strict liability was introduced by the Consumer Protection Act 1987, Part I, implementing EC Directive 85/374.

[50] Viscusi, above, n. 46, pp. 8–16. On the shortcomings of the Consumer Protection Act 1987, see J. Stapleton, 'Products Liability Reform—Real or Illusory' (1986) 6 Ox. J. Legal Stud. 392.　　　　　　　　　　　　　　　　　　　　　　[51] Below, pp. 233–8.

in Chapter 7) and mandatory product standards (discussed here). Further, each of these can be divided into sub-options. Information regulation comprises not only the required disclosure of product characteristics, but also a system of certification to indicate that the product complies with a set of *voluntary* standards, such as those promulgated by the British Standards Institute or its European equivalent (CEN).[52] Mandatory product standards can be formulated as specification, performance, or target standards.

Determining the optimal mode of intervention involves consideration of the interaction between several important variables.[53] The more technologically complex the determinants of quality, the less policy-makers are likely to rely on information regulation. Conversely, the greater the assumed diversity of consumer preferences, the less appropriate are mandatory standards, since, to some extent at least, they will reduce consumer choice. This suggests that, in general and other things being equal, mandatory standards will be favoured for consumer *safety* protection (preferences regarding illness and injury being more homogeneous) and information regulation for control of *quality* characteristics not involving risks of illness and injury (preferences here being less homogeneous). As regards selection of the appropriate type of mandatory standard, there is little to add to the discussion in the previous chapter:[54] account has to be taken of the costs, to the agency and firms respectively, of formulating and monitoring standards, and of the benefits which should accrue from allowing firms greater freedom in meeting the regulatory goal.

## (b) Other Influences

A 'rational' approach to regulatory policy-making might imply a careful application of these considerations, but other influences undoubtedly have some impact. Some may push the choice towards regulatory forms of a more interventionist character and/or stricter standards than would be justified on objective public interest grounds. The first such influence is the publicity given by the media to tragic accidents resulting from certain products (e.g. thalidomide and salmonella). This exerts pressure on politicians and regulators to be seen to react swiftly and decisively. They may gain from an excessively interventionist response without incurring the costs, which will be widely spread among firms and consumers.[55] Paternalism constitutes a second instance: although this is rarely acknowledged in public statements, policy-makers may be sceptical of consumer preferences, especially with regard to products which confer short-term

[52] Cf. above, pp. 137–8.
[53] Hirshhorn, above, n. 46, pp. 65–73; Viscusi, above, n. 46, ch. 2.
[54] Above, pp. 166–8.
[55] Hirshhorn, above, n. 46, p. 68.

satisfaction but generate longer-term risks.[56] Thirdly, politicians and agencies may be subjected to pressure from firms which can gain competitive advantages from product standards in certain forms. For example, a set of mandatory specifications may largely correspond to a firm's existing practice but impose costs of adaptation on other firms; or it may result in a proportionally heavier burden for smaller firms.

Nevertheless, as we saw in the last chapter,[57] EC Law has exerted pressure for consumer product regulation to develop in the opposite direction, away from more interventionist approaches. National systems of mandatory product standards can, of course, constitute barriers to intra-Community trade. To deal with this problem, Community policy-makers have largely abandoned the earlier strategy of harmonizing specification standards, and replaced it by a system of minimum harmonization combined with mutual recognition. Under this system, harmonization is limited to broad, target standards, allowing manufacturers to meet the latter by reference to a set of more detailed national standards, not necessarily those of the importing Member State. For products traded across national boundaries, this effectively creates a system of certification, allowing consumers to choose between products subject to different sets of national standards.[58] The impact on national standard-setting is also likely to be significant.[59] To preserve the international competitiveness of domestic producers, the governments of Member States will be reluctant to insist on costly technical requirements which cannot be justified by assumed consumer preferences and will endeavour to incorporate in national regimes references to voluntary international standards, such as those issued by CEN.

### 3. CONSUMER PRODUCT QUALITY AND SAFETY: FOOD

#### (a) General

Food control occupies a place in the history of social regulation equivalent to that of occupational health and safety: it has deep roots in Victorian interventionism[60] and it has served as a model for other product regimes. Rudimentary target standards featured prominently in the early legislation (notably, a prohibition on the sale of food 'injurious to the health of

---

[56] Cf. above, pp. 51–3.                                      [57] Above, pp. 174–9.

[58] H.-W. Micklitz, 'Perspectives on a European Directive on the Safety of Technical Consumer Goods' (1986) 23 Common Market L. Rev. 617; A. McGee and S. Weatherill, 'The Evolution of the Single Market—Harmonisation or Liberalisation' (1990) 53 Modern LR 578.

[59] Cf. White Paper, Standards, Quality and International Competitiveness (1982, Cmnd. 8621).

[60] F. Tibby, A History of Food Adulteration and Analysis (1934); I. Paulus, The Search for Pure Food: A Sociology of Legislation in Britain (1974).

persons').[61] Then, as advances in technology both increased the risks to consumers and facilitated more sophisticated control procedures, detailed and complex sets of specification and performance standards began to proliferate. Within the last few years, there have been some signs of a reversion to a less interventionist approach,[62] thus following the trend which has characterized occupational health and safety and regulatory systems generally. But the development has been tentative and food suppliers remain subject to a huge mass of detailed and complex standards.[63]

Several reasons may help to explain this phenomenon. Perhaps the most important is the emotive power which questions of food wholesomeness exert on the electorate, and hence the need for politicians to ensure public confidence in the regulatory systems.[64] In the earlier period, adulteration was the main concern;[65] in more recent times, attention has shifted to additives,[66] environmental contaminants,[67] and irradiated foods.[68] Between 1986 and 1990 there was a marked increase in the number of reported cases of food poisoning and the media labelled it as a 'food crisis'.[69] The appointment of expert committees[70] has been a typical governmental response and, as noted elsewhere,[71] such committees can be expected to err on the side of over-regulation.

A second important reason for the retention of a robust interventionist policy has been the impact of EC law. While in other areas the abandonment of the 'old' approach to harmonization has allowed considerable latitude to national systems and has led to some deregulation, in questions of food the momentum for detailed harmonized standards has been maintained and even accelerated. The greater success in promulgating EC Food Directives undoubtedly owes something to the new majority-voting rule introduced by the Single European Act, but the influence at Brussels of powerful pressure groups representing the agricultural and food industries[72] may have been of equal significance. These interests may benefit from the continued emphasis on specification standards.

The complex interaction of motives and forces has resulted in a 'belt and

---

[61] Adulteration of Food Act 1860, s. 1.

[62] C. Scott, 'Continuity and Change in British Food Law' (1990) 53 Modern LR 785.

[63] For details, see A. Painter, *Butterworths Law of Food and Drugs* (looseleaf).

[64] W. Grant, *Pressure Groups, Politics and Democracy in Britain* (1989), pp. 51–5.

[65] Tibby, above, n. 60; Paulus, above, n. 60.

[66] MAFF, *Survey of Consumer Attitudes to Food Additives* (1987).

[67] Seventh Report of the Royal Commission on Environmental Pollution, *Agriculture and Pollution* (1979, Cmnd. 7644).

[68] DHSS Advisory Committee, *Report on the Safety and Wholesomeness of Irradiated Foods* (1986).    [69] Painter, above, n. 63, p. A6.

[70] Esp. the Richmond Committee: see *Report of the Committee on the Micro-biological Safety of Food* (1990).

[71] Above, p. 191.    [72] Grant, above, n. 64, p. 102.

braces' approach to food control which is not always easy to reconcile with public interest justifications for regulation. To illustrate this, we may begin by drawing a broad distinction between the two main problems of market failure posed by the supply of food. On the one hand, there is a *quality* issue, the need to ensure that consumers' subjective preferences are met. On the other hand, there is the *safety* issue: when food creates health risks, regulation may be necessary to correct for externalities or (possibly) to meet a paternalist concern that an individual's diet be satisfactory.

### (b)  Quality

While the *safety* issue may require the imposition of product standards, *quality* is essentially an informational problem and can, to a large degree, be solved by regulation of that type. Indeed, a substantial proportion of the instruments governing food supply can be categorized as information regulation. There are general provisions prohibiting the publication or use of a label which 'falsely describes the food' or 'is likely to mislead as to the nature or substance or quality of the food'.[73] These do not, of course, compel traders positively to supply information and they are complemented by measures requiring the disclosure, *inter alia*, of the ingredients of the food.[74]

However, it is all too easy for such information regulation to slide into product specification standards. Because policy-makers are sceptical of the ability or willingness of consumers to benefit from disclosed information, there is an ever-increasing tendency to prohibit the marketing of a product using a generic name (e.g. Scotch whisky) unless it contains specified ingredients and/or has undergone specified processes.[75] As we saw in an earlier chapter, this may overcome the information problem, but it may do so at the cost of reducing choice and stifling innovation.[76]

Another instance of food quality regulation is to be found in Section 14 of the Food Safety Act 1990, which penalizes traders who sell 'to the purchaser's prejudice any food which is not of the nature or substance or quality demanded by the purchaser'. The provision dates back to the nineteenth century[77] and was intended primarily to combat adulteration which was so prevalent at that time.[78] But, as interpreted by the courts,[79] its protection extends much beyond this, effectively creating a public instrument for enforcing a private, contractual right. The high cost of private enforcement relative to the typically low value of the transaction

---

[73] Food Safety Act 1990, s. 15.
[74] Labelling of Food Regulations, SI 1984/1305 (as amended).
[75] Above, pp. 135–7.                                            [76] Above, p. 136.
[77] Sale of Food and Drugs Act 1875, s. 6.
[78] Paulus, above, n. 60, pp. 36–7.
[79] B. Harvey and D. Parry, *Law of Consumer Protection and Fair Trading* (4th edn., 1992), pp. 390–4.

and the scale economies of public enforcement might justify this, yet consumer purchasers of other low value products have no equivalent protection.

An alternative explanation can be sought in the benefit which the provision confers on agencies responsible for enforcing product *safety* standards. As will soon appear, the agencies have at their disposal a variety of instruments for such purposes, but proof of contravention is often difficult and costly.[80] The evidence indicates that the majority of prosecutions for 'unsound food' are brought under Section 14 even though in many of these a more specific 'safety' offence may have been committed.[81]

## (c) Safety

Traditionally, the British legislators and enforcement agencies have relied heavily on general target standards for dealing with food creating health risks. The main provision imposes criminal liability on 'any person who renders any food [intended for human consumption] injurious to health'.[82] This is complemented by another provision extending liability to those selling, or offering to sell, food which has been rendered injurious to health, is unfit for human consumption, or 'is so contaminated . . . that it would not be reasonable to expect it to be used for human consumption in that state'.[83]

The advantage of this approach, as with target standards generally, is that it gives the enforcement agency discretion in determining what is 'injurious to health' or 'unfit for human consumption', thus enabling it to tailor the regulatory goal of optimal care to the particular circumstances of the case; and suppliers have an incentive to find the cheapest method of providing such care. However, as foods have been subjected to an increasingly wide range of additives and processes, the health effects of which are often uncertain, the information costs of such a highly decentralized approach become much larger. We may then expect suppliers to demand a more detailed set of standards to reduce those costs,[84] particularly if they are cast as specification standards which protect existing modes of production against innovations by competitors. The demand is likely to be endorsed by pressure from consumer interests which, as we have seen, attribute a high value to the wholesomeness of food products.

[80] For many of the relevant offences, *mens rea* must be proved. The 'nature or substance or quality' provision imposed strict liability: *Goodfellow* v. *Johnson* [1966] 1 QB 83. It is, however, now subject to a 'due diligence' defence: below, p. 197.

[81] R. Cranston, *Consumers and the Law* (2nd edn., 1984), p. 262.

[82] Food Safety Act 1990, s. 7.         [83] Ibid. s. 8.

[84] Cf. A. Ogus, 'Information, Error Costs and Regulation' (1992) 12 Int. Rev. Law & Econ. 411.

It is not, therefore, surprising that there exists, alongside the general target standards, a huge array of specification and performance safety standards. There are many detailed regulations prohibiting the use of certain additives in certain foods, and stipulating the maximum amount or concentration of others.[85] The sale of quick-frozen foods is, for example, subjected to specific conditions relating to the quality of the raw materials, the technical equipment used in preparing and quick-freezing the foods, and the storage temperature thereafter.[86]

The control of hygiene provides an excellent illustration of the difficulties inherent in this area. The Food Hygiene Regulations combine some specification standards (e.g. persons handling open food are, in certain cases, required to wear overclothing)[87] with some target standards (e.g. 'a person who engages in the handling of food shall . . . take all such steps as may be reasonably necessary to protect the food from risk of contamination').[88] The problem here is that the circumstances which may give rise to a hygiene risk are very diverse. Specification standards are likely to be either under-inclusive (they fail to deal with some important hazards)[89] or over-inclusive (they are unnecessary in some of the situations to which they apply).[90] Target standards may allow for a better fit, but their use assumes that traders have sufficient information on the risks and the possibilities for dealing with them, and this assumption may be unjustified for smaller firms engaged in supplying food.

Whether the cost of specification standards—which includes the administrative burden of formulating and enforcing them as well as the foreclosing of other, perhaps cheaper means of achieving the same ends— is justified by the benefit of reduced health costs must remain a speculative matter. Critics of the equivalent American regimes, which in some respects appear to be stricter,[91] have argued that the selection of permitted and prohibited additives has been somewhat arbitrary, and that it reflects too

---

[85] Colouring Matter in Food Regulations, SI 1973/1340; Antioxidants in Food Regulations, SI 1978/105; Miscellaneous Additives in Food Regulations, SI 1980/1834; Sweeteners in Food Regulations, SI 1983/1211; Preservatives in Food Regulations, SI 1989/533; Emulsifiers and Stabilisers in Food Regulations, SI 1989/896. In all cases, these instruments have been amended, often to accord with EC Directives.

[86] Quick-Frozen Foodstuffs Regulations, SI 1990/2615, implementing EC Directive 89/108.

[87] Food Hygiene (General) Regulations, SI 1970/1172, Reg. 11.

[88] Ibid. Reg. 9.

[89] e.g. the Food Hygiene Regulations do not deal with microbiological contamination, on which see the Richmond Report, above, n. 70.

[90] Cf. above, p. 169.

[91] Notably, the so-called Delaney clause of the Food, Drug and Cosmetic Act which (for some time at least) was construed as prohibiting any additive which caused cancer in man or animals, however small the threshold risk. See on this R. Merrill, 'Regulating Carcinogens in Food: A Legislative Guide to the Food Safety Provisions of the Federal Food, Drug and Cosmetic Act' (1978) 77 Mich. LR 171.

great an obsession with certain health effects where the risks are extremely small and would be controllable if manufacturers had the incentive to develop the relevant technology.[92]

### (d) A New Approach?

The great majority of the instruments described above remain in force, but the latest major legislative measure, the Food Safety Act 1990, contains some innovatory features which may herald a new, and less interventionist, approach.[93] One is the power conferred on relevant Ministers to issue Codes of Practice governing the Act and Regulations made under it.[94] So far, the Codes issued have been primarily concerned with enforcement procedures,[95] but they could be used to provide guidance for traders and, as such, be analogous to ACOPs which now play such an important role in occupational health and safety.[96] In particular, they could convey valuable information to small traders and yet avoid the problems associated with specification standards.[97]

Another innovation is the new general provision applicable to all quality and safety offences under the Act. Subject to certain conditions, it is now

a defence for the person charged to prove that he took all reasonable precautions and exercised all due diligence to avoid the commission of the offence by himself or by a person under his control.[98]

This creates the possibility that a trader subject to, say, a specification standard may escape liability if she is able to show that the precautions which she took, while not conforming to the detailed requirements of the standard, nevertheless were adequate to meet the goal implicit in it. In other words, it may permit firms to adopt alternative, and perhaps cheaper, methods of abating the risk and hence should promote allocative efficiency by inducing optimal care. Self-regulatory systems for the analysis and control of health risks are already used by many major food suppliers,[99] and the 'due diligence' defence, if interpreted accordingly by the courts, might encourage greater reliance on them.

---

[92] e.g. C. Blank, 'The Delaney Clause: Technical Naiveté and Scientific Advocacy in the Formation of Public Health Policies' (1974) 62 Calif. LR 1084. See also Asch, above, n. 46, pp. 105–8.

[93] Scott, above, n. 62.

[94] Food Safety Act 1990, s. 40.

[95] They are reproduced in Painter, above, n. 63, Division B.

[96] Above, pp. 186–7.

[97] There is also a power to require persons working in the food business to engage in hygiene trading: Food Safety Act 1990, s. 23 and Sched. 1, para. 5(3).

[98] Food Safety Act 1990, s. 21.

[99] Richmond Report, above, n. 70, App. 4.

### 4. CONSUMER PRODUCT QUALITY AND SAFETY:
### OTHER REGIMES

*(a)  General*

The regulation of consumer durable products has differed in important respects from that governing foodstuffs. There are very few mandatory product standards concerned with quality *per se*, that is where a product does not, in ordinary use, generate a risk to health or safety. In relation to this issue, such intervention as has occurred has predominantly been information regulation. Then, as regards safety standards, there has been a much more significant change in policy in the last decade. An approach which concentrated on specification and performance standards, but only in relation to selected categories of consumer products, came gradually to be replaced by a more general regime based predominantly on target standards and an increased use of information (certification) systems.

There are several possible explanations for these differences. The first concerns consumer preferences and their impact on policy-making. With their emotive commitment to food wholesomeness, consumers may constitute a relatively coherent, and therefore powerful, pressure group. They may, however, be less risk-averse regarding the safety of other products, and their preferences as to quality may be less homogeneous, thus reducing their influence on politicians.

Secondly, considerations of administrative rationality may have played an important role. It was already clear in the 1960s that it would be impossible to formulate detailed mandatory standards governing quality, given the diversity of consumer preferences and the enormous range of products available in the market.[100] The selective, piecemeal approach to product safety was very much an *ad hoc* response to consumer complaints regarding particular and overtly dangerous items,[101] and the pressure for a more coherent policy became irresistible.[102]

Thirdly, account must be taken of the response of firms to changes in the nature of product markets and the impact of EC law. Product suppliers will favour specification and performance standards if they result in protection against domestic and foreign competitors. In the formative years of the European Community, such standards may have had this effect. The efforts of the Commission to open up product markets have, as we have seen, taken different forms. In relation to the regulation of food, harmonization has been moderately successful, but, since most of the relevant Directives have imposed specification and performance standards,

---

[100] Cf. Final Report of the [Molony] Committee on Consumer Protection (1962, Cmnd. 1781), paras. 254–6.

[101] Cranston, above, n. 81, p. 313.

[102] Green Paper, *Consumer Safety—A Consultative Document* (1976, Cmnd. 6398).

suppliers using traditional materials and processes have acquired a degree of protection against innovating competitors. This has also been largely true of the safety standards imposed on the construction of motor vehicles,[103] manufacturers constituting a particularly coherent and powerful pressure group.[104]

The suppliers of other products are much more heterogeneous, and agreements on harmonized standards were consequently less easy to obtain. The evolution of a system of mutual recognition of national standards, as an alternative to harmonization, meant that firms supplying to the extended European market would be at a disadvantage if they had to comply with a set of national standards which were more onerous than those of their foreign competitors.[105] During the last decade, it has therefore been in the interest of product suppliers to press for deregulation rather than, as previously, for protective standards.

### (b) The Selective but Interventionist Approach to Product Safety

Mandatory safety standards applicable to durable goods were relatively late arrivals on the regulatory scene. With some notable exceptions,[106] most date from the period after 1961, the year in which the Consumer Protection Act conferred a general power on the Secretary of State to prescribe, in relation to goods, 'such requirements . . . as are in his opinion expedient to prevent or reduce risk of death or personal injury'.[107] To deal with emergencies, the Secretary of State was, in 1978 granted an additional power to issue a temporary prohibition order on goods which he deemed to be 'not safe'.[108] Should it prove to be necessary, such an order might subsequently be replaced by a permanent set of product standards.[109]

As has already been indicated, the policy of the Secretary of State in exercising these statutory powers has been essentially selective and reactive: sets of standards for, and prohibition orders on, particular

---

[103] For details, see P. Wallis *et al.*, *Wilkinson's Road Traffic Offences* (15th edn., 1991), ch. 8.

[104] Not the least because they are largely multinationals: S. Wilks, 'Corporate Strategy and State Support in the European Motor Industry', in L. Hancher and M. Moran (eds.), *Capitalism, Culture and Economic Regulation* (1989), ch. 7.

[105] 1982 White Paper, above, n. 59.

[106] Notably: motor vehicles, although the controls were limited mainly to brakes and lighting (Road Traffic Act 1930, s. 3); paint (Lead Paint (Protection Against Poisoning) Act 1926); heating appliances (Heating Appliances (Fireguards) Act 1952).

[107] S. 1(1)(a), implementing the recommendations of the Interim Report of the [Molony] Committee on Consumer Protection (1960, Cmnd. 1011). The provision was reformulated in the Consumer Safety Act 1978, s. 1, the object of the power becoming then to secure that 'goods are safe'.

[108] Consumer Safety Act 1978, s. 3, re-enacted in the Consumer Protection Act 1987, s. 13.

[109] See e.g. Gas Catalytic Heaters (Safety) Order, SI 1983/1696, which was followed by the Gas Catalytic Heaters (Safety) Regulations, SI 1984/1802.

products have been issued when there is perceived to be a sufficiently strong demand for them. This approach is subject to the obvious objection of arbitrariness. Take, for example, the Toys (Safety) Regulations 1974.[110] They imposed controls to deal with the hazards of nitrate and lead poisoning, electrical current, pile fabrics, sheet metals, spikes and rods, and plastic bags. But do not toys pose a multitude of other risks to children, meriting equivalent treatment? The point is aptly illustrated by an order made in 1983,[111] temporarily prohibiting the sale of scented erasers on the ground that such objects had proved to be a temptation to young children who had choked on them as a result. However, although a number of consumer complaints had been received, no assessment of the risk had been undertaken; and, when data was available, it transpired that, as causes of choking, erasers constituted a very small risk compared with other objects (e.g. money and marbles).[112]

The instruments issued[113] under the statutory powers have imposed a large number of specification and performance standards. As an example of the former, the Electrical Equipment (Safety) Regulations 1975 prescribed that the wiring of certain appliances should meet the specifications set out in relevant BSI Standards.[114] And, as regards performance standards, the Stands for Carry-Cots (Safety) Regulations 1966 required that

A cot-stand shall be such that it will not break or suffer permanent distortion if— (a) a carry-cot is placed in position on the stand; (b) a weight of sixty pounds is so applied that its pressure is equally distributed over the bottom of the carry-cot; and (c) that pressure is maintained for twelve hours.[115]

While it is impossible to pass conclusive judgments on the appropriateness of these particular instruments, we can identify the problems to which standards of these types can give rise. Requiring conformity with BSI Standards may retard innovation and creates no incentives for firms to develop cheaper means of risk abatement. Further, if those Standards reflect closely the practices of some firms but not others, they may have anti-competitive effects. The performance standard is not subject to these objections, but the administrative cost of applying it may outweigh any advantage which it is presumed to have over a target standard (e.g. that cot-stands should be capable of withstanding a reasonable amount of pressure without breakage or distortion).

More generally, there is a suspicion that such standards have been formulated without any serious attempt at the cost–benefit, or cost-

---

[110] SI 1974/1367.  [111] Scented Erasers (Safety) Order, SI 1984/83.
[112] See the penetrating case study in I. Ramsay, *Consumer Protection: Texts and Materials* (1989), pp. 478–82.
[113] For a list and a summary of the provisions, see B. Harvey, *Law of Consumer Protection and Fair Trading* (2nd edn., 1982), pp. 214–8.
[114] SI 1975/1366, Reg. 5.  [115] SI 1966/1610, Reg. 4.

effectiveness, analysis which in the last chapter we identified as the rational approach to standard-setting.[116] Dealing with analogous regimes, American writers have suggested that product standards tend to be too restrictive because policy-makers and regulatory agencies take no account of the indirect cost to consumers of having fewer products available on the market, and tend to ignore alternative strategies, such as certification and mandatory warnings, which serve the additional purpose of inducing consumer self-care.[117] Indeed, some go further and claim on the basis of empirical evidence—which is nevertheless disputed by others[118]—that product regulation has actually increased the rate of accidents, primarily because consumers are lulled into taking less care.[119]

### (c) Reform of Product Safety Regulation

The selective, interventionist approach described in the last section has not been wholly abandoned: some of the relevant instruments remain in force, and new measures, adopting the approach, have been introduced. Nevertheless, there has been a gradual adjustment as the government has worked out the implications of a broader perspective on the product safety problem which emerged in a policy document of 1976.[120] The goals were there defined as securing that:

goods available to the public present no undue risk to consumers; the public are warned about hazards which they may find in products . . . and are advised on how to avoid them; and unsafe goods which are found on the market can be withdrawn from sale, or modified, quickly.[121]

The statement is significant in several respects.

First, the focus on 'undue risk' involves a tacit recognition of the economic concept of optimal safety. Indeed, this was made explicit in the additional observation that

higher product safety standards generally involve higher production costs which ultimately have to be paid for by the consumer. The benefits in each case have to be weighed carefully against the costs.[122]

---

[116] See e.g. the challenge to the Oral Snuff (Safety) Regulations, SI 1989/2347, made in *R v. Secretary of State for Health, ex parte US Tobacco International Inc* [1992] QB 353.

[117] e.g. L. Thomas, 'Revealed Bureaucratic Preference: Priorities of the Consumer Product Safety Commission' (1988) 19 Rand. J. Econ. 102; Viscusi, above, n. 46, which also provides an admirable survey of the evidence and of the literature.

[118] L. Robertson, 'A Critical Analysis of Peltzman's "The Effects of Automobile Safety Regulation" ' (1977) 11 J. Econ. Issues 587; R. Arnould and H. Grabowski, 'Automobile Safety Regulation: A Review of the Evidence' (1983) 5 Res. Law & Econ. 233; M. Kelman, 'On Democracy-Bashing: A Skeptical Lok at the Theoretical and "Empirical" Practice of the Public Choice Movement' (1988) 74 Virginia LR 99, 238–68.

[119] S. Peltzman, 'The Effects of Automobile Safety Regulation' (1975) 83 J. Pol. Econ. 677; P. Linneman, 'The Effects of Consumer Safety Standards: The 1973 Mattress Flammability Standard' (1980) 23 J. Law & Econ. 461; D. Alexander, 'An Empirical Investigation of Lawn Mower Safety Regulation' (1990) 22 Applied Econ. 795.

[120] Green Paper, above, n. 102.     [121] Ibid. para. 3.     [122] Ibid.

Secondly, to implement the goal of optimal safety much more systematic information is required. By 1980, institutional machinery had been set up to gather and process data on the incidence of accidents arising from product use,[123] and, under the Thatcher administration, steps were taken to compile data on the cost to industry of compliance with regulatory requirements.[124]

Thirdly, implicit in the statement is an acknowledgement that mandatory product standards might not always constitute the most effective (economically efficient) means of achieving optimal care. In some cases that goal could be pursued by requiring manufacturers to issue warnings which would induce consumers themselves to take precautions. As we saw in Chapter 7, the policy has resulted in a more widespread use of this regulatory form.[125] In some other cases, the goal might be more successfully met by insisting that defective products be recalled rather than by relying exclusively on fallible *ex ante* standards.[126] In fact, formal powers to order such recalls have not been introduced in Britain, unlike some foreign jurisdictions,[127] although in certain trades a code of practice encourages suppliers to operate such a system.[128]

To overcome the arbitrariness of the selective, piecemeal approach to unsafe products, the government was eventually persuaded to create a general target standard.[129] Its formulation in Section 10 of the Consumer Protection Act 1987 clearly reflects the economic goal of optimal safety. Liability arises if the goods 'are not reasonably safe having regard to all the circumstances', including: (a) the manner in which they are marketed (account thus being taken of the nature of any warnings); (b) the existence of any published standards relating to them; and (c)—most significantly—

the existence of any means by which it would have been reasonable (taking into account the cost, likelihood and extent of any improvement) for the goods to have been made safer.[130]

The reference in (b) indicates that compliance with voluntary standards such as those issued by the BSI or under a Code of Practice, is relevant to, but not conclusive of, the 'reasonably safe' criterion. Another provision in

[123] Notably, the Consumer Safety Unit and the Home Accident Surveillance System.
[124] Above, pp. 164–5.                          [125] Above, pp. 141–4.
[126] For general discussions of recall policies, see: Viscusi, above, n. 46, pp. 62–4; G. Jarrell and S. Peltzman, 'The Impact of Product Recalls on the Wealth of Sellers' (1985) 93 J. Pol. Econ. 512.
[127] For USA, see Viscusi, above, n. 46, p. 62; for Europe, see N. Reich and H.-W. Micklitz, *Consumer Legislation in EC Countries* (1980), p. 80.
[128] e.g. the codes issued by the Society of Motor Manufacturers and Traders and the Association of British Pharmaceutical Industry. See generally T. Watt, 'Improving Recalls of Unsafe Products' (1993) 3 Cons. Pol. Rev. 204.
[129] Cf. White Paper, *The Safety of Goods* (1984, Cmnd. 9302), paras. 33–42.
[130] See, to similar effect, EC Directive 92/59 on General Product Safety, Art. 3.

the 1987 Act nevertheless stipulates that no liability under Section 10 arises if there is compliance with an obligation arising under EC law, a specific safety regulation authorized by statute or a voluntary standard which has been 'approved' by the Secretary of State for this purpose.[131]

As a consequence of this important legislation, many goods are now subject to the general target standard of Section 10, which can be met by compliance with specific, but *optional*, standards. Some goods (e.g. toys, electrical equipment) continue to be subject to a set of specific *mandatory* standards. Nevertheless the latter regimes have also been much affected by the re-orientation of regulatory policy. In the first place, if the goods are the subject of intra-Community trade, under the principle of mutual recognition,[132] it may suffice if they comply with standards set in another Member State. Secondly, the content of the specific mandatory regimes is itself gradually being changed to accommodate the new trend.

Thus, the Low Voltage Electrical Equipment (Safety) Regulations 1989[133]—which supersede the Electrical Equipment (Safety) Regulations considered above—lay down a target standard (electrical equipment shall be 'safe') combined with a highly generalized specification standard ('and constructed in accordance with principles generally accepted within the member States of the European Economic Community as constituting good engineering practice in relation to safety matters').[134] To satisfy these requirements, it is sufficient, but not necessary, for the equipment to meet either harmonized standards, or international safety provisions or the national safety provisions of a Member State, or 'approved' informal standards.[135]

The Toys (Safety) Regulations 1989[136] are also radically different from their predecessors but they simply incorporate the EC-harmonized 'essential safety requirements'. These are predominantly target standards, although there are some specification standards relating to chemical properties.[137] Enforcement is facilitated by a presumption that the essential requirements are satisfied if a toy bears an EC mark, indicating that it meets national standards embodying those requirements.[138]

### (d) Conclusions

It is clear that the reforms described above have done much to place the regulation of product safety on a more rational basis. It now addresses the

---

[131] Consumer Protection Act 1987, s. 10(3). For details of what has been approved, see C. J. Miller, *Product Liability and Consumer Safety Encyclopaedia* (looseleaf), para. vi [3001]. [132] Above, pp. 177–9.

[133] SI 1989/728, implementing Directive 73/23.

[134] SI 1989/728, Reg. 5. For a definition of what is 'safe' and for matters to be taken into account in applying the standards, see also Reg. 8(a) and Sched. 2.

[135] SI 1989/728, Regs. 6–7.   [136] SI 1989/1275, implementing Directive 88/378.

[137] See SI 1989/1275, Sched. 2, para. 2.   [138] SI 1989/1275, Reg. 5.

generality of the problems and, at least in theory, does so by means of reasoned risk assessment. Further, greater freedom has been conferred on manufacturers to devise different means of dealing with safety risks, leading (presumably) to wider consumer choice. Critics nevertheless claim that the process of deregulation has gone too far.[139] They argue that consumers are insufficiently represented in the wider range of institutions which now formulate relevant standards.[140] In addition, when suppliers have the option of compliance with standards set in another country, doubts are sometimes raised regarding the effectiveness of the enforcement agencies in that country.[141]

## 5. ENVIRONMENTAL POLLUTION CONTROL

### (a) Introduction

Pollution control is generally regarded as one of the most important regulatory regimes, and it is not difficult to understand why. The public interest case for some form of intervention is overwhelming: the widespread effects of pollution, in terms of space, time, and population mean that 'private' solutions to externalities—bargaining and the enforcement of tort and property rights—are manifestly inadequate.[142] Moreover, given a popular perception that unchecked growth of industrial activity *might* have catastrophic environmental consequences, for example through global warming, governments are under considerable pressure to introduce regulatory measures which will reassure the electorate.

At the same time, pollution poses problems for standard-setting which are significantly more complex than those experienced in other areas.[143] First, valuing the benefits of environmental protection is highly speculative, particularly when they comprise amenities as well as health, and when account must be taken of the preferences of future generations. The fact that some forms of pollution transcend national boundaries exacerbates the problem. Secondly, there is still much uncertainty regarding the impact of some pollutants, and since abatement costs are often high, it is difficult to reach a consensus on the appropriate trade-off between protection and industrial production. Thirdly, even if agreement can be reached on desirable levels of protection, translating those goals into standards

[139] e.g. Micklitz, above, n. 58.
[140] Cf. S. Weatherill, 'Reinvigorating the Development of Community Product Safety Policy' (1991) 14 J. Cons. Pol. 171.
[141] R. Thomas and S. Weatherill, 'Consumer Regulation Across Borders' (1991) 1 Cons. Pol. Rev. 13, 18–19.
[142] T. Swanson, 'Environmental Economics and Regulations', in O. Lomas (ed.), *Frontiers of Environmental Law* (1991), pp. 133–40.
[143] C. Sunstein, 'Endogenous Preferences, Environmental Law' (1993) 22 J. Legal Stud. 217.

applicable to individual firms is rendered more difficult by several factors. There may be significant variations between the environmental characteristics of different regions. Within any one airshed or watershed, the standard imposed on one firm may depend, to a greater or lesser extent, on the polluting activities of other firms. Finally, there is the question whether account should be taken of the age of industrial plant, given that the adaptation of existing plants often requires a proportionately much higher level of capital expenditure than the fitting of new plants.

The very complexity of public interest decision-making in this area may make it particularly susceptible to private interest influence.[144] Standards adopted in certain forms will impose greater costs on some firms than on others, and thus may be actively sought by those seeking competitive advantages. This is obviously the case where stricter standards are imposed on firms with new plants,[145] but also may apply where, say, a set of specification requirements accord with the existing practices of some firms. The demand from industry for certain regulatory forms may be substantially enhanced if the environmental lobby presses for the same solutions. It is to be expected that the latter will have a preference for more interventionist measures, if only for their symbolic value.[146] They may also support stricter standards for new plants because they assume that such a policy will have a more beneficial, longer-term impact on environmental quality.[147]

We may identify three broad phases in the history of British pollution control.[148] During the first, which lasted approximately until the end of the Second World War, the focus was on the more obvious risks to public health, and the principal regulatory form was a general target standard[149] randomly applied by rudimentary administrative machinery[150] and, for some particularly noxious substances, a set of performance standards, enforced by an expert inspectorate.[151] The second period, from 1947 until the late 1970s, was heralded by land-use planning legislation,[152] implying

[144] On which, see R. Hahn, 'The Political Framework of Environmental Regulation: Towards a Unifying Framework' (1990) 65 Public Choice 21.

[145] Cf. P. Huber, 'The Old-New Division in Risk Regulation' (1983) 63 Virginia LR 1025; M. Maloney and M. McCormick, 'A Positive Theory of Environmental Quality Regulation' (1982) 25 J. Law & Econ. 99.

[146] B. Ackerman and W. Hassler, Clean Coal/Dirty Air (1981). See also, in relation to pollution taxes, below p. 255. For a valuable comparison of the influence of environmentalist groups in the UK and USA, see D. Vogel, National Styles of Regulation: Environmental Policy in Great Britain and the United States (1986), pp. 172–6.

[147] Hahn, above, n. 144, p. 27.

[148] Cf. Vogel, above, n. 146, ch. 1.

[149] The prohibition of 'nuisances' and 'conditions prejudicial to public health' was regularly re-enacted in legislation from the Town Improvement Clauses Act 1847 to the Public Health Act 1936.

[150] W. Cornish and G. de N. Clark, Law and Society in England 1750–1950 (1989), pp. 159–66.     [151] Alkali &c. Works Regulation Act 1906.

[152] Town and Country Planning Act, 1947.

greater state control over environmental concerns, and involved new and more detailed regulatory systems.[153] The features which commentators have identified as characteristic of the 'British' approach to pollution control[154] emerged most clearly during this period: a policy of mainly individualized standards negotiated between firms and regulatory agencies and a 'persuasive', rather than 'confrontational', enforcement strategy.[155] The most recent period has been marked by efforts at administrative rationalization[156] but, more importantly, by some shift away from the traditional approach towards formalized standards, as the control systems have had to meet the challenges of new threats to the environment, the increasing role of EC law, and the demand for more accountability and a greater degree of public participation in standard-setting processes.[157]

We cannot here cover the many different regulatory regimes which comprise modern pollution control.[158] Rather, we shall provide a general account of the techniques and problems of standard-setting, drawing examples primarily from air and water pollution. Economic instruments (taxes, subsidies, and tradeable rights) are considered in Chapter 11.

### (b) Public Interest Goal

Following from earlier discussion,[159] we may assume that the public interest objective of control systems is to achieve the socially optimal level of pollution, where the marginal social costs of pollution abatement are roughly equal to its marginal social benefits, adjusted to meet such distributional considerations as the policy-maker deems appropriate. The legal framework for environmental protection has been slowly evolving towards a formal acceptance of this goal.

The earlier legislation eschewed any general statement of objectives and the policy seems to have been one of containing pollution and its consequences, rather than generating optimal standards.[160] From the mid-1970s, the Royal Commission on Environmental Pollution continued to

---

[153] Notably, under the Rivers (Prevention of Pollution) Act 1961 and the Clean Air Act 1956.

[154] Vogel, above, n. 146, pp. 75–93; 10th Report of the Royal Commission on Environmental Pollution, *Tackling Pollution—Experience and Prospects*, (1984, Cmnd. 9149), paras. 3.13–26.

[155] G. Richardson, A. Ogus, and P. Burrows, *Policing Pollution: A Study of Regulation and Enforcement* (1982), pp. 43–8, 62–4.

[156] Notably by the creation, in 1987, of Her Majesty's Inspectorate of Pollution, and the later proposals to merge that agency with the National Rivers Authority and the Drinking Water Inspectorate.

[157] R. Macrory, 'Environmental Law—Shifting Discretions and the New Formalism', in Lomas, above, n. 142, ch. 2.

[158] For detailed accounts, see: D. Hughes, *Environmental Law* (2nd edn., 1992); N. Haigh, *EEC Environmental Policy and Britain* (2nd edn., 1989).

[159] Above, pp. 153–4.

[160] Richardson *et al.*, above, n. 155, pp. 32–3.

press the government to accept that control measures, particularly for multi-media pollutants, should be designed to induce what it referred to as the 'best practicable environmental option' (BPEO).[161] BPEO was defined as 'the option that provides the most benefit or least damage to the environment as a whole, at acceptable cost, in the long term as well as the short term'.[162]

The economic content of BPEO is clear. In determining 'acceptable costs', the aim is 'to achieve a reasonable balance between the costs of prevention and/or dispersion and the benefits'; and the effect on the 'public purse' should also be taken into account.[163] Nor are distributional considerations to be ignored. Indeed, unusually for policy documents, the Royal Commission explicitly referred to the normative limitations of the Kaldor-Hicks test[164] of allocative efficiency:

Even if the gainers [from a change in pollution] appear to have gained so much that they could easily compensate the losers for their loss, it is still true (because no actual compensation occurs) that the distribution of benefits has been affected by the change. If, therefore, the aggregate costs and benefits to individuals, resulting from the change, are used for a calculation the distribution of benefits must be considered separately and in addition.[165]

As thus interpreted, BPEO is regarded as equivalent to the concept of 'best available techniques not entailing excessive costs' (BATNEEC) which was formulated in an EC Directive as the objective for national controls on air pollution.[166]

General statutory provisions governing environmental protection still tend to be couched in vague language, such as 'maintaining and improving the quality of . . . water'[167] and 'preventing or minimising pollution of the environment'.[168] Nevertheless, under current legislation, BATNEEC is formally incorporated as an objective of standards in all cases where an authorization is required for an industrial process—basically, where a firm discharges a significant quantity of waste; and BPEO is likewise ˌthe goal where a process is designated for central control and involves the release of substances into more than one environmental medium.[169]

---

[161] 5th Report, *Air Pollution Control: An Integrated Approach* (1976, Cmnd. 6371), para. 271; 10th Report, above, n. 154, paras. 3.27–39; and, for an extended discussion, 12th Report, *Best Practicable Environmental Option* (1988, Cm. 310). For critical commentary, see S. Owens, 'The Unified Pollution Inspectorate and Best Practicable Environmental Option in the United Kingdom', in N. Haigh and E. Irwin (eds.), *Integrated Pollution Control in Europe and North America* (1990), ch. 8.

[162] 12th Report, above, n. 161, para. 2.1.

[163] Ibid. paras. 2.5–6.        [164] Cf. above, pp. 24–5.

[165] Royal Commission 12th Report, above, n. 161, para 2.27.

[166] Directive 84/360, on which see Haigh, above, n. 158, pp. 224–7.

[167] Water Resources Act 1991, s. 83(1).

[168] Environmental Protection Act 1990, s. 4(2).     [169] Ibid. s. 7.

### (c) Target Standards

Environmental target standards have characteristics and functions which distinguish them from the target standards used in other regimes. In relation to occupational safety and consumer product regulation, as we have seen, the standard is formulated in very general language, such as a prohibition of conditions or activities which generate an 'unreasonable' risk to health, personal injury, or death. An equivalent approach can be and has been taken to pollution by, for example, prohibiting 'nuisances' or 'conditions prejudicial to public health'.[170] But if such standards are the only legal requirements imposed on firms, in most cases enormous information costs will be incurred, given the complexity and uncertainty inherent in what constitutes optimal pollution; and errors will abound. Happily, for many types of pollution an alternative is available: the quality of the receiving environment can, to some extent at least, be measured, and thus it is possible to formulate a *specific, quantitative* target standard, often referred to as an ambient quality standard (AQS).[171]

Adoption of an AQS may not, however, solve the information problem. Where, as is typically the case, a watershed or airshed receives discharges from a number of sources, the abatement required from each individual source to meet the standard may be impossible to determine without knowledge of what is discharged from other sources. AQSs, then, should not generally be used as standards directly applicable to firms; rather, they should operate as norms constraining the discretion of standard-setters. The knowledge available to the latter regarding polluter behaviour can then be used to design standards—generally performance standards—which, in the aggregate, will be sufficient to meet the requirements of the AQS.

In the formulation of AQSs, an important question arises as to the extent to which there should be variation between regions.[172] In theory, this is to be resolved by reference to the preferences of citizens (including future generations), as users of the environment. There is, however, a 'free-rider' problem in so far as those who demand a cleaner environment may not have to bear the costs of achieving it; and the problem becomes acute where pollution crosses regional or national boundaries. The argument for uniform AQSs is strongest in the latter cases and also where the quality objectives reflect health considerations, as to which citizen preferences may be assumed to be largely homogeneous. Conversely, some regional, or national, variation regarding amenity quality may be

---

[170] Above, n. 149.

[171] For general discussion, see J. Krier, 'Irrational National Air-Quality Standards: Macro and Micro Mistakes' (1974) 22 UCLA LR 323.

[172] Ibid.; E. Rehbinder and R. Stewart, *Environmental Protection Policy* (1985), pp. 220–2.

envisaged to reflect significant differences in demand from populations which are, in broad terms, prepared to bear the costs.

Traditionally, British policy-makers have been hostile to AQSs, arguing that the lack of sufficient scientific knowledge on the effects of some pollutants makes it undesirable to specify concentration levels in statutory form; they are 'unenforceable in practice and would bring the law into disrepute'.[173] This stance reflected a long-held perception that pollution problems could best be solved by close co-operation between industry and regulators and that such co-operation would be jeopardized if the latter were to be made legally accountable.[174] The political pressure from environmentalists and the requirements of EC law have wrought fundamental changes to this attitude.[175]

EC Directives have, for example, laid down air quality limit values relating to the concentration of certain pollutants, although allowing Member States to designate zones for stricter standards where special environmental protection is required.[176] Analogous standards have been established for drinking water[177] and other environmental media. Slowly these AQSs are being formally adopted into British legislation. Thus the Air Quality Standards Regulations 1989 require the Secretary to State to take the necessary steps to implement the air quality limit values,[178] and the Water Supply (Water Quality) Regulations 1989 prescribe maximum concentrations of chemicals and other substances.[179]

### (d) Specification and Performance Standards

The public interest goal of optimal pollution, whether or not it is reflected in an AQS, must be translated into standards directly applicable to a discharging firm's behaviour, and hence into specification or performance standards.

Specification standards create no incentives for firms to control discharges or to develop cheaper modes of abatement. Although for reasons already explored,[180] some firms may prefer them, the public interest case for their use is weak, at least where performance standards—

---

[173] 5th Report of Royal Commission, above, n. 161, paras. 182–3. One advocate of the traditional approach described them as 'a bureaucratic crime against the people. They bear little resemblance to what is or can be done in the circumstances to control or abate pollution. The assumptions behind them are false, and their existence leads to dishonest and irrelevant arguments': R. Scorer, *Pollution in the Air* (1973), pp. 74–5.

[174] T. O'Riordan, *Environmentalism* (2nd edn., 1981), pp. 232–3; Vogel, above, n. 146, pp. 83–5, 91–3.

[175] See esp. White Paper, *The Common Inheritance: Britain's Environmental Strategy* (1990, Cm. 1200), paras. 11.8 (air) and 12.6 (water). See also Macrory, above, n. 157.

[176] Directive 80/779 (for sulphur dioxide and smoke) and 85/203 (for nitrogen dioxide); see Haigh, above, n. 158, pp. 182–200.

[177] Directive 80/778; Haigh, above, n. 158, pp. 42–50.     [178] SI 1989/317.

[179] SI 1989/1147.     [180] Above, pp. 167 and 172.

i.e. controls on emissions—can be applied relatively cheaply.[181] There are nevertheless a number of specification standards currently in force, the majority surviving from earlier legislation: for example, requirements as to the heights of chimneys and the fitting of grit and dust arrestment plants to furnaces.[182] Perhaps the most important instances relate to the use and content of certain fuels.[183]

Performance standards, in the form of prohibitions on the discharge of certain substances, or maximum emission limits, constitute the most widely used pollution control mechanism. The most striking feature of the standards is that, with only a few exceptions,[184] they do not appear in any legislative instrument. The principal legal technique is to require firms to obtain from the regulatory agency a consent or authorization for the emission of pollutants, and for the agency, in an exercise of its statutory discretion, to impose performance standards as a condition for the granting of the consent or authorization.[185] This technique is deeply rooted in the British approach to pollution control and is based on two broad assumptions: that differentiated performance standards are preferable to uniform performance standards; and that they are most effective when negotiated between polluters and the agency.

The public interest justification for differentiated performance standards is that, as a consequence of geographical and other circumstances, there are often significant variations in the damage costs arising from a particular discharge and in the costs of abating it.[186] Damage costs may vary according to the number of firms discharging into an airshed or watershed and/or the relative assimilative capacity of the particular environment. Differences in abatement costs may arise, for example, from the size of the firm (there are economies of scale in abatement) and the age of its plant (older equipment increasing the cost).

An objection sometimes made to differentiated standards is that they will encourage firms to relocate to areas with less stringent emission limits and that this will lead to pollution being spread more evenly. For those who wish to maintain higher levels of environmental quality in certain areas, this would be undesirable. The objection can be easily met if stricter

[181] Richardson et al., above, n. 155, pp. 39–40.

[182] Clean Air Act 1993, ss. 14 and 6, respectively.

[183] e.g. Motor Fuel (Sulphur Content of Gas Oil) Regulations, SI 1976/1989, (as amended) implementing EC Directive 87/219 and Motor Fuel (Lead Content of Petrol) Regulations, SI 1981/1523, (as amended) implementing EC Directive 85/210. For tax solutions to these problems, see below, p. 247.

[184] Notably: Alkali &c. Works Regulation Act 1906 (sulphuric and hydrochloric acid gas); Clean Air (Emission of Grit and Dust from Furnaces) Regulations, SI 1971/162; Road Vehicles (Construction and Use) Regulations, SI 1986/1078, (as amended) implementing EC Directives 78/665, 83/351, and 88/76 (carbon monoxide, hydrocarbons, and nitrous oxide).

[185] Environmental Protection Act 1990, ss. 6–7; Water Resources Act 1991, ss. 85–88.

[186] P. Burrows, The Economic Theory of Pollution Control (1979), pp. 125–131; Richardson et al., above, n. 155, pp. 48–55.

AQSs are set for such areas. There are, however, more potent arguments in favour of uniform standards: they encourage firms to develop cheaper methods of abatement; they are less costly to formulate and administer; and they do not depend on individual bargaining between the agency and polluters, and thus are less vulnerable to manipulation by private interests.

These arguments take us back to the second of the two assumptions underlying the British approach. Until recently, the standards negotiated between agencies and polluters were not available for general inspection.[187] Pressure to render the system of differentiated standards compatible with a greater degree of agency accountability and public participation in decision-making has led to some significant reforms. After considerable delay and vacillation, a statutory requirement that the content of consents for water pollution be published in a public register was introduced in 1984[188] and a similar mechanism has been established for authorizations under the Environmental Protection Act 1990.[189]

These measures were, in part, a response to the EC policy of environmental information dissemination.[190] The UK government has been much less willing to compromise its traditional stance on uniform performance standards.[191] Thus, while under a 1976 Directive uniform emission limits are set for certain dangerous substances discharged into water, Member States can apply their own local limits so long as they meet the relevant AQS.[192] A general framework Directive of 1984 enabled the Council to establish uniform limits for a large variety of atmospheric pollutants from industrial plants,[193] but this is subject to a unanimity voting rule and, unsurprisingly, such limits have not been introduced. Although uniform performance standards have been created to govern emissions from motor vehicles,[194] the circumstances here are exceptional: the pollution sources are highly homogeneous and the market is dominated by a small number of multi-national firms.[195]

## (e) Conclusions

The legal framework, at both EC and national level, may be capable of formulating standards which are adequate to meet the public interest goal

[187] See, for air pollution, M. Frankel, *The Alkali Inspectorate* (1974), and for water pollution, K. Hawkins, *Environment and Enforcement* (1984), pp. 32–3.

[188] The relevant statutory provision was included in the Control of Pollution Act 1974, s. 41. A primary reason for the ten years' delay in implementation was the need to review the conditions stipulated in consents so as to bring them in line with the actual level of discharges! see above, p. 96.                                                  [189] Ss. 20–2.

[190] See Directive 90/313. The policy has led, *inter alia*, to mandatory environmental impact assessments in relation to planning applications for certain projects: Town and Country Planning (Assessment of Environmental Effects) Regulations, SI 1988/1199.

[191] Haigh, above, n. 158, pp. 17–18.

[192] Directive 76/464.                                        [193] Directive 84/360, Art. 8.

[194] Above n. 184.                                            [195] Cf. above, n. 104.

of optimal pollution. Whether it does so is another matter, and doubts arise as to several features of the system.

The acceptance of BPEO and similar appraisal methods suggests that standard-setters are, or should be, attempting to make an appropriate trade-off between the costs and benefits of pollution abatement. But, however good the information they use, many of the variables are bound to be highly speculative. The greater the uncertainty, the more space this allows for private interests to exert an influence on standard-setters. Notwithstanding the political power of environmental groups, it is to be expected that they will have a greater impact on the langauge and rhetoric of the law than on its detailed contents.

At 'ground' level, where the majority of performance standards continue to be formulated, the influence of polluting firms remains dominant. Empirical evidence suggests that agency officials, in exercising their discretion, find it difficult to resist arguments for leniency based on grounds—for example, that a firm is in financial difficulties or that there is high unemployment in the area[196]—which on BPEO-type analysis are strictly irrelevant.[197] Public access to information on the content of individualized standards may influence the *enforcement* behaviour of agency officials. It is, however, unlikely to affect the *formulation* of the standards, except, paradoxically, to reduce their severity, given that officials will not want to see their enforcement role usurped by members of the public.[198]

AQSs represent a (welcome) intrusion of European legal method into the British tradition: they serve as a formal link between EC environmental policy and UK national standards, and provide a new instrument for the accountability of domestic standard-setters. Their efficacy is, however, subject to institutional, political, and legal limitations.[199] Formulating standards at Community level is as speculative and uncertain as at national level and, in the absence of direct democratic constraints on Council decisions, AQSs can too easily be undermined by sectional interests. If the lobbying power of industrialist groups tends to prevail over that of environmentalists at a domestic level, the disparity is likely to be even greater at Community level.[200] This can be explained by reference to private interest theory.[201] Industrialists can co-ordinate their lobbying efforts across national frontiers more cheaply than environmentalists. Further, while the political influence of environmentalists on the European

---

[196] Richardson *et al.*, above, n. 155, pp. 110–13.

[197] 12th Report of Royal Commission, above, n. 161, paras. 2.7–8.

[198] Cf. above, n. 188.

[199] E. Klatte, 'Environmental and Economic Integration in the EC', in Lomas, above, n. 142, ch. 4.

[200] Rehbinder and Stewart, above, n. 172, pp. 270–6.  [201] Above, pp. 70–1.

Commission and Council is blunted by the fact that they have no direct electoral link with these authorities and therefore have no political 'price' to pay for regulatory benefits, the authorities require some co-operation from polluters if effective laws are to be devised, and hence, to a certain degree, will need to placate them.

An additional problem is the absence of effective enforcement machinery at EC level. A European Environment Agency was created in 1990,[202] but its responsibility is mainly that of collecting information from national agencies;[203] it does not have the powers or resources itself to monitor polluter behaviour. It is generally recognized that the Member States have a poor record of implementing European Directives on environmental matters[204] and it cannot be expected that a national agency will pursue a rigorous enforcement policy if it suspects that its foreign equivalents are not doing the same.

[202] EC Regulation 1210/90.

[203] P. Sands, 'European Community Environmental Law: Legislation, the European Court of Justice and Common-Interest Groups' (1990) 53 Modern LR 685, 690–1.

[204] Klatte, above, n. 199, p. 47.

# 10

# Prior Approval

### I. INTRODUCTION

In this chapter we consider situations in which an individual or firm must seek a licence or permit from a regulatory body in order to undertake an activity. The regulatory technique dates back to the medieval guilds, which had effective monopolies over trades and crafts, and to the issuing of 'patents of monopoly' under royal prerogative, enabling certain individuals or groups to carry out trades or activities otherwise prohibited.[1]

Then, as now, this type of control could be used not only to preserve minimum standards of quality but also to limit competition. For the purposes of analysing modern instruments we shall nevertheless distinguish between controls the ostensible aim (i.e. public interest justification) of which is to determine whether the applicants for the licence satisfy certain minimum quality standards—the subject of this chapter—and those which select out a limited number of successful applicants from a larger group, all of whom have adequate qualifications.[2] The latter are used where supply is limited either because the conditions of a natural monopoly exist or because it is government policy artificially to restrict competition: they will be considered in Chapter 15.

The licences which we discuss in this chapter differ from other regulatory forms in a number of important respects:[3] they are issued before the regulated activity has taken place, the ostensible purpose being to *prevent* the occurrence of what is regarded as socially undesirable; the potential quality of performance of *all* those engaged in the activity has to be assessed to ascertain whether it achieves the required standards; typically the conditions for the licence involve only *minimum* and *uniform* standards;[4] and the sanction—prohibition of the occupation or activity—is particularly severe. The administrative costs of scrutinizing all applications is very high and to these must be added the opportunity costs arising from any delay before the licence is granted. Last, and by no means least,

---

[1] S. Kramer, *The English Craft Guilds* (1927); S. Rubin, 'The Legal Web of Professional Regulation', in R. D. Blair and S. Rubin (eds.), *Regulating the Professions* (1980), pp. 31–4; A. I. Ogus, 'Regulatory law: some lessons from the past' (1992) 12 Legal Stud. 1, 8, 14.

[2] S. Breyer, *Regulation and its Reform* (1982), pp. 71–2, 131.

[3] Cf. R. Cranston, 'Reform Through Legislation: the dimension of legislative technique' (1978) 73 Northwestern ULR 873, 894–904.

[4] Although the licensing regime is often combined with a system of ongoing standards which may be differentiated.

significant welfare losses arise if the system is used for the anti-competitive purpose of creating barriers to entry. In short, the benefit from prior scrutiny must be very large to justify, on public interest grounds, these substantial costs.

Two sets of circumstances in which such large benefits are likely to arise may be identified.[5] The first comprises cases (e.g. nuclear accidents) where the consequences of performance failure may be so catastrophic, or the social aversion to them so high, that prior scrutiny and prevention is perceived to be preferable to deterrence from the threat of *ex post* sanctions. In sharp contrast, the second category does not necessarily give rise to large losses in individual cases. The problem, which is particularly acute in relation to the provision of services,[6] is rather that of expressing or measuring a variety of characteristics of performance in such a succinct and yet comprehensive manner that they can be formulated as enforceable standards.[7] The assessment of a multitude of factors is facilitated by the case-by-case approach adopted in the licensing process.

Licensing systems must be distinguished from what are generally referred to as 'registration' or 'certification' systems.[8] A requirement that an individual or firm be 'registered' with an agency, without satisfying any condition of competence or quality, by itself only reduces information costs: it provides easy access to the individual's or firm's address. A 'certification' system, on the other hand, may closely resemble licensing in the conditions which it imposes on applicants. The crucial difference is that it is lawful to engage in an activity which is not certified. Certification thus constitutes an indicator of quality to those consumers who wish to make use of it; but freedom of choice between certified and uncertified activities is preserved. In theory, then, certification is a form of information regulation, the subject-matter of Chapter 7. In practice, as we shall see, in some areas it is effectively equivalent to licensing because there is an insufficient demand from consumers to purchase what is uncertified.

For convenience, we categorize licensing systems under four heads: professional occupations; other occupations and commercial activities; products; and land use. In relation to each we must consider the ostensible public interest justifications—normally forms of market failure—but also private interest explanations, which have been particularly prominent in this area because of the anti-competitive effects of licensing.

[5] See also S. Shavell, 'The Optimal Structure of Law Enforcement' (1993) 36 J. Law & Econ. 255, 279–81.

[6] K. Walsh, 'Quality and Public Services' (1991) 69 Pub. Admin. 503.

[7] R. Stewart, 'Regulation, Innovation and Administrative Law: A Conceptual Framework' (1981) 69 Calif. LR 1256, 1265–6.

[8] T. Moore, 'The Purpose of Licensing' (1961) 4 J. Law & Econ. 93, 104–6; A. D. Wolfson, M. J. Trebilcock, and C. J. Tuohy, 'Regulating the Professions: A Theoretical Framework', in S. Rottenberg (ed.), *Occupational Licensure and Regulation* (1980), pp. 203–6; B. Shimberg, *Occupational Licensing: A Public Perspective* (1982), pp. 15–18.

## 2. LICENSING OF PROFESSIONAL OCCUPATIONS

### (a) Introduction

No clear dividing lines exist between a 'profession', an 'occupation', a 'trade', and an 'activity'. 'Profession' is a value-laden term, and much associated with historical tradition,[9] but occupations which are today generally accepted as falling within this category typically possess some or all of the following characteristics:[10] they require a specialized skill enabling them to offer a specialized service; that skill is acquired by intellectual and practical training; the service calls for a high degree of detachment and integrity; and it involves direct, personal, and fiduciary relations with clients. These characteristics have been used as arguments for special types of licensing systems, including notably the delegation of the power to issue licences to an agency dominated by members of the profession.

### (b) Economic Justifications: Information Deficits

The two principal economic arguments for professional licensing are information deficits and externalities.[11] As regards information, services are in general equivalent to what were described in a previous chapter as 'experience' or 'credence' goods:[12] a purchaser cannot normally verify quality except through consumption, and sometimes not even then. The potential welfare losses arising from undesired low quality may be high if, as with medical care, the service may generate risks to health and safety. It is particularly difficult for the provider of services (and third-party information brokers) to communicate indicators of quality; and in an unregulated market the result is a general lowering of standards.[13] These problems are compounded by the nature of the dependent relationship between a client and many, particularly professional, expert service providers.[14] Typically the client confers a discretion on the expert to diagnose the problem, determine the most appropriate solution, and—if she is competent to do so—provide that solution. Such discretion creates a conflict of interest, since the expert may be financially motivated to provide services which the client, if properly informed, would not have

---

[9] Cf. W. Moore, *The Professions: Roles and Rules* (1970), ch. 1.

[10] Monopolies Commission, Report on the General Effect on the Public Interest of Certain Restrictive Practices . . . in relation to the Supply of Professional Services (1970, Cmnd. 4463), para. 21. See also I. Horowitz, 'The Economic Foundations of Self-Regulation in the Professions', in Blair and Rubin, above, n. 1, pp. 4–6.

[11] Moore, above, n. 8, pp. 104, 109–10; Wolfson *et al.*, above, n. 8, pp. 190–4; H. E. Leland, 'Minimum-Quality Standards and Licensing in Markets with Asymmetric Information', in Rottenberg, above, n. 8, pp. 264–84.

[12] Above, pp. 132–3.                         [13] Cf. above, p. 132.

[14] Wolfson *et al.*, above, n. 8, p. 191; J. H. Beales, 'The Economics of Regulating the Professions', in Blair and Rubin, above, n. 1, pp. 125–30.

wanted—what is often referred to as 'demand generation'. This possibility may be constrained if the client has regular dealings with the supplier, since the latter will have an incentive to establish the client's trust, but not in cases of a 'one-off' transaction.

The private law provides, in principle, the means to combat these problems. The contract between the client and the supplier may contain implied terms on the quality of the service; and there is residual tort liability where the client suffers damage as a result of the supplier's negligence.[15] Further, to deal with potential conflicts of interest, the law imposes on many professionals a fiduciary duty, as a result of which personal profit motives must be subordinated to protection of the client's interests.[16] However, there are significant shortcomings to these solutions. Remedies must be pursued by the client which will be problematic if she has only a vague perception of the difference between the quality of service she has received and that which the private law requires. Moreover, she may find it difficult to find another professional to support her claim or act as expert witness. Finally, because of the difficulty of defining appropriate standards, actions of this kind often give rise to complex and protracted litigation which is very costly.

These arguments appear to raise a strong presumption for regulation—but not necessarily licensing. Certification can overcome the information deficit as well as licensing, and yet it possesses the additional advantage of preserving freedom of choice: consumers who want to can elect for a lower quality service at what will be a lower price.

### (c) Economic Justifications: Externalities

The quality of the service may affect third parties as well as the client. For example, a poorly designed or constructed building may create risks for users of the building who were in no way involved in the original dealings with an architect or engineer; an incompetently drafted will or conveyance may impose losses on individuals far removed from the negligent solicitor; and a failure by a doctor in treating a contagious disease may give rise to an epidemic.

Some frequently encountered 'public interest' arguments for strict controls on entry to certain professions[17] may be construed in terms of externalities. Thus, lawyers have an overriding duty to the courts, and other institutions of the administration of justice, which on occasions must prevail over the interests of clients. And accountants, in carrying out audits, perform that function not only for the company and its share-holders, but also to uphold the general standards of financial reporting

---

[15] A. M. Dugdale and K. M. Stanton, *Professional Negligence* (2nd edn., 1989).
[16] Ibid. ch. 14.
[17] See e.g. Report of the Monopolies Commission, above, n. 10, para. 48.

necessary for commercial life. Finally, there may be psychological benefits accruing to the community generally from the knowledge that quacks and rogues are not allowed to practise.

Such external effects are not, of course, peculiar to low quality professional work, but may arise from a wide range of industrial and commercial activities in relation to which arguments for licensing are rarely made. To justify licensing, it needs to be shown that civil law remedies and other, less restrictive, regulatory techniques are not adequate to meet the problem. Tort liability has little impact in 'public interest' situations where the potential harm is very diffuse. It is not much more effective when the third parties at risk are easily identified, because of the difficulty of establishing that they were owed a duty by the professional, and that the causal link between the negligence and the eventual loss was sufficiently strong.[18] Unless it evolves into an effective licensing system, certification too will prove to be an inadequate solution, because it does not prevent clients from choosing the poorer-quality services which impact on third parties. *Ex post* quality standards, the regulatory technique used for most externality problems, may be a less effective response than licensing where the latter is able, relatively easily and cheaply, to exclude *ex ante* manifest incompetence of a kind which can give rise to high social costs.[19]

### (d) Non-Economic

Paternalist motivations for regulation[20] are rarely made explicit but they may provide a plausible explanation for some occupational licensing systems. Two independent sets of arguments are relevant here.[21] First, policy-makers may consider that individuals systematically misinterpret information that is available to them, by underestimating certain risks, for example. If the goal is then to confer on such individuals the level of welfare they would have desired if the information had been correctly interpreted, this may be done by depriving them of the possibility of opting for a higher risk alternative. Situations which give rise to this concern are likely to have the following characteristics: the variance in the quality offered within the occupation is high; the potential losses arising from such variance are large; and the degree of education or training necessary to evaluate risks arising from the service is also large.

The second argument is that even if information is correctly interpreted individuals may make decisions which, in the opinion of others, are not in their own best interests. As we saw in a previous chapter,[22] there are differences of opinion as to why policy-makers should adopt this stance

---

[18] Dugdale and Stanton, above, n. 15, pp. 77–81, 97–107.
[19] Cf. Report of the Monopolies Commission, above, n. 10, para. 297.
[20] Cf. above, pp. 51–3.
[21] Moore, above, n. 8, pp. 106–9.                    [22] Above, p. 53.

and, in consequence, considerable difficulties as to determining when intervention on this basis is appropriate.

## (e) Private Interest Explanations

Since Milton Friedman's seminal early work on the professions,[23] private interest explanations (and criticisms) of occupational licensing systems have abounded.[24] The efforts of various professional groups and associations to obtain licensing legislation for their occupation are well documented.[25] It is not difficult to understand their enthusiasm. The conditions which applicants must satisfy to obtain a licence (notably training) raise the costs of entry; and of course the more severe the conditions, the higher the costs. The increase in costs will reduce the supply of services and raise prices. The extent of the latter and the extent to which the supplier will profit from the higher prices will depend on the availability in the market of substitutes for the services: the more imperfect the substitute, the higher the price increase, and the greater the profit (rent) earned by the supplier. Given that there are generally only poor substitutes for most professional services, members of licensed professions are often able to earn substantial rents.

Licensing serves the private interest of practitioners in another way. Those who have invested a substantial amount of time in training benefit from 'career insurance', because as that training leads to greater specialization, the diversification of skills and shifting between occupations become more difficult.[26] To the extent that licensing can maintain the returns of the investment in specialisms by constraining the development of substitutes it provides this insurance.

But if the explanation for the introduction of a licensing system is to be sought in the private benefits which it confers on the licensees, is there not an obstacle? Existing members of the hitherto unlicensed profession may not have the qualifications which it is intended to impose as conditions of entry and will not want to incur the additional cost of obtaining those

---

[23] M. Friedman and S. Kuznets, *Income from Independent Professional Practice* (1945). See also M. Friedman, *Capitalism and Freedom* (1962), pp. 144–9.

[24] See esp. A. Maurizi, 'Occupational Licensing and the Public Interest' (1974) 82 J. Pol. Econ. 399; W. Gellhorn, 'The Abuse of Occupational Licensing' (1976) 44 U. Chicago LR 6; L. Shepard, 'Licensing Restrictions and the Cost of Dental Care' (1978) 21 J. Law & Econ. 187; W. D. White, 'Dynamic Elements of Regulation: The Case of Occupational Licensure' (1979) 1 Res. Law & Econ. 15; L. Benham, 'The Demand for Occupational Licensure', in Rottenberg, above, n. 8, pp. 13–25; J. K. Smith, 'Production of Licensing Legislation: An Economic Analysis of Interstate Differences' (1982) 11 J. Legal Stud. 117; R. Van den Bergh and M. Faure, 'Self-Regulation of the Professions in Belgium' (1991) 11 Int. Rev. Law & Econ. 165.

[25] A good example from Britain is osteopathy: see Monopolies and Mergers Commission, *Services of Professionally Regulated Osteopaths* (1989, Cm. 583), pp. 4–5.

[26] Benham, above, n. 24, pp. 14–15.

qualifications. The obstacle is invariably overcome by the insertion of 'grandfather clauses' in the relevant legislation: existing members of the profession are normally exempt from the new controls.[27]

Licensing systems are more difficult to abolish once established than to oppose at the time of introduction.[28] Following the introduction of licensing, there will be a time lag before the new conditions impact on the earnings of practitioners; conversely, if the conditions are removed, the earnings fall immediately. In other words, the present value of losses to practitioners from removing licensing protection is likely to be greater than the present value of gains from introducing such a system.

### (f) Legal Forms

Although variations occur, much of the regulation of occupations in Britain conforms to a standard pattern. Legislation creates a Professional Council, usually dominated by representatives of the occupation,[29] with authority to establish a register of practitioners and to lay down quality standards for practice. The Act then stipulates the conditions which must be satisfied for a practitioner to be entered on the register. What is appropriate in terms of education, training, and practical experience is often left to be determined by the Professional Council, but other requirements, such as age, health, 'good character', and (if the applicant has been trained abroad) language competence, are generally laid down in the statute. If registration is a novelty, or if the conditions for qualification are made stricter than under previous regimes, the legislation includes 'grandfather clauses', provisions which exempt existing practitioners from the new requirements.[30]

The grounds on which the Council may erase a name from the register are invariably made explicit. These generally include, in addition to convictions for criminal offences,[31] 'serious professional misconduct',[32] the meaning of which is left to be determined by the Disciplinary Committee of the Council.[33]

If the profession is governed by a licensing system (in Britain, dentists,

---

[27] For a 'semi-official' recognition that this is necessary to introduce new licensing conditions, see the Report of the [Merrison] Committee of Inquiry into the Regulation of the Medical Profession, (1975, Cmnd. 6018), para. 166.

[28] White, above, n. 24.

[29] For discussion of the self-regulatory aspects, see above, pp. 107–11.

[30] e.g. Insurance Brokers (Registration) Act 1977, s. 3.

[31] Sometimes this is limited to criminal offences (e.g. of dishonesty etc.) which are particularly relevant to the occupation—Estate Agents Act 1979, s. 3; Insurance Brokers (Registration) Act 1977, s. 15—but, more frequently, they cover all criminal offences.

[32] Cp. 'unprofessional conduct': Insurance Brokers (Registration) Act 1977, s. 15.

[33] Subject, of course, to judicial review by the ordinary courts, or appeal to the Judicial Committee of the Privy Council. On 'serious professional misconduct', see esp. *Doughty* v. *General Dental Council* [1988] AC 164.

midwives, patent agents, pharmacists, opticians, solicitors, veterinary surgeons) the legislation[34] makes it a criminal offence for an unregistered person to practise in the occupation. Thus only registered ophthalmic opticians may 'test the sight of another person' or fit contact lenses.[35] But it is often extremely difficult to formulate definitions of activities or practices intended to be conducted *exclusively* by members of the profession. In the case of dentistry, the legislation resorts to a most unhelpful formula: only registered dentists may 'practice . . . dentistry'[36] and the 'practice of dentistry' is deemed to include 'the performance of any such operation and the giving of any such treatment, advice or attendance as is usually performed or given by dentists'.[37] Obviously, legislation cannot prohibit the giving of legal advice by a lay person and consequently the only parts of legal practice which have been or are reserved for the legal professions are: rights of audience in the higher courts; the conduct of litigation; the drawing up of documents for the administration of deceased persons' estates or for the transfer of real property.[38] So, also, it would appear to be impossible to define medical practice in a way which does not overlap with general health care which lay persons obviously, regularly, and properly undertake. For that reason, strictly speaking, medical practice in the United Kingdom is not a licensed occupation; and the same is true of architecture and accountancy.

Under all the relevant legislation, it is an offence to claim falsely to be registered. Most statutes also reserve the use of certain titles—for example, 'medical practitioner'[39]—to those who are enrolled on the register. This, of course, represents the central feature of a certification system: an information signal to the consumer that individuals with specific designations or titles have satisfied certain conditions, but without prohibiting others from practising. Certification may nevertheless become licensing *de facto*. The market demand for uncertified practitioners may be so small that they cease to exist.[40] This phenomenon may itself be a

---

[34] The principal measures are, respectively: Dentists Act 1984; Nurses, Midwives and Health Visitors Act 1979; Patents Act 1977; Pharmacy Act 1954; Opticians Act 1989; Solicitors Act 1974; Veterinary Surgeons Act 1966.

[35] Opticians Act 1989. s. 24.

[36] Dentists Act 1984, s. 38(1).                                        [37] Ibid. s. 37(1).

[38] Solicitors Act 1974, s. 22 (as amended). In pursuance of the goal of opening up legal services to competition (cf. White Paper, *Legal Services: A Framework for the Future* (1989, Cm. 740) ), the Courts and Legal Services Act 1990 enables the right to undertake these (and perhaps other) activities to be conferred on other occupational groups if an authorized body representing such a group is able to convince the Lord Chancellor (in consultation with other designated individuals) that an appropriate regulatory framework exists.

[39] Medical Act 1983, ss. 2 and 49.

[40] The Merrison Committee, above, n. 27, para. 26, considered that licensing of medical practitioners was unnecessary simply because the public would not want to be treated by unregistered individuals.

consequence of other regulatory instruments. One example is the Companies Act 1985, which requires that the mandatory auditing of the accounts of registered companies be undertaken by a member of the Institute of Chartered Accountants.[41] Another is the statutory provision that all doctors performing services for the National Health Service (a monopsonist buyer) must be registered medical practitioners.[42]

Mention should also be made of 'negative' licensing systems, even though strictly speaking they do not come within the category of prior approval regulation. Under such a system, an individual is permitted to engage in an occupation without any test of competence, but should an agency determine *ex post* that he fails to meet a minimum standard of quality, the right to practise may be abolished. Negative licensing has applied to estate agents since 1979, the power of issuing prohibition orders being conferred on the Director General of Fair Trading.[43]

## (g) The EC Dimension

National occupational licensing systems may obviously undermine some key principles of the Treaty of Rome, notably freedom to provide services and freedom of establishment.[44] The argument that such a system does not discriminate against nationals of another member state in that they are free to obtain the requisite qualifications is hardly to the point. On the assumption that, for certain occupations at least, consumers' needs (and therefore appropriate minimum standards) do not vary significantly across the Community, professionals licensed in one state should be free to practise in another.

The goal may be easily stated, and in 1961 a programme to harmonize national systems for professional qualifications was instituted;[45] but, as private interest theory would predict, progress on this programme was painfully slow—in the case of architects it took 17 years to produce a, Directive.[46] Within any one system, a public institution concerned to limit barriers to entry to those which reasonably correlate to public interest justifications has difficulty in confronting a professional association which purports to monopolize wisdom on the issue. Those difficulties are exacerbated when the number of associations, often with different traditions and professional cultures, are multiplied, and many of them

---

[41] S. 389.                          [42] National Health Service Act 1977, s. 128(1).
[43] Estate Agents Act 1979, s. 3.
[44] Arts. 59 and 52, respectively. See generally N. Green, T. Hartley, and J. Usher, *The Legal Foundations of the Single European Market* (1991), ch. 12; R. van den Bergh, 'Self-Regulation in the Medical and Legal Professions and the European Internal Market in Progress', in M. Faure, J. Finsinger, J. Siegers, and R. van den Bergh (eds.), *Regulation of Professions* (1993), pp. 21–43.                          [45] See esp. Directive 64/222.
[46] Directive 85/384.

claim that their own set of conditions is essential for practice in their country.

Given the slowness of progress on harmonization, the Community decided, in 1984, to reorientate the programme. The new and less ambitious approach concentrated on mutual recognition of qualifications but enabled host states to require that migrant practitioners serve an adaptation period, not exceeding three years, or pass an aptitude test.[47] Although much will depend on the rigour of the latter, it is clear that it may allow barriers of entry to be preserved.[48]

*(h) Assessment*

There are obvious difficulties in applying public interest justifications to the British licensing regimes. One is that in relation to, for example, dentists, opticians, solicitors, and veterinary surgeons, externalities are probably less significant than the information and agency problems; and yet, as we have seen, certification should constitute an adequate solution to the latter. In any event, licensing systems do not result in a good correlation between the nature of the input control—the conditions which have to be satisfied to qualify for entry to the profession—and the alleged public interest goal of quality output.[49]

The conditions typically involve a test only of a minimum standard of quality at the outset of an individual's professional career: they provide no guarantee of continuing competence, nor of the ability to adapt to technological change. Although some professional associations are now insisting on some form of continuing education,[50] the requirement is invariably limited to *attendance* at relevant courses, no examination being envisaged. Moreover, initial tests of minimum quality relate to the generality of professional practice and provide no indication of competence in specialist areas which, with technological development, have become increasingly important.[51] Some of the conditions for professional licences are the result more of history and custom than of a rational

---

[47] Directive 89/48, Arts. 4–5. For more detailed discussion, see Green *et al.*, above, n. 44, pp. 163–7.

[48] The aptitude tests for foreign lawyers devised by the Bar Council and the Law Society require *inter alia*, knowledge of English property and trusts law, and it would seem that the majority of successful candidates have been from other jurisdictions within the British Isles.

[49] Shimberg, above, n. 8, ch. 3; Wolfson *et al.*, above, n. 8, pp. 204, 207.

[50] See e.g. the Law Society's Post Admission Training Regulations 1991.

[51] 'The result is undoubtedly that the skills available to consumers are too low for the more complex tasks and too high for the simple ones': Beales, above, n. 14, p. 133. This problem was a major concern of the Merrison Committee on the Medical Profession, above, n. 27, ch. 2. Its recommendation for a 'specialist register' was implemented in 1991 (to bring the UK in line with EC developments) but in an unsatisfactory form, the General Medical Council having only limited control over eligibility for entry: M. Brazier *et al.*, 'The Regulation of Doctors and Lawyers in England and Wales' (1992) Manchester Papers in Politics, p. 10.

decision as to what is desirable. At best such conditions are irrelevant; at worst they constitute a significant and unjustified barrier to entry. The requirement that potential barristers 'eat dinners' at one of the Inns of Court in London is a good example, as it imposes a non-trivial cost on students who have to travel some distance.[52] Finally, even if input controls of this type do provide good indicators of quality, it is unclear how they can be used to constrain demand generation, the problem of providing clients with unnecessary services.

The above arguments suggest that the benefits of licensure are not as great as groups representing the professions often allege.[53] What of its costs? In comparison to other regulatory forms, the administrative and enforcement costs are low: the agency is not concerned with formulating and monitoring gradations of quality—it is simply a question of determining whether an individual has or has not satisfied the qualifying conditions and maintaining the register.

The more interesting and significant questions relate to indirect costs. We saw earlier that restricting entry generates welfare losses. How large those losses are, and whether they exceed the benefits of licensure, will naturally depend on the extent to which supply is constrained, and that will vary from profession to profession. The fact that the agency which determines the conditions of entry is usually dominated by representatives of existing practitioners may give rise to the private interest hypothesis that it will use its power to create rents for the latter. But that hypothesis has still to be validated by empirical evidence. There are several American studies which demonstrate that the introduction of licensing, or the strengthening of licensing laws, resulted in an increase in the earnings of the profession in question.[54] But there are others which show that it had no such impact, or at least that the evidence was ambivalent.[55]

When reviewing British licensing systems in 1970, the Monopolies Commission found no evidence of attempts by professional bodies to set specific limits to the total number of entrants.[56] But, of course, that does not preclude the possibility that these bodies were able to limit supply

---

[52] The alleged public interest justification is that it assists in the absorption of professional ethics: Report of the Royal Commission on Legal Services (1979, Cmnd. 7648), i, pp. 641–2.

[53] Some American studies purport to show that the introduction of licensing does not significantly improve the quality of services: F. McChesney and T. J. Muris, 'The Effect of Advertising on the Quality of Legal Services' (1979) 65 ABA J 1503; S. L. Carroll and R. J. Gaston, 'State Occupational Licensing Provisions and Quality of Service: The Real Estate Business' (1979) 1 Res. Law & Econ. 1.

[54] The pioneering study was carried out by Friedman and Kuznets, above, n. 23. For others, see: Maurizi, above, n. 24; Shepard, above, n. 24; W. D. White, 'The Impact of Occupational Licensure on Clinical Laboratory Personnel' (1978) 13 J. Human Resources 91.

[55] Moore, above, n. 8; W. D. White, 'Mandatory Licensure of Registered Nurses: Introducton and Impact', in Rottenberg, above, n. 8, pp. 47–72.

[56] Above n. 10, para. 86.

under the guise of other goals, such as the raising of examination standards. The institutional arrangements at the English Bar—the requirements to eat dinners and train in London, the difficulties of obtaining pupillage and tenancies, and the low earnings during the early years of practice—have undoubtedly constituted indirect barriers to entry.[57]

Other indirect costs must also be taken into account. Licensing systems enable self-regulatory bodies to impose on members standards which may not be justifiable on public interest grounds. For example, most professional associations have, at some time or another, prohibited their members from advertising, ostensibly on the ground that 'touting' for business is incompatible with the ethical nature of professional practice. As we have seen in another chapter, such bans have led to higher consumer search costs and monopoly rents for practitioners.[58] Licensing tends also to stifle innovation. The self-regulatory bodies tend to be dominated by senior members of the profession who adhere to, and therefore may wish to protect, traditional practices and methods. And, of course, it is necessary to deal with the threat of para-professionals: those who purport to find an alternative solution to the consumer's problems at substantially lower costs.[59] Struggles for territory not only between professionals and para-professionals but also between two or more different professional groups are socially wasteful in that they often give rise to substantial costs without any equivalent welfare gain.[60]

Finally, any system which gives authority to an institution to confer rights to practise on the basis of talents and character creates opportunities for racial and gender discrimination.[61] Within recent years, most licensing bodies have been criticized on this ground and most have been forced to adjust recruitment policies.[62]

### 3. LICENSING OF OTHER OCCUPATIONS AND COMMERCIAL ACTIVITIES

#### (a) General

The extent to which licences or permits must be obtained in order lawfully to practise occupations which are not conventionally regarded as professions and other commercial activities varies enormously from country to

[57] R. Abel, *The Legal Profession in England and Wales* (1988), pp. 60–2; and see A. I. Ogus, 'Regulation of the Legal Profession in England and Wales', in Faure *et al.*, above, n. 44, pp. 317–22.

[58] Above, p.128.

[59] D. B. Hogan, *Regulation of Psychotherapists* (1979) i, pp. 277–9.

[60] Cf. J. B. Corgel, 'Occupational Boundary Setting and the Unauthorised Practice of Law by Real Estate Brokers' (1987) 10 Res. Law & Econ. 161.

[61] S. D. Young, *The Rule of Experts: Occupational Licensing in America* (1987), ch. 12.

[62] For the legal profession, see S. Bailey and M. Gunn, *Smith and Bailey on the Modern English Legal System* (2nd edn., 1991), pp. 167–71.

country.[63] In Belgium, for example, photographers and several retailing trades are so controlled.[64] In the USA, in one state or another, licences are required for over 400 occupations,[65] including such curiosities as ice cream buyers, tattoo artists, astrologers, and fortune-tellers,[66] as well as funeral directors and hairdressers.[67] In Britain,[68] the system is used to control the following occupations and activities (the list is not comprehensive): selling alcoholic liquor, firearms, or (in Scotland) second-hand cars; supplying consumer credit; driving vehicles; offering taxicabs for hire; operating nuclear installations, pet shops, riding establishments, zoos, slaughter-houses, betting shops, premises for gaming, sex shops, massage establish-ments in London, theatres and other places of entertainment, nurseries, or residential care homes; felling trees; catching sea fish and whales; treating, storing, or carrying out research on human embryos.[69]

The legal form resembles that of professional licensure but there are significant differences. First, certification is very rarely used as an alternative to licensing. Secondly, the authority granted power to issue licences is generally a public body, often under the aegis of local government, and thus largely independent of practitioners of the regulated trade. Thirdly, the conditions for obtaining the licence tend to be vaguer, reference being made, in the case of persons, to an individual's 'fitness' for the occupation and, in the case of premises, to their 'suitability' for the activity.

### (b) Public Interest Justifications: Information Problems, Situational Monopolies, and Paternalism

Of the licences for occupations and activities here being considered, it is only a minority which seem designed primarily to protect purchasers who

---

[63] For a valuable, if dated, comparative survey, see C. H. Fulda, 'Controls of Entry into Business and Professions—A Comparative Analysis' (1973) 8 Texas Int. LJ 109.

[64] R. van den Bergh, 'Belgian Public Policy Towards the Retailing Trade', in J.-M. von der Schulenberg and G. Skogh (eds.), *Law and Economics and the Economics of Legal Regulation* (1985), pp. 185–205.     [65] Young, above, n. 61, p. 5.

[66] Hogan, above, n. 59, p. 242.     [67] Moore, above, n. 8, p. 97.

[68] For a valuable, amusing and critical (if also dated) overview, see G. Williams, 'Control by Licensing' [1967] Current Legal Prob. 81. For Australia, see A. J. Duggan, 'Occupational Licensing and the Consumer Interest', in A. J. Duggan and L. W. Darvall (eds.), *Consumer Protection Law and Theory* (1980), pp. 163–81.

[69] The main instruments being, respectively: Licensing Act 1964; Firearms Act 1968; Civic Government (Scotland) Act 1982; Consumer Credit Act 1974; Road Traffic Act 1988; Town Police Clauses Act 1847; Nuclear Installations Act 1965; Pet Animals Act 1951; Riding Establishments Act 1964; Zoo Licensing Act 1981; Slaughterhouses Act 1974; Betting, Gaming and Lotteries Act 1963; Gaming Act 1968; Local Government (Miscellaneous Provisions) Act 1982; London County Council (General Powers) Act 1920; Private Places of Entertainment (Licensing) Act 1967; Theatres Act 1968; Cinemas Act 1985; Nurseries and Child Minding Registration Act 1945; Registered Homes Act 1984; Forestry Act 1967; Sea Fish (Conservation) Act 1967; Human Fertilisation and Embryology Act 1990.

may be susceptible to the information problems which we recognized might justify certification (but not necessarily licensing) of professional services. The fact that these are subject to a licensing regime suggests that the policy-maker, rightly or wrongly, assumes that providing information, by means of certification signals, is not the best way to guarantee consumer welfare.

As regards taxicabs, this unwillingness to allow unconstrained consumer choice may be justified by the peculiar market situation in which transactions often take place. Suppose that taxicabs were unlicensed. An individual hailing a cab in the street would, in practice, be unable to compare the price and other terms with those offered by other cab drivers: in short, the cab driver responding to the call has a *de facto* monopoly position, which can give rise to an extortionate price or other term.[70] It is surely not without significance that the licensing regime does not apply with the same rigour to cabs the rates of hire for which are agreed in advance by telephone;[71] this method facilitates the comparison of prices.

Paternalism would appear to constitute the other main reason for constraining consumer choice. Several of the licensed activities are potentially addictive (drinking alcohol, gambling) and, on one view of paternalism, it is not inconsistent with individual rational choice to recognize that to maximize welfare in the long term it may be preferable for an external force to limit short-term desires.[72] Other licensed services are regularly used by people who, for one reason or another, are vulnerable, and therefore may not be in a good position to determine what is in their own best interests. The licensing of consumer credit may be rationalized, in part at least, on this basis,[73] and equivalent controls on residential care homes are imposed only where the homes are provided for 'persons in need of personal care by reason of old age, disablement, past or present dependence on alcohol or drugs, or past or present mental disorder'.[74]

### (c) Public Interest Justifications: Externalities

The arguments for licensing most frequently used by policy-makers are effectively assertions that the activities in question give rise to important

[70] A 'situational monopoly' in contrast to a 'market-wide monopoly': see M. J. Trebilcock, 'An Economic Approach to the Doctrine of Unconscionability', in B. J. Reiter and J. Swan (eds.), *Studies in Contract Law* (1980), ch. 11.

[71] Transport Act 1985, s. 11.

[72] Cf. above, p. 52. See also D. Miers, 'The Gaming Board for Great Britain: Enforcement and Judicial Restraint', in R. Baldwin and C. McCrudden, *Regulation and Public Law* (1987), p. 83.

[73] Cf. Report of the [Crowther] Committee on Consumer Credit (1971, Cmnd. 4596), para. 6.1.7 (protection against 'improvidence').

[74] Registered Homes Act 1984, s. 1(1).

externalities.[75] For licensing to be justified on this basis it is, however, necessary to demonstrate, or at least assume, that subjecting actors to *ex ante* scrutiny (sometimes with on-going conditions for the validity of the licence) is more effective, i.e. less costly, than other methods of dealing with externalities: private law remedies or other regulatory techniques.

One prominent form of externality is the depletion of natural resources. Over-exploitation of such resources may interfere with the reproductive cycle and thus impose losses on future generations. The controls on catching sea fish and whales and on cutting timber are obvious examples; in relation to the latter, one of the statutory grounds on which the Forestry Commissioners may refuse a licence is 'for the purpose of complying with their duty of promoting the establishment and maintenance in Great Britain of adequate reserves of growing trees'.[76] Private property rights cannot be conferred on the losers in such cases (future generations). As regards other regulatory techniques, it would be possible simply to apply quantity standards to tree owners, but monitoring and enforcement would almost certainly be more costly than combining those standards with *ex ante* control.

While cruelty and other harm to animals may be regarded as an externality, rationalizing the proliferation of licensing systems in this area is more problematic. It is possible, though not obvious, that applying quality standards merely *ex post* would be more expensive in terms of administrative costs. Of course, the explanation may simply reside in the strength of the pro-animal lobby in the United Kingdom.

Using licences to forestall catastrophic losses, of the kind which may arise from nuclear installations or misuse of human embryos, is easier to justify. The sanctions incurred under the private law of torts (damages for injuries sustained by victims) or under conventional safety regulation may constitute inadequate incentives for a firm taking appropriate levels of care where the possibility of incurring the sanction is very low and yet the amount of the sanction very high. This is because the firm's managers may (rationally) decide to gamble that the tiny risk will not materialize and simply declare the firm insolvent should it do so.[77]

The possible externalities arising in the remaining areas of licensed activities have vaguer contours. Excessive drinking leads, among other things, to road accidents, violence, public nuisance, reduced productivity,

---

[75] Cf. P. J. Lloyd, 'The Economics of Regulation of Alcohol Distribution and Consumption in Victoria' (1985) 69 Australian Econ. Rev. 16.

[76] Forestry Act 1967, s. 10(3)(b).

[77] J. C. Coffee, ' "No Soul to Damn: No Body to Kick": An Unscandalized Inquiry into the Problem of Corporate Punishment' (1981) 79 Mich. LR 386, 390; S. Shavell, *Economic Analysis of Accident Law* (1987), pp. 167–70.

and disruption to family life.[78] Sex shops may cause offence to some people particularly if they are located in certain environments. The sale of firearms and certain gaming activities may be linked to crime, and massage parlours to prostitution.

The indirectness of the link between the activity and the social cost might suggest that licensing is a crude and undiscriminating weapon to deal with most of these problems.[79] For example, scrutinizing the credentials of a publican can hardly provide an indication of the level of drinking which will take place at his public house, should the licence be granted. There are, perhaps, answers to this. The possibility of a licence being revoked may be a more effective incentive to minimize the risk of social harm than a monetary sanction which will be applied *ex post*. Then, as regards the link between the licensed activity and crime, the system may substantially reduce the administrative costs of apprehending offenders. For example, to aid the pursuit of armed robbers, the police will at least have information on who may lawfully sell and possess firearms.

One further alleged benefit of licensing ought to be mentioned. There may be practices which are perceived as generating significant social costs, but which are difficult to define for the purposes of traditional quality standards. The flexibility inherent in the processes of granting and reviewing licences can be used to deter such conduct. Goode makes the point in relation to consumer credit licensing: 'the ability, through the licensing power, to nudge business away from practices which, though not unlawful, are generally accepted as undesirable, is obviously beneficial'. But there is a potential cost: 'the danger point is reached when, through the predilections of the particular administrator or his desire for consistency, business procedures are forced into an unnatural straitjacket, so that . . . business initiative is stifled'.[80]

### (d) Private Interest Explanations

By creating barriers to entry, licensing systems can generate rents for existing practitioners and actors. There is no need to repeat the arguments which were fully explored in relation to professional occupations.[81] What special considerations arise in relation to non-professional occupations and other commercial activities?

First, unless numbers are relatively small, non-professionals are likely to constitute a less homogenous group (and therefore a less effective lobby) than professionals, who tend to be bound by an ethic instilled as part of their training. Secondly, to counterbalance this, those engaged in some of the relevant activities can harness their demand for regulation with that of

---

[78] Report of the [Erroll] Departmental Committee on Liquor Licensing (1972, Cmnd. 5154), ch. 4.    [79] Cf. Lloyd, above, n. 75.
[80] R. Goode, *Consumer Credit* (1979), p. 44.    [81] Above, pp. 219–220.

significant sections of the community (with voting power) whose ideology leads them to press for the same control. Limiting the number of sex shops, and trees felled, or imposing rigorous controls on pet shops, is likely to have more voting appeal than (say) the granting of licences to dentists or lawyers. The resulting combination may make strange bedfellows—both breweries, as owners of public houses, and the temperance movement have an interest in limiting the number of 'on-premises licences'[82]—but is no less effective for that. Thirdly, representatives of existing practitioners have considerably less influence on the licence-conferring agency than professionals. The critical question, then, is whether the group is sufficiently powerful to succeed with either or both of the following strategies: persuading legislators (perhaps with the aid of bureaucrats) to write into the relevant statute a clause requiring the agency to 'protect' society against an 'over-provision' of the facility or service;[83] or persuading the agency to exercise its discretion to similar effect. As we shall soon see, both strategies have been effective in some areas.

### (e) Assessment

The comparing of costs and benefits is, as ever, a difficult task. To begin with, it should be observed that the administrative costs of processing applications are often significantly higher for the licence systems here being considered than for professional licences. For the latter, the process is typically confined to receiving and verifying character references and certificates relating to examination and training. What renders an individual a suitable person to carry out some of the licensed non-professional occupations may involve broader and less precise criteria, the testing of which imposes costs on both the applicant and the agency. It is also subject to indeterminacy: 'while it may be relatively easy to screen out those who are obviously unfit, it is very much more difficult . . . to screen out all those who are, or might prove to be, unfit'.[84] The costs are magnified if, as is required for some regulated activities, the agency has to decide, in addition, that the applicant's premises are suitable.

Given the size of these costs and the typically small number of applications which are rejected, some licensing systems may appear as 'sledgehammers to crack nuts'. Consumer credit licensing may be a good example.[85] Under the Consumer Credit Act 1974, all businesses which

---

[82] See the Erroll Committee Report, above, n. 78, pp. 79–80.

[83] e.g. Licensing (Scotland) Act 1976, s. 17(1)(d), on which see J. A. Cairns, 'Over-provision and the Licensing (Scotland) Act 1976' (1987) 7 Int. Rev. Law & Econ. 215.

[84] Miers, above, n. 72, p. 87.

[85] A. I. Ogus and C. K. Rowley, 'The Costs and Benefits of Part III of the Fair Trading Act 1973 and Licensing under the Consumer Credit Act 1974', unpub. research paper for the Office of Fair Trading (1981).

supply consumer credit as well as those which deal with such credit (e.g. debt collectors, credit brokers) must be licensed.[86] The laudable aim of this 'catch-all' approach was to sweep away technical and complex distinctions between different types of consumer credit,[87] but huge numbers are involved. From the inception of the scheme to the end of 1992, 351,850 applications for a licence had been made and 335,816 had been granted.[88] Proposals that negative licensing should replace the existing system for some categories of traders have been made[89] but, as yet, remain unimplemented.

The selection of occupations and activities for controls by licensing inevitably throws up anomalies. Some of these, such as dog licences,[90] can be explained simply as convenient methods of raising revenue.[91] Others are historical vestiges which, once established, are difficult to remove. A licence is needed for the 'reception or treatment [in London] of persons requiring massage manicure chiropody light electric vapour or other baths or other similar treatment'.[92] As one commentator has observed, 'whatever dark suspicions are aroused by the word "massage" can hardly apply to the other treatment mentioned; and I am not clear why manicurists in London need close control when those in Liverpool do not'.[93] The formidable array of controls on places of entertainment is probably best explained on historical grounds[94], although the application of the special safety standards required because of the size of audiences may be facilitated when combined with licences.

The problem of defining precisely the occupation or activity to be governed by the system leads to avoidance behaviour which can involve wasteful expenditure by the licence-avoider and costly monitoring by the regulatory agency. Thus, to avoid being characterized as 'sex shops',[95] certain Soho premises have shelves of 'non-pornographic' books and magazines which no one who enters the shop is interested in purchasing. And, when the hours for consuming alcohol on licensed premises were more rigid, plates of mouldy sausages were placed on tables in some

[86] Consumer Credit Act 1974, ss. 21 and 147.
[87] Crowther Report, above, n. 73, para. 7.2.
[88] Annual Report of the Director General of Fair Trading 1992, 1992–93 HC 719, App. B.
[89] White Paper, *Releasing Enterprise* (1988, Cm. 512), para. 6.8.8.
[90] Dog Licences Act 1959.
[91] 'All licensing statutes owe their existence to a greater or lesser extent to a desire on the part of somebody to raise revenue': Duggan, above, n. 68, p. 165.
[92] London County Council (General Powers) Act 1920, s. 3.
[93] Williams, above, n. 68, p. 90.
[94] See E. Freund, *Administrative Powers over Persons and Property: A Comparative Survey* (1928) p. 505.
[95] ' "Sex shop" means any premises . . . used for a business which consists *to a significant degree* of selling . . . sex articles': Local Government (Miscellaneous Provisions) Act 1982, Sched. 3, para. 4(1) (my italics).

establishments to indicate that the drinkers were 'persons taking table meals' and thus subject to a more liberal regime.[96]

What then of indirect social costs? As with professional licensing, there will be some welfare losses arising from the inability of some consumers to choose a lower quality unlicensed service at a lower price. On the face of it, the fact that the licence-granting body is normally independent of existing practitioners should constrain the use of licences as barriers to entry. However, some interested groups have been adept at having the limiting of supply recognized, formally or informally, as a proper goal of the licensing authority, often by specious arguments that such control serves the public interest. Two systems provide interesting examples of this phenomenon.

Under the Licensing Act 1964, the justices' discretion to grant or refuse 'on-licences' (i.e. for the consumption of alcoholic liquor in public houses) is not constrained. In practice, they take account not only of the suitability of the applicant and of the condition of the premises but also of the 'need' for more public houses, i.e. market demand.[97] A Departmental Committee reviewing the legislation in 1972 considered that this was wholly inappropriate: 'it is one thing to object to market forces determining the overall number of licensed premises; it is quite another to use the justices as the machinery for determining what these market forces are'.[98] Its recommendation that the justices' discretion should be replaced by specific grounds on which applications may be refused has not been implemented. It is not too difficult to speculate why. The brewers, who own most of the public houses and are a very powerful lobby, were vehemently opposed to the recommendation. They argued that if the number of pubs were to be regulated solely by market forces 'the public interest' would suffer: establishments would deteriorate and licensees would engage in sales-pushing.[99]

The licensing of betting shops has given rise to a similar pattern,[100] although here the market considerations are written into the legislation. The authorities may refuse to grant a licence if it would be 'inexpedient having regard to the demand for the time being in the locality for the facilities offered by licensing betting offices'.[101] But if there is insufficient demand, why would anyone apply for a licence? The argument was put by a disappointed applicant to the Divisional Court in R v. *Essex Quarter Sessions, ex parte Thomas*.[102] The response of the court is illuminating. In his judgment, Lord Parker CJ gave two reasons why an application might

---

[96] Licensing Act 1964, s. 68(2).
[97] Erroll Committee Report, above, n. 78, ch. 8.
[98] Ibid. para. 8.32.                                    [99] Ibid. para. 8.09.
[100] See also on gaming facilities, Miers above, n. 72, pp. 81–106.
[101] Betting, Gaming and Lottery Act 1963, Sched. 1, para 19.
[102] [1966] 1 All ER 353.

not be evidence of demand: first, because 'it might be made quite irrespective of demand . . . merely to entice custom away from another betting shop'; and secondly, it 'might merely be made to *stimulate* demand'.[103] The first reason suggests that the judiciary are construing the statutory conditions so as to protect existing licence-holders against competition; the second indicates a paternalist goal.

To sum up: there are powerful public interest arguments for regulating by licence many of the activities considered in this section. In the case of some of them, the administrative costs may be too high relative to the benefits. As regards some others, where the system is used to create inappropriate barriers to entry, there is a substantial mismatch between the public interest goals and the solution adopted. The private interest hypothesis of rent-seeking provides a plausible explanation for the latter.

### 4. LICENSING OF PRODUCTS

Licences could, in theory, be required for a wide range of products. In practice, the instrument has been used principally in two areas: transport and drugs.[104] 'Certificates of fitness' are required for the *use* of, *inter alia*, private motor vehicles (the 'M.O.T.' certificate for cars older than three years), public service vehicles, aircraft and passenger ships.[105] Licences are required for the *manufacture and sale* of pharmaceutical products.[106] Because of its importance and of the controversy to which it has given rise, we shall concentrate on the latter system. First, however, we must consider justifications and explanations for the regulatory form.

### (a) Public Interest Justifications

As we saw in Chapter 7, information deficits may justify the many disclosure regulations which apply to products. Some of these are effectively systems of certification, as that expression is used in this chapter, since they provide a signal that a product has complied with certain minimum standards but do not prohibit the marketing of products which fail to meet those standards.

The more drastic technique of banning products which do not satisfy the *ex ante* minimum standards is less obviously a response to the information problem. The licensing systems here being considered are not primarily designed to protect purchasers of the product, but rather, subsequent

---

[103] Ibid. p. 355 (my italics).

[104] Negative licensing systems (i.e. *ex post* prohibition) are widely used for foodstuffs, cosmetics and poisons: N. Reich and H.-W. Micklitz, *Consumer Legislation in the EC Countries: A Comparative Analysis* (1980), pp. 79–81.

[105] Respectively: Road Traffic Act 1988, s. 47; Public Passenger Vehicles Act 1981, s. 6; Air Navigation Order SI 1989/2004, art. 7(1); Merchant Shipping Act 1894, s. 271(1).

[106] Medicines Act 1968.

users—to that extent, the perceived problem is one of externalities (see below). That is true even in relation to drugs, since in most cases these can be sold only when prescribed by general medical practitioners, who thus are effectively the purchasers.

Nevertheless, the granting of product licences may play an important role in reducing information costs in certain circumstances. For example, although it is not unlawful to *purchase* a car which has failed the M.O.T. test, the absence of the certificate is a signal to the buyer of the low quality of the product. In relation to drugs and public vehicles, ships and aircraft, the argument is less clear, since the purchasers are invariably 'experts'. However, even here, since the products in question involve considerable technological complexity, the information necessary to determine their quality may be secured and assimilated more cheaply by a centralized agency.

The most important public interest justification for licensing products may be sought in the fact that use of such products can generate enormous externalities. In the case of drugs this is a consequence both of the large number of individuals who may consume them, and of the size of the harm—serious illness and death—which may ensue. A third, and critical, factor is the length of time which often elapses between marketing and the harmful consequences. This reduces the effectiveness of other regulatory techniques, such as negative licensing and quality standards, as well as private law remedies, all of which operate *ex post*. The argument applies with less force to public transporting facilities; but the degree of publicity which attaches to disasters in this area and the consequent need to restore public confidence may themselves be regarded as part of the externality.

Cars which fail to satisfy the M.O.T. test can of course cause accidents which generate risks for third parties, but the risks are significantly greater for the drivers of those vehicles. In this case, the externality argument is perhaps less important than paternalism, a justification which is frequently used also in relation to seat belts and crash helmets.[107] The role of doctors in assuming responsibility for decision-making in relation to drugs rules out the paternalist goal in that context.

### (b) Private Interest Explanations

Disasters, like those arising from thalidomide and several major transport accidents, may have electoral implications. Politicians will, then, wish to be seen to promote vigorous and speedy corrective action.[108] In relation to drugs, which as we shall see have a particularly rigorous regime, general medical practitioners may have played a significant role. If drugs were not

---

[107] Cf. J. Kleinig, *Paternalism* (1983), pp. 82–91.
[108] C. Wells, 'Inquests, Inquiries and Indictments: the Official Reception of Death by Disaster' (1991) 11 Legal Stud. 71.

licensed, they would have to bear the information costs of making decisions on which drugs were harmful. Faulty decisions would lead to doctors losing the trust of their patients (and their income, as they are paid according to the number of patients registered with them). A licensing system effectively transfers the information costs to the authorizing agency and reduces, if not eliminates, the risk of making faulty decisions. The medical profession constitutes a powerful political lobby and its influence on the legislation which established the licensing system was substantial.[109]

The introduction of the M.O.T test benefited different sectors of the motor car industry.[110] The system requires a large number of individuals who have to be paid for carrying out the test; to pass the test, repair work has to be carried out on many cars. Perhaps most significantly of all, the system reduces the average lifespan of vehicles, thus increasing the demand for new vehicles. The motor manufacturing industry, traditionally adept at acquiring government support,[111] was then a primary beneficiary.

In relation to the drug licensing regimes, the standard private interest rent-seeking model may have explanatory power. The creation of barriers of entry may protect the manufacturers of existing drugs against competition from new products. The manufacturers may be confident that they can 'capture' the agency with responsibility for issuing licences, given the high degree of dependence of the latter on information which they supply concerning the drugs and the tests carried out.[112] Moreover, larger firms may gain at the expense of smaller firms. The authorization process and the risk that a licence will not be granted increase the cost of research and development (R & D), and this will force firms to be more selective in their investment in R & D projects.[113] The cost may affect smaller firms more severely: the range of R & D projects available to them will be narrower, and returns may be more marginal. The effect may then be to squeeze out smaller firms from R & D.

### (c) Licensing of Pharmaceutical Products

We may now examine in greater detail the regime for licensing pharmaceutical products.[114] In Britain this has been a relatively recent development. Apart from a limited range of dangerous drugs for which a licence

---

[109] H. Teff and C. Munro, *Thalidomide: The Legal Aftermath* (1976), pp. 112–13.

[110] For the general impact of such regulation on the demand for motor vehicles, see D. Rhys, *The Motor Industry: An Economic Survey* (1972), pp. 248–55.

[111] S. Wilks, 'Corporate Strategy and State Support in the European Motor Industry', in L. Hancher and M. Moran (eds.), *Capitalism, Culture and Economic Regulation* (1989), ch. 7.

[112] L. Hancher, *Regulating for Competition* (1990), pp. 120–8.

[113] L. G. Schifrin, 'Lessons from the Drug Lag: A Retrospective Analysis of the 1962 Drug Regulations' (1982) 5 Harv. J. Law & Pub. Pol. 91.

[114] See generally: H. Teff, 'Regulation under the Medicines Act 1968: A Continuing Prescription for Health' (1984) 47 Modern LR 303; H. Teff, 'Drug Approval in England and the United States' (1985) 33 Am. J. Comp. Law 567; Hancher, above, n. 112.

had been required since 1920, the traditional methods of controlling drugs had been quality standards and labelling. The Thalidomide disaster provoked a review of the issue.[115] In 1964, a system of voluntary prior approval was introduced, but that was subsequently replaced by a regime of mandatory licensing under the Medicines Act 1968. Today, most drug manufacturers are multinational enterprises and the international, particularly European, dimension has assumed considerable importance.[116] The American system, while resembling its British counterpart in many features, is more restrictive and less flexible.[117] EC Directives impose on Member States the duty to operate licensing systems conforming to certain standards and processes[118] but, so far, efforts to harmonize principles and procedures and provide for mutual recognition have not proved to be very successful.[119]

Under the Medicines Act 1968, a manufacturer must obtain a product licence before marketing a drug.[120] This is, in fact, the culmination of a three-stage process, for licences are also required for the process of manufacture and for carrying out clinical tests on human beings.[121] While the licences are formally granted by the Ministers of Health, in practice decisions are made by the Committee on Safety of Medicines, a body of experts comprising mainly academics, but also individuals involved in the pharmaceutical industry, who must declare any personal interests. In determining eligibility for the product licence, the authorities must take into consideration the 'safety', 'efficacy', and 'quality' of the drug.[122] Comparisons between the drug for which a licence is sought and other

---

[115] Ministry of Health, *Safety of Drugs: Final Report of the [Cohen] Joint Sub-Committee of the Medical Advisory Committee* (1963).

[116] On this, see: L. Krämer, *EEC Consumer Law* (1986), pp. 206–13; N. Reich (ed.), *The Europeanisation of the Pharmaceutical Market—Chances and Risks* (1988).

[117] See esp. : P. Temin, *Taking Your Medicine: Drug Regulation in the United States* (1980); H. G. Grabowski and J. M. Vernon, *The Regulation of Pharmaceuticals: Balancing the Benefits and Risks* (1983); Breyer, above, n. 2, pp. 141–55. For valuable comparisons between the British and American systems, see Teff (1985), above, n. 114, and J. E. S. Parker, 'Regulating Pharmaceutical Innovation: An Economist's View' (1977) 32 Food Drug Cosmetic Law J. 160.

[118] Directives 65/65, 75/318, and 75/319.

[119] See E. Kaufer, 'The Regulation of New Product Development in the Drug Industry', in G. Majone (ed.), *Deregulation or Re-regulation? Regulatory Reform in Europe and the United States* (1990), pp. 153–75. In 1990 the EC Commission proposed the establishment of a European Agency for the Evaluation of Medicinal Products: *Future System for the Free Movement of Medicinal Drugs in the European Community* COM (90) 283.

[120] Medicines Act 1968, s. 7.

[121] Ibid. ss. 8 and 31. The manufacturer's licence basically requires proof that the premises, facilities, and staff are suitable for the work. Granting of the clinical test licence is dependent on the results of toxicity tests on animals.

[122] Ibid. s. 19(1). Since the legislation is treated as an implementation of the EC Directives, above, n. 118, regard must also be had to the wording of the conditions in those instruments: see esp. Directive 65/65, Art. 5.

drugs may be made as regards relative safety, but not as regards relative efficacy.[123]

In practice, the British authorities recognize that it is not cost-effective to rely exclusively on tests taking place before the product licence is granted, if only because some side effects cannot be identified until the drug has been used by a broader section of the population than is possible under pre-licence tests.[124] Post-marketing monitoring, then, plays an important part in the system, with attempts to minimize risks by limiting the right to prescribe certain drugs to particular hospitals or specialists. The philosophy of the American Food and Drugs Administration is very different: appraisal is made almost entirely on the basis of pre-marketing tests and there is little provision for post-marketing monitoring.[125] This, in combination with other factors, has meant that the period of delay before a drug can be marketed (sometimes referred to as the 'drug lag') is longer in the USA than in Britain (and most other European countries).[126]

The systems of licensing pharmaceutical products have been much studied by economists. Their cost–benefit analysis has led them to condemn the American regime,[127] which as we have just seen is particularly rigorous and time-consuming; but the more flexible British counterpart has not escaped criticism.[128] The analysis has, however, serious limitations and hence conclusions are difficult to reach.[129]

There is no doubt that there has been a decline in the number of new therapeutic drugs marketed since the current licensing systems were introduced in the 1960s,[130] and it is probable (but no more[131]) that the systems are responsible for that decline. Undoubtedly, they have given rise to significant increases in research and development costs, to which must be added the losses arising from the delayed availability of drugs eventually approved: higher health treatment costs and productivity losses.[132] On the other hand, the calculation of the benefits of these measures involves very

---

[123] Medicines Act 1968, s. 19(2).          [124] Teff (1985), above, n. 114, p. 579.
[125] Ibid. and Parker, above, n. 117, pp. 169–71.
[126] See the various studies cited in Temin, above, n. 117, pp. 141–51, and Grabowski and Vernon, above, n. 117, pp. 38–41. One carried out in 1980 revealed that the average FDA approval time for therapeutically important drugs was 23 months; the equivalent average British 'drug lag' was 11 months.
[127] Temin, above, n. 117; Grabowski and Vernon, above, n. 117; Parker, above, n. 117; M. N. Baily, 'Research and Development Costs and Returns: The U.S. Pharmaceutical Industry' (1972) 80 J. Pol. Econ. 70; S. Peltzman, 'An Evaluation of Consumer Protection Legislation: The 1962 Drug Amendments' (1973) 81 J. Pol. Econ. 1049.
[128] K. Hartley and A. Maynard, The Costs and Benefits of Regulating New Product Development in the UK Pharmaceutical Industry (1982).
[129] See esp. Hancher, above, n. 112, pp. 111–13.
[130] Grabowski and Vernon, above, n. 117, pp. 18–21.
[131] An alternative explanation is that a 'technological plateau' had been reached at that time: P. Asch, Consumer Safety Regulation: Putting a Price on Life and Limb (1988), pp. 122, 124.          [132] Cf. Schifrin, above, n. 113, pp. 128–9.

large imponderables:[133] the number of lives or cases of very serious illness which may have been saved will be largely a matter of guesswork; and even if this were known, there is the problem of attributing a value to that benefit.[134] These problems are, moreover, compounded by the extended timescale which governs manifestation of the effects of some drugs.

Global evaluations of drug licensing relative to other regulatory techniques must therefore remain inconclusive. Nevertheless, some less ambitious observations may be in order. First, the fact that there seems to have been little significant differences between the drugs eventually licensed in Britain and the USA, notwithstanding the greater time lag for approval in the latter, does suggest that the British system is more cost-effective than its American counterpart.[135] Secondly, some degree of over-caution in the authorities responsible for issuing licences is probably inevitable. The members of those bodies will bear some of the costs of errors in licensing drugs which prove to be defective; but they will bear none of the costs of errors in not licensing effective drugs.[136]

## 5. LICENSING OF LAND USE

Prior approval is required for a number of specific land uses[137] and also to verify the safety of buildings and sports grounds.[138] Here we confine our attention to the general regime of planning permission which is required for land development under the Town and Country Planning Act 1990 and which is derived from the scheme introduced in 1947.[139] In general, any person who desires to carry out a mining, engineering, or other operation on land, or make a material change to land use, must acquire permission from the local planning authority.[140] In determining the application, the

---

[133] Breyer, above, n. 2, pp. 148–53; Teff (1985), above, n. 114, pp. 587–90.

[134] Cf. above, pp. 156–8. The attempt by Peltzman, above, n. 127, to proxy the benefits by reference to savings of expenditure that otherwise would have been spent on ineffective drugs has been widely criticized as inadequate.

[135] Grabowski and Vernon, above, n. 117, pp. 39–41.          [136] Ibid. 9–13.

[137] e.g. for: mineral workings, oil and gas extraction (Petroleum (Production) Act 1934, Deep Sea Mining (Temporary Provisions) Act 1981); aerodromes (Civil Aviation Act 1982); nuclear installations (Nuclear Installations Act 1965); pipelines (Pipelines Act 1962); caravan sites (Caravan Sites and Control of Development Act 1960); waste disposal sites (Environmental Protection Act 1990, Part II); and a miscellaneous group of other hazardous land uses (Planning (Hazardous Substances) Act 1990; Environmental Protection Act 1990, s. 111).

[138] Building Act 1984; Fire Precautions Act 1971 and Safety of Sports Grounds Act 1975 (both as amended by the Fire Safety and Safety of Places of Sport Act 1987).

[139] Town and Country Planning Act 1947. On the law generally, see M. Purdue, E. Young, J. Rowan-Robinson, *Planning Law and Procedure* (1989). For a comparative survey of European planning systems, see J. Garner (ed.), *Planning Law in Western Europe* (1975); and for US zoning laws, see M. A. Garrett, *Land Use Regulation* (1987), chs. 1–2.

[140] Town and Country Planning Act (hereafter TCPA) 1990, s. 55.

authorities must take into account relevant development plans of the area,[141] environmental assessments where these are required,[142] and 'any other material considerations'.[143] They have discretion to grant the permission subject 'to such conditions as they think fit'[144], although the conditions must be intended to promote a planning purpose, must reasonably relate to the development, and must not be manifestly unreasonable in themselves.[145]

### (a) Public Interest Justifications

The principal public interest justification for public control of land use is the market failure arising from externalities.[146] The use which provides one landowner with profits or non-financial utility may cause disutility to other landowners. This obviously occurs where industrial or commercial use creates disamenities for residential areas. Segregation of land use will, to some extent, occur through the operation of the unregulated market; for example, an industrialist will find that land is cheaper in non-residential areas. Nevertheless, there are often boundary effects between 'natural' zones: the industrial use is likely to impact on the edges of adjacent residential areas.

Externalities also arise within zones. Economic theory predicts that, as a result of market forces, the general tastes of landowners within a given area will be homogeneous.[147] Common interests may then be afflicted by, for example, uncontrolled urban sprawl or unsightly additions to the landscape. Within the framework of common taste, there are bound to be some specific conflicts. One resident may prefer a supermarket or a petrol station to be within easy reach; another may consider that such facilities would spoil the character of the neighbourhood. To this may be added a time dimension. A special characteristic of land use markets is their slowness to adapt to changes in demand. Further, some changes to land use may be irreversible, or at least reversible only at considerable cost.

---

[141] These are authoritative statements of land use policy formulated by planning authorities: see Purdue *et al.*, above, n. 139, ch. 8.

[142] Where the project will have a significant effect on the environment: Town and Country Planning (Assessment of Environmental Effects) Regulations SI 1988/1199, implementing EC Directive 86/337.

[143] TCPA 1990, s. 70(2). On the latter, see M. Loughlin, 'The Scope and Importance of "Material Considerations" ' (1980) 3 Urban Law & Pol. 171.

[144] TCPA 1990, s. 70.

[145] Purdue *et al.*, above, n. 139, ch. 9.

[146] A. Dunham, 'City Planning: An Analysis of the Content of the Master Plan' (1958) 1 J. Law & Econ. 170; R. C. Ellickson, 'Alternatives to Zoning: Covenants, Nuisance Rules and Fines as Land Use Controls' (1973) 40 U. Chicago LR 681, 683–7.

[147] B. Ellickson, 'Jurisdictional Fragmentation and Residential Choice' (1971) 61 Am. Econ. Rev. (Proc.) 334.

Although we cannot know what will determine the utility of future generations, we may have to make some shrewd guesses.

Assuming that such negative externalities exist and are substantial,[148] they cannot normally be dealt with by market transactions and private law devices (e.g. restrictive covenants)[149] because the number of individual landowners involved is so large. Given also the size of costs of relocation and of substantial adaptations to land use which would arise from limiting intervention to *ex post* regulatory controls, there would appear to be a strong prima facie case for planning and licensing land development. Ideally, the authority responsible for these decisions would, if there was a sufficient homogeneity of interest within the community, represent that interest; or, if there was not, would act as 'mediator-arbitrator', seeking a solution which would minimize the costs of the friction.[150]

At the same time, planning and licensing instruments may also be capable of dealing with certain important *positive* externalities (i.e. public goods).[151] There is public provision of many facilities (e.g. roads and drains) which constitute the 'infrastructure' of community life. Taxation constitutes a very imperfect method of allocating the costs according to demand and use. If—which, as we shall see, is legally problematic—developers are compelled to contribute to these costs as a condition of obtaining planning permission, the externality will be internalized and there will be significant welfare gains.

Finally, planning control may be used to achieve non-economic, distributional goals.[152] This can be recognized overtly: the system may be based on the premise that the development value of land is 'owned' not by the landowner but by the community.[153] Even where there is no such overt recognition, the power of the planning authority either to prohibit development or else to stipulate conditions on which permission will be granted may permit it to effect some transfer of resources. For example, a planning application for a commercial development may be granted on the condition that the developer include in the development the creation of some social amenity.[154]

---

[148] A number of American studies purport to demonstrate that the alleged externalities do not exist, or have been greatly exaggerated; they have, however, been contradicted by other studies. For critical reviews, see W. Fischel, *The Economics of Zoning Laws* (1985), ch. 11; and Garrett, above, n. 139, pp. 41-4.          [149] Cf. above, p. 20.

[150] Garrett, above, n. 139, pp. 48-53.

[151] Ibid. 105; M. Loughlin, 'Planning Gain, Law, Policy and Practice' (1981) 1 Ox. J. Legal Stud. 61, 68-71.

[152] J. P. McAuslan, *The Ideologies of Planning Law* (1980), ch. 6.

[153] See *Final Report of the Expert [Uthwatt] Committee on Compensation and Betterment* (1942, Cmd. 6386).

[154] e.g. *Britannia (Cheltenham) Ltd* v. *Secretary of State for the Environment* [1978] JPL 554.

## (b) Private Interest Explanations

Refusals of planning permission and over-restrictive conditions imposed on developments can be used to effect major transfers of wealth.[155] The value of the undeveloped land will decline and, given the restriction on supply, that of other land in the area will probably rise.[156] If it does, existing landowners will benefit at the expense not only of disappointed developers,[157] but also of current and future tenants (who will have to pay higher rents) and future purchasers (who will have to pay higher prices). Whether or not the capital value of these landowners' investments is enhanced, they gain from not having had to pay the price of a market transaction to restrict the competing use: apart from such indirect costs as making representations to the planning authorities, the planning control is 'free' to them.[158]

Although the idealized public interest model of the planning authority stipulates a body which is independent of special interests, it is obviously to be envisaged that the reality will often be very different. Private interest theories of political decision-making would predict outcomes that favour median voters,[159] who in most residential areas are likely to be existing houseowners. On the other hand, this might be balanced by 'regulatory capture': planning decisions are notoriously subject to problems of conflicts of interest and manipulation[160] and, in that respect, commercial property developers are likely to have a considerable advantage.

## (c) Assessment

The structure of the British land planning system would seem, in general, to accord with that required by the public interest model of allocative efficiency. Take, first, the existence of negative externalities. Under the model, the planning authority should grant permission, or subject such permission to conditions, up to the point where the marginal costs of development (including, most significantly, external costs) are equal to its marginal benefits.[161] It will be recalled that the authority is legislatively

---

[155] Fischel, above, n. 148, ch. 7; R. C. Ellickson, 'Suburban Growth Controls: An Economic and Legal Analysis' (1977) 86 Yale LJ 388, 399–403; M. L. Goetz and L. E. Wofford, 'The Motivation for Zoning: Efficiency or Wealth Distribution' (1979) 55 Land Econ. 472.

[156] Depending on the elasticity of demand for land in the area, which in turn is a function of the availability of alternative land in the vicinity.

[157] In general, compensation is not payable for refusals of planning permission. For discussion of the rule and exceptions to it, see Purdue et al., above, n. 139, ch. 13.

[158] Fischel, above, n. 148, pp. 135–7.         [159] Cf. above, pp. 65–6.

[160] M. Grant, Urban Planning Law (1982), p. 258.

[161] F. H. Stephen, 'Property Rules and Liability Rules in the Regulation of Land Development: An Analysis of Development Control in Great Britain and Ontario' (1987) 7 Int. Rev. Law & Econ. 33, 35–6. Stephen, however, assumes that the local planning authority

bound, in reaching its decision, to take account of (i) relevant development plans, (ii) environmental assessments, and (iii) 'any other material considerations'. The appropriate cost–benefit analysis is implicit in (i) and explicit in (ii).[162] Although there is some divergence of opinion on what properly may be regarded as 'other material considerations', there is clear recognition that these include the social costs of development and a tendency to acknowledge that such costs must be balanced against the benefits of development.[163]

Of course, the existence of an appropriate structure does not ensure that efficient solutions will be reached. Development plans are necessarily formulated with a generality that does not allow for the huge variety of possible land uses. If planning authorities are incapable of, or unwilling to engage in, 'fine-tuning', sub-optimal land use will ensue. The American zoning laws, which confer development rights on the basis of local plans, have been criticized on this ground.[164] The adverse consequences could, the critics assert, be avoided if 'market-like' bargaining over such rights could take place between developers and representatives of the community interests.[165] Briefly summarized, the argument is that efficient land use can be achieved at lower cost if the enhanced value of the land to the developer arising from the development were to enable him to purchase the right to that development by paying to the community representative a sum reflecting its social cost.

In fact, within certain limits, bargaining of this kind is possible in Britain and has become increasingly common in recent years.[166] If formally made, the agreement between the developer and the authority attaches to the land and thus its terms are binding on successors in title.[167] Moreover, it escapes the normal procedures for appeals—a fact which has rendered it controversial.[168] The scope of legitimate planning agreements has not been

---

will aim to eliminate the externality, leaving the balancing against benefit to be carried out by the appeal and review processes. This is because he assumes that the authority represents householder interests rather than developer interests. The latter assumption is unclear.

[162] See esp. : TCPA 1990, s.12(6)(c); Town and Country Planning (Structure and Local Plans) Regulations SI 1982/555, Reg. 9; Town and Country Planning (Assessment of Environmental Effects) Regulations SI 1988/1199, Sched. 3.

[163] 'Financial constraints on the economic viability of a desirable planning development are unavoidable facts of life in an imperfect world. It would be unreal and contrary to common sense to insist that they must be excluded from the range of considerations which may properly be regarded as material . . . Virtually all planning decisions involve some kind of balancing exercise': per Kerr LJ, *R* v. *Westminster City Council, ex parte Monahan* [1990] 1 QB 87, 111. See also Loughlin, above, n. 143, and Purdue *et al.*, above, n. 139, pp. 213–19.

[164] Ellickson, above, n. 146; Fischel, above, n. 148.

[165] An application of the Coase Theorem: see above, pp. 17 and 19.

[166] J. Jowell, 'Bargaining in Development Control' [1977] J. Planning Law 414; M. Loughlin, 'Planning Gain: Law, Policy and Practice' (1981) 1 Ox. J. Legal Stud. 61; P. Healey, M. Purdue, I Ennis, *Gains from Planning: Dealing with the Impacts of Development* (1993).                                                        [167] TCPA 1990, s. 106.

fully determined by the courts, but it would seem that the 'price' which the developer pays must be something which is related to a planning purpose and 'reasonable'.[169] To that extent, the instrument falls short of that advocated by those American critics who wish to see planning rights as fully 'fungible'.

Planning permission and the agreements discussed in the last paragraph are frequently used to internalize positive externalities. The power of the planning authorities to refuse permission or resist an agreement can be used to transfer to the developer some, or all, of the public infrastructure costs which are incurred as a result of the development. A developer may, for example, be required to contribute to the cost of laying water mains or providing new or improved highways, where such cost would otherwise fall on the public utility.[170]

Management of the distributional consequences of land development has been a political 'shuttlecock' in the post-war period. Redistributional goals were inherent in the planning system when it was introduced by the Labour government in 1947. The legislation in that year effectively transferred into public ownership the development value of land:[171] subject to certain exceptions, planning permission was required, and a charge payable, for all developments.[172] Given the exorbitant level of that charge (in practice 100 per cent of development value), not unnaturally landowners were disinclined to supply land for development. After many experiments and vicissitudes,[173] the taxation of land development was finally abolished in 1985.

With the abandonment of taxation as the principal instrument for pursuing distributional goals, contests for wealth transfers have to take place, if at all, within the framework of planning law. The extent to which the processes of planning permission and agreements are consistent with the private interest hypothesis of rent-seeking is difficult to determine, not least because of the paucity of empirical evidence on the impact of planning decisions on land prices. On the one hand, the affinity of interests between land developers and typical members of planning authorities

---

[168] See, e.g., Report of the Department of Environment's Property Advisory Group, *Planning Gain* (1981).

[169] *Ex parte Monahan*, above, n. 163; *R* v. *Gillingham BC, ex parte Parham* [1988] J. Planning Law 336.      [170] Purdue *et al.*, above, n. 139, pp. 241-3.

[171] Nevertheless £300 million was made available as compensation for losses suffered by landowners.

[172] See in general White Paper, *The Control of Land Use* (1944, Cmd. 6537).

[173] Development charges were abolished by the Town and Country Planning Act 1953. The more sophisticated betterment levy was introduced in the Land Commission Act 1967, but was repealed as soon as the Conservative party returned to power in 1970. Further attempts to capture development value for the community were made in the Community Land Act 1975 and the Development Land Tax Act 1976. These were in turn repealed in 1980 and 1985 respectively.

suggests that 'regulatory capture' is a real possibility.[174] There are also arguments that the structure of the processes favours the developer as compared with more diffuse environmental interests.[175] On the other hand, as we have seen, the ability of developers to bargain with authorities enhances the efficient allocation of land use and, provided that the social costs of development are properly taken into account by the authorities and adequate procedures are established, this phenomenon may advance public interest goals. Indeed, the 'price' exacted for such bargains may serve to reduce the rents which landowners would otherwise enjoy as a consequence of the development.

[174] Grant, above, n. 160, pp. 258–61; and see *R* v. *St Edmundsbury BC, ex parte Investors in Industry Commercial Properties* [1985] 3 All ER 234.

[175] McAuslan, above, n. 152, ch. 1.

# 11

# Economic Instruments

## 1. INTRODUCTION

The common feature of the forms of social regulation considered in the previous chapters is the use of the criminal law to achieve the public interest goal. Firms engaged in a prohibited activity, breaching an imposed standard, or failing to carry out a required course of conduct are liable, and subject to the problems discussed in Chapter 5, it is assumed that the threat of such proceedings and of the sanctions to which they may give rise is sufficient to induce the desired behaviour. Given the compulsion implicit in this traditional approach, it is often referred to as 'command-and-control' regulation.

The general disenchantment with these traditional regulatory forms which has emerged in the last two decades[1] has led to pressure not only to deregulate but also to experiment with other regulatory forms which encourage the desired behaviour by financial incentives rather than by legal compulsion.[2] Such incentives can be either negative (conduct is legally unconstrained but if a firm chooses to act in an undesired way it must pay a charge) or positive (if a firm chooses to act in a desired way it is awarded a subsidy).

Although the idea has recently gained considerable currency as a method of dealing with externalities, particularly those arising from environmental pollution, it is far from new.[3] Governments have sometimes sought to finance and determine the supply of public goods (for example, highways and public broadcasting services) by imposing charges on users. As regards negative externalities, economists have long recognized that the misallocation of resources can be corrected by imposing a tax on the firms

---

[1] Cf. above, pp. 10–11.

[2] For general discussions of this trend see: J. Braithwaite, 'The Limits of Economism in Controlling Harmful Corporate Conduct' (1982) 16 Law & Soc. Rev. 481; C. Sunstein, *After the Rights Revolution: Reconceiving the Regulatory State* (1990); R. Howse, J. R. Prichard, M. Trebilcock, 'Smaller or Smarter Government?' (1990) 34 U. Toronto LJ 478; R. Howse, 'Retrenchment, Reform or Revolution? The Shift to Incentives and the Future of the Regulatory State' (1993) 31 Alberta LR 455.

[3] Cf. B. Yandle, 'User Charges, Rent Seeking and Public Choice', in R. Wagner (ed.), *Charging for Government: User Charges and Earmarked Taxes in Principle and Practice* (1991), ch. 3.

responsible, thereby ensuring that the external cost of a product or service is 'internalized' in its price.[4]

Those advocating the use of economic instruments (EIs) have argued that they overcome many of the perceived deficiencies of traditional 'command-and-control' regulation (CAC).[5] First, while CAC often gives rise to a complex and detailed set of centrally formulated standards, EIs can function on the basis of broad target goals, with a reduction of information and administrative costs for both the regulators and the firms. Secondly, the greater freedom conferred by EIs on firms creates incentives for technological development. Thirdly, whereas the enforcement of CAC is subject to considerable uncertainty as regards apprehension, prosecution' and the level of sanctions, EIs entail the certain payment of specific sums. Fourthly, negative EIs (i.e. charges) generate funds which can be used to compensate the victims of externalities; CAC regimes rarely allow victims to be compensated.

Notwithstanding the advantages claimed for EIs, they have been relatively infrequently adopted in practice. In this chapter, we shall consider possible explanations: on the one hand, that the merits of EIs are not so pronounced as their advocates claim; and, on the other, that the influence of private interests and other political factors inhibit their adoption. First, however, we must explore in greater detail the various forms of EIs.

### 2. FORMS OF ECONOMIC INSTRUMENTS

#### (a) Charges and Taxes

The most widely used EI form involves the imposition of a charge or tax on individuals or firms. To correct misallocations arising from externalities, the amount set should be equal to the marginal damage which the individual or firm inflicts on others. Because the external cost of the activity is thereby borne by the actor, this should, if the activity takes place within a competitive market, ensure an allocatively efficient level of production and consumption.[6]

From an economic perspective, the principal function of the fiscal instrument is thus to induce a behavioural response. But, of course, taxes

---

[4] The theory is derived from A. Pigou, *The Economics of Welfare* (1920), and hence the expression a 'Pigovian tax'.

[5] For useful summaries of these arguments, see: R. Stewart, 'Regulation, Innovation and Administrative Law: A Conceptual Framework' (1981) 69 Calif. LR 1256, 1326–37; D. Dewees, G. Mathewson and M. Trebilcock, 'Policy Alternatives in Quality Regulation', in D. Dewees (ed.), *The Regulation of Quality: Products, Services, Workplaces and the Environment* (1983), pp. 36–40; Howse, above, n. 2, pp. 458–60.

[6] W. Baumol, 'On Taxation and the Control of Externalities' (1972) 62 Am. Econ. Rev. 307.

are more frequently used simply to produce revenue for general governmental purposes and in such contexts the amounts levied tend to be determined by distributional criteria, notably the ability to pay, rather than by reference to allocational considerations. In consequence, there are difficulties in locating 'genuine' EIs within the mass of fiscal provisions:[7] some instruments may have been intended as revenue taxes, or charges to cover administrative expenditure, but have important incentive effects; others may have been intended as EIs but in practice are dominated by revenue or administrative considerations.

Subject to these difficulties, we may identify three main categories of charges or taxes which have, or may have, important incentive functions, and thus be treated as EIs.[8] They represent interventions at different points in the causal relationship between a given activity and the external costs which it generates and, as such, correspond to the three types of CAC standard (specification, performance, and target) which were discussed in Chapter 8.[9]

The first is imposed on the use of a product which gives rise to an external cost. As was observed in relation to specification standards,[10] the relationship between use of a product and its external cost is inevitably imprecise, and the amount levied may be arbitrary relative to the harm actually caused. This is particularly likely where, as in the case of pollution, the harm varies over time and in relation to the impact of other causes.[11] The differential between the duty levied on leaded and unleaded petrol respectively, which was introduced in Britain in 1987,[12] is a much vaunted[13] example of an effective tax, but it is not obviously related to the environmental costs of leaded fuels. As regards the more traditional duties payable on tobacco and alcohol, these may operate to a greater or lesser extent to internalize the medical and other costs arising from over-consumption which are otherwise borne by general taxpayers,[14] but the

---

[7] Cf. J. Opschoor and H. Vos, *Economic Instruments for Environmental Protection* (1989), pp. 13–14; Yandle, above, n. 3, pp. 38–40. Given the existence of constitutional constraints on the power of the executive to levy taxation 'for or to the use of the Crown' (see Bill of Rights 1688, c. 2, and *Att.-Gen.* v. *Wilts. United Dairies* (1921) 37 TLR 884), the distinction between EIs and revenue taxes might have legal significance. But in the *United Dairies* case and *Congreve* v. *Home Office* [1976] QB 629, the courts treated EIs as subject to those constraints. On the analogous issue in US constitutional law, see *Skinner* v. *Mid-America Pipeline Co* 490 US 212 (1989).

[8] For other attempts at classification, see Opschoor and Vos, above, n. 7, pp. 14–15; S. McKay, M. Pearson, and S. Smith, 'Fiscal Instruments in Environmental Policy' (1990) 11 Fisc. Stud. (No. 4) 1, 6–8; S. Gaines and R. Westin, *Taxation for Environmental Protection* (1991), pp. 8–10. These works provide valuable surveys of the use of EIs for environmental protection purposes in the UK and elsewhere. [9] Above, pp. 150–2.

[10] Above, p. 167. [11] McKay *et al.*, above, n. 8, p. 7.

[12] At the time of writing £0. 0482 per litre (Finance Act 1993, s. 9(3) ).

[13] White Paper, *The Common Inheritance* (1989, Cm. 1200), Annex A22.

[14] Cf. D. Coate and M. Grossman, 'Effects of Beverage Prices and Legal Drinking Ages on Youth Alcohol Use' (1988) 31 J. Law & Econ. 145.

amounts imposed reflect much more the revenue demands of government.[15]

The second category corresponds to performance standards[16] in that it attaches to the quality and/or quantity of harmful substances emanating from a given activity; hence, in relation to pollution, it is often called an 'effluent charge'. While evaluation of the external costs may remain highly problematic, the scaling of the payments to the harmfulness of the discharge as it enters the environment allows for a greater focus on the marginal impact of an activity. Effluent charges are widely used in Continental Europe,[17] but in the UK, apart from one minor existing provision,[18] they are still under consideration as a policy option.[19]

Under the third category, which correlates with target standards,[20] the amount payable is directly related to the harm caused. Clearly, this approach is feasible only where there is a definite and immediate causal relationship between the activity and the harm and where the latter is easily quantifiable. In practice, therefore, it has been adopted predominantly in situations where specific measures have been taken to eliminate the harm and the tax represents the cost of those measures. Reimbursement of the costs incurred by public authorities in the disposal of waste constitutes a frequently adopted example.[21]

### (b)  Subsidies

Subsidies represent the symmetrical opposite of charges and taxes: payments are made *to* individuals or firms to induce them to reduce undesirable activity. Economically, they can have the same effect as charges and taxes: if the payment reflects the marginal cost of eliminating the externality, an efficient allocation of resources should ensue.[22] However, a subsidy may encourage output to grow to a larger size than that which would prevail under a perfect-internalizing charge and in the long run may therefore generate inefficiency.[23] And, of course, the

---

[15]  D. Lee, 'The Political Economy of User Charges: Some Bureaucratic Implications' in Wagner, above, n. 3, pp. 71–3.

[16]  Above, p. 166.

[17]  For details, see Opschoor and Vos, above, n. 7, and Gaines and Westin, above, n. 8.

[18]  Some airports operate a differentiation in landing charges according to the level of aircraft noise (White Paper, above, n. 13, para. 14.31) but a Department of the Environment official has described this as of only 'minor' significance: Opschoor and Vos, above, n. 7, p. 49.

[19]  White Paper, above, n. 13, A17–A19.                    [20]  Above, p. 166.

[21]  See, for the UK, Environmental Protection Act 1990, s. 41, and for other jurisdictions, Opschoor and Vos, above, n. 7, pp. 44–7. On the working of the UK charge scheme for trade effluent into sewers, see G. Richardson, A. Ogus and P. Burrows, *Policing Pollution: A Study of Regulation and Enforcement* (1982), pp. 145–9.

[22]  A. Kneese and K. Mäler, 'Bribes and Charges in Pollution Control: An Aspect of the Coase Controversy' (1973) 13 Nat. Res. J. 705.

[23]  P. Burrows, *The Economic Theory of Pollution Control* (1979), pp. 114–16.

distributional consequences are profoundly different. A tax on a firm increases its costs of production and also generates revenue which can be used to compensate those adversely affected, while the burden of a subsidy scheme falls on general taxpayers. Moreover, such a scheme may create perverse incentives, for example, by inducing firms to increase externalities in order to attract further subsidies.[24]

For these, as well as political-ideological reasons, there has been a decline in the use of subsidies, most notably in the field of environmental protection, where the 'polluter-pay-principle' has become accepted dogma.[25] Even when subsidies were more generally available, there was a problem, as with taxes, in distinguishing those which were intended to operate as EIs from those designed primarily for redistributional purposes, here to increase the wealth or income of specific groups of industries or households.[26] Nevertheless, examples can be given of current subsidies used for EI purposes.[27] They may take the form of a grant (or an interest-free loan) to assist in the purchase of a particular product or equipment— e.g. home thermal insulation grants to limit energy consumption[28]—or the preservation of some public good—e.g. wildlife habitats.[29] Compensation may be offered for a loss of profits resulting from a voluntary restriction on the use of harmful products or processes.[30] Finally, subsidies may operate indirectly through a reduction of tax liability; for example, an accelerated depreciation allowance may be granted for capital expenditure on pollution abatement equipment.[31]

### (c) Tradeable Emission Rights

An EI much discussed in the context of environmental protection is based on the idea that allocative efficiency can be achieved by allowing pollution

---

[24] J. L. Migué, 'Controls Versus Subsidies in the Economic Theory of Regulation' (1977) 20 J. Law & Econ. 213; C. J. Schultze, *The Public Use of Private Interest* (1977), pp. 57–64.

[25] See Treaty of Rome, Art. 130R, inserted by the Single European Act, and White Paper, above, n. 13, A29.

[26] See generally: A. Prest, 'The Economic Rationale of Subsidies to Industries'. in A. Whiting (ed.), *The Economics of Industrial Subsidies* (1976); A. Culyer, *The Political Economy of Social Policy* (1980), pp. 133–6; D. von Stebut, 'Subsidies as an Instrument of Economic Policy', in T. Daintith (ed.), *Law as an Instrument of Economic Policy: Comparative and Critical Approaches* (1988), pp. 137–52.

[27] For a survey within the field of environmental protection, see Opschoor and Vos, above, n. 7, pp. 74–82.

[28] Under the British scheme, they are paid only to households with low incomes: Social Security Act 1990, s. 15.

[29] Wildlife and Countryside Act 1981, s. 38; and see Gaines and Westin, above, n. 8, pp. 169–71.

[30] e.g. to farmers who agree to restrict their use of nitrate in designated nitrate sensitive areas: Water Resources Act 1991, ss. 94–5.

[31] See Gaines and Westin, above, n. 8, pp. 82–8, for the use of this device in Germany.

rights to be traded.[32] Under a 'pure' form of such a system, a public agency would set an absolute limit to the amounts to be discharged into a given airshed or watershed, derived from its perception of optimal ambient quality,[33] and through an auction process sell rights to emit portions of that total to the firms which bid the highest price for them. Once acquired, the rights would be freely tradeable between firms,[34] so that eventually they would be owned by the firms which would value them the most, because they have the highest costs of pollution abatement. Allocative efficiency will be achieved since the lower-cost abaters will find it cheaper to abate than to acquire the pollution rights.

No jurisdiction has yet adopted tradeable emission rights in this form. The nearest to it can be located in the American regime for sulphur dioxide emissions which was introduced in 1990.[35] Firms making such emissions are granted allowances which they may trade among themselves. No provision is, however, made for the auctioning of the allowances. The absence of such provision has been criticized both because efficiency is impaired, the transaction costs of ordinary trading being higher than those of auction-trading, and on the distributional basis that the system will not generate resources to compensate pollution victims.[36]

### 3. EVALUATION

As the above discussion has revealed, environmental protection has been the primary area both for the limited existing experience of EIs and for proposals to adopt them on a more extended basis. In evaluating their merits, and in particular the advantages which they are alleged to possess

---

[32] See esp. : J. Dales, *Pollution, Property and Prices* (1968); T. Tietenberg, *Emissions Trading: An Exercise in Reforming Pollution Policy* (1985).

[33] Cf. above, p. 208.

[34] Purchase of the rights by environmental groups which desire higher standards may also be envisaged, although the 'free rider' problem may inhibit this form of trading.

[35] By the Clean Air Act Amendments of 1990. See generally B. van Dyke, 'Emissions Trading to Reduce Acid Deposition' (1992) 100 Yale LJ 2707. Other systems involving some notion of trading administered by the US Environmental Protection Agency are: 'netting' (a firm creating a new emission source may avoid a standard that would otherwise apply by reducing its emissions from another plant); 'offsets' (new emission sources allowed in over-polluted areas only if existing discharges in that area, either their own or those of another firm, are reduced by a greater amount); 'bubbles' (firms with multiple emission sources within a given airshed are allowed to adjust the level of discharges between those sources so long as the aggregate emission level is not exceeded); 'banking' (firms may 'retain' as credits for future industrial use or trading reductions in emissions exceeding the standards currently imposed). See, on these, R. Hahn and G. Hester, 'Where Did All the Markets Go? An Analysis of EPA's Emissions Trading Program' (1989) 6 Yale J. Reg. 109. For an attempt to apply the 'bubbles' system to UK noise pollution, see *R* v. *Secretary of State for Transport, ex parte Richmond LBC* [1994] 1 All ER 577. [36] van Dyke, above, n. 35, pp. 2717–21.

over CAC regulation, we shall therefore concentrate on their application to that problem. To reduce the complexity of the comparison, we shall assume that CAC regulation seeks to emulate EIs by using differentiated, rather than uniform, standards. As we have seen elsewhere,[37] uniform standards reduce administrative costs but generate significant allocative inefficiencies by failing to take account of differences in abatement costs.

## (a) Information

Regulating pollution by traditional CAC techniques normally involves the agency setting standards which balance the pollution abatement costs to individual firms (PAC) against pollution damage costs (PDC),[38] thus requiring adequate information on both sets of costs. An important advantage claimed for EIs is that, provided the agency can make a reasonable estimate of PDC, it need have no knowledge of PAC. Once a tax[39] has been set so as to reflect the impact on PDC of particular concentrations of pollutant, it is left to individual firms to decide whether it is cheaper to pay the tax or else to abate. Further, the system provides better information for firms on the costs they will incur from pollution: the tax represents a certain sum, whereas what they will have to pay if they contravene a standard depends on such uncertain variables as the enforcement discretion of the agency and the sentencing discretion of the court.

These are powerful arguments, but some qualifications need to be made. First, there is the problem of estimating PDC and thus of setting an appropriate price on discharges. Evaluating environmental harm raises immense difficulties not only because of its geographical and temporal dimensions, but also because of the complex interaction of different polluting sources and such variables as weather and diverse patterns of consumer use.[40] Secondly, without information on PAC, an agency will be unable to predict how much pollution will actually result from a given set of prices and thus how effective those prices will be in relation to the efficiency goal of optimal pollution. To overcome both difficulties, the agency will in practice have to adopt an iterative or 'trial and error' approach: an initial set of prices is established, but these are subsequently modified as their impact is observed and as account is also taken of other variables. The instability of this process will undermine the predictability

---

[37] Cf. above, pp. 210–11.                                    [38] Above, pp. 206–7.

[39] The same applies to subsidies based on reductions to PDC, but not to those which compensate polluters for loss of profits. Under a system of tradeable emission rights, to decide how much pollution to allow the agency must estimate the *aggregate* abatement costs, but need not know how these costs affect individual firms.

[40] Cf. D. Pearce, A. Markandya, and E. Barbier, *Blueprint for a Green Economy* (1989), chs. 3–6.

of the costs imposed on firms, one of the principal benefits claimed for EIs.[41]

Of course, agencies setting standards under a CAC regime face similar difficulties; but the flexibility inherent in negotiating and enforcing individualized standards enables them to adjust to changing conditions in a way that is not possible under a tax system.

### (b) Incentives

Since under a tax or subsidy[42] system the cost to a firm of polluting increases proportionately to the pollution, there is an incentive for the firm to abate as much as possible. It will do so up to the point where the marginal abatement cost is equal to the marginal tax (or subsidy) cost, and there is therefore also an incentive to develop cheaper methods of pollution abatement. A tradeable emission rights regime engenders the same incentives: firms which reduce their abatement costs can profitably sell their rights to firms with higher costs.

In this respect, it would appear that EIs are superior to CAC regulation: although a firm will seek to find the cheapest way of meeting a CAC standard, once that standard has been achieved it has no incentive to reduce pollution further. It is true, as we saw in Chapter 9,[43] that the standards imposed under some CAC regimes are formulated by reference to the 'best available techniques' not entailing excessive cost', but the agency's perceptions of what is 'best' are unlikely to encourage firms to develop new technologies.

### (c) Accidents

A point frequently overlooked in discussions of control instruments is that many cases of serious environmental damage are the result of accidents, rather than deliberate polluting activity.[44] Under CAC regimes, the amount payable by way of penalties can be tailored to reflect the more serious external costs generated by accidents, because it is determined after the accident has occurred. A tax system normally involves an *ex ante* assessment of harm and thus can meet the problem only if the amounts levied reflect the risks of accidental discharges from the individual firm.

As regards industrial health and safety, the contributions levied from firms to finance the compensation payable to victims are in many countries (though not Britain) calculated by reference to the firms' accident

---

[41] P. Burrows, 'Pricing Versus Regulation for Environmental Protection' in A. Culyer (ed.), *Economic Policies and Social Goals* (1974), p. 276. See also Burrows, above, n. 23, pp. 121–9.

[42] Provided that the amount of subsidy reflects the degree of abatement.

[43] Above, p. 207.                    [44] Burrows (1979), above, n. 23, pp. 140–4.

record.[45] It is generally acknowledged that the system is effective, at least when applied to firms large enough for the statistical evidence to be reliable.[46] But that very qualification indicates why a tax system cannot create appropriate incentives for avoiding serious pollution accidents. The infrequency of such accidents would render the system arbitrary: the tax would either be too high, for firms with an accident record, or too low, for firms without one.[47]

### (d) Enforcement

The assertion that EIs are cheaper than CAC systems in terms of enforcement costs is not easily sustained.[48] Both generally[49] entail the monitoring of discharges. The costs in some individual CAC cases may be high, where protracted negotiation or prosecution follows a detected contravention, but that has to be balanced against the administrative burden of collecting taxes in a larger number of cases and dealing with the proceeds. In justifying its hesitation to adopt EIs more widely, the British government referred to the difficulty and expense of the administrative support which would be required.[50] It has been reported that more than half of the revenue derived from the German system of water effluent charges is absorbed by administrative costs.[51]

### (e) Distributional Considerations

One apparently clear advantage of taxes and auctioned tradeable emission rights (but obviously not subsidies) over CAC regulation is that they generate funds which can be used to compensate the victims of pollution. However, the distributional argument for preferring EIs is not so straightforward as may appear. One reason is that the estimation of the distributional consequences of various control instruments is a complex matter: the conditions prevailing in different product, labour, and capital markets as well as the nature of the instruments influence the way in which the ultimate financial burden is shared between shareholders, the labour

---

[45] A. I. Ogus and E. M. Barendt, *The Law of Social Security* (3rd edn., 1988), pp. 254–5. See also Report of the Royal Commission on Civil Liability and Compensation for Personal Injury (1978, Cmnd. 7054).

[46] R. Smith, 'The Feasibility of an "Injury Tax" Approach to Occupational Safety' (1974) 38 Law & Contemp. Prob. 730; J. Mendeloff, *Regulating Safety: An Economic and Political Analysis of Occupational Safety and Health Policy* (1979), pp. 24–8.

[47] Burrows (1979), above, n. 23, p. 142.

[48] Burrows (1979), above, n. 23, pp. 133–5; S. Breyer, *Regulation and Its Reform* (1982), pp. 274, 278–80.

[49] Specification standards and their tax equivalent are exceptions: the monitoring costs of these may be lower but they also reduce the incentives for cost abatement; above, p. 167.

[50] White Paper, above, n. 13, A18.

[51] Opschoor and Vos, above, n. 7, p. 40.

force, and consumers.[52] Secondly, even if EIs might in theory operate to redistribute resources from (say) the shareholders of polluting firms to householder pollution victims, in practice such transfers are limited. Tax revenues tend to be earmarked, if at all, for government clean-up programmes,[53] and schemes which directly compensate pollution victims are rare.[54]

### (f) Empirical Evidence

Although there have been a number of studies of environmental EIs,[55] they provide a far from adequate basis for evaluating the impact of these instruments. One problem is that EIs are generally combined with traditional CAC regimes and it is not possible to isolate the effects of the different approaches.[56] As regards taxes, there is the additional difficulty that the instruments are frequently designed primarily for revenue purposes and the amounts imposed are often significantly lower than would be required for incentive purposes.[57]

Some generalizations have, nevertheless, emerged.[58] The taxes imposed on leaded petrol appear to have had important incentive effects.[59] Effluent charges seem to have made some improvement to water quality, though not to the extent predicted by economists. This is explained on the ground not only that the amounts levied have been too small, but also on the prevalent use of 'grandfather clauses': typically the charges are applied only to new emission sources or to levels of discharges exceeding those current at the time the system is introduced. An exception is the Dutch system, where the charges have been significantly higher and the impact on polluter behaviour significantly greater.[60]

---

[52] For fuller discussion, see: Burrows (1979), above, n. 23, pp. 144–8; D. Dewees, 'Regulating Environmental Quality' in Dewees, above, n. 5, pp. 153–7. See also above, p. 172.

[53] Opschoor and Vos, above, n. 7, ch. 4, *passim*.

[54] Those who suffer damage as the result of a contravention of a CAC standard may seek to recover compensation under the tort of breach of statutory duty, but current legislation severely restricts this remedy: D. Hughes, *Environmental Law* (2nd edn., pp. 38–44).

[55] e.g. those reported in: P. Downing and K. Hanf (eds.), *International Comparisons in Implementing Pollution Laws* (1983); G. Brown and R. Johnson, *The Effluent Charge System in the Federal Republic of Germany* (1983); M. Cropper and W. Oates, 'Environmental Economics: A Survey' (1992) 30 J. Econ. Lit. 675, 689–92.

[56] Opschoor and Vos, above, n. 7, *passim*.

[57] Ibid. 113–14.

[58] Cf. R. Hahn, 'Economic Prescriptions for Environmental Problems: Not Exactly What the Doctor Ordered', in J. Shogren, *The Political Economy of Government Regulation* (1989), ch. 6; Opschoor and Vos, above, n. 7.

[59] McKay *et al.*, above, n. 8, p. 13.

[60] H. Bressers, 'The Role of Effluent Charges in Dutch Water Quality Policy', in Downing and Hanf, above, n. 55.

## 4. POLITICAL AND PRIVATE INTEREST CONSIDERATIONS

Whatever the merits of EIs, it is not difficult to understand the reluctance of legislatures to use them.[61] In general, as we have seen, in formulating regulatory policy politicians are expected to respond to pressures from both sectional interest groups—notably those representing industry—and ideological interest groups, e.g. environmentalists. Although the influence of the former tends to be stronger than that of the latter, some compromise between the respective demands of the two groups normally emerges. In the present context, however, the environmentalist lobby has combined with the industrial lobby in opposing EIs.[62]

The opposition of environmentalists to EIs can be explained on several grounds. First, they expect governments to respond to the pollution crisis by the adoption of immediate and tough measures. Mandatory CAC standards, cast in a suitably rigorous form, are seen to meet this demand; EIs, which rely on voluntary behaviour and are characterized as 'licences to pollute', are not. Secondly, the use of the criminal law and its institutions stigmatizes pollution; EIs, which involve merely administrative intervention, are morally neutral.[63] Thirdly, the assumption of rational economic behaviour which underpins the arguments for EIs is treated with scepticism.

How does economism deal with the crusty general-manager who believes that the old ways of disposing of toxic wastes are the best and that no new-fangled effluent tax is going to change his tried and true practices? Legalism does have a way of dealing with this not-so-uncommon menace to the public health; it takes him to court and threatens to shut his plant down.[64]

Fourthly, as regards taxes, governments cannot be trusted to use the proceeds for environmental purposes; and, as regards subsidies, why should taxpayers support polluters?

The political appeal of this last point is overwhelming and certainly sufficient to dampen the demand by polluting industries for subsidies. Industrial opposition to tax systems is no less difficult to comprehend. Such systems would seem to require polluting firms to pay twice: they pay not only for the technical equipment necessary to abate pollution, but also for

---

[61] Cf. Breyer, above, n. 48, pp. 280–2; Dewees *et al.*, above, n. 5, pp. 38–40; Hahn, above, n. 58; Howse, above, n. 2.

[62] The Netherlands, where effluent charges have been most effective, is an exception. Environmentalists have tended to favour EIs: Hahn, above, n. 58.

[63] S. Kelman, *What Price Incentives? Economists and the Environment* (1985), ch. 2; 'the difference between a pecuniary penalty and a tax is that the former is a sum required in respect of an unlawful act and the latter is a sum required in respect of a lawful act', per Isaacs J., *R v. Bargery* (1908) 6 CLR 41, 54.          [64] Braithwaite, above, n. 2, p. 493.

emissions which they are unable to abate.[65] Moreover, the collection of taxes is a matter of administrative routine and difficult to obstruct. The very effectiveness of tax systems in imposing costs therefore makes them much less attractive to polluters than CAC regimes, the enforcement agencies of which can be persuaded not to prosecute.[66]

Finally, the influence of the agencies themselves in resisting EIs should not be underestimated.[67] The discretion conferred on them by CAC regimes enables them to enjoy power, prestige, and job satisfaction;[68] administration of a tax system provides little by way of equivalent benefit.

[65] Breyer, above, n. 48, p. 281. As he observes, the claim is fallacious: the tax represents the loss that the pollution causes to others.

[66] See also J. Buchanan and G. Tullock, 'Polluters' Profits and Political Response: Direct Controls Versus Taxes' (1975) 65 Am. Econ. Rev. 139. They argue that firms prefer emission standards to emission charges because the former enable them to create barriers to entry, mainly through 'grandfather clauses' (cf. above, p. 169). However, as experience has since revealed (above, p. 254), 'grandfather clauses' are regularly used in tax systems.

[67] Dewees *et al.*, above, n. 5, p. 39.                          [68] Above, p. 69.

# 12

# Private Regulation

## I. ALIENABLE RIGHTS

To understand the concept of 'private' regulation we must return to the distinction drawn in an earlier chapter between private, facilitative law and public, directive law.[1] Clearly, the legislature, and to some extent the judiciary, can attempt to achieve public interest goals, such as economic efficiency or distributional justice, by changing the private law.[2] To correct market failure or to transfer wealth, some alteration in basic entitlements might be undertaken. So, for example, new property rights might be introduced to protect those engaged in creative activity;[3] or strict liability might replace negligence as the tort regime for certain kinds of harm.[4] Provided that individuals are free to modify the rights and obligations by appropriately drafted agreements, these measures are not to be classified as 'regulation' within the meaning which we attribute to this term. They form part of, and are not antithetical to, the market system of economic organization because they enable individual choice to prevail over the collective goals.

## 2. INALIENABLE RIGHTS

Policy-makers may decide that some private rights should not be altered or overridden by agreement; entitlements of this kind are often referred to as 'inalienable rights'.[5] There are three principal legal techniques for creating inalienable rights.[6] First, the courts may, on grounds of public policy, declare to be void or illegal contracts which purport to assign or modify entitlements to property or liberty: an obvious example is that an individual cannot sell himself into slavery or a quasi-servile condition.[7] Secondly, legislation may provide that rights in tort law must prevail over

---

[1] Above, p. 2.

[2] Cf. D. Kennedy, 'Distributive and Paternalist Motives in Contract and Tort Law, With Special Reference to Compulsory Terms and Unequal Bargaining Power' (1982) 41 Maryland LR 563.　　　　　　　　[3] Copyright, Designs and Patents Act 1988, ss. 77–89.

[4] Consumer Protection Act 1987, Part I.

[5] G. Calabresi and A. D. Melamed, 'Property Rules, Liability Rules, and Inalienability: One View of the Cathedral' (1972) 85 Harv. LR 1089, 1111; S. Rose-Ackerman, 'Inalienability and the Theory of Property Rights' (1985) 85 Columbia LR 931.

[6] For other techniques, see Rose-Ackerman, ibid.

[7] *Horwood* v. *Millar's Timber and Trading Co.* [1919] 3 KB 305.

contractual allocations of liability. Thus, under the Unfair Contract Terms Act 1977, a right to claim damages for personal injury or death caused by negligence cannot, in some circumstances, be excluded or restricted by contract.[8] Thirdly, the legislature may insert mandatory terms in certain types of contract. Examples of such obligations include: that goods sold in the course of business to consumers are of merchantable quality;[9] that a debtor under a consumer credit agreement may terminate at any time by serving notice and paying any sums due;[10] that as regards terms and conditions of employment a woman is to be given equal treatment with men in the same employment.[11]

The unenforceability of market transactions which attempt to modify inalienable rights makes it appropriate to classify this form of legal control as 'regulation', and yet it lacks one of the fundamental characteristics which we have used to identify that concept:[12] the state takes no initiative or active role in securing compliance with the specified goal. The parties are free to undertake activity, and even make agreements, which conflict with the legislative (or judicial) norm, in the sense that no public agency can take steps to prevent them. So long as they benefit mutually from such activity or agreement, the norm will not be invoked and individualist choice will prevail over the collective goal. Of course, each party takes the risk that the other will renege, in which case the agreement cannot be judicially enforced[13] and the holder of the inalienable right may seek redress for its infringement. Nevertheless, the party whose right has been infringed may be ill-placed, financially or otherwise, to sue.

### 3. JUDICIAL ROLE

Under a system of 'private' regulation, therefore, the residual power of the judges in the civil courts to protect inalienable rights constitutes the only form of state intervention. The prevailing English tradition of civil procedure, dominated by the adversarial principle[14], means that their role is an essentially passive one and the public interest, on the basis of which an inalienable right may have been created, is not generally represented. Judicial interpretation of the limits of inalienability nevertheless remains crucial and their preference for, or antipathy to, collective goals may have a significant impact on the efficacy of 'private' regulation.

---

[8] S. 2(1). See also Consumer Protection Act 1987, s. 7.
[9] Sale of Goods Act 1979, s. 14(2) and Unfair Contract Terms Act 1977, s. 6(2).
[10] Consumer Credit Act 1974, s. 173(1).
[11] Equal Pay Act 1970, s. 1.                                    [12] Cf. above, p. 2.
[13] In the business world there are, however, very effective extra-legal methods of enforcement: P. S. Atiyah, *An Introduction to the Law of Contract* (4th edn., 1989), p. 347.
[14] J. Jacob, *The English Fabric of Civil Justice* (1987), pp. 5–19.

In the nineteenth century, some common law judges resisted Parliamentary efforts to override freedom of contract.[15] By invoking the maxim '*quilibet potest renunciare juri pro se introducto*', they could hold that, where a provision was enacted solely for the benefit of a class of individuals, a member of that class could agree to waive the relevant term, at least where the legislation did not use clear language preventing such a contracting-out.[16] Modern judges have more respect for collective goals and the doctrine has fallen out of favour. In *Johnson* v. *Moreton* (1978), Lord Simon formulated the general principle

> where it appears that the mischief which Parliament is seeking to remedy is that a situation exists in which the relation of parties cannot properly be left to private contractual regulation, and Parliament therefore provides for statutory regulation, a party cannot contract out of such statutory regulation (albeit exclusively in his own favour), because so to permit would be to reinstate the mischief which the statute was designed to remedy and to render the statutory provision a dead letter.[17]

Analogous issues arise in relation to mandatory contractual terms. The relevant legislation must specify the *type* of contract, such as a lease, which is to contain the terms. Now, of course, parties cannot be compelled to enter into that particular type of contract; they may prefer to create a licence with a set of mainly different, but also overlapping, obligations relating to the possession of property. The preference may indeed, in part, be motivated by a desire of at least one of them to avoid the mandatory terms (e.g. security of tenure) applying to leases. But the courts will not allow them to avoid those terms simply by calling the agreement a 'licence': they characterize the type of contract according to the set of obligations created by it, rather than by the label attaching to it.[18] A similar principle is used to determine whether a particular agreement gives rise to a contract of employment (which gives rise to a large number of compulsory terms) or merely a contract for services as an independent contractor (which does not have to contain those terms).[19]

Nevertheless it is not always easy to apply this principle and there is evidence that, in deciding on which side of the line a particular agreement is to fall, the judges are swayed by their own perceptions of when regulating contracts is appropriate. Recognition that much modern employment legislation is inspired by paternalism or information deficits would seem to explain the contrasting decisions in two reported cases. In *Massey* v. *Crown Life Insurance*,[20] an insurance manager was advised by his accountant to change his relationship with the company with which he

---

[15] P. S. Atiyah, *The Rise and Fall of Freedom of Contract* (1979), ch. 13.
[16] *Graham* v. *Ingleby and Glover* (1848) 1 Exch. 651; *Griffith* v. *Earl of Dudley* (1892) LR 9 QBD 357.    [18] *Street* v. *Mountford* [1985] AC 809.    [17] [1980] AC 37, 69.
[19] *Young and Woods* v. *West* [1980] IRLR 201.    [20] [1978] ICR 590.

was working, such that he would be self-employed. He claimed compensation for unfair dismissal, on the ground that the legal obligations of the contract were those of an employee, notwithstanding the label, and thus necessarily included the provisions of the employment protection legislation. The claim was rejected: '[h]aving made his bed as being self-employed, he must lie on it'.[21] In *Ferguson* v. *Dawson*[22], a general labourer was orally engaged by a firm of building contractors, having been told he was part of 'a lump labour force' (the jargon frequently used to indicate self-employment). His tort claim for damages for personal injuries, based on a breach of a statutory duty owed to employed construction workers, was upheld:

[t]he parties cannot transfer a statute-imposed duty of care for safety of workmen from an employer to the workman himself merely because the parties agree, in effect, that the workman shall be deemed to be self-employed, where the true essence of the contract is, otherwise, a contract of service.[23]

In normative economic terms, efforts of the kind described to override regulation by contractual behaviour are not necessarily inappropriate. Provided that there are no externalities, the contract may generate efficiency by tailoring the regulatory regime to the particular circumstances of the parties. A study has shown how, in the American trucking industry, informal, legally unenforceable contracts are often used to 'fine-tune' the relevant Interstate Commerce Commission regulations.[24]

### 4. RATIONALIZATION

'Private' regulation is peripheral to the subject-matter of this book, but it is appropriate to conclude this short account with some explanation of why and when the legal form is likely to be used. It is a blunt instrument for dealing with significant, market-wide externalities principally because the rights rarely extend to affected third parties, and neither they nor those representing the 'public interest' can normally participate in the legal proceedings. Moreover, the external costs arising from the infringement may greatly exceed the sanctions imposed, damages representing the right-holder's loss,[25] or the unenforceability of a contract, leading to inappro-

---

[21] Per Lord Denning MR, ibid. at 596.          [22] [1976] 3 All ER 817.

[23] Per Megaw LJ, ibid. at 825.

[24] T. M. Palay, 'Avoiding Regulatory Constraint: Contracting Safeguards and the Role of Informal Agreements' (1985) 1 J. Law Econ. & Org. 155.

[25] The conventional measure of damages for the infringement of a private right. Where courts have power to award punitive/exemplary damages, the problem is (to some extent) overcome: R. Cooter and T. Ulen, *Law and Economics* (1988), pp. 388–97. In England, such power is severely limited: *Broome* v. *Cassell* [1972] AC 1027; for discussion and reform proposals, see Law Commission Consultation Paper No. 132, *Aggravated, Exemplary and Restitutionary Damages* (1993).

priate incentives for the infringer, particularly when the cost arising from the sanction has to be discounted by the possibility of the right-holder being unwilling or unable to take legal action.[26]

'Private' regulation is more obviously appropriate for meeting paternalist and distributional goals.[27] Distributional considerations may provide a powerful motive for shifting private law entitlements from wealthier to poorer individuals, thereby strengthening the latters' bargaining position.[28] For example, a householder who has a right in private nuisance to prevent a neighbouring firm from polluting may sell that right for a sum which is higher than that which he would have been prepared to pay the firm not to pollute if he had no such right.[29] Where there are grounds to believe that right-holders may seriously underestimate the value of a right because, for example, they fail to perceive the risks arising from its sale, there is a paternalist argument for rendering that right inalienable.[30]

The attractiveness of this solution, compared with forms of public regulation, lies mainly in its flexibility. The paternalist goal requires that attention be focused on an individual's vulnerability in a particular set of circumstances—it is a 'public' interest in a 'private' interest. The adjudication and enforcement of inalienable private rights, characterized by the exclusion of broader interests, permit a certain degree of tailoring to the assumed needs of the individual in the particular context. The legal formulation of such rights is often couched in language which confers some discretion on the judiciary; for example that the terms of a contract are enforceable only if they are 'reasonable'.[31]

The merits of private regulation should not, however, be exaggerated. The flexibility inherent in the remedy generates uncertainty which, as a non-trivial cost for those trading in an area of private regulation, might inhibit transactions which would benefit the party for whose protection the regulation was designed.[32] The passive and residual nature of the legal control—action is taken by the courts only after the 'event' and only at the initiative of the harmed party—limits its effectiveness. The condition of vulnerability which motivates a paternalistic intervention, at the same time, may paradoxically constitute an obstacle to legal redress.

[26] Cf. A. M. Polinsky, 'Private Versus Public Enforcement of Fines' (1980) 9 J. Legal Stud. 105.　[27] Kennedy, above, n. 2.

[28] Calabresi and Melamed, above, n. 5, pp. 1098–1102.

[29] E. J. Mishan, 'The Economics of Disamenity' (1974) 14 Nat. Res. J. 55, 62–4.

[30] Calabresi and Melamed, above, n. 5, p. 1113.

[31] e.g. Unfair Contract Terms Act 1977, ss. 2(2), 3(2), 4(1), and 6(3).

[32] R. Epstein, 'Unconscionability: A Critical Reappraisal' (1975) 18 J. Law & Econ. 293.

# PART IV

# FORMS OF ECONOMIC REGULATION

# 13

# Public Ownership

## I. INTRODUCTION

On some definitions of 'regulation', public ownership might well be excluded. The public interest which ostensibly justifies interference with ordinary market mechanisms and individual choice is here exercised not by the external legal control of private actors, but rather by the assumption of direct proprietary powers over resources. On another view, public ownership represents 'regulation' in its most complete and radical form: the removal from private hands of the means of production and distribution eliminates the inherent contradiction of forcing, or (more precisely) attempting to force, private interests to serve public goals.[1]

However the definitional issue is resolved, the importance of public ownership as an alternative to traditional forms of regulation cannot be denied. Its institutional structure, while markedly different from those forms, raises the same questions: to what extent can it achieve public interest goals? to what extent can it satisfy private interest demands?

Public enterprise in Britain can be traced back to the Tudor period,[2] but its use became widespread only in the nineteenth century, with the development of gas, electricity, and mechanized transport.[3] The initial response was to rely on supply from the competitive market but to subject undertakers to regulatory constraints regarding prices, profits, and safety.[4] However, a degree of scepticism of the merits of competition developed, particularly in relation to water and gas, as the duplication of facilities, funded by major capital outlays and often with surplus capacity, was perceived to be wasteful.

Public ownership, in the form of municipal corporations, was the favoured alternative for a number of reasons. A private monopoly was not a popular solution, particularly as the experiments with regulatory

---

[1] C. Offe, *Contradictions of the Welfare State* (ed. J. Keane, 1984), ch. 1.

[2] A Charter of 1514 authorized the Corporation of the Elder Brethren of Trinity House to make provision for lighthouses.

[3] W. Robson, 'Public Utility Services', in H. Laski, W. I. Jennings, and W. Robson (eds.), *A Century of Municipal Progress* (1935), ch. 14.

[4] These were normally contained in the private legislation authorizing the particular undertaking; subsequently, general regulatory legislation was passed. See e.g. 7 & 8 Victoria c. 85, which *inter alia* prescribed that if profits on capital stock exceeded 10% the Treasury could revise the scale of railway fares. See, generally, C. Foster, *Privatization, Public Ownership and the Regulation of Natural Monopoly* (1992), chs. 1–2.

institutions, which had been fraught with legal and political difficulties,[5] did not inspire confidence that the power of entrepreneurs could be successfully controlled. In contrast, the municipal corporations had experience in meeting community needs and their boundaries largely coincided with the networks of supply. Moreover, they could raise capital more cheaply than the private sector; and the potential profitability of some of the enterprises, notably gas and electricity, could reduce the burden on ratepayers of other municipal services.

As the twentieth century advanced, localized, independent control inhibited technological development, and municipal ownership of public utilities was gradually superseded by national ownership.[6] So, for example, in 1926 the Central Electricity Board was established to build and operate the national grid, although distribution to users remained in the hands of the municipal corporations and private companies.

The golden age of nationalization, from 1946 to 1951, owed something to the socialist conviction that the major industries should be in public, rather than private hands;[7] but the conditions of those industries provided practical motivations which were even more important.[8] In some cases, such as gas and electricity, nationalization was the continuation of the pre-war policy which located significant economies of scale from larger units of organization,[9] and in relation to a significant part of each industry it involved the transfer from one form of public ownership to another. As regards public transport, the long-term aim was to bring all services into a co-ordinated whole.[10] But the most immediate need was to transfer to public ownership the railways, which suffered from severe under-investment and inefficiency, and the air services, which had always enjoyed considerable government subsidies.[11] None of the other industries which were nationalized during this period—coal, iron, and steel—could be considered as natural monopolies. While transfer to public ownership seemed to be the only way to arrest the serious decline of the coal industry,[12] that was not true of steel, which was relatively prosperous. The

---

[5] H. W. Arthurs, *Without the Law: Administrative Justice and Legal Pluralism in Nineteenth Century England* (1985), ch. 4.                              [6] Robson, above, n. 3.

[7] Cf. C. A. R. Crosland, *The Future of Socialism* (1956), pp. 462–5.

[8] W. A. Robson, *Nationalized Industry and Public Ownership* (1960), ch. 2.

[9] Cf. *Report of the Committee of Enquiry into the Gas Industry* (1945, Cmd. 6699).

[10] The process had begun with the creation of a public corporation, the London Passenger Transport Board, in 1933. The Transport Act 1947 created the British Transport Commission which, until it was abolished in 1962, was to own and control the railways, canals, and a large proportion of the road passenger services.

[11] The nationalization of air services had begun in 1939, following the Report of the [Cadman] Committee of Inquiry into Civil Aviation (1938, Cmd. 5685).

[12] Nationalization had been recommended by a majority of the [Sankey] Coal Industry Royal Commission which reported in 1919 (Cd. 359–60), the year in which the Labour Party adopted a constitution featuring nationalization as a fundamental aim.

nationalization of the latter was motivated more by ideology and, as such, proved to be highly controversial.

With the exception of steel, which was privatized in 1953 and then renationalized in 1967, there was a broad political consensus on public ownership until the mid-1970s. Thereafter, for reasons which will be explored in the last section of this chapter, the Conservative administrations embarked on a radical programme of privatization.

### 2. PUBLIC INTEREST JUSTIFICATIONS FOR PUBLIC OWNERSHIP

*(a) Natural Monopoly*

Of the several public interest justifications advanced for public ownership,[13] that based on natural monopolies is the most important. This phenomenon occurs, it will be recalled,[14] when it is cheaper for production to be undertaken by one firm, rather than by several or many. Although it may be desirable for one firm's monopoly power to be protected when such conditions prevail, it does not, of course, necessarily follow that that firm should be publicly owned. A private firm may be granted the monopoly and the adverse consequences may be constrained by regulation. The argument for a state-owned monopoly must then rest on the hypothesis that those consequences can be dealt with more effectively within the institutional framework of public ownership than by legal controls of private firms.

Historically, the emergence of municipal corporation ownership of the utilities was due, in part at least, to the lack of confidence in the early regulatory bodies,[15] and one reason for the nationalization of the railways was the failure of the pre-war regulatory system to meet the needs of the industry.[16] As we shall see in the next chapter, the more sophisticated regulatory agencies, established to control the prices set and the profits earned by the industries privatized under the Thatcherite programme, have been beset by difficulties, and their decisions have been widely criticized.

It is, indeed, arguable that the imposition of public interest prices and standards may be achieved more effectively by the flexible decision-making inherent in the public ownership framework—considerable

---

[13] See generally: J. R. Prichard and M. J. Trebilcock, 'Crown Corporations in Canada: The Choice of Instrument', in J. R. Prichard (ed.), *Crown Corporations in Canada: The Calculus of Instrumental Choice* (1983), ch. 9; D. Swann, *The Retreat of the State: Deregulation and Privatisation in the UK and US* (1988), pp. 75–85; M. Waterson, *Regulation of the Firm and Natural Monopoly* (1988), pp. 64–5.

[14] Above, pp. 30–3.                    [15] Foster, above, n. 4, pp. 61–3.

[16] H. J. Dyos and D. H. Aldcroft, *British Transport* (1969), pp. 316–19.

internal discretion, subject only to political accountability—than by formalized external legal controls. This is particularly likely where the trading objectives of the enterprise are seriously affected by uncertainty or must closely interact with those of other industries: in such circumstances, it will not be easy for the directions issuing from a regulatory agency, distanced to some degree from the industry, to reflect the complexity of the industrial strategy.[17] Of course, any advantage accruing in this respect from the public ownership form may be offset by costs elsewhere, notably from productive inefficiency.

*(b) Externalities*

An activity which gives rise to significant negative externalities—social costs which are not reflected in the price of the product or services—can normally be controlled adequately by private law liabilities or public regulatory instruments. Public ownership can rarely be justified on this ground alone;[18] but an exception may exist where the size of the externality is potentially very large as, for example, with the escape of radioactive material from a nuclear-powered electricity generation station. If the activity is publicly owned, political accountability should ensure an adequate degree of control and an ability to meet external costs.[19]

The use of public ownership to deal with positive externalities, in other words to supply public goods, is much more common. Public goods, it will be recalled,[20] are those from which individuals may benefit without paying, in the sense that they cannot viably be excluded from consumption. It is sometimes assumed that public ownership of supply is the only means of solving the main problems of public goods: which are deciding how much to supply, and providing adequate compensation for suppliers. This is incorrect.[21] The shortfall in a private supplier's income may be met by a subsidy and an agency may be given power to regulate the quantity and quality of output. In choosing between this form of regulation and public ownership, the key question is which institutional arrangement may more effectively and cheaply assess and reflect the public demand for the goods.[22]

---

[17] Prichard and Trebilcock, above, n. 13, pp. 207–9.

[18] The existence of widespread externalities may, of course, add weight to *other* arguments for public ownership.

[19] The majority, but not all, of the European nuclear generating industries are publicly owned: T. Daintith and L. Hancher, *Energy Strategy in Europe: The Legal Framework* (1986), p. 59.          [20] Cf. above, pp. 33–5.

[21] For general discussions, see: A. J. Culyer, *The Political Economy of Social Policy* (1980), ch. 3; W. Beckerman, 'How Large a Public Sector?', in D. Helm (ed.), *The Economic Borders of the State* (1989), pp. 74–82.

[22] Culyer, above, n. 21, pp. 49–50.

## (c) Other Economic Justifications

As we have seen, one of the main reasons for the nationalization of coal production was to halt the decline of that industry; and the same motivation lay behind the decisions to purchase share holdings in British Leyland and Rolls Royce,[23] and to transfer a significant part of the shipbuilding industry into public ownership.[24] Here also, the payment of subsidies to private firms offers a less radical alternative, but such a solution involves the serious disadvantage that it may act as an incentive for continued or increasing productive inefficiency.[25] On the other hand, if the sickness of the industry is itself largely a consequence of the latter, it is far from certain that public ownership can provide the cure.

The financial support of ailing industries, whether by subsidy or by public ownership, may eliminate the costs arising from insolvency and social dislocation; but in the long term, unless it is being used to correct genuine externalities, it will lead to a serious misallocation of resources.[26] Its use is, in any event, limited by GATT and the Treaty of Rome.[27]

An economic argument for public ownership much deployed in the 1960s was that of 'planning'.[28] Briefly stated, it proceeds from a recognition that co-ordination between certain industries which play a key role in the general economy is essential for growth, to an assertion that such co-ordination is possible only if they are publicly owned. The assertion is questionable: governments can use a variety of methods of influencing and co-ordinating industrial activities in the private sector without assuming the power of ownership.[29]

## (d) Distributional Goals and Cross-Subsidization

In normal conditions, a private firm will not provide services the cost of which cannot be recovered in the prices charged. If prices are related to cost in this way, inhabitants of remoter areas may be unable to afford to pay for some essential services. If supply is considered desirable on distributional grounds,[30] the solution lies in cross-subsidization: a uniform

---

[23] See P. Dunnett, *The Decline of the British Motor Industry* (1980), pp. 133–9.

[24] See B. Hayward, *Government and Shipbuilding* (1979), ch. 7.

[25] The risk is of creating an 'intervention breeding system': A. Prest, 'The Economic Rationale for Subsidising Industry', in A. Whiting, *The Economics of Industrial Subsidies* (1976), p. 73.  [26] Prest, ibid.

[27] See J. Beseler and A. Williams, *Anti-Dumping and Anti-Subsidy Law: The European Communities* (1986), ch. 5.

[28] See generally A. Skuse, *Government Intervention and Industrial Policy* (2nd edn., 1972), ch. 8.

[29] Waterson, above, n. 13, p. 64, citing the example of the Japanese Ministry of International Trade and Industry.

[30] An economic externality argument, based on the social cost of overcrowding in urban areas, may also justify intervention: above, p. 48.

price can be charged which is sufficient to finance supply in high-cost areas. In principle, this can be done without public ownership; a private monopolist can be legally required to provide the relevant service and allowed to charge prices which cover their cost.

Pursuit of the distributional goals by these regulatory means nevertheless involves two disadvantages. First, the agency responsible for reviewing the private firm's prices, and hence the extent of the subsidy, will need access to data which enables it to verify that the subsidy is needed.[31] Secondly, the relative transparency of the agency's price-setting processes may render the subsidy more visible, and, in consequence, provoke opposition from 'ordinary' consumers.[32] The internal processes of public ownership facilitate both the scrutiny of data and the concealment of the subsidy.

## (e) Power and Ideology

Distributional arguments for public ownership may merge into convictions which are fundamentally ideological. Most prominent among these is the conviction that the key industries, particularly those which are natural monopolies, should serve, and be seen to serve, the community at large, and thus should be taken out of the hands of private entrepreneurs. Related to this is a moral antipathy to the profit-making ethos which pervades the private sector. Such ideas were central to Fabian Socialism[33] and were adopted in the famous Clause IV of the Labour Party Constitution, which referred to the goal of securing for workers the 'full fruits of industry . . . on the basis of the common ownership of the means of production, distribution and exchange'.[34] They re-emerged to fuel the nationalization debates in the 1940s,[35] but their influence on Labour Party policy had already waned by 1960,[36] and the attempts to disenshrine the commitment to common ownership from Clause IV are indicative of its current unpopularity.[37]

### 3. PRIVATE INTEREST CONSIDERATIONS

In this chapter, as elsewhere, we will be concerned to explore the hypothesis that public ownership serves to benefit private interests in addition to, or instead of, the public interest. At this stage, however, we can do no more than outline the basic issues, since full consideration requires a more complete understanding of how the legal forms of

---

[31] Swann, above, n. 13, pp. 81–2.
[32] Prichard and Trebilcock, above, n. 13, p. 209.
[33] A. McBriar, *Fabian Socialism and English Politics 1884–1918* (1966).
[34] See G. Radice, *Labour's Path to Power: The New Revisionism* (1989), pp. 61–2.
[35] Cf. TUC Interim Report on Public Ownership (1953), para. 7.
[36] Robson, above, n. 8, ch. 16.          [37] Cf. Radice, above, n. 34, loc. cit.

organization affect the various private interests involved. In the first place, we will investigate the extent to which the absence of both competitive market pressures and regulatory constraints may enable those—managers and other employees—working for a public enterprise to enjoy benefits which otherwise would not accrue to them. Secondly, we will attempt to locate among the consumers of the public firm's products or services those groups which, by exerting pressure through the political processes controlling public enterprise performance, are likely to obtain preferential treatment.

## 4. LEGAL STRUCTURE AND PRODUCTIVE EFFICIENCY

### (a) Forms of Public Ownership

The dividing line between public and private enterprise cannot always be clearly drawn, particularly where some mixture of public and private control is attempted.[38] Nevertheless, we may identify three principal forms of public ownership. First, an enterprise can be placed under direct ministerial control as a government department; the Post Office was so treated until 1969.[39] Secondly, it can be registered as a company under the Companies Act 1985 (and thus be subject to the ordinary principles of company law), with the state holding all, or a significant proportion of, the equity (e.g. British Nuclear Fuels Ltd.[40]). Thirdly, it can be constituted by legislation as a statutory public corporation, in which case its functions and powers are determined by Parliament.[41]

The first of these forms, the governmental department, has been rarely used in recent times for the supply of goods or services which are 'traded' in the sense that the price charged is intended to be related to cost. The commercial character of the enterprise suggests that performance will be enhanced if managers are distanced from political interference and, for their part, Ministers will prefer to limit their identification with activities and decisions which may not be popular.[42] It is for this reason that, where

---

[38] T. Daintith, 'Public and Private Enterprise in the United Kingdom', in W. Friedmann (ed.), *Public and Private Enterprise in Mixed Economies* (1974), pp. 195–202; L. Hancher, 'The Public Sector as Object and Instrument of Economic Policy', in T. Daintith (ed.), *Law as an Instrument of Economic Policy* (1988), pp. 170–1.

[39] On which, see Select Committee on Nationalised Industries, *The Post Office*, (1966–67) HC 340.  [40] Atomic Energy Authority Act 1971.

[41] A public corporation may also be created by exercise of the royal prerogative under a charter of incorporation (e.g. the BBC) but the form is rarely used in modern times, as legislation is normally required to override private rights: Daintith (1974), above, n. 38. pp. 215–16.

[42] Prichard and Trebilcock, above, n. 13, pp. 212–15; R. Zeckhauser and M. Horn 'The Control and Performance of State-Owned Enterprises', in P. MacAvoy *et al.*, *Privatization and State-Owned Enterprises: Lessons from the United States, Great Britain and Canada* (1989), ch. 1. See also *The Post Office*, above, n. 39.

the form has been retained (e.g. for Her Majesty's Stationery Office), the suppliers of the product or services have been separated from the policy functions of government and established as Executive Agencies with formalized performance targets.[43]

The statutory public corporation has been much the most widely used of the instruments of public ownership. An appreciation of its merits relative to those of registered companies requires a more elaborate comparison of the two forms of organization.

### (b) Private Corporations, Public Corporations, and Market Constraints

An important economic goal for any organization, public or private, is what we have already referred to[44] as productive efficiency, the maximization of output relative to input or—to put it another way—the minimization of production costs. According to conventional economic theory,[45] the principal legal form of private organisations, the corporation, creates powerful incentives for pursuit of this goal.

In the first place, the shareholders, as residual owners who benefit financially from the firm's profits, will exert pressure on its managers to reduce inefficiency. In relation to a widely-held company, with a large number of passive shareholders, this may seem to be problematic,[46] but even in this case managerial performance should be constrained by the capital market. Inferior performance will reduce the market value of the firm's shares and will render it vulnerable to takeover by others who can make a profit by acquiring the shares at the lower price, replacing the inefficient management, and thereby inducing the firm to perform to its true potential.[47] In addition, managerial salaries may be related to the firm's profits.

Secondly, productive efficiency may be enhanced by the activities of creditors. Lenders of capital may monitor the firm's performance prior to, or consequent upon, the granting of a loan; and, in the event of solvency problems, may require managerial changes.

Thirdly, if the firm operates in a competitive market, pressure will be exerted by consumers. If the firm does not constrain its costs, the prices of its products will rise and consumers will purchase from another supplier.

---

[43] For an overview, see N. Carter and P. Greer, 'Evaluating Agencies: Next Steps and Performance Indicators' (1993) 71 Pub. Admin. 407.

[44] Above, p. 22.

[45] See e.g. H. Demsetz, *Ownership, Control and the Firm* (1988); T. Eggertsson, *Economic Behavior and Institutions* (1990).

[46] Cf. A. Berle and G. Means, *The Modern Corporation and Private Property* (1932).

[47] H. Manne, 'Mergers and the Market for Corporate Control' (1965) 73 J. Pol. Econ. 110. For some reservations to this prediction, see J. Vickers and G. Yarrow, *Privatization: An Economic Analysis* (1988), pp. 15–24.

The legal structure of public corporations is quite different; although there has been some variation in the statutory provisions, a standard pattern has emerged.[48] Ownership is vested in a Board, the members of which are appointed by the relevant Minister 'from amongst persons appearing to him to be qualified as having had experience of, and having shown capacity in, industrial, commercial or financial matters, applied science, administration, or the organisation of workers'.[49] As individuals, they have no financial interest in the corporation's performance—they are paid salaries and expenses as determined by the Minister and approved by the Treasury—and there are no private shareholders.

We see at once the principal contrast with the private corporate form:[50] there are no residual owners who are financially interested in the profitability of the public firm other than general taxpayers.[51] The latter have to bear the burden if the firm runs at a loss; a statutory corporation must exist until abolished by Parliament—it cannot be wound up for insolvency. Now, while taxpayers may voice their disapproval in the political arena, the losses are spread very thinly among them: as *individuals* they will therefore have little incentive to spend resources on political action; and they are too numerous and diverse to form an effective pressure *group*.[52]

A second source of pressure for the productive efficiency of private firms is also typically absent. Since most public corporations are granted a statutory monopoly, consumers of their products or services cannot generally turn to an alternative supplier. Thirdly, capital can, in general, be raised only from a public source, notably the Treasury.[53] Ministerial and/or Parliamentary approval may be required, but the motivation to insist on efficient performance may be less strong than that of private creditors who have a direct financial interest in the protection of their loans.

---

[48] For a detailed analysis, see: J. Garner, 'Public Corporations in the United Kingdom', in W. Friedmann and J. Garner (eds.), *Government Enterprise: A Comparative Study* (1970), which also contains accounts of legal structures in other jurisdictions; T. Prosser, *Nationalised Industries and Public Control* (1986).

[49] Coal Industry Nationalization Act (hereafter CINA) 1946, s. 2(3). This Morrisonian conception of a public corporation eschews the continental model under which key interest groups (e.g. employees and consumers) are represented: Prosser, above, n. 48, ch. 7.

[50] For general discussion, see: R. Millward, 'Public Ownership, the Theory of Property Rights and the Public Corporation in the U.K. ' (1978) Salford Papers in Economics 78–1; J. Redwood and J. Hatch, *Controlling Public Industries* (1982); H. Gravelle, 'Judicial Review and Public Firms' (1983) 3 Int. Rev. Law & Econ. 187; Waterson, above, n. 13, ch. 4; Vickers and Yarrow, above, n. 47, pp. 26–35.

[51] Cf. *Tamlin* v. *Hannaford* [1950] 1 KB 18.

[52] Gravelle, above, n. 50, pp. 188–9.

[53] See e.g. Gas Act 1948, s. 41.

### (c) Legal Constraints

In the absence of market constraints for productive efficiency, it is clearly necessary to establish some legal or political substitutes; and successive administrations have experimented with a range of different methods.[54] Let us examine, first, the possibilities of legal control.

The legislative provisions governing public corporations have typically imposed two types of obligation which presumptively relate to productive efficiency. The first is to be located in the explicit public interest objectives of the industry, and is formulated in language which is both general and vague: for example, 'to develop and maintain an efficient, co-ordinated and economical system of . . . supply',[55] or 'to secure the efficient development of the . . . industry'.[56] The second, the so-called 'break-even' obligation, has tended to be more precise: 'that the revenues of the Board shall not be less than sufficient for meeting all their outgoings properly chargeable to revenue account . . . on an average of good and bad years'.[57]

To what extent can provisions of this kind be used to effect a judicial review of the activities and decisions of a public corporation? In the United Kingdom judges have traditionally been reluctant to regard matters of economic and social policy as justiciable.[58] However, in recent years they have shown a greater readiness to intervene, and the leading case of *Bromley London BC* v. *Greater London Council* (1982)[59] provides an excellent illustration of the potential, but also the difficulties, of legal control.

In this case the House of Lords had to determine the validity of a GLC resolution which enabled London Transport fares to be reduced by 25 per cent, the resulting deficit being financed by a levy on rates. The relevant legislation, *inter alia* required the GLC to promote 'integrated, efficient and economic' transport services.[60] Their Lordships could not agree on the exact meaning to be attributed to 'economic'. One interpretation was that it required the GLC only to minimize the burden on *both* passengers *and* ratepayers, the allocation of that burden being at the GLC's discretion.[61]

---

[54] Redwood and Hatch, above, n. 50, chs. 4–6; C. Whitehead (ed.), *Reshaping the Nationalised Industries* (1988), chs. 2–4, 12–13.

[55] Gas Act 1948, s. 1(1)(a).          [56] CINA 1946, s. 1(1)(b).

[57] CINA 1946, s. 1(4)(c). In the White Paper, *The Financial and Economic Objectives of the Nationalised Industries* (1961, Cmnd. 1337), para. 19, the government indicated that this test was to be applied over a five-year period, although the requirement was not given statutory force.

[58] See esp. *Roberts* v. *British Railways Board* [1965] 1 WLR 396, 400, per Ungoed-Thomas J.

[59] [1983] 1 AC 768. For valuable commentaries, see: Gravelle, above, n. 50; and M. Loughlin, *Local Government in the Modern State* (1986), pp. 69–78.

[60] Transport (London) Act 1969, s. 1(1).

[61] [1983] 1 AC 768, 828–830, per Lord Diplock.

A second view was that the undertaking must be 'cost-effective', in the sense that to achieve a given end (which might not necessarily be commercial) resources must be used effectively and not wastefully.[62] On a third construction, the industry should be conducted on 'ordinary business principles'; in consequence, losses should be avoided, or at least minimized.[63] The matter was, however, conclusively resolved by the fact that the London Transport Executive was, in the same statute, subjected to a 'break-even' obligation, 'so far as [that was] practicable'.[64] Given the ambiguity of the general duty, this specific obligation was paramount, and led to the conclusion that the fare-cutting policy, being in breach of that obligation as well as inconsistent with 'ordinary business principles', was *ultra vires*.

As the *Bromley* case reveals, broad statutory statements of public interest economic objectives are unreliable as foundations for legal challenges to productive inefficiency. Even if the judges were to agree that 'economic' was to be identified with 'cost-effective', perhaps the closest of the three interpretations to productive efficiency, it is difficult to see how, on the limited information available to a court, appropriate decisions could be made. The 'break-even' obligation is quite different: its meaning is largely free from ambiguity[65] and a determination can be made from an inspection of a properly prepared set of accounts. However, to operate without making a loss does not necessarily imply productive efficiency. It creates no incentive to make a profit and the managers of the corporation may thus be tempted to use up any potential surplus for their own private non-financial interest by, for example, making their working conditions more agreeable and, to avoid hassle, acceding to workforce demands for restrictive practices and higher wage demands.[66]

Finally, for there to be effective legal control of a public corporation, a serious obstacle must be overcome: there must be someone willing and able to pursue an appropriate remedy. We have already seen that those who must bear the consequences of productive inefficiency, mainly consumers and taxpayers, are unlikely, as *individuals*, to have a sufficient financial incentive to act, and that co-ordinating effective group action is costly and difficult for them. Even if these problems are overcome, they may not have standing to apply for judicial review. Until relatively recently, English law adopted a cautious and somewhat arbitrary approach

---

[62] See e.g. Lord Brandon, ibid. at 852.

[63] See, especially, Lord Scarman, ibid. at 845–6.

[64] Transport (London) Act 1969, s. 7(3).

[65] It leaves some questions unresolved, e.g. whether the depreciation of assets is to be calculated on a 'historical cost' or a 'replacement cost' basis. On this, see the 1961 White Paper, above, n. 57, which, in para. 19, directed that the latter basis be adopted.

[66] Millward, above, n. 50, p. 12.

to this question,[67] with the result that aggrieved taxpayers, in particular, were denied access to the courts.[68] A more liberal approach now prevails: in exercising its discretion as to whether an applicant for judicial review has 'a sufficient interest in the matter to which the application relates',[69] the court has regard to the strength of the claim as well as the nature of the applicant's interest.[70] It follows that, although consumers and taxpayers may not suffer an automatic exclusion, nevertheless to acquire standing they may still have to show that the acts or decisions of the public corporation were manifestly or flagrantly unlawful.

### (d) Ministerial Responsibility and Accountability

The standard post-war legislative framework for the nationalized industries relied predominantly on two agents of control: ministerial responsibility and accountability to Parliament. As regards the first of these, although the policy was one of an 'arm's length' relationship between the Minister and the Board, nevertheless he was given a wide variety of residual powers, including those of reviewing borrowing and investment decisions, and of issuing formal directions on matters of national interest.[71] The effectiveness of this method of control was blunted by several factors.[72] The 'arm's length' relationship meant that it was hardly possible for the Minister (and his staff) to monitor production costs.[73] His interest in the efficiency of the industry might be limited to his own (perhaps short) term of office, and, most importantly, it might conflict with other political and economic goals, such as price restraint.[74]

While not everyone might agree with one writer's conclusion that the sovereignty of Parliament, and in particular its control of public money, is the 'great myth of the British constitution',[75] there is nevertheless general recognition that it has not been very effective in influencing the efficiency

---

[67] P. Craig, *Administrative Law* (2nd edn., 1989), pp. 349–55.

[68] See e.g. *R* v. *Customs and Excise Comrs, ex parte Cooke and Stevenson* [1970] 1 WLR 450. Ratepayers were treated more generously on the grounds that they were typically less numerous than taxpayers and were owed a 'fiduciary duty' by local authorities: *Prescott* v. *Birmingham Corporation* [1955] Ch 210.

[69] Supreme Court Act 1981, s. 31(3), incorporating the test originally prescribed in SI 1977/1955.

[70] *R* v. *Inland Revenue Comrs, ex parte National Federation of Self-Employed* [1982] AC 617.

[71] For details, see C. Drake, 'The Public Corporation as an Organ of Government Policy', in Friedmann and Garner, above, n. 48, pp. 30–41.

[72] Millward, above, n. 50.

[73] Gravelle, above, n. 50, p. 188, contrasting such decisions with those on e.g. investment and prices, where less detailed information is required.

[74] This was a particular problem in the 1960s and early 1970s: see NEDO, *Study of the UK Nationalised Industries: Their Role in the Economy and Control in the Future* (1976), p. 31.

[75] I. Harden, 'Money and the Constitution: Financial Control, Reporting and Audit' (1993) 13 Legal Stud. 16, 33.

of publicly owned industries. In part, this has been a consequence of institutional factors:[76] the abolition of the Select Committee on Nationalised Industries when the more broadly select committee structure was introduced in 1979 diluted the focus and expertise of parliamentary scrutiny of the nationalized industries, and the restrictions on the powers of the Public Accounts Committee in relation to these industries. In part, it can be explained by reference to private interest theory: politicians are likely to be more responsive to the interests of groups which benefit from productive inefficiency (employees, managers, and other input suppliers) than those which must bear the losses (taxpayers and consumers), because the financial stake of the former per individual is greater, and they are better organized.[77]

### (e) Financial Constraints

To counteract the perceived weaknesses of the institutional methods of control, governments in the period 1961 to 1978 experimented with a number of financial devices. The main focus of these was the problem of capital expenditure: unless constrained, managers might engage in unprofitable expansion if that would advance their own non-financial interests, such as minimizing worker and consumer complaints.[78] An early attempt to counter this tendency was for the government to set financial targets, in the form of a desirable rate of return on the industry's assets.[79] In an effort to render such targets equivalent to those operating in the private sector, these were subsequently complemented by commercial-type appraisals of particular investment projects.[80] Measures of this kind were, however, beset by difficulties. What is to be regarded as a desirable rate of return, for this purpose, is, as we shall see in another context,[81] a highly complex matter, not least because public corporations are often expected to pursue some social objectives which do not easily lend themselves to commercial criteria. Also, with the information problem posed by the arm's length relationship, it is not clear that Ministers are in the best position to make the necessary judgements.

A second line of attack was the use of external financing limits: from 1975, a ceiling was imposed on the amount that could be borrowed from

[76] V. Flegmann, 'Parliamentary Accountability', in Whitehead, above, n. 54, ch. 12; Prosser, above, n. 48, ch. 10.                    [77] Gravelle, above, n. 50, p. 189.
[78] Millward, above, n. 50, pp. 18–19; C. K. Rowley and G. K. Yarrow, 'Property Rights, Regulation and Public Enterprise: The Case of the British Steel Industry 1957–1975' (1981) 1 Int. Rev. Law & Econ. 63, 80.
[79] It was introduced following a proposal in the 1961 White Paper, above, n. 57, para. 23.
[80] For detailed discussion, see White Papers, Nationalised Industries: A Review of Economic and Financial Objectives (1967, Cmnd. 3437), paras. 6–16, and The Nationalised Industries (1978, Cmnd. 7131), paras. 58–65; and Redwood and Hatch, above, n. 50, pp. 73–80.                    [81] Below, pp. 307–9.

government during any one financial year.[82] This can be considered as equivalent to the type of control which creditors might exert on private enterprises; it might serve to lower wage demands and induce other efficiencies in production. On the other hand, operating within the limit might be achieved by other means: by lowering the quality of the service provided, for example, or by deferring essential maintenance expenditure.[83]

While not abandoning financial targets and external limits, the Thatcher administration sought to overcome the problems these devices created for government control by establishing new forms of independent financial management and strengthening existing forms.[84] The National Audit Act 1983 created the National Audit Office, comprising the Comptroller and Auditor General—now independent of both Parliament and the Executive—and his staff. His functions extend beyond the traditional financial audit, the scrutinizing of accounts of public bodies, to what has become known as 'value for money' audit, legislatively defined as an examination 'into the economy, efficiency and effectiveness with which [a public body] . . . has used its resources in discharging its functions'.[85] On the face of it, this statutory provision may seem to be as general and vague as those which gave rise to interpretational problems in the context of judicial review,[86] but the National Audit Office has developed a framework for analysis in which its meaning is clearly identified with productive efficiency.[87] Moreover, the accumulation of expertise within the Office, and the continuity of experience, substantially reduce the difficulties faced by judges in 'one-off' legal challenges.

### (f) Consumers and Performance Indicators

Attempts to find a proxy for the pressure which consumer choice exerts on private firms in a competitive market have been plentiful, but not, as yet, very successful. The legislation governing nationalized industries has typically established consumer councils or user consultative committees,[88] but their role has been predominantly limited to that of receiving

---

[82] See the 1978 White Paper, above, n. 80, paras. 79–82; and Redwood and Hatch, above, n. 50, ch. 5. The device was part of a general strategy on the Public Sector Borrowing Requirement: White Paper, *Cash Limits* (1976, Cmnd. 6440).

[83] The failure to renew the sewerage systems has been attributed to the cash limits imposed on the water industry: J. Rees and M. Synnott, 'Privatisation and Social Objectives: The Water Industry', in Whitehead, above, n. 54, pp. 185–6.

[84] Harden, above, n. 75, pp. 22–7.

[85] National Audit Act 1983, s. 6(1).      [86] Above, p. 274.

[87] 'Economy' is construed to mean minimizing the cost of resources acquired or used, and 'efficiency' maximizing output for a given input or minimizing input for a given output: National Audit Office, *NAO a Framework for Value for Money Audits*, cited in Harden, above, n. 75, p. 24.      [88] e.g. Gas Act 1948, s. 9.

complaints and transmitting them to the Board. In consequence, their impact on the policy and performance of public corporations has been slight.[89]

More imaginative, if also flawed, have been the efforts to create and apply performance indicators in the public sector.[90] The impetus for this form of control began well before the Conservative administrations of the 1980s,[91] but reached a high-water mark with the publication of Mr Major's 'Citizen's Charter'.[92] Two categories of performance indicators may be identified. The first, which lays down standards for the quality of service provided, relates more to the issue of allocative efficiency, and we shall return to it in that context.[93] The second deals directly with productive efficiency, and covers such matters as the efficient use of manpower, land, energy, and materials. The Boards of nationalized industries have always been encouraged to specify and publish indicators of the latter kind, and often have done so in their annual reports. But the efficacy of the system may be doubted. The data provided has tended to focus on actual results, rather than targets; and where targets have been specified, they have mostly been formulated internally, and have not been the subject of external scrutiny.[94] In short, in relation to productive efficiency, performance indicators have served principally as a valuable source of information for bodies like the National Audit Office.

*(g) Efficiency Reviews*

One of the first measures of the Thatcher government was to enable the Secretary of State for Trade and Industry to refer public corporations to the Monopolies and Mergers Commission for investigation of 'the efficiency and costs of . . . the service provided . . . or possible abuse of a monopoly situation'.[95] A substantial number of such efficiency reviews have taken place. The Commission has been adept at locating structural or procedural weaknesses in a corporation's financial management system,[96] but has been less successful in applying objective efficiency criteria. The

---

[89] Prosser, above, n. 48, ch. 8. See also the experiment in the 1970s of nominating consumer representatives to the Board: White Paper (1978), above, n. 80, paras. 26, 30–9.

[90] See generally: Prosser, above, n. 48, pp. 176–88; I. Harden, *The Contracting State* (1992), pp. 64–8.

[91] See e.g. : White Paper (1967), above, n. 80, para. 32; White Paper (1978), above, n. 80, paras. 76–8; and, more generally, Redwood and Hatch, above, n. 50, ch. 6.

[92] (1991, Cm. 1599); also Cabinet Office, *Service to the Public* (1988). For critical evaluation, see A. Barron and C. Scott, 'The Citizen's Charter Programme' (1992) 55 Modern LR 526.  [93] Below, p. 285.

[94] Redwood and Hatch, above, n. 50, p. 115; Harden, above, n. 90, p. 65.

[95] Competition Act 1980, s. 11(1). See generally B. Wharton, 'Efficiency Reviews and the Role of the Monopolies and Mergers Commission', in Whitehead, above, n. 54, ch. 4. In addition, the Minister can, and does, commission reviews by management consultants: ibid. 60.

[96] See e.g. Report on Central Electricity Generating Board, 1980–81 HC 315.

main problem has been in finding suitable comparators: it is, for example, not obvious that the input costs in one nationalized industry can provide guidance on what is desirable in another; and comparisons with previous performance within the same industry are subject to the obvious objection that they cannot by themselves indicate what levels of efficiency can be attained.

A further problem concerns the consequences of a review. Although in theory the Secretary of State has power formally to require a public corporation to take remedial action where the Commission has found that it has been pursuing a course of conduct which operates against the public interest,[97] this is not normally done. Rather, the investigatee is invited to comment on criticisms contained in the review and to indicate the steps which it proposes to take to implement those recommendations which it accepts. The Commission itself is not involved in any follow-up discussion or investigation, and it is left to government or more general political forces to apply pressure for change.

### (h) Conclusions

The absence of reliable comparators which has hindered the efficiency reviews carried out by the Monopolies and Mergers Commission also constitutes an obstacle to forming definitive judgments on the productive efficiency of public corporations. Nevertheless, with some exceptions,[98] economists have tended to conclude on the basis of available data that they perform poorly in comparison with private enterprise.[99] Admittedly, most of such data relates to the period before the drive to efficiency which characterized the Thatcherian decade, and there is some evidence of improved performance in response to the more recent measures described above.[100]

Our analysis suggests that the problems which are intrinsic to public ownership cannot be overcome by conventional legal restraints, given the limited competence of judges to appraise efficiency within the context of judicial review. Government control tends to be thwarted by information problems and the pursuance of conflicting goals; and the influence of politicians may be subverted to meet the demands of interest groups which

---

[97] Competition Act 1980, s. 12.

[98] e.g. R. Millward, 'The Comparative Performance of Public and Private Ownership' in J. Kay, C. Mayer, and D. Thompson, *Privatisation and Regulation—The UK Experience* (1986), ch. 6. See also the study of a number of organizations which had been transferred from public to private ownership reported in A. Dunsire, K. Hartley, and D. Parker, 'Organizational Status and Performance: Summary of the Findings' (1991) 69 Pub. Admin. 21. The authors found that in most cases improvements in productive efficiency had not been achieved.

[99] R. Pryke, 'The Comparative Performance of Public and Private Enterprise', in Kay *et al.*, above, n. 98; Rowley and Yarrow, above, n. 78, pp. 71–6; Vickers and Yarrow, above, n.47, pp. 147–50.          [100] Whitehead, above, n. 54, *passim.*

benefit from inefficiency. Bodies such as the National Audit Office and the Monopolies and Mergers Commission, which are independent of government and Parliament and which possess sufficient expertise to undertake a rigorous scrutiny of a public corporation's performance, undoubtedly offer the best model for effective control. Yet they have no power to insist on remedial action, a consequence presumably of the reluctance in Britain to establish a clear public law framework for the control of public enterprise.[101] As one commentator has observed, 'the relationship between the government and the nationalized industries has always been one which, while formally regulated by statute, in effect is a product of constant marginal adjustment of behaviour, custom and practice'.[102]

### 5. ALLOCATIVE EFFICIENCY

#### (a) General

Subject to externalities and information deficits, it is assumed that private firms operating in competitive markets will generate allocative efficiency. The profit-making motive of such firms implies that they will supply goods or services up to the point where the marginal benefit to consumers equals the marginal cost of supply. At this equilibrium point, resources cannot be reallocated to increase welfare without some losses being incurred—in other words, the resources are being put to their most valuable use.

Some important characteristics of public ownership may inhibit realization of this economic goal. In the first place, where—as is often the case—the public corporation is a monopoly supplier, it will, unless constrained, generate efficiency losses. Secondly, in the absence of profit-making incentives, the motivation of the managers of public corporations to meet consumer demand may be dulled. Thirdly, as a result either of explicit statutory obligations or of policies imposed by government, the managers may have to pursue goals which conflict with allocative efficiency, for example, by using cross-subsidization to finance services which would otherwise be loss-making.

Before addressing these issues, we must make it clear that allocative efficiency should not be regarded as an exclusive or overriding goal for public corporations.[103] Public ownership may have been selected specifically because it was considered the most appropriate legal form to achieve

---

[101] Cf. N. Lewis, 'Regulating Non-Government Bodies: Privatization, Accountability and the Public-Private Divide', in J. Jowell and D. Oliver (eds.), *The Changing Constitution* (2nd edn., 1989), pp. 233-6.

[102] M. Elliott, 'The Control of Public Expenditure', ibid. 182-3.

[103] For general discussion of this issue, see: W. G. Shepherd, *Public Enterprise: Economic Analysis of Theory and Practice* (1976), ch. 3; R. Schmalensee, *The Control of Natural Monopolies* (1979), ch. 2; Foster, above, n. 4, pp. 362-5.

distributional goals. This applies most obviously to social services; but even in relation to more commercial enterprises, such as utilities, it may be felt desirable to supply certain categories of consumers at below-cost prices. Allocative efficiency nevertheless remains an important goal where such other aims do not intrude; and where they do, it is necessary to consider methods of minimizing inefficiency losses.

### (b) Monopoly and Prices

If a public corporation is a monopoly supplier, it may, like a private monopolist, set its prices above marginal cost, thereby creating 'dead-weight' welfare losses: consumers who would have purchased the commodity at the lower marginal cost price will spend the money in ways which give them less satisfaction.[104] On the face of it, this might appear to be an unlikely scenario, since the managers of such corporations do not have the same profit-making incentive as private entrepreneurs to drive the price upward. On the other hand, if their working life is made easier by reducing demand for the products or services, this can create an alternative motivation for charging excessive prices.

If the sole concern was this classical problem of monopoly pricing, the solution would not be hard to find: the public corporation should be compelled to set prices which relate to marginal cost. Since account must be taken of changes in demand requiring, for example, increased output, and therefore perhaps increased investment, this should be long-run marginal cost, rather than short-run marginal cost. However, as we have seen,[105] a significant feature of natural monopolies is that, at least up to a certain point, long-run marginal costs may continue to decline, so that for certain levels of output, those costs are less than the supplier's long-run *average* costs. If the supplier is not allowed to charge a price which exceeds her long-run marginal cost, she will not obtain an adequate return on investments already made and will not be able to finance ongoing investments.[106]

The dilemma, then, afflicting the pricing decisions of public corporations, and (as we will discuss in the next chapter) regulators setting prices for private natural monopolies, is to find an alternative to the marginal cost principle which avoids the losses associated with monopolistic pricing.[107] One possibility is to allow price discrimination. This occurs when consumers are charged different prices relative to what they are willing to

---

[104] Cf. above, p. 23. Another consequence, generally regarded as undesirable, is that some or all of the consumer surplus (the difference between what consumers would be willing to pay and the marginal cost price) is transferred to the supplier.

[105] Above, pp. 30–1.

[106] Waterson, above, n. 13, pp. 65–7; W. K. Viscusi, J. M. Vernon, and J. E. Harrington, *Economics of Regulation and Antitrust* (1992), pp. 330–8.

[107] Waterson, above, n. 13, pp. 68–70; Viscusi *et al.*, above, n. 106, pp. 337–47.

pay, even though the cost of supplying them remains the same. Provided that information is available, and account is taken, of the price elasticity of the consumer demand for the product or service, this can be demonstrated to be allocatively efficient.[108] An objection to it can nevertheless be made on distributional grounds: it involves transferring part or all of the consumer surplus—the difference between what consumers would be willing to pay and the marginal cost price—to the supplier.

The information necessary for efficient price discrimination is often not available. A second solution lies in a dual tariff system under which consumers are charged a fixed fee for the right to consume, and a per-unit price for the amount they consume. The latter can reflect marginal cost and the fee can be set so as to enable the enterprise to cover the deficit. There is, however, a distributional problem with this solution: the fee may impose an undue burden on low-consumption purchasers.

Finally, the losses resulting from marginal cost pricing may be met by a subsidy funded by taxpayers. This may be considered distributionally more attractive than the last solution, but it will encounter political opposition. Also, unless a lump sum tax is used to raise the necessary revenue, it will generate other misallocations in the economy;[109] and, as we have seen, deficit funding of this kind can create incentives for productive inefficiency.

To what extent have the law and government policy influenced the choice between these various solutions? Legislation does not, of course, prescribe how public corporations should determine prices; but their discretion has been constrained. As part of its attempt to exert a greater influence on financial management in the late 1960s, the government issued a guideline to nationalized industries whereby prices should *relate* to long-run marginal cost, but should nevertheless be sufficient to cover full accounting costs (and therefore, by implication, long-run average costs).[110]

To achieve this goal, there was no legal impediment to adoption of the dual tariff system, and it has been widely used by public utilities, although the standing charge component has had to be fixed at a level which does not impose too great a burden on poorer consumers.[111] On the other hand, the price discrimination solution might seem to be prohibited by legislative provisions which, for example, prescribe that in fixing tariffs a Board 'shall not show undue preference to any person or class of persons and shall not exercise any undue discrimination against any person or class of persons'.[112] Judicial interpretation of this provision has confirmed that

[108] So-called 'Ramsey' pricing (F. Ramsey, 'A Contribution to the Theory of Taxation' (1927) 37 Econ. J. 47); in non-technical terms, the higher the price elasticity, the closer the price must be set to marginal cost. [109] Viscusi *et al.*, above, n. 106, p. 338.
[110] See White Paper (1967), above, n. 80, para 21.
[111] G. Reid and K. Allen, *Nationalised Industries* (1970), pp. 41–2.
[112] Electricity Act 1947, s. 37(8).

'undue discrimination' carries the economic meaning given above—charging different prices where the costs of supply do not vary.[113] Nevertheless, in the vast majority of cases it is possible to show that the relevant costs vary to some extent, and therefore the legislative prohibition may have had little impact in practice.

The obvious implication of the statutory 'break-even' obligation was that the taxpayer subsidy solution should not be adopted. But meeting this obligation, as well as complying with government guidance on pricing policy, was thwarted by the government's own policy of price restraint in the public sector.[114] In practice, therefore, at least until the 1980s, tax subsidies were often used to compensate for sub-optimal prices.

### (c)  Distributional Goals and Subsidization

As we have seen, a distributional goal of a public corporation may be to provide products or services at a lower-than-cost price to some consumers. There are two main methods available: the difference between the price charged to the targeted consumers and the cost of supply may be funded either by a general subsidy from public funds, or by cross-subsidization from the prices paid by other consumers. Since both methods may create significant allocative inefficiencies, one might expect that they would be the subject of clear legal or policy constraints. In fact, the issue is clouded by vagueness and uncertainty.[115]

Take first the general subsidy approach. If this is allowed on an *ad hoc*, *ex post* basis—the money being allocated from general funds as and when needed—the problem of allocative inefficiency is compounded by the lack of control.[116] In principle, the phenomenon is checked by the statutory break-even obligation; in practice, as we have seen, that obligation has not always been effectively enforced. As regards explicit *ex ante* allocations, the *Bromley* decision[117] may be authority for the proposition that if the corporation is subject to a break-even obligation, it cannot deliberately lower its general prices in the expectation that the resulting deficit will be covered by such an allocation. But it does not follow from this that an enterprise must break even on all its operations; and governments have

---

[113] *South of Scotland Electricity Board* v. *British Oxygen Co Ltd* [1956] 3 All ER 199. The House of Lords there held that the provision invalidated discriminatory increases of price, as well as total prices. See, further, Foster, above, n. 4, pp. 292–4.

[114] NEDO Study, above, n. 74, p. 31. See also White Paper (1978), above, n. 80, paras. 66–8.

[115] Cf. A. Harrison, 'The Framework of Control', in Whitehead, above, n. 54, pp. 38–40.

[116] 'To subsidise [certain] . . . consumers via an overall deficit, which is then covered on an overall basis by an equivalent ex post allocation of funds, is to run the danger of trying to let the water out of a boat by boring a hole in the bottom': J. R. Nelson, in Shepherd, above, n. 103, p. 65.       [117] Above, p. 274.

often made specific subsidies available to maintain 'uneconomic' services.[118]

The alternative cross-subsidization method, whereby a uniform price is set so that lower-cost consumers effectively assume the burden of supplying higher-cost consumers, may be a lesser evil in so far as the corporation itself has to extract the subsidy.[119] But the principles governing use of the device are even more obscure. There is nothing in the legislation to prevent the practice, although it has been argued that the statutory requirements regarding the preparation and publication of a corporation's accounts should at least disclose its occurrence.[120] Government policy has been ambivalent. In the 1967 White Paper on Nationalized Industries it said that:

in a few cases, cross-subsidisation may be justified by statutory requirements or by wider economic or social considerations. But—these cases apart—to cross-subsidise loss-making services amounts to taxing remunerative services . . . and is as objectionable as subsidising from general taxation services which have no social justification.[121]

But it has never been prepared to define 'wider economic or social considerations', or indeed to give any clear guidance on the matter. This can hardly be regarded as satisfactory: whatever view be taken of the nature of relationship between government and public corporations, it should not be for the latter to form judgements on distributional equity.

### (d) Performance and Quality Standards

The inefficiencies arising from monopolies may relate to quality as well as price.[122] This follows from the obvious proposition that consumers are concerned not with price *per se*, but with the utility to be derived from a specific quality of product or service at a certain price. And, of course, external controls on prices will be seriously flawed if the monopolist is able to meet the control by reducing quality.

Concern with the quality of a public corporation's products and services has been a relatively recent phenomenon. The legislation typically lays down a general standard regarding the obligation to supply—'to satisfy, so

---

[118] C. Nash, 'British Rail and the Administration of Subsidies', in Whitehead, above, n. 54, ch. 6.

[119] Which thus should act as a constraint on productive inefficiency. Nevertheless, if the public corporation is competing with private suppliers, such cross-subsidization will constitute unfair competition: Daintith, above, n. 38, pp. 255–60.

[120] Ibid. 257–9.

[121] Above, n. 80, para. 18. See also White Paper (1978), above, n. 80, para. 68: 'arbitrary cross-subsidisation between different groups of consumers . . . should be avoided'.

[122] See generally A. Kahn, *The Economics of Regulation* i (1970), pp. 21–5.

far as it is economical to do so, all reasonable demands . . . within their area'[123]—and specific safety standards relating to the supply,[124] but no more. There may be good reasons for the neglect of the quality issue.[125] A monopolist, public or private, has no incentive to reduce quality so long as she is allowed to pass on the cost to consumers.[126] Moreover, as regards public services, consumer criticisms of quality may be more effective (especially if channelled through the Consumer Councils) than complaints concerning prices. This is because, while service deficiencies may be manifest, there is bound to be considerable disagreement on what are appropriate price levels. Nevertheless, such pressures may fall well short of what can be achieved by consumers in private competitive markets where suppliers are driven to quality improvements by exploiting technological developments.

Against this background we must consider what quality controls can be, and have been, imposed on public enterprises. The difficulty of devising quality control mechanisms which can replicate the assumed consumer demand needs to be recognized at the outset. In the first place, it is not easy to assess that demand. In part, this is a consequence of the fact that the products or services supplied by public enterprise often contain a public good dimension:[127] because some of those who benefit will not have to pay the full price of providing that benefit, they will have an incentive to overstate the quality demanded.[128] Secondly, some quality aspects elude measurement and are difficult to monitor; for example, the cleanliness of facilities, or the politeness of staff. Thirdly, most public corporations supply services rather than products, and the specification of service quality is particularly problematic.[129] Unlike products, services cannot be stored—production and consumption are not separated in time. In consequence, they cannot be sampled prior to delivery and it is difficult to adapt to fluctuations in demand.

Notwithstanding these obstacles, as we have already seen,[130] efforts have increasingly been made to subject public corporations to performance indicators. Until recently, such indicators were formulated by the corporations themselves. Although consumer councils often collaborated in the exercise,[131] the indicators were often vague and tended to reflect

[123] Gas Act 1948, s. 1(1)(a).
[124] e.g. the Gas (Safety) Regulations, SI 1972/1178. The public corporation is normally also subject to general health and safety legislation.
[125] Kahn, above, n. 122, pp. 24–5.
[126] In such a case, the quality may be higher than that implicit in consumer preferences: Schmalensee, above n. 103, p. 33.               [127] Cf. above, p. 34.
[128] Schmalensee, above, n. 103, p. 33.
[129] K. Walsh, 'Quality and Public Services' (1991) 69 Pub. Admin. 503.
[130] Above, p. 279.
[131] See National Consumer Council, *Consumer Performance Indicators for the Nationalised Industries* (1981).

existing practices, rather than set more exacting targets for the future.[132] The government became more involved in the 1980s. It now sets quality objectives for some public services—for example, British Rail Network SouthEast is expected to ensure that 92 per cent of trains arrive within five minutes of the scheduled time,[133] requires charter documents to be published by the main public services, specifying standards of service delivery,[134] and has established a unit within the Cabinet Office to co-ordinate the Citizen's Charter programme.[135] Further, it is envisaged that services which meet the required standards will be entitled to a 'Chartermark', a symbol of quality analogous to that used by the British Standards Institute in relation to privately manufactured products.[136]

It should be noted that, in contrast to equivalent measures taken with respect to the regulated privatized utilities,[137] the performance standards do not appear to be legally enforceable obligations.[138] Although provision is made in some charter documents for compensation to be paid to consumers in the event of breach of certain standards, it is unclear what other steps, if any, will be taken to deal with inadequate performance. It is, of course, too early to judge the efficacy of the Citizen's Charter programme. From a theoretical perspective, it may be considered as an imaginative attempt to construct a proxy for market discipline. On the other hand, given the problems of formulating and enforcing quality standards, it may be that the programme will serve mainly the symbolic purpose of conferring some legitimacy on public enterprise in a political environment which, as we shall now see, has been dominated by the ethos of privatization.[139]

## 6. PRIVATIZATION

Privatization is not a form of regulation, and therefore does not, strictly speaking, come within the scope of this work. Nevertheless it merits discussion[140] both as a necessary introduction to the regulation of the

---

[132] Redwood and Hatch, above, n. 50, pp. 107–13.

[133] *Citizen's Charter*, above, n. 92, p. 17.

[134] See e.g. British Railways Board, *The British Rail Passenger's Charter* (1992).

[135] *Citizen's Charter*, above, n. 92, p. 7.

[136] Cf. above, pp. 137 and 200.

[137] Competition and Service (Utilities) Act 1992: below, p. 316.

[138] Unless, which is unclear, they are incorporated into the contracts between supplier and consumer: Barron and Scott, above, n. 92, p. 529. On this issue generally, see Harden, above, n. 90.

[139] Cf. R. Hambleton and P. Hoggett, 'Rethinking Consumerism in Public Services' (1993) 3 Cons. Pol. Rev. 103.

[140] There is already a huge literature on the subject. See: for a detailed historical account, R. Fraser (ed.), *Privatization: The UK Experience and International Trends* (1988); for legal analysis, C. Graham and T. Prosser, *Privatizing Public Enterprise: Constitutions, the State, and Regulation in a Comparative Perspective* (1991); for general evaluative analysis, Kay *et*

privatized utilities which will be examined in the next chapter, and as a corollary to our analysis of public ownership: the arguments and character of privatization may shed further light on that legal form of control; and we shall also be concerned to investigate whether they are consistent with public interest goals or, rather, serve to advance private interests.

### (a) Reasons for Privatization

Until 1974 there was a broad political consensus that public ownership was the most appropriate legal form for dealing with natural monopolies. A new approach, critical of that philosophy, and which was to dominate Conservative Party policy from that date until the present, had its origin in a general discontent with the poor performance of the British economy. This was thought to be a consequence of too much public expenditure and too much interference with the market.[141] Privatization began to emerge as a possible solution when the problem of imposing effective financial constraints on the nationalized industries proved to be more intractable than had been envisaged, and the Chairmen of their Boards became resistant to proposals for tighter control.[142] Leading Conservatives[143] were then able to invoke the theoretical arguments and empirical evidence relating to public ownership which we have considered above.

While economic theory undoubtedly inspired the privatization programme, pragmatic and ideological factors also played an important role.[144] The government urgently needed to reduce the public sector borrowing requirement and it was politically easier to do this by selling public assets, rather than by cutting public expenditure. The sale of public assets would also lead to wider share ownership, a goal which would advance not only the Conservative vision of a property-owning democracy,[145] but also, in so far as it applied to employees, a more generally held ideal of greater participation by the workforce in the decisions of industry.[146] Conversely, and paradoxically, privatization can be seen to relate to the Conservative attack on trade union power.[147] Determination of pay awards

al., above, n. 98, Swann, above, n. 13; Vickers and Yarrow, above, n. 47, C. Veljanovski, *Selling the State* (1987), M. Pirie, *Privatization* (1988), C. Veljanovski (ed.), *Privatisation and Competition: A Market Perspective* (1989), M. Beesley, *Privatization, Regulation and Deregulation* (1992), Foster, above, n. 4; and for a survey of the literature, D. Marsh, 'Privatization under Mrs Thatcher: A Review of the Literature' (1991) 60 Pub. Admin. 459.

[141] K. Joseph, *Reversing the Trend* (1975).

[142] J. Moore, 'Why Privatise?', in Kay *et al.*, above, n. 98, pp. 85–6; Swann, above, n. 13, pp. 236–7.

[143] Moore, above, n. 142, p. 82. The first full statement of the government's privatization aims appears to have been in the White Paper, *Privatisation of the Water Authorities in England and Wales* (1986, Cmnd. 9734), para. 3.

[144] S. Brittan, 'The Politics and Economics of Privatisation' (1984) 55 Pol. Q. 109.

[145] Cf. Swann, above, n. 13, p. 235.    [146] Moore, above, n. 142, pp. 87–90.

[147] M. Debek, 'Privatization as a Political Priority: The British Experience' (1993) 41 Pol. Stud. 24, 36–8.

in the public sector had always been a problem, not the least because trade unions in formulating wage demands could assume that public funds were available if the corporation's income were insufficient to meet the claim. Eliminating the possibility of public subsidy would, it was envisaged, constrain such demands.

### (b) Modes of Privatization: General

Deciding which industries to privatize and how to carry out the task were interrelated issues.[148] The obvious starting point was to sell publicly owned shares in private corporations (e.g. British Petroleum and the British Sugar Corporation). Such action was relatively uncontroversial, since the enterprises were only partly public and no regulatory machinery was necessary to deal with the consequences. The latter consideration applied also to statutory corporations (e.g. British Aerospace and British Rail (Hotels) Ltd.) which were clearly not natural monopolies in the sense that competition already existed, or would certainly emerge. Provided that they were sufficiently profitable to effect an easy sale on the Stock Exchange, these were obvious candidates for early privatization.[149]

Public corporations which were, or were claimed to be, natural monopolies and sufficiently profitable for privatization to be feasible[150]— thus the principal public utilities, telecommunications, electricity, water, gas—arrived later on the agenda primarily because they threw up a complex set of questions, concerning the nature of the sale, the prospects of competition, and the need for regulation.

### (c) Modes of Privatization: Sale of Shares

The major privatizations have been effected by legislatively transforming the public corporation into a private limited corporation, the authorized share capital of which is owned by the Secretary of State. Provision is then made for the sale of the shares on the Stock Exchange. Public interest considerations suggest that such sales should be effected with a minimum of administrative costs and at prices which permitted demand to match supply. The flotations of the 1980s have been criticized on both counts.[151] Huge sums were spent not only on promotion but also on underwriting fees. The latter was particularly wasteful, given that the government's

---

[148] Graham and Prosser, above, n. 140, pp. 74–8. It should be noted that the concept of 'privatization' can be used to describe a far wider range of methods than the sale of shares: see Pirie, above, n. 140, Part II, who identifies 21 such methods.

[149] Cf. British Aerospace Act 1980; Transport Act 1981.

[150] For the argument that loss-making should not preclude privatization, see Pirie, above, n. 140, pp. 69–70.

[151] Veljanovski (1987), above, n. 140, pp. 100–1, 106–10 (whose criticism of underpricing is nevertheless qualified); Vickers and Yarrow, above, n. 47, ch. 7.

capacity to bear the risk of insufficient sales was greater than that of the private underwriters. The underpricing of the shares[152] resulted in a substantial redistribution of wealth to the successful applicants, who made large windfall profits, from taxpayers and from the consumers who would have benefited from better services if the prices had been higher.

Such redistribution is subject to the public interest objections that: it is arbitrary, there being no obvious social reason why applicants (who include foreign investors) should thus benefit; it encourages unproductive wealth-seeking activity; and there are substantial costs, administrative and allocative, in collecting the amount of tax representing the extent of underpricing.[153] Unlike some of their foreign counterparts, the British government was under no constitutional or legal constraint regarding the sale of national assets.[154] What motivated its policy of underpricing?[155] As private interest theory would predict, there were political gains to be made from conferring overt profits on applicants, when the costs were more widely spread and less visible. This was reinforced by a strategy of maximizing the number of small investors and offering them favourable terms of purchase: payments could be made in instalments; vouchers redeemable by the privatized utility were available as a substitute for dividends or bonus shares; and, when a share issue was over-subscribed, the applications from institutional investors were scaled down more heavily than was the case for small investors.[156]

### (d) Modes of Privatization: Generating Competition

Determining to what extent privatization should be complemented by efforts to encourage competition within the relevant industries gives rise to complex theoretical and technical issues. On the face of it, if the industry is clearly characterized by conditions of natural monopoly, for reasons which have already been discussed,[157] competition is inefficient and ought to be prevented and the adverse consequences of the privatized monopoly should be controlled entirely by regulation. However, it is necessary to reach such a conclusion only if 'competition' is here construed to mean market-wide competition. An alternative—'yardstick competition'—exists

---

[152] In most cases, flotation was by offer for sale at a fixed price. Partly in response to criticisms of underpricing, the government subsequently adopted (e.g. for the sale of British Aerospace) the alternative device of a tender offer whereby shares are allocated on the basis either of the amounts bid by individual applicants or of a common striking price calculated as sufficient to clear the market when all the bids have been received.

[153] Vickers and Yarrow, above, n. 47, p. 180.

[154] For a detailed comparison with France, where such constraints exist, see Graham and Prosser, above, n. 140, chs. 2–3.

[155] Cf. Graham and Prosser, above, n. 140, pp. 90–1.

[156] For details, see Fraser, above, n. 140, ch. 3, *passim*.

[157] Above, pp. 30–1.

whereby a firm with a natural monopoly is broken up into separate entities which supply different regions.[158] Each entity retains its monopoly but only in relation to its own region. This arrangement does not obviate the need for regulation, but it facilitates the regulators' task, since the performance of one entity can be compared with that of another.

Another possibility, which will be fully considered in Chapter 15, is to retain the monopoly but to create competition between private firms for the right of exclusive supply over a limited period. Such competition for franchises can achieve some, though not all, of the aims of normal supply competition.

Further, as was pointed out earlier,[159] it is rash to assume that because an industry has traditionally been regarded as a natural monopoly it should always be treated as such. First, it may be possible to separate those parts of the industrial process which possess the characteristics of a natural monopoly (for example, the transmission of electricity) from those which do not (for example, the generation of electricity). Secondly, technological developments may render competition viable; thus in relation to tele-communications, satellites and microwave systems provide an alternative to traditional cable networks.

Where the conditions of natural monopoly are not present, is it sufficient merely to privatize the public corporations and repeal any statutory barriers to entry? Assuming application of the ordinary principles and procedures of competition law, will an adequate level of competition emerge? On one view, that law is inadequate to contain the propensity of the incumbent privatized firm to engage in anti-competitive practices like predatory pricing, and thus thwart effective entry; the government should enact measures, or regulation should be designed, actively to promote competition.[160] On another view, it does not matter if one firm holds a dominant position in the market, provided that other firms are free to enter it, and can also exit at low cost.[161]

While the public interest arguments considered in the preceding paragraphs might suggest that privatization should be accompanied by a strong proactive approach to competition, government policy has been ambivalent, and not always consistent. The degree of commitment to competition and the measures taken to encourage it have varied from one privatization programme to another.

---

[158] Vickers and Yarrow, above, n. 47, pp. 115–18. To some extent, it is possible to require the regional entities to compete for customers along the common boundaries. For this, and for other possibilities of indirect competition, see C. Veljanovski, 'Privatization: Monopoly Money or Competition?', in Veljanovski (1989), above, n. 140, pp. 39–44.

[159] Above, p. 31.

[160] J. Vickers and G. Yarrow, Privatization and Natural Monopolies (1985), p. 19.

[161] The so-called theory of 'contestable markets', the conditions of which are unlikely to be present: above, p. 32.

The principal privatization statutes have imposed a duty on the Secretary of State (as well as the regulators) to promote competition, but in some cases it is circumscribed. In relation to water, for example, it is merely 'to facilitate effective competition, with respect to such matters *as he considers appropriate.*'[162] The approach to competition in the gas distribution industry has been even more restrictive.[163] The 1986 privatization legislation permitted entry by suppliers other than British Gas (BG) only in relation to larger industrial and commercial consumers (the 'contract' market);[164] and even here no effective competition has emerged. While efforts have been made by the Director General of Gas Supply and others with regulatory powers (the Monopolies and Mergers Commission, the Director General of Fair Trading) to effect changes in BG's operations in the contract market to facilitate entry by other suppliers,[165] it is unclear at the time of writing whether these will bear fruit. As regards domestic and small business consumers (the 'tariff market'), the Secretary of State was, in 1992, given powers to abolish BG's monopoly;[166] but action to implement this is still awaited.

Some restructuring of privatized industries has occurred. Thus, the supply and installation of telecommunications equipment have been divorced from the provision of services[167] and the ensuing competition in the equipment market has resulted in lower prices and increased consumer choice.[168] So also the generation of electricity has been separated from its distribution,[169] but the government's decision to create from the generating functions of the Central Electricity Generating Board (CEGB) effectively only two firms (NatPower and PowerGen) has severely limited the potential for competition.[170] The break-up of the distribution functions of CEGB into twelve regional companies and the similar arrangements made in relation to water[171] have introduced a form of 'yardstick' competition

---

[162] Water Act 1989, s. 7(3)(e) (my italics).

[163] 'So far British Gas represents the height of "monopoly mongering" in the privatisation programme': Veljanovski, above, n. 158, p. 29.

[164] Gas Act 1986, s. 4(2)(d).

[165] For a useful summary, see I. Powe, 'Competition in Gas Supply: Paradox or Policy?' (1992) 4 Cons. Pol. Rev. 4.

[166] Competition and Service (Utilities) Act 1992, s. 37.

[167] This was done prior to privatization in the British Telecommunications Act 1981.

[168] Vickers and Yarrow, above, n. 47, p. 231. Additional steps had to be taken to prevent British Telecom exploiting its position as dominant supplier, and the licence issued to it when it was privatized in 1984 contained requirements of fair trading, e.g. that it should not, through cross-subsidization, engage in predatory pricing: B. Carsberg, 'Injecting Competition into Telecommunications', in Veljanovski (1989), above, n. 140, p. 84.

[169] See generally White Paper, *Privatising Electricity* (1988, Cm. 322), paras. 32–43.

[170] Cf. Veljanovski, above, n. 158, pp. 33–5.

[171] There are 28 regionally based water companies appointed under Water Act 1989, s. 11. See on this, White Paper (1986), above, n. 143, para. 56.

into industries characterized by natural monopoly. However, notwith-standing criticism by economists,[172] equivalent steps have not been taken in relation to gas distribution.[173]

Some of the variations in government policy recorded above may reflect genuine economic differences between the relevant industries; for example, while electricity and gas provide alternative sources of energy and, to some extent at least, must compete against each other, there is no substitute for water.[174] On the other hand, some of them may be attributed to political considerations and the attitude of the actors involved.[175] The desire of the government to make rapid progress with its privatization programme inhibited coherence and necessarily led to a rethinking of competition policy. At the same time, there were political gains in maximizing the proceeds of the privatization sales, and this was incompatible with an aggressively pro-competition policy, which would have rendered investment in the privatized companies less attractive. There is evidence, too, that the government was keen to satisfy the demands of those private interests (e.g. the managers of the privatized firms) which would benefit from protection, and whose lobbying power was greater than that of groups who would be losers, notably consumers.[176]

### (e) Conclusions

It would obviously be inappropriate to attempt here any overall assessment of the privatization programme, since the important regulatory arrangements remain to be considered in the next chapter. Some tentative conclusions may nevertheless be reached on the matters discussed in this chapter.[177]

It would seem that most of the government's shorter-term privatization aims have been achieved: the sales of public assets have reduced the public sector borrowing requirement; trade union power has declined within the privatized industries;[178] and a larger number of individuals own, or have owned,[179] shares.[180] More germane to our concerns is the question of whether the industrial performance of the privatized firms has improved. Understandably, given the recentness of the reforms and the complexity of the issues, opinions of commentators differ widely. We have seen that the

---

[172] e.g Vickers and Yarrow, above, n. 47, pp. 237–8, 268–70.

[173] A proposal that British Gas should be split into twelve regional companies was made by the Director General of Gas Supply in 1993.

[174] White Paper (1986), above, n. 143, para. 55.

[175] Vickers and Yarrow, above, n. 47, pp. 428–9.          [176] Ibid. 236, 268, 428.

[177] The following paragraph relies heavily on the review provided in Marsh, above, n. 140.

[178] Although it is not clear how much of this is a consequence of privatization: cf. D. Thomas, 'The Union Response to Denationalisation', in Kay et al., above, n. 98, ch. 16.

[179] On average, some 60% of the successful applicants resold the shares within a short time of purchase: see Marsh, above, n. 140, p. 474.

[180] According to government figures, 20.5% of the adult population in 1988, compared with 7% in 1979: Fraser, above, n. 140, p. 14.

level of competition in the privatized industries falls short of that which is regarded as desirable by many economists. That may itself help to explain research findings which suggest that there have not been widespread changes in managerial structures.[181] Some commentators point to general increases in profitability;[182] others have found relatively little evidence of improved productive efficiency.[183]

[181] Dunsire *et al.*, above, n. 98.

[182] e.g. C. Veljanovski in D. Gayle and J. Goodrich (eds.), *Privatisation in Global Perspective* (1990), pp. 63–79; and D. Pitt, 'An Essentially Contestable Organisation! British Telecom and the Privatisation Debate', in J. Richardson (ed.), *Privatisation and Deregulation in Canada and Britain* (1990), pp. 55–76.

[183] Dunsire *et al.*, above, n. 98; J. Foreman-Peck and D. Manning, 'How Well Is BT Performing: An International Comparison of Total Factor Productivity' (1988) 9(3) Fiscal Stud. 54.

# 14

# Price Controls

## I. INTRODUCTION

Almost without exaggeration it may be said that, wherever there have been governments, attempts have been made to control prices; the history of this regulatory form thus spans at least five millennia.[1] For the purposes of our analysis of modern instruments, a fundamental distinction must be drawn between controls which prevail over prices which would have emerged in ordinary competitive markets, and those which are imposed on monopolists and others operating in an uncompetitive market. The former are typically instituted in pursuance either of the distributional goal of making certain commodities available to low-income individuals (section 2) or of certain macro-economic goals, notably the control of inflation (section 3). They have been the object of stringent criticisms by economists, and in recent years have fallen out of favour. In contrast, the latter (section 4) have become increasingly important as the privatization of public enterprises, particularly the utilities, has not generated sufficient competition[2] for prices to be determined by market forces alone.

Price controls can take a variety of forms but, broadly speaking, they fall into two principal categories:[3] one which purports to prescribe a *fair rate of return* (FRR) for suppliers, having regard in particular to the investment necessary to produce the commodity; and the other, often referred to as the *historical method* (HM), which limits price increases to what is reasonable, taking into account the extent to which suppliers can control their costs. As will be seen, the two methods cannot be kept entirely distinct, since in practice FRR controls have to take account of inflation and uncontrollable costs, and HM controls sometimes slide into a consideration of what is a fair return. Subject to this caveat, we will consider important examples of FRR in Section 2 (rent controls) and Section 4 (the regulation of American utilities) and of HM in Section 3 (control of inflation) and Section 4 (the regulation of British utilities).

---

[1] R. Schuettinger, 'The Historical Record: A Survey of Wage and Price Controls Over Five Centuries', in M. Walker (ed.), *The Illusion of Wage and Price Control* (1976), pp. 59–97.

[2] Cf. above, pp. 292–3.

[3] Cf. S. Breyer, *Regulation and Its Reform* (1982), chs. 2 and 3 respectively.

## 2. PRICE CONTROLS FOR DISTRIBUTIONAL PURPOSES

### (a) General

Pressure is often brought to bear on governments to deal with cases of alleged abuse, where traders charge 'unfair' or 'unconscionable' prices. If the transactions take place in competitive markets, the existence of competition should ensure that the prices do not significantly exceed the marginal costs of supply, provided that the consumer has adequate information on the prices which the trader and other suppliers charge and she is not the victim of oppressive conduct (duress or undue influence). Private law doctrines or regulatory regimes which render contracts unenforceable or illegal simply on the ground that the price is 'unfair' or 'unconscionable' are therefore poorly targeted: they tackle the symptom, but not the cause, of the problem.[4] Efforts should instead be concentrated on controlling anti-competitive practices and oppressive conduct and, where appropriate, compelling disclosure of relevant information.

Suppose, however, that the competitive market price, which reflects the marginal cost of supply, is higher than many low-income individuals can afford, and that the commodity in question is a basic essential for life (e.g. food, clothing, housing). Can price controls be used to ensure an adequate supply for these individuals?[5]

To begin with, it should be noted that price controls constitute only one of several alternative instruments available for distributional problems of this kind, all of them funded predominantly from tax revenue. First, as to a large extent occurs in relation to health care and education, the means of production and distribution can be taken into public ownership, with consumers paying only a small, or nominal, price. Secondly, subsidies can be paid to private suppliers, enabling them to sell the commodity to low-income individuals at reduced prices. Thirdly, such individuals can be issued with vouchers, exchangeable for the relevant commodity. Finally, more general redistributive measures to raise the income of poorer people can be undertaken through the social security system.

We cannot here discuss the relative merits of these various devices,[6] but standard economic analysis suggests that controlling prices is likely to be

---

[4] R. Epstein, 'Unconscionability: A Critical Reappraisal' (1975) 18 J. Law & Econ. 293; M. Trebilcock, 'An Economic Approach to the Doctrine of Unconscionability', in B. Reiter and J. Swan (eds.), *Studies in Contract Law* (1980), ch. 11. As the following discussion will reveal, they may also give rise to significant welfare losses.

[5] See generally: K. Hartley, *Problems of Economic Policy* (1977), pp. 122–35; D. Swann, 'Price Control and the Consumer Interest: An Economic View', in M. Goyens (ed.), *Price Information and Public Price Controls, Consumers and Market Performance* (1986), pp. 155–61.

[6] For such discussion, see e.g. N. Barr, *The Economics of the Welfare State* (1987).

the least effective solution.[7] Under ordinary conditions, the imposition of a ceiling price below the natural market equilibrium price will mean that some sellers will no longer find it profitable to supply the market, and there will be a reduction in the quantity of the commodity produced. There will also be an excess of demand over supply; and some method other than pricing has to be devised for allocating the commodity among those wanting to purchase it. If this is done simply on a 'first come, first served' basis, allocation is arbitrary and will impose on individuals the costs of racing and/or queuing.[8] The other possibilities are a formal rationing system or some institutional determination of need, both of which involve substantial administrative costs. More fundamentally, there will be allocative inefficiency: the reduction in supply will mean that society will be deprived of the production of a commodity which is valued higher than it costs to produce.

Nor should the secondary effects of price controls be ignored. In particular, suppliers will be tempted to maintain the gains that they would have made from uncontrolled prices by other means: 'black markets' (i.e. systems of unlawful pricing) are likely to emerge; alternatively, traders may attempt to reduce the quality of the commodity. To deal with these phenomena, the price controls will have to be buttressed by other regulation which consumes resources in its formulation and enforcement.

In short, as one economist has observed, '[t]he analysis of maximum price controls shows that in a world of scarcity, the basic forces of demand and supply cannot be eliminated by passing a law'.[9]

*(b) Rent Control*

During wartime, when the supply side of the market was seriously disrupted, price controls, often combined with rationing, were imposed on a wide variety of goods.[10] In Britain, the most important incidence of price control being used for distributional purposes in modern peacetime conditions has been in relation to private rented accommodation; and it is this area of law which we will use to illustrate the general arguments outlined above.

Rent controls have had a long and complex history.[11] Suffice it here to

---

[7] Cf. R. Albon and D. C. Stafford, *Rent Control* (1987), pp. 16–19.

[8] Y. Barzel, 'A Theory of Rationing by Waiting' (1974) 17 J. Law & Econ. 73. It should be noted that, since the opportunity costs of higher earners are greater than those of low or non-earners, this method will favour the latter, which might be regarded as distributionally desirable. [9] Hartley, above, n. 5, p. 126.

[10] Prices of Goods Act 1939; Goods and Services (Price Control) Act 1941. See generally J. Mitchell, *Price Determination and Prices Policy* (1978), pp. 39–42. As she there indicates, many such controls were ineffective (it was too easy to market 'new' products which escaped the controls) and led to productive inefficiency (because traders were invariably allowed to pass costs on to consumers). [11] M. Davey, *Residential Rents* (1990), ch. 2.

focus on the system of 'fair rents' operative under the provisions of the Rent Acts of 1965 and 1977.[12] These enable parties to regulated tenancy agreements to apply to a rent officer (with a right of appeal to a rent assessment committee) for determination of what is a 'fair rent' for the relevant premises. In making the assessment, regard is to be had to all circumstances (other than personal circumstances) and in particular to the age, character, locality, and state of repair of the premises, and also to the provision (if any) of furniture.[13] This part of the statutory test is unexceptional; the circumstances in question are those which should be reflected in a freely determined market rent. However, the legislation then postulates a criterion which departs significantly from market principles.

For the purposes of the determination it shall be assumed that the number of persons seeking to become tenants of similar dwelling-houses in the locality on the terms (other than those relating to rent) of the regulated premises is not substantially greater than the number of such dwelling-houses in the locality which are available for letting on such terms.[14]

This part of the test, often referred to as the 'scarcity factor', requires the assessment to be made on the assumption that demand does not exceed supply and thus, where applicable, to substitute for a rent reflecting actual market conditions one based on some hypothetical market equilibrium. The legislation does not indicate how the latter determination is to be made and a variety of methods has been used.[15] One which involves deducting from the market rent a percentage assumed to reflect the scarcity factor tends to arbitrariness, in that scarcity is 'incapable of measurement except by way of an intelligent guess'.[16] A second is akin to the method used by American regulators to determine prices chargeable by private utilities:[17] the assessor estimates what sum would constitute a fair rate of return on the landlord's investment, calculated by reference either to the capital value of the premises or else what would be the current cost of constructing them. This, too has been discredited, mainly on the grounds that it is difficult to identify a suitable basis for assessing capital value, and that construction cost is an unreliable alternative.[18] The most favoured method is to have regard to the rents payable for equivalent premises in comparable areas.[19] Were there to be a market equilibrium in the comparator area, this would be unobjectionable, but in practice such

---

[12] For more detailed, legal analysis, see ibid. ch. 5.

[13] Rent Act 1965, s. 27(1): Rent Act 1977, s. 70(1).

[14] Rent Act 1965, s. 27(2); Rent Act 1977, s. 70(2).

[15] Report of the [Francis] Committee on the Rent Acts (1971, Cmnd. 4609), pp. 58–62; Davey, above, n. 11, pp. 76–85.        [16] Francis Report, above, n. 15, p. 58.

[17] Below, pp. 307–9.

[18] *Crofton Investment Trust* v. *Greater London Rent Assessment Committee* [1967] 2 QB 955.        [19] *Mason* v. *Skilling* [1974] 1 WLR 1437.

areas are themselves subject to the scarcity element,[20] and the reference is therefore generally to the 'fair rents' registered there. The method may thereby generate horizontal equity between landlords (and tenants) in different areas, but by itself cannot provide a satisfactorily objective basis for what is the appropriate rent.

Given the difficulties inherent in the scarcity factor test and the large amount of litigation to which they give rise, the 'fair rents' system is costly to administer. No doubt it has conferred benefits on existing tenants, particularly those with security of tenure; but it has also led to undesired consequences. While the original intention may have been to allow market rents generally to prevail, and to intervene only in cases where landlords appeared to be exploiting conditions of unusual scarcity,[21] the impact of rent controls has been much more widespread. Before 1988, they had been applied to a substantial and ever increasing proportion of regulated tenancies; at the same time, there was a steady decline in the size of the private rented sector.[22] In the light of the economic arguments summarized above, it is not difficult to explain the phenomena.[23] Landlords, unable to obtain a market-determined return on their property, convert it, as soon as they are able, to an alternative and more valuable use (e.g. owner-occupation). The resulting shortage creates a greater demand for 'fair rents'; and the spiral continues. The law, by forcing assessors to calculate 'fair rents' as if there were no shortage, accelerates the process: it 'specifically excludes from the reckoning the one economic factor likely to produce any easing of a situation of shortage'.[24]

The benefit which rent control conferred on existing tenants and the decline in the stock available for those seeking a tenancy combined to create disincentives for labour mobility and may have raised the level of unemployment.[25] Other predictable consequences also occurred. There was a general decline in the quality of the private housing stock available for rental.[26] Although black markets as such could hardly emerge, it being

[20] M. Davey, 'A Farewell to Fair Rents' [1992] J. Social Welfare & Fam. Law 497, 502.
[21] P. Watchman, 'Fair Rents and Market Scarcity' [1985] Conv. 199. See also D. Donnison, *The Government of Housing* (1967), pp. 265–7.
[22] Davey, above, n. 20, pp. 498–9.
[23] For a different view, see R. Lee, 'Rent Control—The Economic Impact of Social Legislation' (1992) 12 Ox. J. Legal Stud. 543. He argues that the traditional economic analysis oversimplifies the motivations of many landlords and that the decline of private renting may be attributable to other causes, especially the problems created by tenants having security of tenure.                              [24] F. G. Pennance, *Verdict on Rent Control* (1972), p. xv.
[25] P. Minford, P. Ashton and M. Peel, 'The Effects of Housing Distortions on Unemployment' (1986), cited in Albon and Stafford, above, n. 7, p. 64. The authors estimated that if the rental market had been decontrolled and council house rents raised to free market levels, unemployment would have fallen by about 2%.
[26] Albon and Stafford, above, n. 7, p. 89. On the legislative attempts to impose quality controls, see A. Arden and M. Partington, *Housing Law* (1983), Part 3.

too difficult to enter into clandestine transactions for long-term occupation, other forms of avoidance behaviour became rife and costly to control. A favourite device was to encourage the potential occupier to enter into a licence, which escaped the regulatory regime, rather than a tenancy agreement. This raised an additional problem of legal characterization. The courts have been intolerant of attempts to dress up tenancy agreements as licences and have held that the category of a transaction is to be determined by its essence (i.e. the obligations to which it gives rise) rather than the label that is attached to it.[27] But formulating the appropriate distinctions and detecting instances of unlawful avoidance are costly undertakings.

Recognition of the harmful effects of rent control in a White Paper of 1987[28] was followed by the Housing Act 1988, which abolished the system, although it continues to apply to relevant agreements entered into before that Act came into force.

### 3. COUNTER-INFLATION MEASURES

In an earlier chapter, we considered the public interest arguments for controlling inflation.[29] As was there indicated, in recent times monetarist theory has won favour with governments, and limiting both the money supply and public expenditure has become the principal policy for dealing with the problem. Nevertheless, in the period 1945 to 1979 there was widespread use of price (and wage) controls.[30] Prior to 1973, British governments had experimented with a variety of prices and incomes policies, most of them relying on voluntary agreements with industry and trade unions.[31] In that year there was introduced a formal price control system, more comprehensive and complex than any other attempted in conditions of peacetime. In 1977 it was replaced by another regime, equally comprehensive but more flexible, that was to last until Mrs Thatcher's assumption of power in 1979. The two models provide an excellent illustration of the difficulties inherent in the historical method of price control.

### (a) The Historical Method Generally

It is easy to understand why the historical method (HM) has been preferred to a fair rate of return (FRR) as the principal regulatory device

---

[27] *Street* v. *Mountford* [1985] AC 809, and see above, p. 259.

[28] *Housing: The Government's Proposals* (Cm. 214).

[29] Above, pp. 44–6.

[30] See generally: for Britain, Mitchell, above, n. 10, ch. 9; for Sweden, L. Jonung, *The Political Economy of Price Controls* (1990); for the USA, H. Rockoff, *Drastic Measures: A History of Wage and Price Controls in the United States* (1984).

[31] See generally A. Fels, *The British Prices and Incomes Board* (1972).

for controlling inflation.[32] HM not only relates directly to the problem of inflation through its focus on price increases, but also involves a much simpler set of tests which can be applied to a large number of firms. FRR, on the other hand, normally requires a detailed investigation of an individual firm's accounts and the criteria for determining what is 'fair' are often highly complex.

In its simplest form, HM imposes an absolute and uniform price freeze: traders are not allowed to increase prices beyond the highest that were charged during a base period. Although occasionally used to deal with economic crises,[33] this crude approach can at best operate for only a short period.[34] In most instances, traders have little control over the costs of production. Inevitably, therefore, the system has to proceed on a more discriminating basis by attempting to distinguish between 'justifiable' and 'unjustifiable' price increases.

### (b) The 1973 Model

The first of our two models, the Counter-Inflation Act 1973, and the Price Code issued under its provisions,[35] adopted a three-pronged approach to the problem of defining unjustifiable increases.[36] First, it removed from the ambit of control cases for which reference to prices charged in the base period were likely to be arbitrary: where the cost to the supplier was subject to seasonal factors (fresh food) or fluctuations in the exchange rate (the first sale of imported goods) and where there was no recognizable pattern of trading (second-hand sales[37] and auctions).[38] Secondly, the Price Commission (the agency entrusted with the relevant powers) was to permit increases to the prices of controlled goods and services only to the extent that they reflected a demonstrable increase in 'allowable', i.e. uncontainable, costs. While 'allowable' costs were defined to include those for materials, components, energy, rent of premises, interest charges, and certain bought-in services (e.g. transport and insurance), originally only fifty per cent of labour costs could be passed on to consumers—thus assuming improved productivity—and nothing at all for selling costs or depreciation.[39] Thirdly, net profit margins were not to exceed the average of those attained in the best two of the preceding five trading years.[40]

---

[32] Cf. Breyer, above, n. 3, p. 62.

[33] e.g. Prices and Incomes (General Conditions) (No. 2) Order, SI 1966/1477, made under Prices and Incomes Act 1966; Counter-Inflation (Temporary Provisions) Act 1972, s. 2.

[34] Breyer, above, n. 3, pp. 60–1.

[35] Counter-Inflation (Price and Pay Code) Order, SI 1973/658.

[36] For details and critical analysis, see B. Bracewell-Milnes, *Pay and Price Control Guide* (1973).    [37] But the sale of second-hand vehicles by distributors was controlled.

[38] 1973 Price and Pay Code, above, n. 35, paras. 5–8.

[39] Ibid. paras. 25, 29.    [40] Ibid. para. 50.

To evaluate the merits of this model, we should begin by recognizing that, like many regulatory systems, it creates incentives and opportunities for avoidance behaviour. It may be possible to make explicit provision prohibiting the more obvious instances of such conduct; for example, the Price Code stipulated that

quality change in goods or services, quantity change in sales unit, or artificial creation of new products should not be used as a means of avoiding the requirements of the Code. Where the Commission form the opinion that this has been done, they may seek price reductions, or disallow or reduce price increases.[41]

But, with limited resources available for routine monitoring, the Commission was unlikely to detect behaviour of this kind.[42] In any event, imaginative traders are likely to find other devices which will be almost impossible to control. For example, to come within the exemption granted to imported goods, some suppliers wrote invoices which purported to sell the relevant goods to a subsidiary or agent overseas from whom the goods were then repurchased at an increased, but decontrolled, price.[43]

Perversities of this kind may be costly in three different respects. First, the firm itself uses up valuable resources in engaging in avoidance behaviour. Secondly, the Price Commission has the expense of attempting to detect such behaviour, at least where it is unlawful and monitoring is feasible. Thirdly, as avoidance devices become more widely known and their use more common, so the legal system itself may be brought into disrepute, with serious lasting side-effects.[44]

Subject to this last problem, it may nevertheless be argued that the costs arising from avoidance behaviour may be justified if the system succeeds in reducing inflation. Economists have tended to conclude that while, in the short term, price controls have this desired effect, in the longer term they have no significant impact on the rate of inflation.[45] This is primarily because individuals' *expectations* of continuing inflation are not affected by a form of control which they assume, on the basis of previous experience, will not endure. Therefore, as soon as the control is relaxed, they engage in wage demands, spending 'sprees', and other forms of behaviour which have the effect of returning the rate of inflation to its pre-control level.

---

[41] 1973 Price and Pay Code, para. 48.

[42] This applies also to the dissolution of a company and the formation of a 'new' one, a device which was legislated for only in a subsequent version of the Code.

[43] M. Parkin, 'Wage and Price Controls: The Lessons from Britain', in Walker, above, n. 1, p. 122.

[44] Parkin, ibid. 128–9, who equates legislative controls of prices and incomes with 'attempting by statute to repeal the law of gravity'.

[45] M. Darby, 'Price and Wage Controls: The First Two Years' (1976) 2 J. Mon. Econ. 235, and 'Price and Wage Controls: Further Evidence', ibid. 269; Hartley, above, n. 5, pp. 78–80; Parkin, above, n. 43, pp. 115–20; Jonung, above, n. 30, ch. 9.

Account must also be taken of other economic consequences. In principle, price controls should encourage productive efficiency, particularly where, as under the 1973 Price Code, a productivity factor is deducted from allowable costs. The evidence suggests that the 1973 regime indeed had that effect,[46] but the 50 per cent deduction rule proved to be too Draconian for firms with no slack to reduce and subsequently it was amended so that first 80 per cent, and then 100 per cent, of labour costs became recoverable.[47] The history of the productivity factor serves to illustrate a general problem with regulation of this kind, described by a former chairman of the Price Commission:

As times go on, refinements and reliefs have to be introduced to meet the hard cases. The legislation—or Code—gets longer and longer. But broadly you cannot relax to help hard cases without relaxing to benefit the others as well. In the end the control becomes largely ineffective. So one ends up with a more and more complex control which achieves less and less. This is precisely what happened with price control.[48]

Criticisms of the allocative effects have been equally stringent.[49] Attempts to avoid the controls and to exploit loopholes within them push resources away from their socially most valuable uses. Where the controls have their desired effect, and consumers pay less than they would have done in an unregulated market, demand will exceed supply and the consequences which we described in relation to rent controls[50] will ensue. Admittedly, one such consequence, the absence of an incentive to invest in supply of the product, can be met by allowing the supplier to charge a reasonable proportion of investment against allowable costs—this was authorized in a revised version of the Price Code.[51] Finally, such a comprehensive control system requires a very large number of staff to administer[52] and enforce the code and deal with the many queries it is likely to generate.

## (c) The 1977 Model

A different approach was taken in the Price Commission Act 1977 and its

---

[46] Mitchell, above, n. 10, p. 187.
[47] See Counter-Inflation (Price Code) Orders of 1974 and 1976, SI 1974/2113 and SI 1976/1170, respectively.
[48] A. Cockfield, 'The Price Commission and the Price Control' (1978) 117 Three Banks Rev. 3, 23.
[49] J. Carr, 'Wage and Price Controls: Panacea for Inflation or Prescription for Disaster', in Walker, above, n. 1, pp. 41–8; Parkin, above, n. 43, pp. 121–2; R. Evely, 'The Effects of the Price Code' (1976) 77 Nat. Inst. Econ. Rev. 50.          [50] Above, pp. 296–7.
[51] See the 1974 Order, above, n. 47, paras. 79–81.
[52] The larger firms were required to notify the agency (the Price Commission) of proposed price increases and obtain its approval before charging the higher prices: Counter-Inflation (Notification of Increases in Prices and Charges) Order, SI 1973/664.

much altered Price Code.[53] This new model reflected dissatisfaction with the rigidities of the 1973 Code, but also a perception that more attention had to be given to profit motive and competition as the best means of promoting efficiency and growth.[54] Thus under the 1977 Act, the Commission was to perform its functions 'with a view to restraining prices of goods and charges for services so far as that appears [to it] to be consistent with the making of adequate profits by efficient suppliers'.[55] Further, in deciding whether to permit price increases, the Commission was not to apply specific or arithmetical rules, as under the 1973 model, but rather 'to have regard to' a number of general considerations, which included[56]

(a) the need to recover costs incurred in efficiently supplying goods and services . . . ; (b) the desirability of encouraging reductions in costs by improvements in the use of resources . . . ; (c) the need to earn . . . profits which provide a return on the capital employed . . . [sufficient to cover capital costs and encourage innovation] . . . ; (e) the desirability of maintaining the quality of goods and services and satisfying the demands of users of goods and services; (f) the need to safeguard the interests of users . . . by promoting competition between suppliers . . . ; (g) the desirability of establishing and maintaining a balance between the supply of goods and services and the demand for them.

In short, under the 1977 Act, the system was changed from one in which the regulatory agency applied detailed rules formulated to achieve the desired goals, to one in which it exercised a broad discretion constrained by general guidelines incorporating those goals.[57] Thus it can be seen that guideline (b) was aimed at productive efficiency, while (a), (c), (e), and (g) attempted to counter the misallocations to which the earlier system may have given rise. Guideline (f) is of particular interest. Competition had been largely ignored under the 1973 Act; now it was given considerable prominence, such that firms operating in competitive markets were generally left free to raise their prices without being scrutinized by the Price Commission.[58] Indeed, the new price control system was seen as complementing the work of the Monopolies Commission, the principal agency for implementing competition policy.[59]

[53] Counter-Inflation (Price Code) Order, SI 1977/1272.
[54] J. D. Gribbin, 'The Operation of Price Control in the United Kingdom' (1981) 52 Annals of Public and Co-operative Economy 425, 438–439.
[55] S. 2(1)(a).                                                                 [56] S 2(2).
[57] On the choice between discretion and rules in this area of regulation, see R. Kagan, *Regulatory Justice: Implementing a Wage-Price Freeze* (1978), esp. ch. 5.
[58] Gribbin, above, n. 54, p. 439. See also, by the same author, 'The United Kingdom 1977 Price Commission Act and Competition Policy' (1978) 23 Antitrust Bull. 405.
[59] Ibid. 411. The argument for a separate system controlling the prices set by uncompetitive firms, outside the operation of the ordinary competition laws, was that investigations under the latter took too long.

The discretionary character of the 1977 model and the selective approach which focused on prices set in insufficiently competitive markets obviously led to a significant reduction in administrative costs. Although there is relatively little evidence available to confirm this,[60] it may also be assumed that such an approach would have avoided many of the other adverse consequences which predictably resulted from the 1973 model. Nevertheless, it should be noted that discretionary price control systems generate their own problems. Firms subject to them will not have available clear and authoritative information on what price increases will and will not be treated as lawful; and the planning of business will become difficult.[61] Moreover, as the Swedish experience indicates,[62] the absence of specific rules is likely to lead to a bargaining process between the agency and relevant firms, enabling those with substantial lobbying power to extract distributional gains from the system.

### 4. PRICE CONTROLS IN MONOPOLISTIC MARKETS

#### (a) General

The advent of the Thatcher government, with its policy of deregulation, may have dealt a death-blow to the two systems of price control so far considered; but the concomitant policy of privatization revived the need for such control, albeit in a very different form. Since, as we saw in the last chapter,[63] the major British utilities were allowed to retain a predominantly monopolistic power, new regulatory structures had to be put in place to curb that power, and the problem of devising principles for determining appropriate prices came again to the fore. Not that the problem was a new one: prior to the utilities being publicly owned, the nineteenth-century regulatory commissions had exerted control over prices;[64] and, more recently, the pricing policies of the nationalized industries had been the subject of lively debate.[65] Reference could also be made to the considerable American experience of rate regulation.

Viewed from a public interest perspective, the prices set for a monopolist firm by regulators should aim to induce allocative and productive efficiency. More specifically, the firm should meet the demand for its products at minimum cost, with customers paying on average no more than that cost; and the prices should be sensitive to changes in the conditions of supply and demand, thus creating incentives for efficient

---

[60] The short life of the system may have discouraged detailed analysis. For a general appraisal, see Gribbin (1978), above, n. 58.  [61] Kagan, above, n. 57, p. 172.
[62] Jonung, above, n. 30, ch. 8.  [63] Above, pp. 289–93.
[64] Above, p. 265.  [65] Above, pp. 282–4.

consumption.[66] In an unregulated, competitive market, the prices charged by firms should, in principle, fulfil these goals: on average they will be set at a level sufficient to cover costs (including investment), and competition will ensure that such costs are minimized and excess profits eliminated. Of course, there is always an element of uncertainty concerning the future conditions of supply and demand, and investment decisions made on the basis of such imperfect information may, at particular times as conditions of supply and demand change, generate earnings which are either more or less than the 'ideal' competitive return. Such outcomes are partly the result of luck—where unforeseeable external events are responsible for the changes—and partly the result of astute decision-making, some firms construing the limited information available better than others. The ability of some firms to earn higher returns provides a valuable incentive for astute decision-making; in any event the advantage is unlikely to endure, as other firms will adjust to meet the changed circumstances.

The regulatory system can be envisaged as a long-term contract between the regulatory agency and the monopolistic firm, with the latter agreeing to meet the reasonable demands of consumers at minimum cost in return for the agency allowing it to charge prices sufficient to cover those costs.[67] The aim is then for the terms of this 'contract' to mirror what would have occurred in an unregulated competitive market. The task of accomplishing this aim is nevertheless a formidable one. Difficulties arise from the fact that the agency's access to information concerning a firm's activities is limited. The agency will not always be well placed to make decisions on whether the costs incurred by the firm were reasonable and thus to be covered by the prices set. For example, in relation to a firm's statement on labour costs, how is the agency to judge whether the same output could have been achieved by a smaller number of managers and employees? Another difficulty is to determine a rate of return for the firm sufficient for it to be able to attract investors. Moreover, if the agency succeeds in setting prices just sufficient to cover costs, this will eliminate the incentive which firms in unregulated competitive markets have for astute decision-making: the agency will not allow the astute regulated firm to earn higher than normal returns.[68]

So far we have treated the agency's task as if it were simply to control the prices which monopolist firms can charge. In fact, it is more complex, and price controls in this context normally have three dimensions. First, there is the *rate level* issue: the agency is concerned to ensure that the total earnings of firms are appropriate in the light of their costs. Secondly, and

---

[66] P. Joskow and R. Schmalensee, 'Incentive Regulation for Electric Utilities' (1986) 4 Yale J. Reg. 1, 14–15.                                                                  [67] Ibid. 8–9.

[68] In practice, the problem can sometimes be met by 'regulatory lag', i.e. the fixing of prices for periods between agency reviews: see below, p. 309.

distinct from this, there is the *rate structure* issue: the agency may also have to determine how those total earnings are to be derived as between different products or services which the firm supplies and as between different groups of consumers. This may have implications for allocative efficiency. For example, should the agency insist that firms engage in peak load pricing, i.e. varying prices according to the time of consumption, to encourage demand to shift to off-peak periods? But it may also involve distributional considerations: should private consumers be charged at the same rate as industrial users? Should there be any cross-subsidization as between lower-cost consumers (e.g. urban households) and higher-cost consumers (e.g. rural households)?[69] Thirdly, there is the *quality* issue. As we have seen in other contexts, price controls invariably create incentives for firms to reduce the quality of the relevant product; in consequence, agencies must have the power to formulate and enforce appropriate standards of performance.

Finally, in devising appropriate regulatory structures, account must also be taken of private interest considerations. It may be predicted that suppliers, who profit from higher prices, will be able to exert greater influence on agencies than consumers, who benefit from price controls. The broader the discretion enjoyed by agencies in the price-fixing process, the more susceptible they will be to that influence.[70]

A number of different methods for determining the rate level issue have been used or proposed. We concentrate here on the standard American fair rate of return method and the method currently favoured in Britain, the price cap. We then consider briefly the legal techniques for dealing with the issues of rate structure and quality.

### (b) Fair Rate of Return Method

The fair rate of return method constitutes the most ambitious and complex attempt to find a regulatory equivalent to the operation of prices in unregulated competitive markets. Developed by the American Regulatory Commissions and the courts to meet the general legislative requirement that the rates set by utilities should be 'just and reasonable', its challenges and pitfalls have attracted much attention from economists.[71]

While the formulae used have varied over time and between different

---

[69] Cf. above, pp. 284–5.

[70] Cf. J. Vickers and G. Yarrow, *Privatization: An Economic Analysis* (1988), p. 108.

[71] See: A. Kahn, *The Economics of Regulation* (1970), i, pp. 26–54; A. Klevorick, 'The "Optimal" Fair Rate of Return' (1971) 2 Bell J. Econ. 122; R. Schmalensee, *The Control of Natural Monopolies* (1979), ch. 3; P. Joskow and R. Noll, 'Regulation in Theory and Practice: An Overview', in G. Fromm (ed.), *Studies in Public Regulation* (1981), ch. 1; Breyer, above, n. 3, ch. 2; Joskow and Schmalensee, above, n. 66; W. K. Viscusi, J. M. Vernon, and J. E. Harrington, *Economics of Regulation and Antitrust* (1992), ch. 12.

agencies,[72] in essence they allow regulated firms to acquire, as total revenue, such a sum as will cover annual expenditure plus a reasonable profit on capital investment. This can be formulated as

$$E + (r \times RB)$$

where $E$ is the firm's annual expenditure, and includes operating costs, depreciation, and taxes, $r$ is a multiplier, representing the 'fair' rate of return; and $RB$ the rate base, which is the attributed value of the capital investment.

Although the assessment of $E$ and $RB$ has given rise to some difficulties,[73] most controversy has arisen in relation to $r$. Given that the aim is to reflect the level of return which would attract adequate investment in the context of a competitive market, how is this to be determined? Three methods have been used.[74] The first, and most traditional,[75] has regard to the average rates of return in 'comparable' industries, but in relation to many regulated industries, particularly utilities, it is difficult to know what is truly 'comparable'. The second, which is known as the discounted cash flow method, is based on the level of return which has been necessary to attract investors to the same industry in the past.[76] This is subject to the obvious objections that the past is not necessarily a good guide to investment behaviour in the present or future, and that it takes no account of external factors such as the general economic climate. The third method, the capital asset pricing model, was devised in particular to meet this last problem.[77] It looks to the returns investors obtain from a portfolio of investments, as modified by the difference between the returns from shares in utilities and those from other, more general, market shares. This may provide an indication of what is a 'fair' rate of return in a generalized sense, but, like other methods, it is an imperfect criterion for determining the rate of return that

---

[72] For a detailed survey, see *Corpus Juris Secundum*, vol. 73B, Public Utilities.

[73] The main problem has been whether *RB* should be assessed on the book value of historical investment or on the replacement value of its assets (i.e. the present cost of obtaining the service which the plant or equipment provides). In principle, the replacement method should constitute the more accurate estimate, but its assessment gives rise to much complexity and, following a decision of the US Supreme Court (*Federal Power Commission* v. *Hope Natural Gas* 320 US 591), the historical method is generally used, with some adjustment for inflation: Breyer, above, n. 3, pp. 38–40.

[74] For general discussion, see: E. Solomon, 'Alternative Rate of Return Concepts and Their Implications for Utility Regulation' (1970) 1 Bell J. Econ. 65; and Breyer, above, n. 3, pp. 43–7.

[75] Approved by the US Supreme Court in the *Hope Natural Gas* case, above, n. 73.

[76] See, e.g. *City of Pittsburgh* v. *Pennsylvania Utility Commission* 222 A 2d 114.

[77] For its use, see e.g. *Hibbing Taconite Co* v. *Minnesota Public Service Commission* 302 NW 2d 5.

investors will demand from the particular industry at a particular point in time.

Whichever of these methods of assessment is used, critics argue that the fair rate of return approach to price control is not conducive to allocative and productive efficiency.[78] The first, and most obvious, weakness arises from the inclusion of $E$ in the formula. If the regulated firm is able simply to pass on its current costs to consumers, it will have no incentive to constrain them and, as we have seen, there is a limit to the agencies' competence to determine what costs are reasonably incurred. Some consider that the problem is alleviated by the phenomenon of 'regulatory lag': the price fixed by agencies typically remains in force for several years, and this enables firms to retain profits earned during that period by reducing costs below the level used to calculate that price. But if the firm anticipates that a price review will take place in the near future, it would be folly so to reduce its costs if that will result in a lower $E$ assessment.[79] Next, it is asserted that the multiplicand $RB$ creates an incentive for firms to over-invest in capital.[80] Obviously, if a firm is allowed to enlarge $RB$, the prices it is allowed to charge and hence its profits will increase proportionately; and, again, the agency is not well placed to judge whether the additional investment is justified. Finally, account must be taken of the huge administrative costs of a system which requires the agency to scrutinize the firm's behaviour and history so closely, and which also generates a considerable amount of litigation.

The considerable information demands which the system imposes on agencies give rise to another problem. Since the demands can generally be met only with the co-operation of firms, the latter are placed in a powerful position which they can exploit by negotiating laxer controls. Hence the allegation that the American regulatory commissions have often been 'captured' by private interests.[81]

## (c) Price Cap Method

When, in 1982, the Conservative government was formulating its plans to privatize British Telecom, it sought the advice of an economist, Professor Littlechild, as to the appropriate method of controlling the firm's profits.

---

[78] For summaries of the arguments, see: Schmalensee, above, n. 71, pp. 33–7; Breyer, above, n. 3, pp. 47–50.

[79] Hence the argument that agencies should adopt some form of sliding scale whereby firms are allowed to keep a proportion of profits earned by cost reduction: Schmalensee, above, n. 71, pp. 126–30. For more recent suggestions to deal with the incentive problem, see Joskow and Schmalensee, above, n. 66.

[80] The so-called 'Averch-Johnson' effect, derived from H. Averch and L. Johnson, 'Behavior of the Firm under Regulatory Constraint' (1962) 52 Am. Econ. Rev. 1052.

[81] e.g. Joskow and Noll, above, n. 71.

In his report,[82] Littlechild critically evaluated several approaches[83] in terms particularly of efficiency and administrative burden. On both counts, he concluded that the fair rate of return method was inferior to what he referred to as 'local tariff reduction', but which later became better known as the price cap method, or simply $RPI - X$. The latter, which is a variant of the historical method and therefore akin to the measures used to control inflation, requires the firm to increase its prices for each year within a given period by no more than the retail price index ($RPI$) minus a variable factor ($X$) which is the agency's assessment of the firm's cost-efficiency potential. For Littlechild, such a system was

easy to understand, relatively cheap and simple to monitor, [would] preserve the incentives of efficiency, and . . . can be focused precisely on the areas of concern so as not to restrict the operation of the business in other respects.[84]

He also assumed that, because the system would reduce the amount of information which the agency would require from firms, it would be less prone to capture by them.

With some modification, the method was adopted to regulate the prices of all the major utilities privatised in the 1980s. In most cases, price control in this form was intended to be a temporary phenomenon, pending the opening up of the relevant markets to effective competition. As we have seen,[85] for a variety of reasons such competition has not emerged, and the system is likely to remain in force for the foreseeable future.

Discussion of the operation of the system must begin with an account of the legislative and institutional arrangements.[86] Although the wording and detailed provisions of the privatization statutes differ, a general pattern has emerged. The Secretary of State is given power to issue licences or authorization for individual firms to supply the product or service, and an office,[87] headed by a Director General, is established to regulate such supply. In carrying out their functions, the Secretary of State and the Director have the duties, *inter alia*, of ensuring adequate quantity and quality of supply, facilitating competition, promoting efficiency and

[82] S. Littlechild, *Regulation of British Telecommunications' Profitability* (1983).
[83] Viz. maximum rate of return, output-related profits levy, profits ceiling, local tariff reduction, and no formal regulation.
[84] Littlechild, above, n. 82, p. 37. See also M. Beesley and S. Littlechild, 'The Regulation of Privatized Monopolies in the United Kingdom', in M. Beesley, *Privatization, Regulation and Deregulation* (1992), ch. 4.
[85] Above, pp. 290–3.
[86] For a general account, see C. Graham and T. Prosser, *Privatizing Public Enterprises* (1991), pp. 185–97 and ch. 7. There is currently a paucity of specialist legal texts on the subject, but readers should find useful Price Waterhouse, *Regulated Industries: The UK Framework* (1992) and C. Veljanovski, *The Future of Industry Regulation in the UK* (1993).
[87] Notably Office of Telecommunications (OFTEL); Office of Gas Supply (OFGAS); Office of Water Services (OFWAT); Office of Electricity Regulation (OFFER).

economy, and protecting the interests of consumers.[88] The last of these duties explicitly covers prices; but there is no indication, on the face of the legislation, as to how they should be controlled. Rather, the matter is regulated by the terms of the licence granted to the supplier. These are initially set by the Secretary of State, but are then subject to amendment by agreement between the Director and the licensee, with a reference to the Monopolies and Mergers Commission if agreement cannot be reached, and an ultimate power of review in the Secretary of State.[89]

The $RPI - X$ method has, therefore, no formal legislative status, but has been adopted as an exercise of discretion in the various operating licences. The discretion involves deciding what prices should be subject to the price cap, as well as the specific formula to be applied. As regards the first of these questions, the principle has been to exclude from the control prices of commodities for which the supplier faces competition.[90] The formula itself has undergone significant variation as it has been adapted to meet the differing circumstances of the privatised industries. Thus, in the cases of airports, gas, and electricity, the formula became effectively

$$RPI - X + Y + cf$$

$Y$ reflecting a cost that is outside the control of the firm and which the government therefore considers should be passed directly on to consumers,[91] and $cf$ a correcting factor, where previous forecasts have proved to be erroneous.[92]

Let us now examine the content of the formula, and its operation, in more detail. In the first place, it should be observed that, like other historical methods of price control, it regulates price *increases*, rather than prices *per se*. While this has the merit of simplifying the assessment process, it 'fossilizes' the pre-regulation prices the level of which cannot always be assumed to have been economically appropriate.[93] The basis for

[88] See e.g. Gas Act 1986, s. 4, and Electricity Act 1989, s. 3.

[89] e.g. Gas Act 1986, ss. 23–7; Electricity Act 1989, ss. 11–15. The arrangements differ from the American equivalents in that (i) the government plays a more important role, and (ii) there are no formal, adjudicative hearings.

[90] It is not, however, clear what degree of competition is adequate for this purpose. The initial decision to exclude from the control British Telecom's charges for trunk and international calls was reversed, following doubts about the effectiveness of competition from Mercury. And, unless the current efforts to generate more competition for the supply by British Gas to the 'contract' market (i.e. large industrial customers)—see above, p. 292—prove successful, the continued exclusion of this area of its operations from the control is in doubt.

[91] The cost of additional security (for airports), of purchasing electricity from generators (for electricity suppliers), and of changes in the gas price index (for gas suppliers).

[92] Veljanovski, above, n. 86, pp. 28–9.

[93] D. Helm, 'A Regulatory Rule: RPI Minus X', in C. Whitehead (ed.), *Reshaping The Nationalised Industries* (1988), p. 112. As he points out, there was evidence of many distortions in the pre-privatization price levels.

allowable increases is uncontrollable costs. For this purpose, the Retail Price Index (*RPI*) is readily available, but it is calculated by reference to some items (e.g. food) which are irrelevant to the regulated industries and to some others (e.g. material inputs) which represent a proportionally much higher cost for those industries than they do for average households.[94] It is for this reason that the formula, in some cases, had to be adapted by the inclusion of the 'cost pass through' factor ($Y$).[95]

The crux of the control system is $X$,[96] and yet no clear and definitive principles have been formulated on how it should be assessed. One reason for this is that those who are responsible for setting the figure—initially the Secretary of State, subsequently the Directors—have to pursue conflicting aims. Although the principal objective is to determine the cost-reduction potential of the particular firm, this has to be balanced against the need to provide an adequate return for shareholders and to encourage an appropriate degree of investment by the firm;[97] account must also be taken of changes in the level of demand for the products or services.

We cannot here enter into details of the decisions by regulators on the value of $X$ for the different industries,[98] but the experience of several years' operation of the system does permit some generalized comments. First, the complexity of the controls has grown as regulators have felt it necessary not only to adjust $X$ to accommodate changing circumstances but also to differentiate between different services within an industry. Secondly, as a consequence of this relative instability, planning by the industries has become difficult.[99] This, combined with the increased severity of some $X$ determinations, has led to acrimony between managers and regulators, and several references to the Monopolies and Merger Commission.[100] Thirdly, and perhaps most significantly, the efforts of the regulators to assess the cost-reduction potential of firms have blurred the distinction between the price cap method and the fair rate of return method. No doubt it is possible for regulators, in carrying out this task, to

---

[94] Helm, above, n. 93, 111.

[95] On which see Beesley and Littlechild, above, n. 84, pp. 67–8.

[96] For general discussion, see: Helm, above, n. 93, pp. 112–14; Beesley and Littlechild, above, n. 84, pp. 58–63; Vickers and Yarrow, above, n. 70, pp. 214–16; J. Dorken, 'RPI-X: Then and Now', in T. Gilland (ed.), *Incentive Regulation: Reviewing RPI–X and Promoting Competition* (1992), pp. 20–37.

[97] This is of particular importance in relation to water supply. It was widely recognized that, at the time of privatization, the industry suffered from under-investment and the problem was compounded by the need to meet increasingly stringent quality standards. In consequence, $X$ was given a negative value; i.e. the formula was $RPI + X$. See I. Byatt, 'Office of Water Services: Regulation of Water and Sewerage', in C. Veljanovski (ed.), *Regulators and the Market: An Assessment of the Growth of Regulation in the UK* (1991), ch. 9. [98] These may be found in the Price Waterhouse brief, above, n. 86.

[99] '[W]hat we never, ever expected was that the goal posts were going to be moved all the time': spokesman for British Gas, *Financial Times*, 6 July 1992, quoted in Veljanovski, above, n. 86, p. 24. [100] Ibid, pp. 22–6.

adopt the principle of 'yardstick competition' and have regard to the performance of comparable industries,[101] but, as we have seen elsewhere,[102] this is subject to the problem of deciding what is 'comparable'. Regulators have preferred the alternative strategy of scrutinizing prices in the light of what is needed to satisfy shareholders, with the result that elements of the American approach have entered 'by the backdoor'.[103] Moreover, the periodical review of $X$ may create perverse incentives akin to those for which rate of return regulation has been criticized: a firm can aim to make quick and substantial profits immediately after a review, and then, as the next review approaches, increase its costs.[104]

These points are fundamental to an evaluation of the price cap method. The main thrust of Littlechild's case for the latter was its assumed advantage over the fair rate of return approach. If maintaining a clear distinction between the two systems proved to be a false hope, so also did the expectation that the price cap method would be 'easy to understand'. Conclusions on its alleged incentives for efficiency are more difficult to reach. The prices charged by the majority of the privatized industries have declined in real terms,[105] but there is an unresolved debate as to whether the allocatively efficient level has been attained.[106] As regards productive efficiency, it is impossible to disentangle the effects of price control from other changes associated with privatisation. The administrative costs of the British system are significantly lower than those of the American equivalents.[107] On the other hand, the institutional structure in Britain has been criticized for the weakness of its accountability and for the lack of procedural safeguards.[108] This problem, the reliance of regulators on information provided by firms, and the history of bargaining between them[109] all suggest that the system may not be as resistant to the influence of private interests as its proponents hoped.

*(d) Rate Structure*

Most utilities provide a variety of services for different categories of consumers (e.g. industrialists and private households), often by means of

---

[101] Strongly urged by D. Glynn, 'Long Run Regulation of Natural Monopoly: The Case of the Water Industry', in Gilland, above, n. 96, pp. 80–4. [102] Above, p. 308.

[103] Helm, above, n. 93, p. 113; Vickers and Yarrow, above, n. 70, p. 207; Veljanovski, above, n. 86, p. 34.

[104] C. Foster *Privatization, Public Ownership and the Regulation of Natural Monopoly* (1992), pp. 215–16. [105] Veljanovski, above, n. 86, Table 12, p. 40.

[106] Cf. M. Beesley 'Privatization: Reflections on UK Experience', in Beesley, above, n. 84, pp. 45–7.

[107] See the figures quoted in M. Waterson, *Regulation of the Firm and Natural Monopoly* (1988), p. 105.

[108] Veljanovski, above, n. 86, ch. 6; Foster, above, n. 104, ch. 8. See further above, pp. 112–17 and below, p. 341.

[109] C. Veljanovski, 'The Regulation Game', in Veljanovski, above, n. 97, pp. 13–25.

common systems of distribution. The question of how prices should be structured between the services and consumer categories (and within the levels set by the price controls) raises issues of both allocative efficiency and distributional justice.[110] These issues were explored in our discussion of the pricing policy of publicly owned firms[111] and in this chapter it is necessary only to see how the regulatory structures for the privatized industries affect them.

It should be observed, first, that there is a broad similarity between the statutes governing the nationalized industries and privatized industries respectively in so far as they impose a duty to respond to reasonable demands for supply and they prohibit, in relation to the fixing of tariffs, 'undue preference' and 'undue discrimination'.[112] One consequence has been that the privatized utilities have been able to maintain the policy of their public predecessors in having a uniform tariff relating to the geographical location of customers, notwithstanding that this involves some cross-subsidization, from those in urban areas to those in remoter rural areas, for example, and necessarily sacrifices some efficiency to distributional goals.[113]

Although the regulators whose general remit includes rate structure issues have not seen fit to intervene on the above form of cross-subsidization, they have played a prominent role in the determination of some related questions which have been thrown up by the process of privatization.[114] To illustrate the nature of the problem and the impact of the regulatory system, we may use two examples drawn from British Telecom's pricing strategy.

The introduction of competition into the telecommunications industry meant that BT had to grant access to its network to other firms (notably Mercury). It was the task of the Director General of Telecommunications (DGT) to determine what price BT should charge Mercury.[115] In cases of a common facility, such as this, the simple solution of charging the user a proportion of the costs based on usage (the number of call minutes) is allocatively inefficient, since the variable of usage does not reflect the marginal cost of the commodity purchased.[116] The guideline set for the

[110] See generally: Schmalensee, above, n. 71, pp. 29–31; Viscusi *et al.*, above, n. 71, pp. 368–78.

[111] Above, pp. 281–5.

[112] Cf. e.g. Gas Act 1948, ss. 1(1)(a) and 53(7), with Gas Act 1986, ss. 9(1) and 14(3).

[113] See, for gas, C. Price and M. Gibson, 'Privatisation and Regulation 2: British Gas', in Whitehead, above, n. 93, pp. 168–9.

[114] See generally M. Cave and R. Mills, *Cost Allocation in Regulated Industries* (1992).

[115] See M. Beesley and B. Laidlaw, 'The British Telecom/Mercury Interconnect Determination', in Beesley, above. n. 84, ch. 15.

[116] Viscusi *et al.*, above, n. 71, pp. 368–9.

DGT in BT's licence[117] clearly envisaged something more sophisticated than this, and could have been interpreted by the DGT to incorporate a goal of marginal cost and therefore allocatively efficient pricing. In fact the DGT's decision resulted in a set of charges which commentators consider fell significantly below marginal cost[118], the assumption being that he was motivated more by the desire to facilitate competition between Mercury and BT than by the efficiency goal.[119]

The second example concerns the relationship between the prices charged by BT for different services, and demonstrates the difficulty of reaching an appropriate trade-off between conflicting public interest goals. Under the discretion conferred by the legislation on regulators, they may apply the $RPI - X$ formula to the aggregate 'basket' of services or else select different price caps for different services. If, as was the case with the initial BT licence, the first of these options is taken, the firm may operate a more flexible pricing policy. In terms of allocative efficiency, this has the advantage that it enables the firm to rebalance its prices to bring them more closely in line with costs.[120]

BT thus proposed gradually to eliminate the cross-subsidization between business consumers and households by proportionally higher increases to the charges for local calls and line rentals. The DGT responded by persuading BT to agree to a separate price cap on the latter services. There is some evidence of distributional motives for this intervention,[121] and legally this was permissible as the legislation requires him 'to promote the interests of consumers, purchasers and other users . . . (including, in particular, those who are disabled or of pensionable age) in respect of the prices charged'.[122] But there was also the economic argument based on predatory pricing: higher charges for rentals and local calls would enable BT to reduce its tariffs for long-distance calls and thus to drive its competitor in that market (Mercury) out of business.

### (e) Quality

The problem of quality in relation to the supply of products or services by a monopolist was fully considered in the last chapter. As indicated there, the

[117] BT was to be paid 'the cost of anything done pursuant to or in connection with the agreement including fully allocated costs attributable to the services to be provided and taking into account relevant overheads and a reasonable rate of return on attributable assets': BT 1984 Licence, clause 13.5(a), quoted in Cave and Mills, above, n. 114, p. 29.

[118] Beesley and Laidlaw, above, n. 115, p. 305.

[119] Beesley and Littlechild, above, n. 84, pp. 46–7. As the authors there indicate, no explanation for the cost basis was given, 'perhaps to avoid any statement that might evoke a test of the decision by the courts'.

[120] Vickers and Yarrow, above, n. 70, p. 224.

[121] Cave and Mills, above, n. 114, p. 33.

[122] Telecommunications Act 1984, s. 3(2)(a).

government has made a considerable effort in recent years to address this issue, and to formulate performance indicators and quality standards.

The problem was recognized in the earlier privatization statutes relating to telecommunications and gas; but, following the pattern established for the nationalized industries, they did nothing more than to impose on the Secretary of State and the Directors vague duties relating to safety and the quality of products and services supplied.[123] The lack of more specific instruments clearly frustrated the attempts of the regulators to persuade their relevant industries to adopt clearly defined performance and quality targets.[124]

A new approach was taken in the legislation governing electricity and water; these enabled the Director and Secretary of State, respectively, to issue performance and quality standards.[125] The approach was consolidated in the Competition and Service (Utilities) Act 1992, the regulators now having power not only to prescribe standards of performance,[126] but also to collect from suppliers information relating to such performance and to direct that it be made available to consumers.[127] In relation to electricity and water, the standards may be set only after the Directors have undertaken research to discover 'the views of a representative sample of persons likely to be affected'.[128]

The regime which now governs the privatized utilities contrasts significantly with that applicable to public enterprise.[129] As we have seen, the standards applicable to the latter are not the subject of formal legal instruments and have largely been set by the industries themselves.[130] It is true that the regulations issued so far under the new regime[131] have tended to reflect pre-existing voluntary standards; but the legislation clearly envisages that the regulators will assume a more interventionist stance, not the least because of their duty to obtain the views of consumers.

Regulators also play a key role in the enforcement of performance standards. For this purpose, a distinction is drawn between 'standards of performance in individual cases' (SPIC) and 'overall performance standards' (OPS). SPICs are laid down in formal regulations and confer rights of

---

[123] Telecommunications Act 1984, s. 3(2)(a); Gas Act 1986, s. 4(2)(a) and (c).

[124] See e.g. the Report of the Director General of Gas Supply for 1989 (Cm. 142), p. 19.

[125] Electricity Act 1989, s. 41; Water Industry Act 1991, ss. 38 and 67. The supply of water had, of course, always been subject to quality standards: see e.g. Water Act 1973, s. 11.

[126] Although in the case of water this power remains with the Secretary of State.

[127] Ss. 1–3 (telecommunications), 11–13 (gas), 21 (electricity), 27 (water).

[128] Ss. 20 and 26.

[129] T. Boorman, 'The Price-Quality Trade-Off in Electricity Supply' (1993) 3 Cons. Pol. Rev. 11.          [130] Above, pp. 286–7.

[131] See esp. Electricity (Standards of Performance) Regulations, SI 1991/1344, and Water Supply and Sewerage Services (Customer Service Standards) Regulations, SI 1989/1159.

compensation on individual consumers,[132] with a reference to the Directors in the event of a dispute. OPCs are more general targets and may vary as between firms or regions;[133] they are incorporated into the licences authorizing supply and, as such, are enforceable by the Directors in civil proceedings.[134]

It is too early to judge the efficacy of the new regime. The institutional framework established by the 1992 Act is, perhaps, as good as any that could have been devised. It remains to be seen whether the regulators will exercise their powers in pursuance of public interest goals, or rather, allow the influence of suppliers' private interests to prevail. We have drawn attention elsewhere to the fundamental difficulties in formulating and enforcing quality standards, particularly in relation to services.[135] It is worth reiterating that misallocations can arise—and private interests can benefit—from excess quality, just as much as from inferior quality: consumers suffer welfare losses if they have to pay for the additional costs of a level of quality which they do not want.[136] The regulators' task in acting as a proxy for consumers in this respect is clearly not an easy one.

---

[132] e.g. under the Electricity Regulations, above, n. 131, supplies must be restored after a fault within 24 hours. Failure to achieve this results in a payment of £20 to domestic customers and £50 to non-domestic customers, plus £10 for each further delay of 12 hours.

[133] e.g. the target of reading electricity meters at least once a year is 93% for Southern Electricity and 99% for East Midlands Electricity: S. Bailey, Annotations to Competition and Service (Utilities) Act 1992, Current Law Statutes, 43–38.

[134] Competition and Service (Utilities) Act 1992, s. 9.

[135] Above, pp. 285–6.                    [136] Schmalensee, above, n. 71, p. 33.

# 15

# Public Franchise Allocation

## I. INTRODUCTION

For economic or other reasons, policy-makers may consider it appropriate to limit the number of suppliers operating in particular markets. One possibility is to create a public corporation with an exclusive right of supply, but, as we saw in Chapter 13, public ownership has many disadvantages. The main alternative is for the right to be conferred on one or more private firms; and if this solution is adopted, it is necessary to devise institutions and principles for selecting the firms and for determining the conditions under which they are to operate.

The rights of supply are often referred to in legislation as 'licences'. They are, however, significantly different from the 'licences' which are used as instruments of prior approval and which, as such, were discussed in Chapter 10. The ostensible purpose of prior approval licences is not to limit competition but rather to ensure that all suppliers or their products competing in the market satisfy certain minimum standards.[1] Licences which are the subject-matter of this chapter do impose conditions regarding the quality and price of the services to be supplied, but there is normally no expectation that the licensee will compete with other suppliers; to avoid ambiguity, we will refer to them as 'public franchises'.

Public franchises may be conferred without formal processes or principles of allocation. In the Tudor and early Stuart periods this was often done as an act of royal prerogative.[2] For the Crown, this proved to be a lucrative source of revenue which, unlike taxation, was not subject to parliamentary scrutiny. As such, the practice provoked a constitutional crisis,[3] and from the end of the seventeenth century legislation was required for the granting of monopoly rights.

In modern times, legislation has created monopoly (or near-monopoly) rights, but to deal with the adverse consequences this has invariably been accompanied by an elaborate regulatory regime. The privatization legislation of the 1980s constitutes a prime example. This, as we have seen,[4] in addition to abolishing the public corporations and creating private firms to

---

[1] Although in practice, as we found in Ch. 10, they sometimes have the effect of limiting competition: cf. above, pp. 219–20.

[2] W. Holdsworth, *History of English Law*, iv (1924), pp. 340–54.

[3] See esp. the *Case of Monopolies* (1602) 11 Co. Rep. 84B.

[4] Cf. above, pp. 289 and 291.

inherit their assets and liabilities, also automatically conferred a franchise on those firms. The huge investments represented by the assets made it inevitable that the firms would also succeed to the right of supply without recourse to any additional principle or process of allocation. The lack of competition in the allocation process and its relative absence from the markets in which the privatized firms operated made it necessary to institute the price and quality regulatory regimes which were discussed in Chapter 14.

In this chapter, we consider systems under which public franchises are allocated by special agencies, using criteria which, to a greater or lesser extent, are formalized. As will be seen, the systems are diverse in character and operation. An evaluation of their design and impact can best be undertaken in the light of an important theory of public franchising which has emerged from the economics literature.[5] According to this theory, if franchises are allocated by a suitably devised process of competitive tendering, this will obviate—or at least reduce—the need for regulation. Briefly put, the argument is that competitive tendering can be used as a substitute for conventional market competition: to enjoy the monopoly right *ex post*, the supplier must engage in competition *ex ante* to secure that right. Such competition should, it is contended, force firms to supply their goods or services on terms which are consistent with allocative and productive efficiency. The public franchise process may then be analogous to the decisions made by a householder who, before entering into a contract for work to be done on his premises, obtains estimates from a number of competing builders, and selects the one which offers the most attractive combination of price and quality.[6]

The terms of the successful bid, particularly those affecting price and quality, then become conditions of the franchise which, like any other contract, governs the ongoing behaviour of the supplier. Contract can thus replace conventional regulation as the instrument of legal control, and unlike regulation which typically involves resort to, or a threat of, the criminal process, it relies on termination or non-renewal of the franchise as the principal sanction for inadequate performance.

In our analysis of public franchising, we shall focus on several systems

[5] The theory can be traced back to E. Chadwick, 'Research of different principles of legislation and administration in Europe of competition for the field as compared with competition within the field of service' (1859) 22 J. Royal Stat. Soc. (Series A) 381. The leading modern exponents are: H. Demsetz, 'Why Regulate Utilities?' (1968) 11 J. Law & Econ. 55; and R. Posner, 'The Appropriate Scope of Regulation in the Cable Television Industry' (1972) 3 Bell J. Econ. 98. See also S. Domberger, 'Economic Regulation Through Franchise Contracts', in J. Kay, C. Mayer, and D. Thompson (eds.), *Privatisation and Regulation: The UK Experience* (1986), ch. 14.

[6] M. Waterson, *Regulation of the Firm and Natural Monopoly* (1988), pp. 106–7. The analogy is not perfect, since, unlike the public franchise case, the householder does not normally envisage an ongoing relationship.

which are, or have been, used in Britain: that governing bus and coach routes which was established by the Road Traffic Act 1930 and which survived until the deregulation measures in the 1980s;[7] the licensing of domestic airline routes under the Civil Aviation (Licensing) Act 1960 and the Civil Aviation Act 1971;[8] and the contrasting regimes of franchises for television services introduced by the Television Act 1955, the Cable and Broadcasting Act 1984, and the Broadcasting Act 1990.[9] Reference will also be made to the franchising of passenger services to be introduced under the Railways Act 1993,[10] although at the time of writing the details of the scheme have not yet been announced.

We first consider the public interest justifications and private interest explanations for public franchising (section 2). This is followed by discussions of the criteria (section 3) and processes (section 4) adopted for allocating franchises, and of issues concerning the nature and enforcement of the franchise contract (section 5). The chapter concludes with an evaluation of franchising as a regulatory instrument (section 6).

## 2. JUSTIFICATIONS AND EXPLANATIONS FOR PUBLIC FRANCHISING

### (a) Natural Monopoly and 'Cream-Skimming'

In accordance with conventional economic analysis, there is a strong case for limiting the right to supply where the conditions of a natural monopoly exist in a particular market.[11] Determination of such conditions is a highly technical matter, but there is a general consensus among commentators that the bus, airline, and broadcasting industries do not satisfy the conventional criteria of a natural monopoly.[12] As was indicated in an earlier chapter,[13] the possibility of 'cream-skimming' (suppliers concentrating on those areas of the market where, for geographical or other reasons, the costs of supply are lowest) may enhance the case for treating certain industries as natural monopolies, especially where on distributional grounds it is deemed desirable to maintain certain levels of supply for such

[7] See generally S. Glaister and C. Mulley, *Public Control of the British Bus Industry* (1983).

[8] See generally R. Baldwin, *Regulating the Airlines: Administrative Justice and Agency Discretion* (1985).

[9] See generally T. Gibbons, *Regulating the Media* (1991), pp. 58–97.

[10] For commentaries written prior to the passing of the Act, see: A. Dnes, *On the Wrong Tracks: The Government's Proposals for Franchising Passenger Rail* (1993); L. Stafford, 'Rail Privatisation: Efficiency, Quality and the Consumer' (1993) 3 Cons. Pol. Rev. 17.

[11] Cf. above, pp. 30–3 and 267–8.

[12] See: (for buses) Glaister and Mulley, above, n. 7, pp. 123–7, and K. Gwilliam, 'Deregulation of the Bus Industry' (1989) 23 J. Transport Econ. & Pol. 29; (for airlines) S. Breyer, *Regulation and Its Reform* (1982), ch. 11; (for television) M. Cave, 'An Introduction to Television Economics', in G. Hughes and D. Vines (eds.), *Deregulation and the Future of Commercial Television* (1989), pp. 11–14.          [13] Above, p. 32.

areas. The argument has been invoked to justify franchising,[14] but the distributional goal can be achieved by means other than limiting entry, notably through the provision of publicly financed subsidies.[15]

## (b) Technological Scarcity

There are situations where, for technological reasons, the number of firms willing to supply the market exceed the number who can do so. Broadcasting on the electro-magnetic spectrum constitutes the classic example. Until recently, this was the only medium available for broadcasting and there was a limit to the number of stations which could be accommodated on adjacent frequencies without mutual interference. Thus, when commercial broadcasting was introduced alongside the publicly-owned BBC, limiting suppliers by a system of franchises was the obvious solution.

It is true that, as Coase argued in a famous article,[16] the existence of technological scarcity is not a conclusive justification for regulation: a private and marketable property right could be created in a frequency. However, the latter system would create difficulties in the formulation and trading of broadcasting property rights,[17] and it would still be necessary to devise principles and processes for the initial distribution.

## (c) 'Excessive Competition'

Historically, the principal argument used to justify the franchising of bus and domestic airline routes was that, if unregulated, competition would be 'excessive' or 'destructive'.[18] This justification is ambiguous and can refer to several different problems, most of which can be met by other means.[19] The first is predatory pricing, in which firms reduce their prices in order to drive competitors out of the market, only to raise them again when they hold monopolistic power. While such practices may justify intervention, this is properly a task for competition law;[20] limiting entry may actually

[14] e.g. Second Report of the Royal Commission on Transport (1929, Cmd. 3416), para. 86. See also Report of the [Thesiger] Committee on the Licensing of Road Passenger Services (1953) which acknowledged that the 1930 bus franchising system had been 'remarkably successful' in maintaining non-profitable routes.
[15] A. Kahn, *The Economics of Regulation*, ii (1971), pp. 220–6; and see Transport Act 1985, s. 63.
[16] R. Coase, 'The Federal Communications Commission' (1959) 2 J. Law & Econ. 1.
[17] N. Johnson, 'Towers of Babel: The Chaos in Radio Spectrum Utilization and Allocation' (1969) 34 Law & Contemp. Prob. 505.
[18] Cf. Final Report of Royal Commission on Transport (1931, Cmd. 3751) paras. 50–1; Report of the [Maybury] Committee on the Development of Civil Aviation in the United Kingdom (1937, Cmd. 5351), paras. 125–6. See also the [Salter] Report on the Conference on Rail and Road Transport (1932), para. 94, which used the same argument to justify the licensing of road hauliers.
[19] Kahn, above, n. 15, pp. 172–8; Breyer, above, n. 12, pp. 30–2.
[20] Cf. T. Frazer, *Monopoly, Competition and the Law* (1988), pp. 63–6.

facilitate predatory pricing.[21] Secondly, the 'excessive competition' concept has been applied to market distortions arising from the fact that some other areas of the market are subject to regulatory controls. For example, the licensing of bus routes in 1930 was in part due to pressure exerted by the railway and tramway industries which were subject to rigorous controls and thus, it was argued, subject to competitive disadvantages.[22] The obvious solution to this problem is to modify the regulatory controls to eliminate the distortion. Thirdly, it has been used in relation to some harmful effects, some of them externalities, which are said to be induced by competition in some markets. Thus, for example, in relation to transport, it is sometimes claimed that price competition leads to firms skimping on safety and reliability.[23] The problem is not peculiar to specific markets, like transport, but occurs more generally, where consumers are unable readily to detect variations in quality.[24] Limiting entry is an unnecessarily heavy-handed response to such a problem; a more appropriate remedy may be sought in information or quality controls.[25]

### (d) Private Interest Considerations

If public franchising systems are designed so as to accord perfectly with the economic theory described earlier in this chapter,[26] franchisees would be unable to earn rents of the kind typically associated with uncompetitive markets. However, as will be seen, there is a considerable divergence between what that theory prescribes and the form and practice of the systems actually adopted. Unsurprisingly, therefore, commentators have sought to explain the existence of these systems, particularly where they cannot easily be justified on the public interest grounds considered above, by reference to the hypothesis that regulation is the result of rent-seeking behaviour by private interest groups.

The system of bus route franchising established in the 1930 Road Traffic Act provides an excellent illustration.[27] The large and powerful bus operators had a clear interest in subscribing to a system which would limit the very free competition existing at that time. To this must be added the interest of the railway and tramway companies, which not only suffered as a consequence of the competition, but also had developed their own bus

---

[21] Breyer, above, n. 12, p. 32.

[22] Glaister and Mulley, above, n. 7, pp. 21–2.

[23] Royal Commission on Transport, above, n. 14, para. 86.

[24] G. Akerlof, 'The Market for "Lemons": Qualitative Uncertainty and Market Mechanism' (1970) Q. J. Econ. 488; and see above, pp. 38–41.

[25] For some of the harmful effects, private rights may be adequate: see e.g. the classic 19th-cent. case of *Limpus* v. *London General Omnibus Co.* (1862) 1 H & C 526.

[26] Above, p. 319.

[27] K. Button, 'Economic Theories of Regulation and the Regulation of the United Kingdom's Bus Industry' (1989) 34 Antitrust Bull. 489.

services. These industries were, indeed, well represented on the committees whose recommendations played a key role in the policy debates.[28]

## 3. CRITERIA FOR ALLOCATING PUBLIC FRANCHISES

### (a) Public Interest Goals

In establishing the criteria and processes for allocating public franchises, the policy-maker may be assumed to pursue public interest goals. Of course, we would expect the by now familiar concepts of allocative efficiency and productive efficiency to be a prominent concern, and the economic theory of franchising provides a model for achieving such goals. But, in the present context, there are other public interest considerations which may also play an important role. Account may have to be taken of distributional justice. Distributional questions arise particularly when some forms or areas of supply are more profitable than others and 'cream-skimming' is therefore possible. Then, in relation to broadcasting, there are special considerations arising from the power of the media to influence public opinion and political activity: freedom of speech, independence from political parties, and a balanced presentation of news programmes all become important values.[29]

### (b) Types of Allocation Systems

Two broad categories of allocation systems may be distinguished. The first, often referred to as *public interest franchising*,[30] is the more widely used of these: the agency responsible for conferring the franchise attempts to select from the competing firms those which, in its view, would best serve a wide range of 'public interest' goals. In practice, priority is accorded to the range and quality of the services promised and the financial soundness of the firm. This traditional approach is to be contrasted with *price bidding franchising*, which comes closer to the model derived from the economic theory of franchising but which, in its purest form, has been adopted only infrequently. Here the rights of supply are conferred on those among the competing firms which will charge consumers the lowest price for their products or services, or, alternatively, which are prepared to pay (into public funds) the highest price for acquiring the right.

In fact, as will be seen, there is a difference of emphasis, rather than of kind, between the two approaches. Given the monopoly position of the franchisee, the public interest method cannot ignore the pricing issue.

---

[28] Glaister and Mulley, above, n. 7, ch. 3. The same was true of the Salter Conference, above, n. 18, which recommended the licensing of road hauliers: see A. A. Walters, 'Commentary on the Report of the Committee on Carriers' Licensing' (1966) 29 Modern LR 68.          [29] See generally Gibbons, above, n. 9, ch. 2.

[30] Cf. Breyer, above, n. 12, ch. 4.

Under price bidding systems, the agency defining the product to be franchised, comparing bids, and formulating the terms of the franchise will find it difficult not to take some account of the quality of what is offered.

### (c) Public Interest Franchising

In selecting from the competitive bids, the authority responsible for awarding the franchises is acting as agent for the purchasers of the service and, ideally, the legislation should require it to reflect consumer preferences. Although this is sometimes made explicit,[31] and provisions enable it to consult bodies representing consumer interests,[32] there is clearly a limit to its capacity to perform this task. Inevitably it is driven to making subjective judgements on what is desirable in the public interest.

This is not to imply that such judgements are necessarily arbitrary: the legislation can specify matters to which the agency should have regard in exercising its discretion and expect a reasoned decision on the basis of them. This is relatively unproblematic where the service in question has a largely homogeneous quality. For example, the demand for air services on particular routes can be determined without undue difficulty, and the quality of service is unlikely to vary greatly between one airline and another. The modern statutory criteria thus concentrate on the fitness of the operator to operate the service. The Civil Aviation Authority (CAA) is required to reject a licence application if it is not satisfied that:

(a) the applicant is, having regard [to his experience in aviation] . . . a fit person to operate aircraft under the authority of the licence . . . ; or (b) the resources of the applicant and the financial arrangements made by him are adequate for discharging his actual and potential obligations in respect of the business activities in which he is engaged (if any) and in which he may be expected to engage if he is granted the licence[33]

As the dimensions to quality, or public interest, increase in number and complexity, so the task for the legislature in formulating appropriate criteria, and for the agency in making reasoned decisions on the basis of them, becomes more problematic.[34] In relation to the desirability of bus services on particular routes, the Traffic Commissioners were to have regard to

---

[31] e.g. the Civil Aviation Authority is under a duty to perform its functions 'in the manner which it considers is best calculated—(a) to secure that British airlines provide air transport services which satisfy all substantial categories of public demand . . . and (d) . . . to further the reasonable interests of users of air transport services': Civil Aviation Act 1971, s. 3(1).

[32] See e.g. Television Act 1954, s. 8.

[33] Civil Aviation Act 1971, s. 22(2); cf. Railways Act 1993, s. 26(3).

[34] V. Goldberg, 'Competitive Bidding and the Production of Precontract Information' (1976) 7 Bell J. Econ. 250, 252-4.

(a) the suitability of the routes . . . ; (b) the extent, if any, to which the needs of the proposed routes . . . are already adequately served; (c) the extent to which the proposed service is necessary or desirable in the public interest; (d) the needs of the area as a whole in relation to traffic . . . and the co-ordination of all forms of passenger transport, including transport by rail.[35]

Of course, with the multi-faceted public interest dimension to broadcasting, the specification and measurement of quality becomes even more difficult.[36] The solution adopted in the Television Act 1954 was to confer an almost[37] unfettered discretion on the agency regarding the selection of franchisees, but to require that standards of quality, decency, impartiality, and so forth be included in the contract awarded to the successful bidder.[38] A quite different approach was taken in the legislation governing cable television.[39] In deciding whether or to whom to grant a licence, the agency was to take into account not only 'all matters appearing to them to be relevant', but also the extent to which certain specified qualities were planned to be included in programmes, for example, range and diversity, educational or local orientation.[40] It is not, however, clear that the proliferation of criteria induces better or more consistent decision-making. As Breyer has written of the American system which articulates a larger number of quality indicators,

[t]he effect of many standards . . . is virtually the same as having none at all. There is no clear indication of which standards are more important, how they are to be individually applied, or how varying degrees of conformity are to be balanced. The existence of so many standards effectively allows the agency near-total discretion in making a selection.[41]

### (d) Price Bidding Franchising

The public interest method of allocating franchises does not, in principle, take account of prices in the selection of franchisees, although conditions

---

[35] Road Traffic Act 1930, s. 72(3).

[36] Breyer, above, n. 12, pp. 78–81; C. Veljanovski, 'Cable Television: Agency Franchising and Economics', in R. Baldwin and C. McCrudden (eds.), Regulation and Public Law (1987), pp. 291–3. In relation to commercial terrestrial services, the problem of measuring consumer demand is aggravated by the fact that firms derive their revenue from advertising rather than consumer payments: Cave, above, n. 12, pp. 19–23.

[37] There were a few categories of 'disqualified person', notably foreigners, advertising agents and sound broadcasters: s. 5.

[38] S. 3. Certain changes were made in the Broadcasting Act 1980 (consolidated in the Broadcasting Act 1981), but the discretion of the agency remained largely unaltered. A similar system was applied to independent local radio: see on this R. Baldwin, M. Cave, and T. Jones, 'The Regulation of Independent Local Radio and Its Reform' (1987) 7 Int. Rev. Law & Econ. 177.

[39] For the changes to the system of terrestrial service franchises effected by the Broadcasting Act 1990, see below, p. 327.

[40] Cable and Broadcasting Act 1984, s. 7.          [41] Above n. 12, p. 79.

regarding pricing are often imposed in the contracts. In contrast, under the price bidding approach, prices are the principal criterion for awarding the contract. There are, in fact, two variants to this approach. Under the first, which we may label *monopoly price bidding* (MPB), the agency selects the firm which is prepared to pay the highest price to acquire the franchise.[42] Under the second, *consumer price bidding* (CPB), it is awarded to the firm that promises to charge consumers the lowest price for its services. CPB does not appear to have been adopted in any British legislation.

For many economists, price bidding is preferable to public interest franchising because it should generate allocative efficiency and productive efficiency: the price competition will eliminate monopoly rents and force suppliers to minimize the costs of production. Why then have price bidding schemes, particularly the CPB variant, been adopted so rarely? One possible explanation can be derived from private interest theory: firms which profit from public interest franchising, or other forms of regulation, may have sufficient influence to resist the introduction of schemes which will eliminate their rents.[43] The fact that governments receive payments under MPB schemes, but not CPB, may also help to explain why the former approach to price bidding is invariably adopted.[44]

There are, however, problems with price bidding which have not always been sufficiently recognised by its advocates.[45] The MPB approach does not ensure that the pricing of the franchisee's services will be allocatively efficient, because once the award has been made, the firm's determination of its prices is unregulated. Of course, this problem can be met by the agency either requiring information regarding pricing policy at the time of the bid and inserting appropriate conditions into the franchise contract, or else controlling the firm's prices on an ongoing basis. But both of these alternatives impose on the agency the considerable demands of price controls which we encountered in the last chapter and which franchising is designed to avoid.

These arguments do not apply to the CPB approach, but this, as well as MPB, has to confront the problem of verifying non-price dimensions of supply. In the first place, the agency has to be confident that the financial

---

[42] Or which is prepared to accept from public sources the lowest subsidy for running a non-profitable service, as is envisaged under Railways Act 1993, s. 136(7).

[43] T. Hazlett, 'The Rationality of U.S. Regulation of the Broadcast Spectrum' (1990) 33 J. Law & Econ. 133.

[44] Cf. A. Dnes, 'Bidding for Commercial Broadcasting: An Analysis of U.K. Experience' (1993) 40 Sc. J. Pol. Econ 104. The Tudor and early Stuart practice of royal prerogative franchising provides a further example: above, p. 318.

[45] See esp. O. Williamson, 'Franchise Bidding for Natural Monopolies—in General and with Respect to CATV' (1976) 7 Bell J. Econ 73; Goldberg (1976), above, n. 34; V. Goldberg, 'Regulation and Administered Contracts' (1977) 8 Bell J. Econ. 426; R. Schmalensee, *Regulation of Natural Monopoly* (1979), pp. 68–73.

structure of the firm is adequate to supply at the price bid.[46] Secondly, as we have seen, the services which are the subject of franchises are not always of a sufficiently homogeneous character as to render trivial differences of quality. Competition as to price alone will, then, create incentives for firms to reduce quality. The problem may be containable in relation to rail passenger franchises, since it is envisaged that the bids will be for contracts of specified frequency and quality of service.[47] But, predictably, the problem proved to be a major obstacle when proposals to use a price bidding scheme to replace the public interest approach to broadcasting franchises[48] were being considered.

What emerged in the Broadcasting Act 1990 in relation to commercial television[49] was a hybrid system. For a bid to be considered, it must first pass a quality threshold, which includes the requirements: that sufficient time be allocated to news and current affairs, other programmes of 'high quality', and religious and regional programmes; and that 'programmes so included are calculated to appeal to a wide variety of tastes and interests'.[50] The agency, after considering all the bids which pass this threshold, is then to award the franchise to the applicant submitting the highest bid.[51] However, the franchise may be awarded to another applicant if 'exceptional circumstances' make such a decision appropriate.[52] The phrase 'exceptional circumstances' is not defined, but it includes cases where the quality of service promised by the preferred applicant is 'exceptionally high', or where it is 'substantially higher' than that proposed by the highest bidder.[53] Parliament thus recoiled from embarking on a 'pure' price bidding system; and the problematic issue of quality, while not the principal criterion as under public interest franchising, continues to play an important role.

---

[46] See *R* v. *Independent Television Commission, ex parte TSW Broadcasting, The Times*, 30 Mar. 1992.

[47] White Paper, *New Opportunities for the Railways* (1992, Cm. 2012), para. 26. For doubts, see Dnes, above, n. 10, pp. 21–2.

[48] White Paper, *Broadcasting in the '90s: Competition, Choice and Quality* (1988, Cm. 517), which was influenced by the Report of the [Peacock] Committee on Financing the BBC (1986, Cmnd. 9824).

[49] The MPB system is used for national independent radio services without a quality threshold (although diversity of programmes is a relevant consideration): Broadcasting Act 1990, ss. 98–100. Local radio services are not now governed by a competitive franchising system because it is considered that the spectrum is wide enough to enable a large number of stations to compete against each other. Licences are thus awarded principally on the basis of financial and technical viability: ibid. ss. 104–5, and see Gibbons, above, n. 9, p. 86.

[50] Broadcasting Act 1990, s. 16(2).

[51] Ibid. s. 17(1).

[52] Ibid. s. 17(3).

[53] Ibid. s. 17(4).

## 4. THE ALLOCATION PROCESS AND COMPETITION

### (a) General

Fair competition is the key requirement of a franchise allocating process. This is a consequence not only of the legal value associated with procedural justice,[54] but also of the economic justifications for the system; in the absence of such competition, allocative and productive efficiency will be jeopardized. Fair competition will also reduce the impact of, and discourage, rent-seeking behaviour.

The goal of fair competition raises issues both of substance and of procedure. Where, as in the case of railways, the services have been operated by a publicly owned monopoly, competition is jeopardised if it is allowed to bid for the franchise, since its assets and experience would give it a considerable advantage over entrants. Although the government's proposal for a blanket exclusion of British Rail from the franchising systems was defeated in the House of Lords, the resulting compromise preserves the spirit of the proposal. The franchising agency is given power to exclude British Rail or a wholly owned subsidiary from bidding, where this is considered desirable for the purposes of promoting competition.[55]

As regards procedure, it is important that the criteria for conferring the franchises should be reasonably certain and available to applicants, that consistent decisions be formulated in accordance with the criteria and on the basis of information contained in the applications, and that members of the awarding agency should have no interest in the outcome. Some would argue that a public hearing is also desirable.[56] The general principles of administrative law should ensure that most of these requirements are met,[57] although the fact that applicants' interest in the proceedings can be characterized as only 'contractual' may create conceptual barriers to an effective remedy.[58]

The record of the British franchising systems in meeting process standards has been mixed. As regards the agencies responsible for domestic airline route franchises, there was, for some time, a problem of independence from government. Inconsistency between government policy and agency policy made it difficult for the latter to articulate clear guidelines on the criteria for awarding franchises,[59] but eventually a

---

[54] N. Lewis, 'I.B.A. Programme Contract Awards' [1975] Public Law 317; Baldwin, above, n. 8, pp. 251–63.                    [55] Railways Act 1993, s. 25(4)–(5).

[56] For discussion of this issue, see: Lewis, above, n. 54, pp. 333–8; Baldwin, above, n. 8, pp. 192–204.                    [57] Cf. above, pp. 114–15.

[58] Lewis, above, n. 54, pp. 325–6; T. Daintith, 'Regulation by Contract: The New Prerogative' [1979] Current Law Prob. 41.

[59] Under the Civil Aviation (Licensing) Act 1960, a right of appeal lay from the agency's decision to the Minister and, during the period 1962–71, 30% of such appeals succeeded: Baldwin, above, n. 8, p. 41. To reduce difficulties created by differences between government

compromise was reached and such guidelines were published.[60] Similarly the Traffic Commissioners, responsible for allocating franchises for bus routes, were slow to develop a coherent policy.[61] Although such a policy did eventually emerge, it was never published, perhaps because it accorded priority to existing operators and eschewed competition.[62] Unsurprisingly, given the extent to which it benefited the bus industry, the system largely escaped criticism,[63] but that was not true of commercial television franchising under the Television Act 1954.

Crude criteria for the selection process were laid down though they were not publicised until well after the event, yet in an atmosphere of prevailing mystery it was not possible to divine which were given priority and how seriously they were taken. The reasons for the choice of companies did not illuminate the dominating standards and would certainly not have satisfied a court of law were a requirement to state reasons imposed.[64]

### (b) Renewal of Franchises

We have seen that there is a problem of ensuring fair competition if, as in the case of railways, a system of franchising is introduced and an existing operator is allowed to bid. The same problem arises when the period of a franchise contract comes to an end and the incumbent is seeking renewal.[65] Under public interest franchising systems, where decisions involve a broad discretion and a variety of criteria, a newcomer is likely to be placed at a disadvantage *vis-à-vis* the incumbent as regards experience of the business and its market, and knowledge of the agency and its processes. There is, indeed, evidence that agencies have tended to prefer the status quo by routinely renewing the franchises of established operators, or at least requiring newcomers to make a particularly powerful case.[66] This might

and agency policy, the Civil Aviation Act 1971 provided that the Minister might give written guidance to the agency. That this did not solve the problem is evident from *Laker Airways Ltd v. Department of Trade* [1977] QB 643, where the Court of Appeal held that the written guidance could not override the objectives which bound the agency.

[60] Baldwin, above, n. 8, pp. 166–76.

[61] The Minister of Transport, to whom appeals could be made, was originally opposed to the formulation of general principles: 'the circumstances of individual services differ so widely that it is not desirable, or even practical, . . . to formulate any rules or conditions that could be of universal application' (statement of October 1931, quoted in I. Savage, *The Deregulation of Bus Services* (1985), p. 5).

[62] See esp. D. N. Chester, *The Control of Public Road Passenger Transport* (1937).

[63] Button, above, n. 27, p. 506.

[64] Lewis, above, n. 54, p. 320. See also A. Briggs and J. Spicer, *The Franchise Affair* (1986), ch. 2. On the analogous system for local radio, see Baldwin *et al.*, above, n. 38: their statistical analysis of the franchises awarded 1981–83 failed to establish a correlation between the probability of success and particular characteristics of applicants, or to identify any significant difference between those that succeeded and those that failed: ibid. p. 184.

[65] Williamson, above, n. 45, pp. 83–90; Breyer, above, n. 12, pp. 89–94.

[66] See: (for buses), Chester, above, n. 62; (for domestic airline routes), Baldwin, above, n. 8, p. 212.

suggest that the agency has been 'captured' by the incumbent;[67] but there may be a public interest argument for such preference. Incumbents invariably have a greater degree of investment in the franchised activity, and if this factor is disregarded there will be no incentive to seek out and invest in developing markets. On the other hand, if there is too great an emphasis on existing investment, incumbent firms will have an incentive to over-invest and newcomers may be deterred from competing.

Appropriate investment incentives constitute an intractable problem which applies to price bidding schemes as much as to public interest schemes. The price bid will reflect the supplier's predicted costs during the next franchise period and, given the existing investment of the incumbent, her costs should be lower than those of a newcomer. To meet this problem, Posner has suggested that the bids should be appraised on the basis that the newcomer, if successful, will purchase the incumbent's system and a provision to that effect can then be incorporated in the franchise contract.[68] But he appears to underestimate the difficulties to which such a solution would give rise; in particular, how would plant and equipment be valued? and how could the compulsory sale be applied to the incumbent's labour force?[69]

## 5. THE FRANCHISE CONTRACT

Under a franchising system, the contract between the agency and the franchisee replaces conventional regulation as the principal instrument of legal control. Advocates of the system, inspired by the efficacy, flexibility, and low administrative costs of conventional private contracts made in competitive markets, have assumed that it is superior to regulation[70] which, as we saw in the last chapter, imposes high information and enforcement costs on agencies. This contention must be evaluated as we here explore the nature and operation of the franchise contract.

### (a) Content of Contract

It is inherent in the concept of competitive franchising that applicants should be bound by the terms of their successful bids, and these are normally incorporated in the franchise contract. However, while the conditions stipulated for the competition and the terms of the bids may capture much that is required by the public interest goals, inevitably there will be a gap between what is regarded as socially desirable and the obligations that can be derived from consensual agreement. The gap has to

[67] For consideration of this, see: (on buses) Button, above, n. 27, p. 506; and (on airlines) Baldwin, above, n. 8, pp. 219–31.                    [68] Above, n. 5, p. 116.
[69] Williamson, above, n. 45, pp. 84–9.
[70] See esp. Demsetz, above, n. 5, pp. 64–5.

be filled by controls unilaterally imposed on franchisees, whether by additional conditions incorporated in the contract or by conventional regulation.

The relative scope of the consensually derived obligations and the unilaterally imposed standards, respectively, obviously varies according to the type of franchising system. Where franchises are allocated on the basis of public interest criteria or under an MPB bidding scheme, the firm's consumer pricing strategy is not generally of direct relevance and, in consequence, a power to regulate prices is usually conferred on the agency.[71] Quality controls are necessary under both types of price bidding scheme and are invariably imposed also under public interest schemes, since the criteria for allocation can rarely capture all that is desirable. Thus, for example, the suppliers of public transport are subjected to standards relating to safety and noise,[72] and broadcasters to standards relating to freedom of speech, decency, political impartiality, and cultural diversity.[73] To avoid 'cream-skimming', it may be necessary to require franchisees to maintain supply in certain forms or in certain areas.[74] Where such supply is not clearly profitable, the agencies have used their regulatory powers to encourage, or at least permit, cross-subsidisation.[75] Franchisees may also be obliged, on distributional grounds, to offer some services to certain categories of consumers at discounted prices.[76]

## (b) Duration of Contract

The duration of franchise contracts is specified in the recent broadcasting legislation;[77] in other systems it has been left to the discretion of the agency. Determining the optimal length is an important, but also complex,

---

[71] For buses, see Road Traffic Act 1930, s. 72(4)(a), and Glaister and Mulley, above, n. 7, pp. 66–7; and for railways, Railways Act 1993, s. 28(1). The duration and content of advertisements, the equivalent of prices in relation to non-subscriber broadcasting services, is regulated under Broadcasting Act 1990, s. 9. The fares on domestic airline routes were regulated under the Civil Aviation (Licensing) Act 1960 and the Civil Aviation Act 1971. In 1984, the government decided that, given increased competition, this was no longer necessary (White Paper, *Airline Competition Policy* (1984, Cmnd. 9366) ) and all that remains is a residual control exercised by the Director General of Fair Trading and the Monopolies and Mergers Commission under the Fair Trading Act 1973.

[72] Road Traffic Act 1930, s. 72(4), and see ss. 67–71 regarding the licensing of vehicles; Civil Aviation Act 1971, ss. 26–9.

[73] Television Act 1954, s. 3(1); Cable and Broadcasting Act 1984, s. 10; Broadcasting Act 1990, ss. 6–9.

[74] For general discussion, see Goldberg (1977), above, n. 45, pp. 439–41.

[75] See: (for buses) Glaister and Mulley, above, n. 7, pp. 127–30; (for domestic airline routes) Report of the [Edwards] Committee of Inquiry, *British Air Transport in the Seventies* (1969, Cmnd. 4018), paras. 665–9; (for broadcasting) Broadcasting Act 1990, s. 26; and (for general discussion), above, pp. 284–5.

[76] Railways Act 1993, s. 28(4)–(5).

[77] e.g. 10 years for Channel 3 television and 8 years for radio: Broadcasting Act 1990, ss. 20(1), 86(3).

issue, as it involves consideration of several factors.[78] First, there is the impact on the competitive process: if the period is too short, it will reduce the number of bids; but if it is too long, it will give the incumbent a substantial advantage in terms of knowledge and experience. Secondly, there is the question of investment: the period must be sufficiently long to enable the franchisee to obtain a reasonable return on investment (and thus to encourage it); but not so as to enable him to acquire and exploit monopolistic power.[79] Finally, duration affects the nature of the contract and the costs of administering it: a short-term contract can be more specific and thus easier to enforce; a long-term contract needs to be more flexible so that both the agency and the franchisee can adapt to changing circumstances.

### (c) Enforcement of Contract

Decisions on the appropriate duration of a franchise contract thus place considerable informational demands on the agency (or legislature). This, by itself, may suggest that the advantages of the contractual form over traditional regulation may not be as great as is often claimed. Enforcement of the contract raises problems of a more fundamental character.[80]

Consider first the agency's task of ensuring compliance. As regards prices, this is relatively straightforward, but quality standards are quite a different matter.[81] Some, like those relating to broadcasting, involve highly subjective judgements; others, for example those relating to the reliability of transport services, require extensive monitoring.

What then happens if serious breaches are detected? It is here that the weakness of the contractual basis of the regulatory structure is most clearly revealed. English law suffers from its failure to develop an independent set of principles to govern public contracts, in particular to deal with breaches.[82] The conventional private law remedy of damages is inefficacious because the principal losses are incurred by consumers, not the franchisor (the agency). The legislation invariably confers on the agency the power to revoke or suspend a franchise if its conditions are not

[78] Williamson, above, n. 45, pp. 79–84; Waterson, above, n. 6, pp. 114–16; Domberger, above, n. 5, pp. 278–80.

[79] To the same end, it is desirable to restrict the number of franchises which a single firm can earn. See, e.g. Broadcasting Act 1990, Sched. 2, although, under pressure from the industry, the government has controversially relaxed the control imposed on Channel 3 licences: SI 1993/3199.

[80] For general discussion, see Domberger, above, n. 5, pp. 280–2; and Waterson, above, n. 6, pp. 111–12.

[81] Cf. Goldberg (1977), above, n. 45, p. 442.

[82] Cf. P. Craig, Administrative Law (2nd edn., 1989), p. 509. French law provides a striking contrast: see L. N. Brown and J. Bell, French Administrative Law (4th edn., 1991), pp. 196–201.

complied with,[83] but in the vast majority of cases this is an empty threat. The remedy is so Draconian that it will be entertained by agencies only in cases of outrageous breaches,[84] not the least because it will normally be impossible to find a substitute franchisee within a short timescale.

The imposition of financial penalties on the defaulting franchisee would seem to be a more attractive solution. The existence of the equitable doctrine constraining courts from enforcing penalty clauses[85] means that legislation is normally required for this purpose. In fact, it is only very recently that Parliament has enacted provisions to this effect,[86] and it remains to be seen whether, and to what extent, they will be invoked.

The problems of enforcing franchise contracts may have a significant impact on the allocation process. If applicants realise that compliance with the contract conditions will not be insisted on, they will be motivated to make over-optimistic bids, thus undermining the notion of 'fair competition'.[87] As one commentator has observed,

The history of franchising is not short of cases of unrealistic bidding designed to get 'a foot in the door' in the knowledge that once the contract is secured, more favourable terms can then be negotiated and the base-period pricing adjusted towards monopoly levels.[88]

## 6. CONCLUSIONS

Drawing together the strands of arguments in this chapter, we can now reach some tentative conclusions on the merits of public franchising, as illustrated by the British schemes which we have been considering.

We may begin by observing that public franchising can be, and has been, used where the public interest arguments for limiting supply (notably natural monopoly) are not strong. In such cases, the introduction and retention of the scheme are best explained by reference to the influence of private interests which benefit from the barriers to entry.

The licensing of bus and coach routes under the Road Traffic Act 1930 was clearly subject to such influence. The system was abolished in the 1980s.[89] Have the consequences of deregulation shed any light on the

---

[83] e.g. Road Traffic Act 1930, s. 74; Civil Aviation Act 1971, s. 23; Broadcasting Act 1990, s. 42.                [84] Veljanovski, above, n. 36, p. 294.

[85] *Dunlop Pneumatic Tyre Co. Ltd* v. *New Garage* [1915] AC 79.

[86] Broadcasting Act 1990, ss. 41, 55, 81, 110, and 120, which confer on the Independent Television Commission a power to impose a financial penalty on licensees not exceeding, for a first offence, 3% of qualifying revenue received during the last complete accounting period (5% for subsequent offences). See also Railways Act 1993, s. 55(8).

[87] Waterson, above, n. 6, p. 112.                [88] Domberger, above, n. 5, p. 280.

[89] Transport Act 1980 (express coach services); Transport Act 1985 (local bus services, except in London).

public interest arguments for franchising? Some generalizations can be drawn from the considerable literature which has accumulated on the subject.[90] There has been a notable increase in the number and quality of express, long-distance coach services and a significant reduction in the fares charged for them. The impact on local services has been mixed. In general, fares have not been reduced, perhaps because the degree of competition envisaged has not materialized. On the other hand, there has been an improvement in productive efficiency and an expansion of services on more popular routes, without any significant reduction on less popular routes. Overall, then, from this evidence it may be inferred that, on public interest grounds, a public franchising system cannot be justified.

In relation to domestic airline routes and broadcasting, where the case for limiting supply may have been somewhat stronger, the public interest method of allocating franchises was, until 1990, universally adopted. The main problem here has been the lack of attention to process values, in particular the absence of consistent and coherent decision-making based on fully articulated criteria. If, as may be surmised, the result has been some divergence from the principle of fair competition inherent in the economic theory of franchising, then the systems have generated significant welfare losses. However, there has been a marked trend in recent years towards greater institutional 'rationality' in the procedures for allocating franchises, and the problem may be less serious than it once was.

As we have seen, an influential group of economists has pleaded the merits of price bidding franchises as being superior not only to the public interest method of allocation, but also to the traditional regulatory solutions to the natural monopoly problem. On our analysis, their claims have been much exaggerated. The reluctance of policy-makers to adopt such schemes, particularly in 'purer' forms, might reflect the influence of private interests that would stand to lose if the more traditional approach were abandoned. But it might indicate a recognition that the systems give rise to difficulties and administrative burdens no less severe than those arising from conventional regulatory regimes. Among these may be highlighted the array of quality standards which, perforce, have to supplement the prices agreed and the problematic issue of contract enforcement.

[90] Gwilliam, above, n. 12; Button, above, n. 27; Savage, above, n. 61; E. Davis, 'Express Coaching Since 1980: Liberalisation in Practice', in Kay *et al.*, above, n. 5, ch. 7; A. Harrison, 'Deregulating Bus Services', in C. Whitehead (ed.), *Reshaping The Nationalised Industries* (1988), ch. 8; J. Vickers and G. Yarrow, *Privatization: An Economic Analysis* (1988), pp. 366–84; D. Banister and L. Pickup, 'Bus Transport in the Metropolitan Areas and London', in P. Bell and P. Cloke (eds.), *Deregulation and Transport* (1990), ch. 4; M. Beesley, *Privatization, Regulation and Deregulation* (1992), ch. 9.

# PART V

# EPILOGUE

# 16

# The Future of Regulation

Over the last fifteen years, there has been a significant transformation in the style and institutions of regulatory law. The details have been documented in the preceding chapters. Here we shall draw together the principal themes and attempt to identify some implications for the future.

## I. THE AGENDA FOR REGULATORY REFORM

In earlier generations there seemed to have been an almost irresistible momentum for extending and intensifying regulatory controls, leading one commentator to observe that 'the urge to regulate is stronger than the sex drive'.[1] Whether the impetus originated in the ever-increasing expectations of an electorate impatient for governments to cure a variety of ills or else in the opportunistic support of sections of industry which could anticipate profit from the resulting measures, it was not easily arrested: the perceived imperfections of the solutions tended to fuel the demand for more regulation, rather than less.[2] The consequences were: as regards social regulation, a proliferation of detailed standards and much use of prior approval regimes; and, in relation to natural monopolies, an almost exclusive reliance on public ownership.

Allegations of 'regulatory failure' may be made too glibly and the achievements of legislation in the areas of, for example, consumer and environmental protection should not be lightly dismissed. Nevertheless, traditional modes of regulation had serious flaws. First, there was an unjustified degree of confidence in the ability of government bureaucracies to devise appropriate solutions, with adverse consequences not only for the management of publicly-owned industries but also in the mass of detailed specification and performance standards which were costly to administer and which often inhibited innovation. Secondly, there was an uncritical acceptance of forms of social regulation which created significant barriers to entry or had other anti-competitive effects. Thirdly, regulatory rule-makers sometimes failed adequately to predict behavioural responses to interventionist measures which would defeat their object; the reduction in

---

[1] A. Schwartz, 'Unconscionability and Imperfect Information: A Research Agenda' (1991) 19 Can. Bus. LJ 437, 438.

[2] A phenomenon documented by MacDonagh in his study of 19th-cent. regulation: above, p. 7.

the supply of housing in the rented sector consequent on rent controls is the most notable example.[3] Fourthly, the tendency, in the light of political needs, to adopt pragmatic and often hasty solutions to well-publicized risks necessarily impeded a 'rational' cost-benefit approach to standard-setting.

It will be for future historians to provide definitive explanations of how and why these issues reached the political agenda and resulted in the reforms which have occurred. It will suffice here to summarize the main tendencies of these reforms. The most important facet of the new approach has undoubtedly been the privatization programme necessarily entailing, where insufficient competition has been generated, new regulatory regimes, but administered by agencies with (some) independence from government. Social regulation has developed along less interventionist lines. Large numbers of detailed specification and performance standards have been replaced by broader target standards; and greater use has been made of information regulation. On the other hand, the possibilities of substituting economic instruments (notably taxes) for traditional command-and-control techniques have not been sufficiently explored. Moreover, prior approval regimes remain largely intact, although in some cases there have been efforts to transform them into certification systems, thus allowing for greater consumer choice.

### 2. TOWARDS 'RATIONAL' SOCIAL REGULATION?

The future thrust of reform in the area of social regulation—at least while the current administration remains in power—has been signalled by the recent Deregulation Initiative. This led to the publication, in January 1994, of the Deregulation and Contracting Out Bill. If passed in its current form, this would entail not only the abolition of a number of specific regulatory controls but also, more controversially, a general power for a relevant Minister by statutory instrument to eliminate or reduce the burden of other legislative controls if, in his opinion, this would not involve 'removing any necessary protection'.[4]

Of equal significance, for our purposes, has been the contemporaneous publication of several documents in which the government sets out, in the most explicit terms, its strategy on social regulation.[5] The tone is set by the Prime Minister's personal contribution:

All regulation imposes costs on businesses. So there should always be a presumption *against* regulation unless it is strictly necessary to protect the interests of the consumer and the wider public. But in the past there has sometimes been a

---

[3] Above, pp. 297–9.                                              [4] Clause 1(1).
[5] Deregulation Initiative, *Thinking About Regulating: A Guide to Good Regulation* (1993) and *Regulation in the Balance: A Guide to Risk Assessment* (1993); Dept. of Trade and Industry, *Deregulation: Cutting Red Tape* (1994).

tendency to go too far and impose regulatory burdens well in excess of what is really required. This damages small business, restricts market entry and stifles the innovation and growth our economy needs. The temptation to over-regulate must be restricted.[6]

What is envisaged to lead to 'good' regulation is then tabulated in a set of succinct guidelines for policy-makers.

Good regulation—10 points to think about
1 Identify the issue . . . Keep the regulation in proportion to the problem.
2 Keep it simple . . . Go for goal-based regulation.
3 Provide flexibility for the future . . . set the objective rather than the detailed way of making sure the regulation is kept to.
4 Keep it short.
5 Try to anticipate the effects on competition or trade.
6 Minimise costs of compliance.
7 Integrate with previous regulations.
8 Make sure the regulation can be effectively managed and enforced.
9 Make sure that the regulation will work and that you will know if it does not.
10 Allow enough time.[7]

Both the Prime Minister's statement and the guidelines indicate a concern to overcome what we have identified as being the most significant defects in traditional social regulation. One central notion is that of proportionality: the costs of regulation should be justified by the benefits; and 'costs' in this context include those resulting from reduced competition, as well as the more direct burdens on business. As regards benefits, special attention is given, in another document, to risk assessment and management.[8] The guidance is broadly consistent with the public interest model for standard-setting outlined in Chapter 8,[9] care being taken to emphasize the uncertainties involved and the need to take account of less obvious behavioural responses to regulation, such as changes in demand. For example, if the costs of rail travel increase as a consequence of stricter safety controls, some passengers may shift to road transport, where the risks are greater.[10]

Another main concern is flexibility, suggesting a preference for target standards (leaving firms free to devise the cheapest means of achieving the target) but also an investigation of other regulatory options, including voluntary Codes of Practice, self-regulation, and economic instruments.[11]

The articulation of these guidelines is itself a significant advance on previous, blander statements of regulatory policy.[12] It is a matter for

---

[6] *Thinking About Regulating*, above, n. 5, Foreword.   [7] Ibid. pp. 20–1.
[8] *Regulation in the Balance*, above, n. 5.   [9] Above, pp. 152–60.
[10] *Regulation in the Balance*, above, n. 5, p. 6.
[11] *Thinking About Regulating*, above, n. 5, pp. 5–7.
[12] Cf. Green Paper, *Consumer Safety—A Consultative Document* (1976, Cmnd. 6398).

speculation whether a better match between public interest goals and regulatory instruments will in fact emerge. A number of doubts arise concerning the content of the guidelines and their implementation.

The guidelines contain an overt presumption against regulation. This might have been thought necessary to counteract previous policy but it creates a serious risk of sub-optimal control. That risk is increased by the evident bias in the evaluation process towards costs and away from benefits. The compliance costs as they affect firms, particularly small businesses, must be quantified; benefits need only be described in vague terms.[13] The consultation exercises envisaged concentrate correspondingly on acquiring information from the regulated industries, rather than from groups representing beneficiaries.[14] The desire to protect small businesses and, at the same time, to encourage more flexible modes of control must be set against the empirical evidence which suggests that small firms have a poor record of compliance with target standards and voluntary Codes of Conduct.[15]

In short, while the government blueprint has many features reflecting a 'rational' approach to social regulation, it also facilitates undue influence being exercised by powerful private interest groups.

### 3. TOWARDS 'RATIONAL' ECONOMIC REGULATION?

There has been no equivalent government statement on 'good' economic regulation. This is hardly surprising, given that privatization and the introduction of the new regulatory regimes have been so recent and that government policy towards the utilities is still relatively unstable. There remains considerable uncertainty on several aspects of this policy: the degree of competition which will emerge in, or be forced on, the relevant markets; the extent to which distributional goals should intrude, by, for example, cross-subsidization; and, most fundamentally, securing an appropriate balance between providing an adequate return to investors in the privatized utilities and achieving allocative efficiency.

The application of the principal regulatory device, the control of price increases by means of the $RPI - X$ formula, has been subjected to almost continuous modification in the light of the circumstances affecting the different utilities. Originally designed to avoid the complexities and perverse incentives arising under the American rate-of-return systems, it has generated its own set of problems. The principles on which the regulators do or should exercise their discretion in determining the value of $X$, the variable representing the firms' potential for cost reduction, remain

---

[13] Cf. above, pp. 164–5.
[14] *Thinking About Regulating*, above, n. 5, pp. 13–15, and Annex F.
[15] See, in relation to occupational health and safety, above, p. 189.

unclear. In consequence, the operation of the price cap has been too dependent on negotiations between the regulators and the firms, with outcomes tending to reflect pragmatic compromises rather than public interest goals.

To develop a more 'rational' approach to economic regulation, therefore, the priority must be to establish a more coherent institutional framework. Although it is appropriate for the regulators to retain a broad discretion in determining the price cap, because that will preserve their independence from political influences, the general principles for exercising that discretion should be laid down in legislation. Further, to reduce the possibility of 'capture', the utilities should be subjected to more stringent requirements relating to the disclosure of accounts and other information; and, with access to that information, consumer interests should play a more active role in the regulatory process. The extent to which the process should be rendered justiciable, by allowing appeals on the merits of the regulator's decision to be brought by consumer interests as well as the firms, is debatable. For reasons which have already been explored,[16] traditional judicial review procedures are not obviously appropriate. An alternative solution lies in enhancing and formalizing the existing appellate functions of the Monopolies and Mergers Commission so that, for example, its decisions are made binding on the regulator.

[16] Above, pp. 116–17.

# Index of Names

# Subject Index

use of 79–98, 245, 255
*see also* command-and-control regulation
crises, regulation and 9, 56, 191, 193, 234, 236, 255
cross-subsidization 32, 269–70, 284–5, 314–15, 331

deregulation 10–12, 75, 102, 164–5, 178–9, 198–9, 204, 333–4, 338–9
destructive competition, *see* excessive competition
Director General of Fair Trading, *see under* regulatory agencies
distributional justice 26, 46–51, 125, 140, 159–60, 182, 207, 240, 243, 248–9, 253–4, 261, 269–70, 281–2, 284–5, 296, 307, 314–15, 320–1, 323, 331
drugs, *see* product licensing: pharmaceutical products

economic instruments 5, 245–56, 339
charges, *see* taxes *below*
evaluation 250–4
political considerations 255–6
private interest considerations 255–6
subsidies 48, 248–9
taxes 48, 246–8
tradeable emission rights 249–50
economic planning 45–6, 269
economic regulation 5, 265–334, 340–1
education and training 34–5, 48
efficiency:
allocative 24–5, 29, 38, 111, 207, 281–7, 297, 303, 307, 309, 313–15, 326
Kaldor–Hicks test of 24–5, 59, 62, 72–3, 207
Pareto test of 24–5, 59, 62, 72–3
productive 22, 111, 272–81, 303, 309, 313, 326
election of politicians 63–6, 74, 173
electoral systems 65
electrical equipment, *see under* product quality and safety
electricity 8, 31, 292–3, 311, 316
enforcement of regulation 56, 171, 197, 206, 212, 253, 256, 332
*see also under* criminal law; European Community
environmental pollution control 19–20, 35, 36–7, 48, 168, 204–13, 249–54
ambient quality standards (AQS) 208–13
best available techniques not entailing excessive cost (BATNEEC) 84, 170, 207, 252
best practicable environmental option (BPEO) 207, 212
history of 10, 205–6

information dissemination 211
performance standards 210
pollution taxes 247–8, 251–6
public interest goal 206–7
specification standards 209–10
target standards 208–9
tradeable emission rights 249–50
European Commission 103, 127, 146, 175–6, 198, 212–13
European Committee on Standardization 138, 178, 191–2
European Community:
arguments for regulation by 100–4
competitive regulation 178–9
co-ordination regulation 101–3
enforcement 102, 175, 177, 179, 203–4, 213
freedom of trade within 12, 101–2, 137, 174–5, 222
general 11–12
harmonization of regulation 11–12, 130–2, 137, 175–7, 192–3, 198–9, 222, 236
impact of private interests on 103–4
integration regulation 101–3, 175
mutual recognition 12, 102, 177–9, 192, 199, 203, 223, 236
subsidiarity 102
European Union, *see* European Community
excessive competition 321–2
Executive Agencies 272
experience goods 132, 134, 190
externalities:
negative 18–19, 35–8, 52, 102, 123, 152, 179, 181–2, 189, 217–18, 227–9, 234, 239–40, 245–6, 268
pecuniary 37–8
positive 21, 36, 123–4, 140–1, 240, 268; *see also* public goods
technological 37–8

fiduciary obligations 17, 217
financial regulation, *see* consumer credit; information regulation: securities and financial disclosure
food controls 11, 192–7
new approach to 197
quality 194–5
safety 195–7
*see also under* information regulation
franchise contracts, *see under* public franchising
future generations 35, 48–9, 54, 158–9, 204, 228, 240

gas 8, 292, 311, 316
grandfather clauses 169, 172, 220, 254
guilds 7, 214